Blindness and Children is a summary and interpretation of the research literature on infants and children with visual impairments. It concludes that many aspects of "delayed" development are the result not of visual impairment itself, but of environmental variables that tend to accompany visual impairment. Hence, many of the typical developmental delays may be ameliorated or avoided by the appropriate structuring of the child's experiences. The book is developmentally oriented and treats all of the major areas of child development. The author's premise is that a truly useful body of knowledge about the development of children with visual impairments not only must characterize normative development, but must account for the factors associated with relatively good or poor developmental progress. Thus, the research literature is examined for evidence of variables that may account for individual differences, particularly variables related to the child's several environments.

Blindness and children

Blindness and children

An individual differences approach

DAVID H. WARREN

Department of Psychology
University of California, Riverside

CAMBRIDGE
UNIVERSITY PRESS

Published by the Press Syndicate of the University of Cambridge
The Pitt Building, Trumpington Street, Cambridge CB2 1RP
40 West 20th Street, New York, NY 10011-4211, USA
10 Stamford Road, Oakleigh, Melbourne 3166, Australia

First published 1994

Printed in the United States of America

Library of Congress Cataloging-in-Publication Data
Warren, David H.
Blindness and children : an individual differences approach /
David H. Warren.
p.   cm.
Includes bibliographical references and indexes.
ISBN 0-521-45109-4 – ISBN 0-521-45719-X (pbk.)
1. Children, blind.   2. Handicapped children – Development.
I. Title
HV1596.2.W36   1994
155.45'11 – dc20   93-42678
                                                            CIP

A catalog record for this book is available from the British Library.

ISBN 0-521-45109-4 hardback
ISBN 0-521-45719-X paperback

Contents

Preface

Ten years have passed since 1984, when my previous book on blindness and children, *Blindness and Early Childhood Development*, was published. Those ten years have seen a welcome surge of research on children with visual impairments, and that is reason enough to write a sequel. But *Blindness and Children: An Individual Differences Approach* is not just a sequel. It takes an entirely different approach to analyzing the research literature. As the title suggests, this analysis and summary of the literature is based on the premise that it is the variation within the population of children with visual impairments that we should be studying, not the norm. I believe that a truly useful body of research-based knowledge about this population must focus not on the norm, or the usual, but on the unusual. It should focus on children whose development is unusually advanced and on those whose development is unusually delayed. It should focus on the factors in those children's experience that have caused their development to vary in a positive or negative direction. Only with that kind of knowledge base will we be prepared to intervene in the lives of children with visual impairments in order to allow them to achieve their optimal potential.

Above all, the message that this analysis contains is one of optimism: optimism on the part of researchers that they can provide service professionals and parents with sound advice about how to structure children's experiences; optimism on the part of service professionals that their expertise can make a positive impact, rather than just avoid a negative outcome; and above all, optimism on the part of parents that their children with visual impairments need not be bound to the delayed development that our current norms suggest, but that if provided appropriate environments and experiences, these children can truly achieve an optimal developmental course.

In doing the analysis in this book, I have been buoyed by the results of researchers who have attended carefully to the differences that exist among their research "subjects," and particularly by those who have sought the reasons for those differences. They have, increasingly, made a difference in the body of knowledge that we now have. I hope that this book will persuade the entire research community that the quest for the understanding of individual differences and their causality is paramount. If this happens, I believe that ten years from now we not only will have a dramatically more useful body of knowledge, but will also see that children with visual impairments indeed do have more potential than the normative research suggests.

There is just one more thing to be said: during the course of this project I have enjoyed the unflagging support and confidence of my wife, Katherine, and I dedicate this book to her.

Introduction

The purpose of this book is to explore what is known about the variables that affect the development of children with visual impairments.[1] I take as a starting point the premise that children face a number of adaptive tasks that must be met in the course of development. That is, the world presents children with situations for which they must develop appropriate adaptive behaviors. This approach concentrates on the children themselves and on the variables that affect the quality of their adaptation to these tasks, rather than (as in past treatments) on comparisons of children who have visual impairments with those children who are sighted.

The comparative approach

In my book entitled *Blindness and Early Childhood Development* (Warren, 1977, 1984), my approach was explicitly comparative. That is, the capabilities and characteristics of blind and visually impaired children were evaluated in relation to the corresponding capabilities and characteristics of sighted children, all in relation to chronological age (CA).[2]

---

[1] A word about terminology is needed. Usage of the terms "visual impairment," "visual handicap," and "blind" has varied over the years. My preference is to use the term "visual impairment" to refer generically to all individuals whose vision falls within the range generally called "legally blind." Within this range, I will use the term "blind" to refer to individuals whose vision is reported as light perception (LP) or less, and I will use the term "partial vision" to refer to those who have more than LP. In some studies the term "low vision" is used for children who have a significant visual loss but who do not fall under the definition of legal blindness.

[2] A procedural note is required about CA, particularly in infancy. In any analysis of the development of infants with visual impairments, it is necessary to address prematur-

This approach implicitly assumes a "blindness as deficit" model, in which the differences revealed are attributed to the variable that differentiates the two groups, namely the presence or absence of vision. Using this approach, one then concludes what the effects of the absence of vision are.

This approach has advantages and disadvantages. The chief advantage is that the frame of reference is clear – it is the developmental psychology, and the accompanying developmental norms, of the sighted child. For most areas of development, there is a vast accumulation of information about what the course of development looks like. Therefore, it is relatively easy to study the normative development of children with visual impairments and to compare the evidence with that for sighted children.

The attractiveness of this approach is demonstrated by the fact that most of the existing research on the development of children with visual impairments has used it. Often both visually impaired and sighted children, matched for CA as well as other variables, are included in the same

---

ity. This would not be an issue if all infants were born at full term, but this is not the case. In many studies, a substantial proportion of infants in the research sample have been born prematurely and have lost vision very early as a consequence of retinopathy of prematurity (ROP, formerly referred to as retrolental fibroplasia, RLF). Usually an analytic procedure called "correction for prematurity" is used. The logic of this procedure is that if an infant is born prematurely, then it is less mature than a full-term infant. For example, at six months of chronological age an infant that was born three months prematurely is indeed six months old, but in terms of its maturational development, it may be considered to be only three months old. If this premature infant performs an activity at six months uncorrected birth age, the correction for prematurity yields credit for that activity at three months rather than six.

Of course this approach is somewhat simplistic since this infant has also had the advantage of three months' extra experience. The issue thus becomes entangled with the age-old problem of the relative contributions of maturation and experience. In the case of a prematurely born infant, this issue becomes even more complicated by the fact that his or her experience in the first several months is certainly different from that of the full-term infant.

There is no perfect answer to the question of how to count age for the prematurely born infant. The typical treatment, however, has been to correct CA for prematurity, and in the ensuing sections in which the issue is of any importance, I will take the same approach. Thus, if it is specified that corrected age is being used, I will use the reported age. If no such specification is made, I will assume that birth was at term unless the cause of visual loss was reported as ROP. In this case, I will use an age-correction factor of three months.

study, and the same basic data are acquired from both. Then the results of the group with visual impairment are simply compared with those of the sighted group. Sometimes only children with visual impairments are studied, but their results are evaluated with reference to known sighted norms as determined by other research. In short, this approach seeks comparisons *between populations*, in this case that of sighted children and that of children with visual impairments.

The differential approach

The main alternative to the comparative approach is called the differential approach because it seeks to explain differences *within a population*. The differential approach addresses the major questions: what is the nature, and what are the causes, of the variation within the population?

The first step in this approach is careful description of the characteristics of the population. A critical element of proper description is variation: what are the extremes in the population, and what is the nature of the distribution? Description restricted to averages is incomplete and often misleading.

The second step is to identify the correlates, and if possible the causality, of the variation. If six-year-old children show a particular distribution of cognitive skills, then what can be said about the causes of this variation, about why some children are in the high end and others in the low end of the distribution?

It is in the search for causality that the difficulties of the differential approach emerge. These occur in part because there are so many possible causal factors. In any area of development, there are general genetic factors involved as well as variations in the specific heredity of individual members of the population. On the environmental side, the variations in experience are virtually endless. Add to this already complex picture the additional variables related to visual impairment, such as partial vision or a period of early vision, and the array of potential causal variables that might affect development is staggering.

Nevertheless, it is exactly this complex of causal variables that should occupy our attention in attempting to understand the development of children with visual impairments. The comparative approach, with its emphasis on CA and visual status, tends to draw our attention away from the variables on which we should be focusing. Thus, one major advantage of the differential approach is that it reminds us that there is a great deal of developmental variation within the population of visually impaired children. Some children adapt with apparent ease; others have difficulty. Some learn well, others not so well. Some are socially gregarious, some are not. Our quest should be for an understanding of the variables that produce these differences within the population of children with visual impairments.

The differential model has a second major advantage in that it is well suited to generating knowledge that can help us intervene in the circumstances of children to optimize their development. In order to do this effectively we must understand causality, and we will not understand causality without exploring the differences among children. With its focus on the factors that produce variation in development, the differential approach allows causal relationships to be understood.

The search for theory

The literature on the development of children with visual impairments is remarkably devoid of explicit concern for theory. It has generally been assumed that when visually impaired children acquire characteristics at later ages than sighted children, they are proceeding through the same steps of development in the same order but at a slower pace. In fact, much practice and many intervention programs have been based on this premise. Their goal is to intervene in order to cause children with visual impairments to show the same rate of development as sighted children. The implicit theory that guides this reasoning can be called the *developmental lag* theory.

This theory should not be accepted without question, however. Let us examine the bases for alternative approaches to theory. One, at the other extreme from the simplistic notion of developmental lag, is that the development of children with visual impairments is totally different from that of sighted children, and that there is nothing at all to be gained by making any reference to the development of sighted children.

This is surely an unnecessarily pessimistic view. The development of all children is governed to some degree by maturation, and since development occurs within environments that, though they differ in specifics, have major domains in common, we should expect some basic commonalities of development among all children.

The intermediate possibility, which I take as a reasonable starting point, is that the principles and basic dynamics of development are fundamentally the same for children with and without visual impairments. It does not follow that development *on the average* will actually be identical, since there are important ways in which the environments, not to mention the perceptual capabilities, of the two populations may differ. In any case, an account of average development is not our major concern. Rather, our goal is to understand the variations in development that occur in children with visual impairments.

Researchers in the field of mental retardation have wrestled with the comparable problem, and there may be some benefit in drawing the analogy. One approach (e.g., Zigler & Balla, 1982) has been to hypothesize that the generally lower intelligence of retarded children at a given CA represents a developmental delay. That is, the nine-year-old with a mental age (MA) of six years has achieved the same structure and quality of cognitive abilities that the average six-year-old child has, but the nine-year-old has taken three additional years to reach that level. The parallel to the developmental lag theory with visual impairments is evident.

As more refined research methodologies and approaches to theory have led to better understandings among developmental psychologists about the roles of the child's environments such as family interactions, relationships with peers, and learning dynamics, the prevailing view of the development of children with mental retardation has come to include attention to these additional dynamics (Hodapp & Zigler, in press). Thus, development is not regarded a simple matter of the child's age and cognitive skills; rather, it is seen as determined by the complex relationships among the child's environments, the child's developing abilities and characteristics, and particularly how other people respond to the child's disability. This approach to the development of children with mental retardation is a much more complex undertaking in that it subjugates CA to a very minor role in the overall spectrum of factors that determine developmental level, and forces the relationships among many other variables to be evaluated.

General systems analysis has been offered in recent years as a theoretical framework for approaching developmental issues (Sameroff, 1989; Thelen, 1989). An important element in this approach is the notion of "self-reorganization." "Adaptive self-reorganization occurs when the system encounters new constants in the environment that cannot be balanced by existing system mechanisms" (Sameroff, 1989, p. 223). That is, if the environment presents a changed set of circumstances, the child will tend to change in the direction of adaptation to those circumstances. Similarly, as new capabilities develop, they are applied to the environmental circumstances in new ways, in effect changing the nature of the child's adaptation.

This framework offers a particularly attractive way to think about the development of children with visual impairments, because it draws our attention to the dynamic interplay between the child's capabilities and the circumstances provided by the environment. We can address the fundamental questions: how, with his or her changing abilities, does the child engage the environment? How, in its variety, does the environment afford opportunities for and impose expectations on the child? What, given these dynamically changing features, is the resulting nature of development? Children with visual impairments have certain abilities and characteristics, and they encounter a variety of environmental circumstances to which they must adapt. What is the nature of the resulting adaptation, and how does that adaptation change with changes in the child's abilities and characteristics, on the one hand, and with changes in the environmental circumstances, on the other? These are the issues to which this book is directed.

Adaptive tasks: a new way of approaching the issues

I wish to propose an approach to the analysis of development that is entirely new for research on children with visual impairments. This approach rejects the simplistic comparative CA model. It also rejects the other extreme, that there is nothing to be learned from the development of sighted children. Instead, it assumes that the variables that are related to visual impairment are simply additional sources of variance in the development of children. These variables are considered along with those that must be evaluated in accounting for the development of sighted children.

Briefly stated, the premises of the adaptive tasks approach are the following:

1. the developing child faces a set of adaptive tasks;
2. the child faces these adaptive tasks armed with a set of personal capabilities and characteristics;

3. the environment shapes not only the nature of the adaptive tasks but also the child's set of capabilities and characteristics; and

4. for the child with a visual impairment, there are variations on the tasks, the capabilities and characteristics, and the environmental circumstances that must be taken into account to understand development and its causality.

The adaptive tasks of infancy and childhood

All children, whether sighted or with visual impairments, face the problem of adapting to the tasks of existence. These tasks may be loosely grouped into several domains:

The physical world. The child must be able to perceive the characteristics of the physical world in order to adapt to the constraints and opportunities that it presents. The child needs to interact physically with the physical world and in order to do so must acquire motor skills, including skills of travel as well as of haptic exploration and manipulation. A major part of the child's adaptation to the physical world is cognitive: the child must acquire an understanding of the properties of the world, including specifically its spatial properties.

Cognitive skills. The child must acquire the abilities of logical reasoning. These depend, though only in part, on the acquisition of language as a tool of cognitive processes; language, in particular, is almost inextricably tied up with concept formation. Other aspects of cognitive skills, the so-called executive functions, are memory, attention, and information-processing strategies. Creativity and intelligence round out the picture of cognitive skills.

The social world. The child must perceive and understand the characteristics of the social world and social relationships, and his or her role and responsibility in them, in order to adapt to the constraints and opportunities that the social world places and provides. The child must learn the behaviors that facilitate successful social interactions, from the acquisition of social bonds to verbal and nonverbal social skills. In addition, the child must gain a sense of self. This includes an image of the child's own body as well as the ability to conceptualize the self in relation to other people and objects.

The child's capabilities and characteristics

In the course of development, children acquire certain capabilities and characteristics that shape their adaptation in these domains. These capabilities and characteristics include self-concept, cognitive skills, perceptual abilities, language skills, motor skills, mannerisms, information-acquisition and processing strategies, and personality characteristics.

The child's environments

The child's environments vary in ways that may directly alter the nature of adaptation and / or that may interact with the child's own characteristics to do so. For example, the physical environment varies in the amount and variety of stimulation it provides the senses. The social–emotional climate of the family varies, as do the parents' reactions to the child's visual impairment. The learning environment varies in such respects as the opportunities that are provided to learn, reinforcement characteristics, and the degree of challenge and other expectations placed on the child.

Variables related to visual impairment

In addition to these factors common to all children, several broad categories of factors are specifically related to visual impairment. These include the age at which the visual loss occurred, the presence of any residual visual capability, etiological factors, and the presence of any additional handicaps. These affect the child's environments as well as his or her capabilities and characteristics.

I am convinced that the basic unit of analysis in producing a developmental theory for children with visual impairments (and perhaps for children in general) must be the adaptive task. This conviction dictates the following series of analytic steps.

The first step is to identify and organize the set of adaptive tasks in some meaningful way. In identifying the key adaptive tasks, it is necessary to find a balance between too much and too little detail. Organization presents an even greater problem. One tempting extreme is to be too tightly guided by the developmental sequence of the sighted child. The other extreme is to ignore all of what is known about normative development. Both extremes are seductive and must be avoided.

The second step is a logical analysis of each adaptive task in the context of visual loss. What is the nature of the task when vision is impaired? What personal capabilities and characteristics facilitate or interfere with the task?

The third step is to evaluate the relevant literature. What is the evidence about the achievement of the basic adaptive tasks for children with visual impairments? What is the nature of the variation that occurs within the population of children with visual impairments? What are the environmental circumstances that shape children's activities? What additional factors specifically related to visual loss, such as partial vision or additional impairments, shape development?

The application of these three steps should allow us, to the extent that the existing research allows, to propose a theory of the development of children with visual impairments. However, because much of the existing research has, either explicitly or implicitly, used the comparative approach, we can anticipate that the research base will fall short of what is needed.

Therefore, the final step is to chart the course for the future. Are there significant gaps in the literature, where we do not know about important features of development or the variables that influence them? To what issues should future researchers turn their attention in order to fill in the significant gaps?

Organizational plan of the book

The bulk of the book is divided into parts that correspond to the major domains of adaptive tasks: dealing with the physical world, acquisition of cognitive skills, and dealing with the social world. Within each part, each of several chapters addresses a major area of development. Each chapter begins with a general summary of the various accomplishments that the child (whether visually impaired or not) must make. This summary is followed by an analysis of the available research with visually impaired children that addresses these accomplishments. These analyses are oriented to individual differences: what is known about the factors, including those related to visual impairment, that lead to more or less effective achievement of the adaptive tasks?

While it has its advantages, the organization by adaptive tasks creates a major problem. The problem is that the interrelations among adaptive areas can be neglected. For example, basic perceptual abilities are prerequisite to accomplishments in several other areas. Acquisition of a basic understanding of the properties of the physical world clearly depends on effective perceptual processing of information about it; effective social interaction just as clearly depends on the ability to perceive aspects of the social situation. I point out these interrelationships by cross-referencing among sections.

In the final section, Chapter 12 reviews several short- and long-term longitudinal studies. These are especially valuable in addressing important issues of developmental continuity. Finally, Chapter 13 summarizes the impact of individual differences variables across the domains of adaptive tasks.

My intention is not to produce an exhaustive catalog of all research that uses children with visual impairments as subjects. Many studies that are valuable in other respects are not useful to an analysis based on individual differences. This is the case when they report only central tendencies but no indices of variation or, more important, information about the possible causes of variation. Thus, many studies reviewed in my previous treatments of the literature (Warren, 1977, 1984) do not appear in the present analysis.

Instead, my goal is threefold:

1. to provide a picture of the development of children with visual impairments, with an emphasis on the variations within the population, and to address the causes of the variation;
2. to demonstrate that research attuned to individual differences is ultimately more supportive of effective intervention in the environments of children with visual impairments, so as to optimize their highest level of attainment in the various areas of development; and
3. to present a picture of what we do know and of what we do not know *about what we ought to know.* I hope that this analysis will help chart a course for future research.

Part I

Interaction with the physical world

Coming to know about the physical world is a long process that begins early in infancy and is not completed for years. The child's contact with the physical world comes via the senses, and thus the first set of questions has to do with the quality of the infant's perceptual capabilities. Perception is not the end of the matter, though – the infant and child also have to acquire the skills to engage in motor and locomotor interaction with the environment. Throughout, the child gradually gains the ability to conceptualize the physical world through thought, rather than just acting upon it. A large and important part of this growing ability to conceptualize is the perception and understanding of the spatial aspects of the physical world. In Part I we address each of these major issues in separate chapters.

1

Perception of the physical world

The mediating role of perception in human behavior is vast, and this is particularly true in issues of development. Perceptual information, acquired via the senses, serves the direct function of mediating physical interaction with the environment by manual and locomotor behaviors. Only slightly less directly, perceptual information is the basis for the child's learning about and acquiring a conceptual understanding of the properties of the physical world. Because of the pervasive involvement of perception in other areas of development, it is useful to treat this topic first. We will start with perceptual development in infancy and then move to issues of perception in older children.

Perceptual development in infancy

The past several decades have seen tremendous growth in our knowledge about the perceptual capabilities of the neonate and young infant. Generally, the more we learn, the more we come to be impressed with the infant's capabilities. Not surprisingly, the bulk of research attention has been devoted to the development of visual perception, from the anatomical basics such as visual acuity and lens accommodation to capabilities that show integration of immediate sensory information with previous experience, such as the perception of pattern or distance relationships. Auditory perception has not been neglected, however, and we have good information about the neonate's and young infant's ability to make basic auditory discriminations of amplitude and pitch, and about more complex types of auditory perception such as speech sounds and spatial localization.

Although there is much less research with infants with visual impairments, there is nevertheless sufficient information available about the basic perceptual abilities to draw important conclusions.

Table 1 summarizes key observations that various investigators have reported, mainly from case studies, about blind infants' responsiveness to various auditory and tactile stimuli. Identification of the stimulus is followed by the nature of the response that the infant is reported to have made. Note that some entries show no response – these can be as significant as those in which a definite response does occur. We will discuss first the evidence about responsiveness to sound stimuli, then move to tactile stimuli and other topics.

Responsiveness to sound stimuli

In evaluating the evidence about the perception of sound stimuli, it is useful to distinguish among three levels of responsiveness. At the level of *simple reaction*, we can infer that the infant's auditory system can detect the stimulus. At a second level, *discriminative reaction*, we can also infer that the infant can discriminate the stimulus from other stimuli. At the third level, the infant makes an *interactive behavior* (either positive or negative) to the stimulus, presumably to engage (or avoid) the stimulus. At this level, we can infer that the stimulus carries some meaning for the infant. Throughout, we must take care to observe responses of which the infant is capable – it is a mistake to conclude that perception does not occur based on the infant's failure to make a response that he or she cannot yet perform.

Applying this approach to the perception of sound stimuli by infants with visual impairments, the following points become evident.

Simple reaction. Various sound stimuli evoke at least simple reactions throughout the developmental sequence. In the earliest months, tests have usually involved the mother's voice: some reaction is always evident, whether it is smiling, quieting, a head turn, or an arm movement. Reactions to sounds other than the human voice have not been studied in the earliest months, but responsiveness occurs to a "noise-making object" and to plastic keys by four months and to rattle toys by five months of age. The occasional observation that no response occurs at all (e.g., Fraiberg, Siegel, & Gibson, 1966) is the exception. In short, there is no reason to doubt that basic auditory responsiveness begins in the earliest days of life.

Table 1. *Evidence of responsiveness of infants with visual impairments to auditory (A) and tactual (T) stimuli*

Stimulus	Response	Citation
One month		
(A) Mother's voice	Head turn, arms out	1
(A) Mother's voice	Smile	3
(T) Chance hand encounters	Hand movements	3
Two months		
(A) Mother's voice	Quieting	6
(A) Other voices	No response	6
(A) Mother's voice	Arm movements, head turn	1
(A) Parent's voice	Smile	9
(A) Parents' voices	Smile (unreliable)	3
(T) Tactile contact with mother (proliferates through 5 months)	Active seeking	3
(T) Tactile contact with mother	Smile	3
Three months		
(A) Mother's voice	Arm movements, smile	1
(A) Mother's voice	Smile (unreliable)	4
(A) Other voice	No response	4
Four months		
(A) Noise-making object	Reach, grasp (lost by 6 months)	11
(A) Mother's voice	Arm movements	1
(A) Sister's voice	Smile	8
(A) Parent's voice	Smile	4
(T) Touch mother's nose	Grunt	1
(T) Pacifier	Moves hand to hand and mouth	1
Five months		
(A) Plastic key rattle	Reach, retrieve, mouth (but 1 week later, no response unless also touched)	6
(T) Keys touching hand or mouth	Grasp	1
(T) Parent's face	Hand exploration (5 to 8 months progressively more discriminating and intentional)	3

Table 1 *(cont.)*

Stimulus	Response	Citation
Six months		
(A) Noise-making object	No response	11
(A) Rattle	Smile	2
(A) Clock chime	Slight movement toward	2
(A) Sounding toy	Attention, but no head or hand activity	5
(A) Removal of sounding toy from grasp	No response	5
(T) Tickle on chest	Smile	2
(T) Drop toy	No response	5
Seven months		
(A) Bell, rattle	Finger movements, no reach	3
(A) Crumpling paper, scratching pillow	Attention	2
(T) Drops cookie	Search, find, mouth	1
(T) Mother hold	Quiet, touch face	3
(T) Stranger hold	Squirm, whimper, cry	3
(T) Drop toy, sound or not	Random, fragile search	5
(T) Toy, touch back of hand	Grasp	10
Eight months		
(A) Mother's voice	Smile, movements, vocalization	3
(A) Stranger's voice	Freeze	3
(A) Sounding toy	Alert, hand movements, no reach	3
(A) Sounding toy	Head orientation, no reach	3
(A) Sounding toy	Finger, arm movements, grasp (8th to 11th month, increasing tactile activity to sound cues)	10 3
(T) Stranger hold	Freeze (8th to 11th month, increasingly organized tactile search)	4 3
Nine months		
(A) Sounding toy	Hand pantomime, no reach	5
Ten months		
(A) Sounding toy	Reach (median for group)	3

Table 1 *(cont.)*

Stimulus	Response	Citation
Eleven months		
(A) Mother's voice	Response only if also tickle	2
(A) Sounding toy	Reach, then (shortly thereafter) crawl	5

Note: All ages are corrected for prematurity where appropriate. Key to citations: 1, Als et al. (1980a); 2, Burlingham (1964); 3, Fraiberg (1968); 4, Fraiberg and Freedman (1964); 5, Fraiberg, Siegel, and Gibson (1966); 6, Freedman, Fox-Kolenda, Margileth, and Miller (1969); 7, Freedman (1964); 8, Gesell, Ilg, and Bullis (1949); 9, Parmalee (1955); 10, Schwartz (1984); 11, Urwin (1973).

Discriminative reaction. Here the evidence is almost as clear. As early as two and three months of age, the smile begins to differentiate, occurring in response to the mother's (or father's) voice but not to those of strangers. Strangers' voices are certainly perceptible to the infant's auditory system, so we can infer that the infant can discriminate between parent and stranger based on voice cues. (This not only tells us something about the discriminative capabilities of the infant's auditory system, but also demonstrates the infant's capability to learn, presumably to associate positive experiences selectively to the parents' voices.) At no age beyond a month is there any evidence of the inability to discriminate between parents' (or other familiar people's) and strangers' voices.

For sounds other than voices, the picture is not as clear. We can see a hint of discrimination in two items reported by Burlingham (1964) at six months: the infant smiled (a positive response) upon hearing plastic keys rattled, but only oriented (a neutral response) upon hearing a clock chime. Such a difference in response suggests discrimination between the two kinds of sound.

Overall, there are simply too few data reported to reach reliable empirical conclusions about the infant's capability to discriminate among various nonvoice stimuli. Logically, it is fair to argue that the subtleties of differences among human voices are at least as fine as those that differentiate other sounds, and so if the infant can discriminate between subtly differing voices, presumably he or she can also discriminate among other sound-making sources.

Interactive behavior. The third level involves the overt reaction of engaging or avoiding a stimulus. Here, we see only fleeting responses in the early months that might be interpreted as engaging the stimulus interactively. Examples are the head turn and arm movement in response to the mother's voice at one month and again at two, three, and four months; the reach and grasp for a sound-making object at four months; the reach and retrieval of plastic keys at five months; and the directional reach and grasp of a sound-making object at five months. A seven-month-old infant crumples paper and scratches the pillow, listening to the sounds thus produced. By eight and nine months of age, the infant begins to make anticipatory hand motions in response to sounds. On the negative side, Fraiberg et al. (1966) emphasized that reaching to sound stimuli did not occur in their sample until a median age of around nine months.

Summary. The evidence clearly shows the blind infant's ability to perceive and discriminate sound stimuli. There is no evidence to controvert the thesis that perceptual discriminative capabilities exist at birth, and that they develop gradually over the first year in a way that is not different from the development of the sighted infant.

As for interactive reactions, in which the infant is either attracted to interact with or motivated to avoid sound stimuli, it is obvious that these behaviors are slower to develop than the basic perceptual discriminations. In this respect, the picture is no different from that for sighted infants. It is only with experience that the infant comes to associate either positive or negative affect with particular auditory stimuli. Although it may take several more months for these behaviors to become fully organized and successful, it seems clear from the evidence that the blind infant is indeed motivated to interact with a variety of sound-producing stimuli (and succeeds to a degree in doing so), on a timetable not notably different from that of the sighted infant. If reaching or other specific responses are slow to become organized, this cannot be a result of the lack of auditory ability.

In short, there is nothing in the evidence about basic auditory functioning that should lead us to expect any difficulty in the development of basic auditory abilities in the blind infant, or in the development of other abilities that depend on auditory perception.

Responsiveness to tactual stimuli

The evidence of responsiveness to tactual stimuli is not as extensive as that regarding response to sound, but we can take the same three-level approach to evaluating tactual perception, again keeping in mind the necessity of looking at responses that are within the infant's behavioral repertoire. In the case of touch, the attempt to disentangle behavior from perceptual experience is even more complex because much tactual stimulation comes to the hand, and at the same time the hand is the primary agent of responsiveness, particularly at the level of interactive reaction. Key findings are included in Table 1.

Simple reaction. There is evidence of tactile responsiveness from the earliest months, ranging from reports of smiling in response to tactile contact with the mother at two months, to grasping objects that come into contact with the hand at five months, to smiling in response to a tickle of the chest at six months.

Discriminative reaction. There is almost no evidence that bears directly on the issue of tactual discrimination. However, discrimination is prerequisite to the interactive behaviors to be noted and can thus be inferred from them.

Interactive behavior. Here there is clear positive evidence throughout the age range when the touching stimulus is human. At the young end, infants actively seek tactile contact with the mother at two months, followed by tactile recognition of the mother's face at four months. Fraiberg (1968) reported increasingly discriminative hand exploration of the parent's face in the period from five to eight months, and beginning around seven months, there is good evidence of aversive reactions (e.g., freezing, whimpering) to being held by strangers, in contrast to quieting and manual interaction in response to being held by the mother.

For response to objects the evidence is less extensive, but an early example is grasping a pacifier and moving it to the mouth at four months and grasping a set of keys at five (Als, Tronick, & Brazelton, 1980a). Als et al. also observed successful search for a dropped cookie at seven months. Fraiberg et al. (1966) also noted the onset of a fragile manual search for a dropped toy at seven months, and thereafter an increase in the infant's attempts to retrieve previously touched stimuli.

Summary. At the level of simple reactions, the available evidence supports the notion that the tactual perceptual capabilities of the blind infant are intact and develop without problem. As for interactive behaviors, it is clear that the blind infant learns the significance of the parent's touch very early. He or she not only discriminates between the parent's touch and that of other people, but modulates his or her own behavior appropriately, choosing to engage the parent from the early months and, around midyear, to avoid the tactual stimulation of other people. Thus, tactual development appears to be entirely normal, and it should serve the acquisition of other behaviors that may depend on it.

Integration of the senses

Here the question is the nature and degree of organization among the several sensory modalities – are they independent or interactive in their perception of events, and if they are interactive, what is the nature of their interaction and how does it develop? The issue is of interest because of the role that vision plays in the developing interaction of touch and hearing in the sighted infant, and the possibility that lack of this function of vision constitutes a risk for the blind infant.

An impressive example of interaction in a sighted infant was noted by Wertheimer (1961), who reported that within the first 10 min after birth, a neonate looked to the side on which a clicking sound occurred with greater than chance frequency. This evidence of an innate linkage between vision and audition has been replicated under more controlled conditions by Muir (1982), who showed that two-day-old neonates not only show directional head-turn responses to sounds presented to the left and right, but also make graded reactions to different amounts of deviation of the sound from the midline. Interestingly, the directional responsiveness decreased during the second and third months, to reemerge strongly in the fourth month (Muir, Abraham, Forbes, & Harris, 1979).

Bower (1974) advanced a theory of the "primitive unity" of the senses. He suggested that at birth, vision and hearing are equivalent with respect to what they denote to the neonate about external events, and moreover that there is no real distinction between these modalities as separate sources of information. Furthermore, the motor (hand) system is linked to the nondifferentiated visual-auditory system. In support of his position, Bower cited the evidence of Ball and Tronick (1971) that a sighted infant in the second week interposed her hands between her face and a "looming" object. He argued that this behavior could not be learned and so must be based on an innate linkage between the visual and motor systems.

Bower (1974) extended the notion of primitive unity to infants born without sight, citing evidence that a 16-week-old infant turned her eyes toward a sound source (Freedman, 1964), and that another 16-week-old infant reached out to grasp noise-making objects (Urwin, 1973).

Although these arguments are based on the results of only two infants, the theoretical position is provocative and worthy of attention. In both cases, the early evidence of motor responsiveness to sound disappeared by midyear, only to reappear later in the first year. Bower attributed this development to the processes of differentiation, and later reintegration, of the senses: "Taken together, these observations suggest that the object-specifying properties of audition decline after birth, to be reconstructed toward the end of the first year" (Bower, 1974, p. 170).

However interesting it may be from a theoretical point of view, the case for early auditory-motor unity as argued by Bower may not be of much practical importance since, as he reported, in the Urwin case this behavior disappeared by six months "despite considerable reinforcement and practice, and had not reappeared by the age of ten months" (Bower, 1974, p. 169). It may be that blind infants must indeed construct the significance of auditorially specified objects in relation to their own motor behavior during the latter part of the first year, without benefit of vision.

Nielsen (1991) observed that while infants normally attend to external sounds, when they were enclosed in her "little room" and isolated from external auditory stimulation, they tended to listen to the sounds created by their own activities. Nielsen suggested that the use of such a restricted environment might promote the integration of auditory-tactual spatial relationships by allowing the infants' attention to focus on their own activities rather than being distracted by events in extended space. Nielsen's assumption is that the integration of external relationships would then develop once internal relationships were well established.

What of the infant with some visual capability? Here the situation may be different, since even a small amount of vision may serve to mediate the young infant's visual attention to external spatial events (Freedman, 1972; Hart, 1983). Unfortunately there is no research reported on the role of partial vision in responsiveness to sound stimuli in the early months.

Moving to midyear, there is not much more evidence, although Fraiberg (1968), noting that infants with partial vision generally move through the developmental sequence more like sighted than blind infants, implied that the coordination of reaching to sound occurs around midyear.

Summary. With respect to the developing integration of the senses, there is unfortunately little evidence to go on. Vision no doubt plays an important role for the infant with sight, and the scanty evidence from infants with visual impairments does suggest that partial vision may be of benefit.

In the future it may prove useful to distinguish between integration of the senses with respect to the perception of aspects of the self and aspects of the external environment. We will see in Chapter 3 that the blind infant's progress through the stages of object constancy seems to bog down when the infant has to escape from engaging the spatial environment in an egocentric manner.

Analyzing responses

To this point, we have discussed the evidence in terms of the infant's *perceptual* capabilities. The evidence clearly supports the conclusion that neither auditory nor tactual perception follows a different developmental course than for the sighted infant. There may be differences in the developing integration of hearing and tactual perception and motor development that accompany visual loss, although much too little is known about this.

What, then, should we make of the conclusions that appear in earlier literature, that the blind infant is delayed, particularly in auditory perception (e.g., Fraiberg, 1968)? The answer lies not in the perceptual capabilities themselves, but in the infant's means of responding to perceptual stimuli.

Consider the behaviors that may occur in response to auditory and tactile stimuli. Generally speaking, the responses that have been studied are affective responses (e.g., smiling, avoidance), attentive responses (e.g., quieting, head turn), and hand activity (from fragmentary hand movements and manual search to successful reaching and grasping). We can consider each of these in turn, looking at what we can learn about the infant's increasingly organized patterns of behavior.

Affective responses. There is ample evidence in the first several months that affective responses, particularly smiling, occur in response to both auditory and tactile stimuli (Fraiberg, 1968). Nor do affective responses decrease in frequency: throughout the first year, the infant not only shows positive affect selectively to some auditory and tactile stimuli, but also begins to respond with negative affect to both the touch and the sound of strangers (Fraiberg & Freedman, 1964).

Attentive responses. There is less mention of attentive responses in the literature, possibly because they may tend, when accompanying more easily observable responses, to be overshadowed by the latter. For example, head orientation to sound may occur, but if it is followed by a reach of the hand, the latter is more likely to be reported than the former.

Nonetheless, some very early attentive reactions, such as the head turn, have been reported to the sound of the mother's voice at two and three months (Als et al., 1980a). There are numerous reports of head orientation to sounding objects, without other more overt behaviors, at around six months (e.g., Fraiberg et al., 1966).

Particularly when more overt responses are not available, researchers must look carefully for attentive responses, since these may give important evidence about the perception of stimuli even in the absence of more active behaviors.

Manual responses. Many researchers have interpreted hand activity, particularly reaching to objects, as an indicator of perceptual responsiveness. It is dangerous to assume that because reaching to a sound stimulus does not occur, the sound has not been perceived. This danger has been recognized in the literature: for example, Fraiberg et al. (1966) discussed the ineffectiveness of sound stimuli to elicit reaching responses before nine months of age or so, even though it is clear from other evidence that the infant certainly can perceive the sound in question. In Chapter 2, we will examine the development of reaching in its own right, rather than just as an indicator of perceptual capabilities.

Perceptual development after infancy

A general summary statement can be made about the research on postinfancy development of basic perceptual skills: there is not much to report. Of course the ways in which perceptual information is used in the service of other functions change dramatically, and we will address these in later chapters; but postinfancy developments of the basic perceptual skills are largely uninteresting.

Auditory perception

Sound discrimination. Hayes (1933) reported the results of threshold detection tests for blind boys and girls, whose ages and visual characteristics were not reported. The data contain no evidence of general gender or age differences in absolute thresholds.

Phonemic discrimination improves over the 6- to 11-year age range (Hare, Hammill, & Crandell, 1970), but not further over the 10- to 15-year age range (Stankov & Spilsbury, 1978). Phonemic discrimination is not related to visual acuity (Hare et al., 1970; Gibbs & Rice, 1974); although Stankov and Spilsbury (1978) found partially sighted children to be worse than totally blind children in phonemic discrimination, subject selection factors render this finding suspect.

Sound localization. Hayes (1935) found no clear differences in sound localization based on the amount of partial vision or intelligence in a sample ranging from school age to adult. Using a finer measure of localization ability, Spiegelman (1976) found that children who had a history of early visual experience were significantly better at localizing sound sources than those who had lost vision in early infancy as a result of retinopathy of prematurity (ROP).

Auditory localization involves not only auditory discrimination, but also reference to a spatial framework, and numerous studies show an advantage to individuals with early visual experience in tests of spatial performance (for reviews see McLinden, 1988; Warren, Anooshian, & Bollinger, 1973). We will review the general evidence related to perception of spatial structure in Chapter 4.

The obstacle sense. In the 1940s and 1950s Dallenbach and his colleagues conducted a series of investigations that resulted in the understanding that what had sometimes been called "facial vision" in fact depends on the use of auditory cues (e.g., Supa, Cotzin, & Dallenbach, 1944), and the term "obstacle sense" came into use. Worchel, Mauney, and Andrew (1950) evaluated the obstacle sense in blind children ranging in age from 8 to 23 years. They had the subjects walk toward a large object and stop when they were within arm's reach. About three-quarters were successful, but it was not reported whether success varied with age or with the age of visual loss.

More recently, Ashmead, Hill, and Talor (1989) tested elementary school children who were blind from birth in two echodetection experiments. In one, the ability to detect disks suspended to the right or left of the head was evaluated. Performance was above chance for four of nine younger children and for five of six older children. The other experiment was more functional, in that the child had to walk along a path and detect whether a box was present in the path. Younger children (up to age seven) were generally not successful, but most of the older children performed well. The difference between younger and older children may have resulted from the fact that the latter were more likely to have had formal orientation and mobility training that may have increased their attention to echo cues.

It is surprising that not more research has been done to evaluate the child's functional use of auditory information during the process of walking about in the physical environment.

Summary. No overall patterns emerge from this small amount of literature. Sporadic age-related improvements have been found, for example in phoneme discrimination. Of more interest are the apparent relationship of sound localization to early vision and the possible effect of orientation and mobility training on the use of echo information.

Tactual perception

Several dimensions of tactual perception have been investigated in children with visual impairments. Given the frequent use of tactile materials in educational and other settings, these issues have clear functional significance.

Tactile sensitivity. Several researchers (e.g., Axelrod, 1959; Nolan, 1960a; Nolan & Morris, 1960) have studied indices of skin and fingertip sensitivity in school-age children. While age-related improvements occur in younger children, other variables such as gender and visual history generally do not have significant effects. Similar age trends also tend to emerge on tests of cutaneous localization (Jones, 1972; Renshaw, Wherry, & Newlin, 1930).

Size and length discrimination. Berlá and Murr (1975) studied the discriminability of line width for the purpose of determining parameters for the design of maps and other tangible educational materials. The children were all braille readers ranging in age from 10 to 20 years. Discrimination thresholds did not vary with grade level or gender. However, discrimination performance did improve over the testing session, suggesting that performance is facilitated by short-term practice.

In a test of length discrimination, Duran and Tufenkjian (1970) found that thresholds were not related to age, IQ, or gender. The children had at most LP and had for the most part lost vision within the first two years of life. Although the children used a variety of methods to determine the length of the rods, no variation in the quality of performance was reported in relation to strategy use. On the other hand, Hanninen (1970, 1976) did find length discrimination performance to improve with age. Hanninen's hypothesis that coarse textures would lead to underestimation and fine textures to overestimation of length was not supported.

Moving to size discrimination, Morris and Nolan (1963) required fourth to twelfth grade children to choose a size match for a tactually presented form. The children had at most LP. Generally the older children performed better than the younger ones. Block (1972) also studied the tactual size-discrimination ability of school-age children who varied in the age of visual loss and the amount of useful vision. The children tended to overestimate size consistently, and this tendency increased with age.

Form discrimination. Information about age trends in form discrimination is available from several studies using the Tactile-Kinesthetic-Discrimination Test (TKT), which requires same–different judgments for pairs of geometric forms embossed on plastic sheets. Hammill and Crandell (1969) used the TKT to evaluate the relationships between tactual form discrimination and several other variables in children ranging in age from 6 to 11 years (Crandell, Hammill, Witkowski, & Barkovich, 1968 extended the age range to 21 years). Performance was related to MA but not to grade level. Relationships to the age at visual loss were not reported.

Tactual factors in reading braille

Hammill and Crandell (1969) also found that their braille readers, who tended to have greater visual loss, performed better than large-print readers on the TKT: presumably the experience of reading leads to more effective tactual discrimination. A related study of the tactual abilities of good and poor braille readers was reported by Weiner (1963). The poor readers read at least a grade below their actual grade placement, whereas the good readers read at or above grade placement. The good readers performed significantly better than the poor readers on several tasks of tactual discrimination. Correlational analysis did not reveal patterns of significant relationships to IQ or other subject characteristics.

Weiner suggested that some children performed better on the tactual tests because of greater fingertip sensitivity, which also allowed them to become better braille readers. The question of causality is complex, however. It seems just as likely that children who spend more time practicing become better braille readers and that they develop better tactual abilities as a result. The "educability" of tactual functions, as well as of other perceptual abilities, is an important question that has received too little attention. It is important to know about the possible effects of practice on discriminative functions, and how practice might interact with naturally occurring differences in sensitivity.

The role of other tactual factors, such as handedness, in reading braille has also received research attention. Hermelin and O'Connor (1971a) evaluated the relative speed and accuracy of reading braille text passages with the left and right hands. In blind children ages 8 to 10 years, performance with the left hand was both faster and more accurate than with the right hand; the difference between hands was also greater for the middle finger than for the forefinger. That braille reading was possible at all when using the middle finger, which all children claimed never to have used before, is impressive evidence of transfer. The evidence of laterality suggested to Hermelin and O'Connor that braille characters are processed by the brain primarily as spatial arrangements (a task thought to be mediated by the right hemisphere) rather than primarily as verbal material (a left-hemisphere task). Some caution should be exercised, however. The assumption of hemispheric specificity for these tasks is an easy but dangerous one even in regard to sighted individuals, and there is no independent evidence upon which to base this assumption for blind children.

Mommers (1980) replicated and extended the Hermelin and O'Connor (1971a) work, exploring the relative effectiveness of braille reading using the left and right index and middle fingers. In another condition the child was allowed free choice of fingers and hands. The blind children were all right-handed and ranged in age from 7 to 12. Both word lists and numeral lists were used. For a majority of the sample, performance was better for the left index (and middle) finger, and for numeral lists better for the right index (and middle) finger. However, a substantial proportion of the sample showed the reverse handedness effect. These hand-dominance effects were secondary, however: of the 25 children, 22 preferred to use both hands, and when this was allowed, performance was significantly better than under any of the more restricted hand/finger conditions.

Davidson, Wiles-Kettenmann, Haber, and Appelle (1980) investigated the relationship between tactual scanning strategies and braille reading proficiency. The subjects, whose average IQ was 92, ranged in age from 13 to 21 years of age. They were divided into four reading-proficiency groups, which also differed in mean IQ. Reading passages were selected to represent grade levels 2, 4, 8, and 12. Each subject read each of the passages aloud, in order of increasing difficulty, after which a retention test was administered to assess recall and recognition.

Each subject's hand movements while reading were analyzed from video recordings. Strategies were classified according to whether just one forefinger was used, or if both forefingers were used, whether they were used for part or all of the line. On this measure, subjects were very consistent in their choice of strategies, but there was no relationship between strategy and reading level or the incidence of reading errors or memory measures. The incidence of regresses (skipping backward to reread) and fixations (stopping for at least one second) was also recorded. Fixations were exceedingly rare, and regresses did not differentiate the strategy groups.

Davidson et al. (1980) suggested that these results show the linearity of the braille reading process, noting in particular that regresses place a burden on haptic short-term memory. The nondifferentiation of reading success on the basis of strategy suggests that consistency, in this respect, is a virtue – any reasonable strategy, used consistently, may yield success.

Summary. These results are straightforward and uncomplicated. There are clearly some variations in braille reading skill depending on the hand–finger combinations that are used, and individual children have distinct preferences. However, the amount of transfer of skill to non-preferred fingers is impressive. There is clearly a great deal of flexibility possible; and a variety of scanning strategies, consistently used, are useful.

The other senses

There is negligible work on the senses of taste and smell of children with visual impairments. We review studies of balance in Chapter 2.

Summary

As was noted at the beginning of this part on postinfancy perceptual development, there is nothing of great excitement to report. As expected, some general age trends appear in various studies, but other individual differences are notably absent in the findings. And overall, there is no finding that would make us anticipate difficulty in any other developmental area that depends on basic perceptual abilities in the nonvisual modalities.

Of course, there are aspects of perception that involve cognitive processes, such as the perception of spatial relationships. Material of this sort is covered in Chapters 3 and 4, and there are indeed significant variations in such abilities associated with factors related to visual impairment.

Sensory compensation

There is an enduring popular belief, sometimes referred to as "sensory compensation," that blindness is accompanied by an improvement in the basic acuity of the other senses, particularly hearing and touch. Over the past half-century, numerous studies have compared blind and sighted children and adults. There are occasional reports in which a sample of blind children shows superior performance in the discrimination of some stimulus property; these are balanced by reports in which there are no differences. There is no consistent pattern to the occasional differences, and on balance, no preponderance of evidence supports either the notion of sensory compensation or, for that matter, the alternative. In short, basic sensory discriminative abilities are much the same in blind, partially sighted, and sighted samples.

On the other hand, blind children are sometimes found to perform better on various tasks involving complex auditory stimulation (Miller, 1992). Better-developed habits of attention are often cited as the reason for these advantages, given that the evidence is firmly against differences in basic sensory discrimination. Miller provided an excellent review of the evidence, including close attention to individual differences variables, and concluded that neither attention nor strategy differences can account for all of the findings.

2

Motor and locomotor interaction with the physical world

In order to interact with the physical world effectively, the child must acquire motors skills, including travel as well as haptic exploration and manipulation. Success clearly depends in part on the effectiveness of perceptual skills, which we reviewed in Chapter 1; just as clearly, concepts of spatial relations must be involved.

Our approach is to treat first the infancy period, focusing on reaching and grasping, then locomotion. Then we move to issues of motor and locomotor development in the postinfancy period. Finally, we turn briefly to the phenomenon of stereotypic behaviors in children with visual impairments.

Infancy

Reaching and grasping

Our focus is on the manner in which the infant reaches for and grasps objects. These activities clearly depend on physical control of the musculature, but in addition, a fundamental prerequisite for these behaviors is adequate processing of the perceptual information that emanates from objects, whether that stimulation comes via the auditory, the visual, the tactual, or even the olfactory sense.

For sighted infants, a major milestone in this development typically occurs around four to five months of age, when the infant begins to reach for interesting objects that are seen. Reaching for objects that are only heard typically emerges later, in the last third of the first year (Freedman, 1971; Freedman, Fox-Kolenda, Margileth, & Miller, 1969).

What is the situation for infants with visual impairments?

Manual behaviors. The evidence is mixed with respect to two major indices, bimanual midline activity and reaching for objects. Fraiberg (1977) observed delays in the initiation of blind infants' bimanual activity, noting that by three months the typical sighted infant's hands are engaged in midline interaction, and that by five and a half months the infant can transfer an object from hand to hand. In this age range, Fraiberg's blind infants showed only chance midline hand encounters and no coordination of the activities of the two hands until a number of months later. However, other evidence is contradictory. On the Cattell Scale, the item "transfers object hand to hand" has a five-month norm for sighted infants. In their major study of children with visual impairments, Norris, Spaulding, and Brodie (1957) found that fewer than 50% succeeded at six months, but that performance jumped to more than 75% at nine months. A large proportion of the Norris et al. sample was blind due to ROP, and correction for prematurity would show 75% passing the item by six or seven months, about what would be expected based on the Cattell norms. Ferrell's (Ferrell et al., 1990) report of a median age of seven months for the "transfers object hand to hand" item is also clearly more consonant with the estimate of Norris et al. (1957) than that of Fraiberg. Thus, with respect to midline bimanual activity, there is a discrepancy between Fraiberg's conclusions and those from other work. However, the Norris and Ferrell results are based on data from much larger samples and are probably more representative.

Reaching for objects is another major developmental indicator. Norris et al. found an interesting disparity between Cattell items that involved grasping and those that involved reaching. The children with visual impairments showed the onset of grasping indicators at very close to the same time as the Cattell norms, whereas they were delayed in the reaching items. In fact, fewer than 25% of the infants passed the "unilateral reach" at the normative age of six months. By nine months, more than 75% of the Norris infants did so. It should be noted that a large majority of this sample was blind from ROP and that no age correction for prematurity was used. If a three-month correction factor is applied, then even the unilateral reaching item shows age-appropriate achievement according to the Cattell norms. It is difficult to know what to make of this evidence, since it is unfortunately unclear what stimulus was used to elicit the reaching response.

Summary. Although the evidence about manual behaviors is mixed, the outcomes from larger samples such as those of Norris and Ferrell tend to show some indications of developmental lag. These are generally not of the magnitude suggested by Fraiberg, however. The answer to the apparent disparity may lie in the variance. Both Ferrell and Norris found considerable variability within their samples. It is likely that Fraiberg's observations, based on very few cases, fell within these ranges of variability. In any case, results from larger samples tend to be more reliable. Unfortunately, there is as yet little indication of the importance of partial vision in facilitating the development of manual behaviors; as the VIIRC project (Ferrell et al., 1990) develops, this picture should become clearer.

Reaching to sound. Infants with vision are apparently slower to reach to audible objects than to visible objects. Freedman et al. (1969) studied sighted infants from 5 to 12 months of age, observing their behavior in a situation in which a bell was sounded and the infant was allowed to handle it, upon which the bell was removed from the infant's grasp and hidden while the infant was temporarily distracted. While hidden, the bell was again sounded. It was not until 40 weeks of age that more than half of the infants actively searched for the bell. Sound, in contrast to visual information, was a relatively ineffective stimulus for object search in sighted infants until around nine months of age.

Other evidence suggests the earlier development of reaching to sound. Wishart, Bower, and Dunkeld (1978) found that sighted infants reach to sounding objects in the four- to five-month period, then do not reach in the next five months, then begin effective reaching again around 10 months of age. However, Stack, Muir, and Sherriff (1986) found a gradually increasing frequency and accuracy of reaching by sighted infants to sounding objects in the dark over the two- to seven-month age range.

The tasks used in these various studies are sufficiently different that some discrepancies in outcomes are not surprising. However, this also means that generalizations are not yet possible about the development of reaching to sounding objects in sighted infants.

Not surprisingly, the evidence about the development of reaching to sounds in blind infants is similarly mixed. Several investigators have reported that reaching to sound develops more slowly than other aspects of motor development (Fraiberg & Freedman, 1964; Wills, 1970). Fraiberg et al. (1966) used three tasks to investigate the effectiveness of various stimuli in eliciting reaching. *Touch alone:* a soundless object was presented to the hand, then withdrawn. *Sound alone:* a sound-making object was sounded and placed in front of the infant, with no tactile contact. *Sound and touch:* a sound-making object was sounded and was touched to the infant's hand, and then was placed in front of the infant. Numerous variations on these tasks occurred, including some using the infant's own toys as stimuli, but the basic results were as follows.

One infant showed the following sequence. For *touch alone* and *sound and touch,* a fleeting "hand pantomime" was observed at six to seven months when the object was removed; unsystematic and fragile exploratory activities began in the seven- to eight-month range, and systematic and successful reaching began around eight months. By contrast, although at six months the infant was attentive to the object in the *sound alone* condition, no hand activity occurred until about eight months, when a brief "hand pantomime" was seen. Not until 11 months did successful reaching for a sounding object occur. The median age for successful reach to sound was nine months for the group of 10 infants, but the sequence of task success was routinely the same as for the infant described here.

Bigelow (1986) used a more differentiated set of reaching tasks. The five children ranged from 11 to 32 months at the onset of testing and therefore were older than Fraiberg's infants when they were beginning to reach to sound. On the other hand, Bigelow's infants apparently did not have the benefit of an "educational" program as Fraiberg's infants did, and slower development might be expected. Indeed, despite their more advanced age, it was clear that some of Bigelow's infants had not yet mastered the behaviors that all of Fraiberg's sample had achieved by the end of the first year. A further precaution about strict comparison of Bigelow's and Fraiberg's results is that Bigelow used a considerably stricter criterion for success on any given task.

In addition to her corroboration of the late reach to sound, a major point of interest in Bigelow's work is the task variations she used. In addition to the basic task, in which the sound was presented straight ahead of the infant at chest level, variations included lateral and vertical presentation, and moving and intermittent stimuli. A general summary of the results is as follows.

Reaching to vertically displaced stimuli appeared later than to laterally displaced stimuli. Lateral displacements did not differ from midline presentation, but reaching in both of these tasks occurred on the first month's test and differences might have been revealed by earlier testing. The difficulty of vertical displacements is not surprising in view of the generally lesser discrimination by human observers of vertical locations of sounds.

Response to sideways movement occurred later than to stationary midline presentation. Reaching to a moving and intermittently sounding stimulus occurred later than to a moving and continuously sounding stimulus, which in turn was later than reaching to the midline stationary intermittent stimulus. Paradoxically, a stationary object sounding intermittently at midline was most difficult of all; no infant was successful in the duration of the testing.

Much more research must be done for a complete understanding of the development of reaching to sounds. Bigelow's infants were already too old at the outset of testing for us to differentiate effectively among all task variations and to ascertain the age of initial success on some tasks. Nevertheless, the results are clear as to the age ordering of some of the stimulus variations, and even more important, Bigelow's work serves as a model for dissecting the effects of stimulus variations with a small sample of subjects. This work is important and should be followed up vigorously.

Based on evidence noted in Chapter 1, it is clear that these difficulties are not due to deficiencies in basic auditory perception. Sound-producing objects are perceived, but they are largely ineffective in eliciting reaching.

Despite the evidence of Fraiberg and Bigelow showing delayed reaching to sound, three contradictory studies should be noted. Bower (1974) cited results of a study by Urwin, who reported that one blind infant reached to grasp sounding objects at the age of four months. By six months this behavior had ceased, despite experimental efforts to sustain it, and did not reappear until the end of the first year. Second, Als, Tronick, and Brazelton (1980b) reported that one full-term congenitally blind infant developed progressively more refined reaching toward the mother on the basis of auditory cues by five months of age. No significant interruption in the reaching behavior was noted. In this case, the mother had engaged in a great deal of social interaction and had apparently established a very strong affective bond with the infant. Finally, Schwartz (1984) reported the case of Andrew, who began to reach for sounds at 19 weeks (corrected age, actual age 35 weeks). Andrew showed generally delayed motor development, including manual activity, due to cerebral palsy (CP). Upon initiation of an experiential program, he began to reach to sound and quickly was successful in grasping sounding objects. No subsequent loss of these abilities was reported.

Reaching to sounds is an important issue. If it is indeed the case that there is an early period for the blind infant in which sounds generally do elicit reaching, then this should be clearly established, as should the circumstances and conditions under which the behavior may disappear and then reappear. Detailed observations of more blind infants are clearly needed to inform our knowledge in this area, and the role of partial vision must be explored.

Given the obvious importance of vision to the sighted infant during this period, it is tempting to attribute the blind infant's failure to reach to sounds solely to the lack of visual stimulation. However, other information should be considered before we accept this conclusion.

Hart (1983) proposed a motor basis for the late reaching observed in blind infants. Hart observed that a common characteristic of blind infants, particularly those with incubator experience, is resistance to lying in the prone position. This observation was echoed by Adelson and Fraiberg (1974). Hart further cited evidence linking experience in the prone position to effective development of the motor strength and coordination that are prerequisite for reaching. Lying in the supine position leaves the arms free to wave about and possibly reach for objects, but the unconstrained activity of the arms in this position does not require the development of the musculature of chest, shoulders, and arms that mediates more versatile arm activity.

Lying in the prone position, the blind infant may indeed be less likely to reach outward spontaneously than in the supine position, precisely because of the added muscular requirements. What is required, apparently, is a combination of the more demanding prone position and an effective stimulus for reaching outward. Freedman (1972) noted that five- to six-month-old infants with any degree of light perception were more likely to wave their hands across the visual field than those without any visual function. Even a minor amount of visual capability may thus serve a useful function. Hart (1983) also noted the importance of any degree of vision: "The vision can be stimulated to encourage the head righting, prone position, reaching and other movement" (p. 7). Fraiberg et al. (1966) also noted that infants with "even a small amount of useful vision follow closely the developmental patterns of sighted children. Light perception alone affords an advantage to the blind infant" (p. 331).

A summary of the evidence about reaching to sound is difficult. Given the lack of agreement about this development for sighted infants, the discrepancies in the literature for blind infants are not surprising. On the one hand, several investigators have found reaching to sounds only toward the end of the first year, whereas others have reported isolated cases of earlier reaching. None of the studies has examined more than a few cases. Clearly this development is characterized by sufficient variability that trying to identify a norm is hopeless without far more data. The norm should not be the research goal, however; it is important to understand the relationship of the development of reaching to such factors as muscular strength, affect, and partial vision.

Artificial sensory devices. The question occurs whether nonvisual stimulation of any sort might serve as an effective stimulus to encourage the blind infant's tendency to reach to events in the external environment. In the past couple of decades several electronic devices have been developed to deliver to the visually impaired person information that would ordinarily be obtained by the use of vision. One of these, the commercially available Sonicguide, has been adapted for research and applied use by several investigators. The Sonicguide is a sonar-based system that delivers, via earphones or ear tubes, a complex auditory signal containing information about the distance, direction, and surface characteristics of objects in its range (Kay, 1974). The effectiveness of the Sonicguide in stimulating development has been studied for a number of areas. For the present, our treatment will be restricted to the question of whether its use facilitates the development of reaching. Other research uses of the Sonicguide are considered in subsequent sections.

Bower opened the issue with his provocatively titled article "Blind Babies See with Their Ears" (1977). A blind infant was fitted with a modified Sonicguide at 16 weeks of age. In the initial session, the infant was reported to perform a variety of motor and oculomotor behaviors in response to objects mediated by the Sonicguide, and in particular to swipe manually at moving objects. Subsequent development was reported to include two-handed reaching at six months.

The credibility of Bower's report was questioned by Kay, the inventor of the Sonicguide, who pointed out that the physical capabilities of the equipment used by Bower were not sufficient to deliver the information that Bower's infant needed to perform the tasks as reported (Kay & Strelow, 1977). It suffices here to say that there is little case to be made on the basis of Bower's initial report. Fortunately, a considerable amount of subsequent research has shed more light on the subject.

Aitken and Bower (1982) reported two sets of work, one with infants on a very short-term basis (one to seven hours of Sonicguide experience) and the other with longer-term experience. Only the short-term study is relevant here. While wearing the Sonicguide, infants at five, six, and eight months of age were reported to reach accurately to objects at midline, and the six- and eight-month-olds also reached to objects in lateral locations, while the youngest "swiped" at such objects. All of these ages for reaching for midline objects are on the low side compared to Fraiberg's "reaching to sound" task, which was achieved at a median age of nine months (Fraiberg et al., 1966).

Taken at face value, the Aitken and Bower reports of reaching based on Sonicguide information at these ages seem impressive. The attractive conclusion is that auditory information about spatial structure provided by the Sonicguide can effectively substitute for vision for young blind infants. However, several reservations should be expressed. First, it is not clear that the infants were indeed totally blind, and as we have already seen, even a small amount of residual vision may make a difference in the development of reaching. Second, the parents of these infants were reported to be highly motivated to help their babies (as witnessed by their willingness to travel an average of 400 miles to visit the laboratory), and may therefore have provided unusually stimulating perceptual and social environments for their infants. This factor itself might well have produced earlier reaching to objects based on sound cues alone, as suggested by Als et al. (1980a). Both of these factors would have operated to produce earlier reaching even without the Sonicguide, and since no pretest of reaching to sound cues without the Sonicguide was reported, it is uncertain what the infants' preexisting developmental level might have been. Third, the Aitken and Bower results have been attributed to experimental artifact and/or misinterpretation of the data (Kay, 1984).

A number of other studies help clarify the issues. Sampaio (1989) reported the results of several infants, including a five- and a six-month-old. The younger showed evidence of reaching to a midline object in a third of the trials and orientation movements of the head in other trials.

The six-month-old did not show reaching behavior until after five one-hour sessions with the Sonicguide, distributed over a month's time. Both infants, though, showed fragmentary hand movements reminiscent of Fraiberg's reports of the clutching that occurs before reaching itself emerges.

Harris, Humphrey, Muir, and Dodwell (1985) studied an infant born prematurely that was subsequently a victim of ROP. At six months of age, she did not reach to sounds, although generally her developmental indices on the Bayley Motor Scale were in the low-normal range. Although she quieted in response to the initial sounds of the Sonicguide, she showed no orientation responses, and in particular no reaching. At this point an intensive training program without the Sonicguide began, and by nine months (at Fraiberg's median age for reaching to sounds), she showed considerable success in reaching to sounds. Upon reintroduction of the Sonicguide at this point, she was able to reach to objects mediated by the device after a short period of further training. Harris et al. (1985) concluded that, contrary to the Bower reports, this infant did not make spontaneous use of the Sonicguide's information, and that subsequent successful use of the device depended on an extensive program of training with natural sounds.

The same research group reported data from another blind infant who was initially exposed to the Sonicguide at eight months of age (Humphrey, Dodwell, Muir, & Humphrey, 1988). At that time he had begun to reach for sounding objects. Upon initial presentation of an object in the field of the Sonicguide, he reached for the headband of the device; in the second session he made tactual contact with the object, first accidentally and then apparently intentionally. Again, though, there was no evidence that the Sonicguide stimulated more advanced reaching than had already occurred without the device.

Still another report is available from Ferrell (1980). Only one of Ferrell's infants was young enough to bear on the question of reaching. This infant was introduced to the Sonicguide at six months of age and began reaching to objects based on Sonicguide input at eight months, before she reached to objects without the device.

There has been much effort devoted to evaluation of the Sonicguide as a possible means of accelerating the development of reaching in blind infants. Of all of the infants tested, only two (Sampaio's five-month-old and Ferrell's six-month-old) present credible evidence that reaching to objects based on Sonicguide information was developmentally facilitated. Ferrell's conclusion that "the Sonicguide is certainly not the panacea that has been suggested" (1984, p. 216) seems appropriate. Electronic devices such as the Sonicguide may indeed play a role in assisting the infant's perception of the external environment. Nevertheless, most studies suggest that such devices cannot hasten development and depend on effective prior developmental achievement. It seems clear that research should be devoted to how best to stimulate development by the provision of appropriate natural experience and opportunity, rather than how to substitute for experience and opportunity by artificial means.

Summary. It is difficult to summarize the work on reaching and grasping succinctly because of the contradictions that exist in the research literature. Particularly for reaching outward for external stimuli, there are some indications that blind infants may lag normatively behind sighted infants. However, this is not a safe conclusion because so few infants have been studied and because collectively the results are so diverse. The counterinstances are also provocative in suggesting that patterns of environmental circumstances may elicit reaching earlier in some cases, and we have to wonder what the norms would be if more ideal environmental circumstances were provided for all blind infants.

Finally, it must be noted that reaching should not be considered as strictly a perceptual–motor act, but rather as one that involves conceptual and affective factors as well. Fraiberg (1968) argued that auditory information does not signify the existence of an external object for the blind infant before 10 months. It is not that the infant cannot perceive the stimulus or cannot physically perform the reaching behavior, but that the infant does not reach to a sounding object because the stimulus does not denote an object to be reached for. In Chapter 3 we will consider the infant's budding understanding of the nature of the physical world.

Motor and locomotor development

The neonate's motor activity is characterized by reflexive action; there is little voluntary behavior. Shortly after midyear the typical infant is beginning to crawl, and by a year, to walk; by two years, a wide variety of motor and locomotor capabilities have normally appeared.

The debate over the factors that cause or allow locomotor development to proceed in these early stages has been with us for decades and will continue. It is clear that both physical maturation and opportunity are critical. Without adequate physical development, no richness of opportunity will elicit progressively more capable behaviors; and no matter how physically robust the infant may be, the developmental expression of motor activities is impossible without the opportunity to "operate on" the world, whether reaching for stimulating objects or moving about in the environment.

The term "locomotion" refers to self-produced motion of the entire body with respect to the environment. Active movement of an arm or leg does not qualify, nor does passive movement of the entire body (as in being carried about). Thus, our concern in the infancy period will be with the development of crawling and walking.

The development of these behaviors depends at very least on the physical readiness of the musculature. Without the physical capability to support the body on hands and knees, crawling cannot occur, and later, unless the legs are capable of supporting and balancing the body, walking cannot, either. Evidence from decades of normative research suggests that the physical capabilities basic to crawling normally develop by midway in the first year, and that those requisite for taking the first steps normally develop by around the end of it.

Even given the necessary physical capabilities, crawling and walking do not typically occur without adequate perceptual stimulation. The infant crawls not for the sake of the activity itself, but rather in order to accomplish a goal, perhaps to get a toy beyond reach. Nor is walking an end in itself: the child walks in order to approach and attain objects in the physical environment. Clearly the perception of stimuli that signify events in the external environment is as critical in initiation of these activities as is the attainment of physical readiness to crawl or walk.

One of the most durable findings in the research literature on visual impairment and infancy is the slowness of locomotion to occur. Most infants crawl before they walk. It is clear from the work of Fraiberg (1977) and others that crawling is generally delayed in blind infants. Fraiberg's infants generally did not begin to crawl until near the end of the first year of life, and this finding has been corroborated by other investigators (e.g., Ferrell et al., 1990; Freedman & Cannady, 1971; Norris et al., 1957).

Whereas sighted infants typically begin to walk around a year of age,

Table 2. *Selected data for visually impaired subjects from VIIRC study*

Task	Median age (months)	SIR[a]
Reaches for and grasps toy	6.5	2.9
Transfers object hand to hand	7.0	2.0
Searches for a dropped toy	12.0	4.5
Says first word	10.0	2.5
Crawls	10.0	3.1
Walks alone without support	15.0	4.5

[a]SIR refers to semi-interquartile range, which is one-half of the difference between the first and third quartile values. For example, for the item "crawls," half of the sample had crawled by 10 months of age, and 50% of the sample began to crawl at some point within a 6.2-month range that extends to either side of the median age.

Source: Ferrell et al. (1990).

there is much evidence that blind infants typically do not do so until significantly later. The item "walks alone, few steps" showed a median age of 15.3 months (range 11.5 to 19) for Adelson and Fraiberg's sample of blind infants, compared to the Bayley median of 11.7 (range 9 to 17 months). Urwin's (1978) totally blind infant began to walk at 15 months. The intensive sample of Norris et al. (1957) showed somewhat slower accomplishments: "walks alone, few steps" was not accomplished by at least half of the infants until 18 months (these ages are corrected for prematurity). On the relatively more positive side, the more recent sample of Ferrell et al. (1990) showed a median age of 15 months for the item "walks alone without support" (see Table 2).

It should be noted that the problem in delayed walking apparently is not with the prerequisite ability to stand. For example, for their group of 10 infants, Adelson and Fraiberg (1974) reported a median age for "stands alone" of 13 months (range 9 to 15.5 months), compared to the Bayley median for sighted infants of 11 months (range 9 to 16 months).

For a full understanding of these developments it is not sufficient to look just at median ages of achievement; we must look at the age ranges as well, since these represent differences among individuals within samples. In particular, it is evident that some blind infants achieve these milestones virtually as early as sighted infants do. It is on the high end that major differences occur, and statistically, the fact that the age range extends upward further for samples of blind infants tends to pull the median age of the group up. Thus, lack of vision is clearly not the only factor at work. There are numerous other variables whose effects must be understood.

There is surprisingly little work on the overall orientation and mobility characteristics of preschool children with visual impairments, but the research program of Brambring and his colleagues holds great promise. Brambring, Dobslaw, Hauptmeier, Hecker, Latta-Weber, and Troester (1989) have under development the Bielefeld Developmental Test for Blind Infants and Preschoolers and the associated Bielefeld Parents' Questionnaire. These have been used to evaluate the orientation and mobility performance of infants and preschoolers from 9 to 48 months of age. Subscales assess crawling, walking, and more advanced locomotor behaviors. The subjects to date are children who have at most LP. Four-fifths are blind from birth, which was premature in 40% of the cases.

The results show a regular improvement with increasing age on the overall orientation and mobility scale. Brambring et al. noted a high variance within age groups, but as yet, little information is available about the factors that may influence individual variation. This important project will continue to generate useful data, particularly as it expands to include infants and preschoolers with a broader set of visual characteristics.

We now turn to two major questions. First, what accounts for the relatively slow development of locomotion by some blind infants? Second, what factors are associated with faster development? We address these issues by considering several alternative hypotheses about factors involved in locomotor development in blind infants and by examining the available evidence for each of them.

Vision. An apparently attractive but naive hypothesis is that the lack of visual capability is the simple cause of delayed development. This hypothesis is attractive because it *is* simple, but it has two fatal flaws. First, it does not recognize the empirical evidence; that some blind infants begin to walk as early as some sighted infants is sufficient to discredit the hypothesis. Second, the statement that "walking is slow because vision is absent" is simply a statement of relationship. It contains no seeds of explanation and consequently is theoretically sterile.

However, it is reasonable to ask whether residual vision facilitates the development of locomotion. Given the importance of the issue, there is surprisingly little empirical evidence. Hart (1983), reporting preliminary evidence, noted not only that infants with "any amount of vision seem to reach their developmental milestones more quickly than those who are totally blind," but also that "some of the blind children who have developed more quickly have later turned out to have some degree of vision" (p. 7). Hart also suggested that this earlier motor progress may be facilitated by "greater tolerance of the prone position, greater head righting, more motor movement," and that these children may be "easier to intervene with because the vision can be stimulated to encourage the head righting, prone position, reaching and other movement" (p. 7).

Hart's evidence suggests that any degree of visual function should facilitate the development of locomotion. Support for this comes from Fraiberg (1968), who noted that babies with some visual function tend to follow the pattern of development of sighted infants with only minor lags. In his comparison of partially sighted with totally blind infants, Keeler (1958) found that the former did not show the typical patterns of delayed motor development that the latter did. Given the importance of the issue, it is critical that research be directed toward ascertaining the dynamics of these influences, the extent to which these dynamics may be facilitated by intervention with infants with some partial vision, and how effectively similar influences might be brought to bear even with infants who are totally blind.

Overall motor slowdown. Another obvious hypothesis is that blind infants are generally slow to develop motor capabilities, and that the slowness to crawl and walk is simply one facet in an overall pattern of delay in every area of motor development.

The evidence contradicts this general hypothesis. There is not a generalized slowdown of motor development; the idiosyncrasies of motor development are in large part specific to the locomotor area. For example, Adelson and Fraiberg (1974) compared the development of their group of 10 congenitally blind infants with that of the group studied by Norris et al. (1957), as well as with the Bayley norms for sighted infants. The development of the 10 infants was only slightly delayed with respect to that of sighted infants in areas of muscular and postural development ("sits alone momentarily," "rolls from back to stomach," "sits alone steadily," "stepping movements," and "stands alone"). However, on the two items that were clearly related to locomotor activities ("walks alone, 3 steps," "walks alone, across room") the blind infants were delayed. The evidence does not show a general delay in motor development, but rather one specific to walking.

Muscular readiness. Another possibility is that the large muscles required for locomotion are slow to develop. If this is true, then all activities that depend on large-muscle groups should be delayed.

Several pieces of evidence contradict this hypothesis. Adelson and Fraiberg (1974) reported substantial lags for behaviors related to actual walking, but that other behaviors that depend on large muscles showed much less delay in relation to sighted norms. With respect to crawling, Fraiberg noted that each of her infants showed the same phenomenon late in the first year: "In spite of demonstrated postural readiness for creeping, at a point where the baby can support himself well on hands and knees, the blind baby is unable to creep" (1968, p. 279). Fraiberg argued that the infant's failure to crawl at this point is due *not* to muscular or postural limitations, but rather to the infant's failure to reach outward to sound cues, a point to which we will return.

Hart (1983) presented a different argument. She noted that many of the infants she studied were resistant to the prone position, and that the more they occupied the supine position, the greater the resistance to the prone position was. This lack of experience in the prone position, she argued, causes their delay in developing reaching behaviors. Experience in the prone position develops the musculature and postural stability that is requisite for reaching while on hands and knees, as well as for initiating crawling movements. In fact, some infants who were given increased experience in the prone position not only reached within the normal time frame but developed the musculature necessary for appropriate head posture as well.

Thus, part of the picture seems clear. The Adelson and Fraiberg (1974) evidence shows some delays in nonwalking gross motor development (e.g., standing), delays that may well be due to poor muscular development. This interpretation is consonant with Hart's (1983) emphasis on the importance of the prone position for the development of muscular and postural readiness for reaching and crawling. What does not fit neatly into this picture is Fraiberg's (1968) observation that her infants were ready to crawl from a muscular and postural point of view well before they began to reach and then crawl. If Hart's results prove to have generality, then in any case the practical answer would seem to lie in emphasizing the prone position, in order to facilitate the development of reaching.

The other senses. When vision is intact, the infant can see objects in the distal environment, and no doubt this is a major source of stimulation to begin locomotion. For the blind infant, vision cannot play this role, and in the partially sighted infant the role of vision in furnishing information about the distal environment is reduced. In these circumstances, we may ask about the role of the other sensory modalities in providing information to motivate locomotion. Hearing and smell are the only sensory modalities capable of providing information about the distal environment. I know of no reported evidence about the possible role of olfaction in stimulating locomotion in blind infants, although the issue may not be trivial. Thus, we turn our attention to the role that audition might play.

The prevalent pattern among Fraiberg's infants was for crawling to begin shortly after the infant began to reach for sounds. Fraiberg and her colleagues made the argument that sound does not serve as an effective stimulus for reaching until late in the first year, and that this is because the infant does not understand that external sound can denote objects that can be reached for. As soon as the arm motion of reaching to sounds begins, the same motion serves to enable crawling. According to this view, the problem is a cognitive rather than a perceptual one. It is a problem nonetheless, and one that resisted the vigorous efforts of the Fraiberg educational program, which included every attempt to induce the blind infant to reach for sounding objects earlier than the last quarter of the first year. On the other hand, Hart (1983) found earlier reaching (presumably to auditory stimuli) and earlier crawling when experience in the prone position was emphasized, and she suggested that the problem may be more postural and muscular than a failure of auditory stimuli to evoke motor responses. Contrary evidence is also offered by Schwartz (1984), whose two very different infants both began to crawl at about 14 months. One (C) had in fact not begun to reach for sounds by this time, whereas the other (A) had begun to reach for sounds at around five months. In neither case was crawling closely related to reaching to sounds. The latter infant had some CP involvement, to be sure, but the example of these two infants serves only to underscore the importance of attending to individual differences among infants.

Artificial sensory devices. In the previous section on reaching, we considered the possibility that artificial sensory devices might provide information about environmental events sufficient to stimulate the earlier onset of reaching. The corresponding question may be asked about locomotion. Unfortunately, there is less evidence about this than about reaching. Of the three "long term" infants studied by Aitken and Bower (1982), one began Sonicguide use at 6 months, then crawled at 14 and walked at 16 months. The second began Sonicguide use at 8 months and had not begun walking by 20 months; the third began Sonicguide use at 13 months and showed no appreciable developmental progress at all. It is possible that the second infant's use of a rolling "walker" actually interfered with the development of walking proper, and it was noted that the third infant's parents were extremely overprotective and probably did not allow the infant sufficient opportunity to develop his motor skills, regardless of the sensory device.

Ferrell (1980) reported the results of four infants who ranged in age from 6 to 26 months when Sonicguide use began. Regarding the development of locomotor skills, one infant had attained most motor skills before introduction of the Sonicguide at 26 months of age; a second received the Sonicguide at 14 months, began to crawl a month later, but had not begun to walk by 36 months. Another received the Sonicguide at 14.5 months, began to crawl at 16 months and to walk at 22 months. The fourth received the Sonicguide at 6 months, began to crawl at 12 months, and walked at 16 months. Despite this generally negative evidence about the effectiveness of the Sonicguide in facilitating locomotor behavior, Ferrell did note that all of the infants "appeared much more confident of their movements when wearing the Sonicguide" (p. 217), and that all of the children showed a better head-up posture while wearing the device.

Although Ferrell's project was not specifically designed to test whether the use of an artificial sensory device might elicit earlier locomotor behaviors, her conclusion about this question is cogent: "The results are not impressive" (p. 217). In fact, these blind infants showed locomotor behaviors well within the age range when they might have been expected to without the Sonicguide.

This conclusion, in fact, serves to summarize the findings available to date: there is no compelling evidence that use of the Sonicguide stimulates the development of locomotor abilities earlier than they might be expected to emerge spontaneously.

Opportunity. A final hypothesis is that the key factor in the delayed locomotor development of some blind infants is the restriction of opportunity. In their extensive study, Norris et al. (1957) noted that developmental lags occur in various areas, including locomotion, and that these areas have in common that they require specific experience and stimulation to elicit appropriate development. With regard to the item "moves about on floor," Norris et al. reported that "well over half of the children . . . observed at nine months received credit. . . . Children who did not develop some means of getting about on the floor at the 'normal' age were typically those who were not given appropriate opportunities for doing so" (p. 39). Further with regard to the locomotor item "walks alone," Norris et al. noted a broad span of age of attainment, ranging from well within sighted norms to serious delay until four or five years of age. Again, lack of appropriate opportunity was implicated as a major factor in the cases of most serious delay.

Opportunity is also cited as a factor by other authors. Adelson and Fraiberg (1974), comparing their group of 10 with the Norris et al. intensive sample, found that median age of attainment did not differ appreciably in areas of nonlocomotor gross motor development. On the clearly locomotor items, the Adelson and Fraiberg sample was clearly superior, although the difference diminishes when the Norris et al. ages are corrected for prematurity. The two samples differed in several ways, but Adelson and Fraiberg attributed their group's superior performance to "the cumulative effects of the intervention program. Delays in mobility and locomotion were lessened when we were successful in providing early auditory-tactile experiences that sustained interest in the external world, encouraged physical activity, and ultimately permitted sound to serve as a lure for forward progression" (p. 121).

As previously noted, Hart (1983) attributed the earlier gross motor development of some of her infants to their experience in the prone position. The chance to exercise muscles and master postures is certainly another variety of opportunity.

Yet another striking example is provided by Freedman and Cannady (1971) in their study of seven blind infants. The development of these infants was compared to the McGraw (1945) norms for the crawling substages for sighted infants. Three of the infants were congenitally blind, four (including one of the blind infants and one of the nonblind Rubella infants) were "environmentally deprived," and three (including the blind and environmentally deprived infant) were Rubella babies. Of the blind subjects, only the environmentally deprived infant (with Rubella) fell consistently outside of the McGraw norms. By contrast, all of the Rubella babies and all of the environmentally deprived infants were consistently slower than the McGraw norms at each substage of the development of crawling. The conclusions are striking within the limitations of the small sample: blindness without environmental deprivation did not produce marked delays, whereas environmental deprivation, with or without blindness, was implicated in the serious delays shown by four infants.

Summary. The evidence is compelling that, in general, blind infants are slower to crawl and walk than sighted infants; the critical question is why. It is clear from the evidence that lack of vision does not necessarily create a handicap, although total blindness creates a higher risk than partial vision. Muscular readiness is of course a prerequisite for locomotion, but it is also more related to opportunity than to visual loss. Artificial sensory aids are clearly not the answer. The conclusion seems warranted that the most important factor in determining the locomotor capabilities of the visually impaired infant is *opportunity*. Simply put, restriction of opportunity causes developmental delays in locomotion.

Locomotor abilities in the postinfancy period

In preschool and school-age children, locomotor abilities are prerequisite to many activities. Effective mobility in the environment is perhaps the most obvious of these. More generally, though, there is the issue of physical fitness, which is prerequisite not only to general health but to the enjoyment of a variety of recreational opportunities.

Locomotor abilities and physical fitness

There have been numerous studies of the general locomotor abilities of preschool and school-age children with visual impairments, and in general these show poor levels of physical fitness. Buell (1950) found various areas of motor performance in which children with visual impairments did not meet sighted norms. He attributed these difficulties to the child's failure to engage in sufficient physical activity before entering school. In turn, the limited physical activity was attributed to parental overprotection. Buell advised that "insofar as motor performance is concerned, parental neglect is to be preferred to overprotection" (p. 71).

More recently, the Project UNIQUE test of physical fitness was developed by Short and Winnick (1986). The children were 10 to 17 years old and included both boys and girls. One group was legally blind, while a "partially sighted" group ranged in acuity from 20/70 to 20/200 (these children were thus not legally blind). The children had no additional handicaps or physical disabilities. Generally, the overall fitness level of both groups was lower than that of sighted children. Boys generally scored better than girls except in flexibility, and fitness generally improved with increasing age (note the contrast with the results from Jankowski & Evans, 1981, discussed later in this section). On nonrunning items, the two vision groups did not differ, but on running items the children with more severe visual loss did not score as well, even taking the different means of assisted running into account. Short and Winnick clearly implicated reduced opportunity for physical exercise as the major factor in producing this pattern of results.

The opportunities for physical exercise apparently differ across school settings. Buell (1982) concluded that many public schools do not have adequate programs in physical education for students with visual impairments, and that their fitness may suffer in an integrated school. This point is well supported by Seeyle (1983), who used the Kraus–Weber Minimum Physical Fitness Test with partially sighted and blind elementary and junior high school students, drawn from a metropolitan public school system. Whereas the partially sighted children performed reasonably well, with a pass rate of 84% for the test as a whole, only 46% of the blind group passed. It was noted that even the partially sighted students did not for the most part participate in the physical education activities of sighted students and apparently did not have separate activities for fitness.

Short and Winnick (1988) analyzed the data from their 1986 study further in terms of the educational placement of the children. Placement was either in segregated residential or nonresidential schools for handicapped students, or in integrated schools. Although the pattern of results was mixed, there was if anything a tendency for better performance by children in segregated schools. Short and Winnick, like Buell (1982), concluded that exercise programs in integrated schools are generally not adequate for students with visual impairments.

The situation is not necessarily better in special schools, however. Jankowski and Evans (1981) tested a sample of 20 blind children (whose characteristics were not further specified), from 4 to 18 years old, from a "progressively run" school for children with visual impairments. Despite the excellent physical facilities of the school and the requirement of two 30-min periods of physical activity per week, the vast majority of the children were overweight, had low grip strength, low oxygen uptake, and (based on a finding of increasing percentage of body fat with increasing age) generally showed a developmentally "increasingly sedentary lifestyle." Jankowski and Evans suggested that a daily program of vigorous exercise would bring the physical fitness of these children into acceptable limits within about eight months.

It is clear that the characteristics of the physical environment play an important part in determining the level of physical activity of children with visual impairments, just as they do for sighted children. Schneekloth (1989) assessed the motor proficiency level of 7- to 13-year-old blind and partially sighted children, the frequency and kinds of their behaviors in unstructured play, and the nature of their interaction with the physical environment. Time sampling of unstructured play was conducted over a six-week period. Analyses revealed that although most of the children showed basic motor proficiency, the higher their proficiency was, the higher were the frequency, diversity, and complexity of gross motor behaviors exhibited. Some differences in the nature of play emerged between the vision groups. The blind children spent more of their play time alone than the partially sighted children. The play interactions of the visually impaired children also tended to occur more with adults than with other children.

The blind children, though they were clearly capable as measured by the motor proficiency test, tended to show less active and passive activity than the partially sighted children. Schneekloth concluded that "developmental delays seen in the visually impaired children may not result from their handicapping condition alone. Rather, . . . some of the delay can be attributed to lack of experience, particularly in gross motor interactions with the environment" (p. 197). Schneekloth stressed the need for specially designed environments for children with visual impairments, thus echoing the point made by Buell (1982).

Nor is the social environment inconsequential in the visually impaired child's level of physical activity. Nixon (1988) conducted in-depth interviews with the parents of partially sighted and blind children enrolled in public schools. The children had generally lost vision within the first few years, ranged in age from 7 to 19 years, and included both boys and girls. Parental attitudes toward the involvement of their children in physical education and organized sports ranged from "strong encouragers" downward to "tolerators" and "discouragers." Half of the children were not involved in any type of sport. A strong relationship was found between parental attitudes and the children's participation. This is true within the population of sighted children and their parents as well, but the dynamics may be even stronger in the case of participation in organized sports by children with visual impairments, simply because of the logistics of that participation. Parental attitudes clearly influenced the degree of the child's participation in school-based physical education activities as well. Among the "tolerators" and "discouragers," the prevalent attitude seemed to be more a matter of devaluation of physical activities in relation to academic activities than of discouragement of physical activities because they might be dangerous or inappropriate. That is to say, the issue was more the value of physical activity in general than the child's visual impairment. The dynamics are the same as for sighted children, but the effects of parental interest may be more serious in children with visual impairments.

Summary. The evidence clearly supports the conclusion that children with visual impairments are at risk for poor physical fitness. Investigators agree that poor fitness is not a necessary consequence of visual impairment. The relationship of fitness to partial vision is not clear in the evidence. The opportunities that the child has for engaging in physical activities, and the encouragement that they receive to do so, are the keys. Fitness and physical activity vary in complex ways across school situations, and although some general trends emerge, it is undoubtedly not the type of school but rather the nature of the opportunities and the encouragement provided that make the major difference.

Aspects of locomotor success

The various types of postural and locomotor abilities involved in general mobility success have been evaluated in numerous research projects, and there is clear variation associated with several factors. These include aspects of visual experience such as early vision and residual vision, and particularly experience, including the effects of training programs.

Posture and balance. The ability to maintain posture is fundamental to effective locomotion. Gipsman (1979) evaluated the ability of partially sighted and blind children (who had lost sight by age two) to adjust their posture to the upright. The child was seated in a chair whose tilt was adjustable and was instructed to adjust him- or herself to upright by means of a hand control. All children were tested without vision. There was no difference between 12- to 14-year-old partially sighted and blind children, but in a younger group (8 to 10 years), the performance of the blind children was worse. All children showed improvement over a three- to five-week practice period. Not surprisingly, Hill, Spencer, and Baybutt (1985) found a significant correlation between teacher-rated posture and travel efficiency.

Leonard (1969) assessed static and mobile balancing in children who varied widely in residual vision and who ranged in age from 11 to 20 years. The mobile balancing test required the child to walk along a narrow beam, using any vision available. The relationship between the balancing scores was complex: while poor static balance predicted poor mobile balance, good mobile balance did not necessarily accompany good static balance. Children with very little vision performed poorly on the test of mobile balance, but those with more visual function did not necessarily perform well. This suggests that other factors in addition to residual vision affect balance performance. Boys were generally better than girls, and no relationships to age were reported. Pereira (1990) also showed that balance performance was significantly facilitated by some residual vision for children as young as age six.

Thus, with respect to posture and balance, the research tends to show the value of partial vision in successful performance.

Components of locomotion. In an extensive study, Cratty (1967) evaluated several basic elements of locomotor behavior. The subjects varied widely in age (8 to 86), visual characteristics, and mobility history. One test was of the subject's ability to walk, without vision, in a straight line in an open area, unconstrained by environmental elements. The tendency in this situation is to veer to one side or the other. The data were not broken down by chronological age, but the influence of several individual differences variables is of interest. Formal mobility training was not a predictor of success. Subjects who traveled with a guide dog were markedly worse in straight-line locomotion than those who traveled either with a cane or a sighted guide. It is somewhat surprising that those who had lost vision at birth veered less than those who had lost their sight later.

In the same study, Cratty evaluated sensitivity to the incline and decline of paths. Generally the pattern of results was the same as that for walking in a straight line, with one interesting exception. People who reported using dog guides for travel were better able to perceive a slight gradient than those who used a cane, who were in turn better than those who traveled with sighted guides.

Cratty, Peterson, Harris, and Schoner (1968) reported that on a task that involved walking through curved pathways with varying radii of curvature, adventitiously blind children made fewer errors than congenitally blind children. Cratty et al. suggested that a concept of laterality is prerequisite for this task, and that laterality is less developed in congenitally blind children. We will review evidence about the development of laterality in Chapter 11.

In a test of more complex spatial performance, Worchel (1951) studied blind children in the age range of 8 to 21 years and of mixed gender. Half were blind from birth, several had lost sight within three years, and the rest ranged upward in the age of visual loss. In a triangle relocation test, the child was led over two legs of a right triangle and was asked to return unassisted to the starting point. Neither age of visual loss, gender, nor age was a significant predictor of performance. It should be noted that this task involved not only locomotor control, but also the ability to conceptualize spatial relationships. We will review the evidence about spatial concepts in Chapter 4.

Training. It is an important question whether components of locomotor behavior are amenable to training, and several important studies have been reported. Cratty (1969) administered a training program to children ranging in age from 7 to 14 years. They were pre- and post-tested on various tasks. A control group received no training during an eight-week period before retesting, while the training group participated in an eight-week program involving straight-line walking and executing various turns. Feedback was given after each trial.

Both straight-line walking and turn performance improved significantly over the course of the training. A triangle relocation task similar to that used by Worchel (1951) was used in the pre- and post-tests. Although no specific training was provided for this task, the performance of the children in the training group improved significantly. Other aspects of mobility, orientation, and spatial relations were also reported to show improvement in the trained group, although formal measures were not reported.

Two quite different approaches to training also warrant mention. Duehl (1979) administered an eight-week program of creative dance training to four congenitally blind children, age 8 to 10 years, and used the Cratty and Sams (1968) test as a pre- and post-test. In the program the children enacted various concepts by body movements. The post-test showed substantial improvements in many areas of motor performance and control, and the research suggests that some of the motor awkwardness and developmental delay reported by other researchers may be avoided or overcome by such programs.

More specifically related to mobility skills, Clark (1992) conducted a 16-week training study with four five-year-old children who had lost sight due to ROP. The purpose of the study was to examine the effectiveness of training with a "precane" mobility device, in comparison to training with a long cane. Various aspects of mobility behavior were evaluated in appropriate baseline and posttraining sessions. Training with the precane device (the Connecticut precane, designed to be held in front of the body using both hands) was more effective than that with the long cane, although the children generally showed gains from both types of training. The skills acquired during training persisted after training for at least six weeks; further persistence was not evaluated. Furthermore, the skills acquired during training were found to generalize to nontraining settings.

Summary. There is a great deal of variability in components of locomotor effectiveness. It is clear, for example from the research program of Cratty and his colleagues, that a good deal of this variability is related to aspects of visual experience, such as a period of early vision or the availability of some residual vision. This is a complex issue, though, and it is evident that visual experience factors do not completely account for locomotor effectiveness.

In particular, it is an important but open question what the developmental continuities might be between motor and locomotor indices in infancy and the acquisition of locomotor skills in childhood. It is tempting to suppose that relatively precocious infants have better locomotor skills in childhood, but there is no evidence one way or the other. Only the longitudinal study, as difficult as it is to conduct, will yield information on this question. It is also important to know what the relationships are between the quality of children's spatial concepts and spatial behaviors (see Chapter 4).

Finally, the successes reported in various training studies indicate the importance of experience in the development of effective spatial behaviors. This is certainly no surprise, but it is still an open issue whether spatial awareness training (which is demonstrably successful in short-term studies) has longer-term effectiveness, and also whether such training is more effective at some developmental levels than at others. It is reasonable to suppose that the general maxim "the earlier the better" applies in this area, but the evidence is not available to test this hypothesis. Perhaps the most reasonable general conclusion is that effective locomotor skills cannot develop optimally without ample opportunity and the encouragement to engage that opportunity.

Stereotypic behaviors

The term *stereotypic behaviors*, or *mannerisms*, covers a wide range of activities, including movements of parts of the body such as eye rubbing, head turning, and hand gestures, and larger body movements such as rocking or swaying. These terms are also used to refer to more complex and involved sequences of movements. The common factor is the repetitiveness of the behaviors. The term *blindism*, which has been used in the past, is a misnomer since behaviors that often occur in children with visual impairments are not discriminable from those observed in some autistic children, or even from behaviors observed in children without apparent problems of either a perceptual or an emotional nature. Nevertheless, many children with visual impairments show a substantial frequency of stereotypic behaviors, and these are often a concern because they may be inhibiting to normal social interactions, may interfere with the child's attention to events in the external world, or may result in physical injury.

Hypotheses. Several general hypotheses have been advanced to account for the occurrence of stereotypic behaviors in children with visual impairments. One is that these behaviors represent attempts to increase the general level of sensory stimulation (e.g., Burlingham, 1967; Curson, 1979; Smith, Chethik, & Adelson, 1969). That is, because of the low level of visual stimulation, more sensory stimulation is sought via other senses, including feedback from motor activity. An efferent variant of this hypothesis is that repetitive behaviors occur because they provide a vehicle for "motor discharge" (e.g., Burlingham, 1965).

Though this formulation makes sense and is supported by data, the same data do not generally contradict an alternative hypothesis, that mannerisms are a result of social rather than sensory deprivation. Experimental evidence in support of this hypothesis comes from studies of animals that show stereotypic behaviors if they are raised in conditions of social deprivation even within a relatively rich sensory environment (e.g., Berkson, 1973).

Still another hypothesis is that mannerisms are a form of self-regulation in the face of overstimulation. Knight (1972) argued that children both with and without sight tend to regress to behaviors characteristic of earlier developmental stages when placed in stressful situations. Stone (1964), studying institutionalized, retarded children blind from ROP, distinguished between two patterns of stereotypic behaviors, which he designated "withdrawal" and "alerting." The former was characterized by a regular frequency of movement and a loss of awareness of the environment; it often occurred in response to stressful situations. Electroencephalogram (EEG) patterns indicating a drowsy state accompanied these behaviors in some children, suggesting to Stone that the repetitive pattern served to produce a protective condition of insensitivity to a stressful external environment. The behaviors accompanying the "alerting" form were less rhythmic and more complex, and they tended to occur in response to novel objects. The accompanying EEG patterns were more characteristic of attentiveness.

Thus there are several hypothesized causes of stereotypic behaviors in children with (as well as without) visual impairments, and given the evidence of multiple causation, it is undoubtedly an oversimplification to regard these behaviors categorically.

Causal factors. The incidence of mannerisms has been found to be related to several factors. For example, Guess (1966) found that mannerisms are associated with sensory deficit and locomotor restraint. He studied groups of blind and sighted, retarded, institutionalized boys ranging in age from 6 to 20 years. There was a negative correlation between locomotor behavior and self-manipulation, and there was a positive correlation between locomotor behavior and manipulation of the environment. The factors that bear on self versus environmental manipulation were not clarified, although Guess did find less self-stimulatory behavior in the group of sighted children and suggested that visual loss was implicated in producing a greater incidence of stereotypic behaviors.

Troester, Brambring, and Beelmann (1991) used a questionnaire to reach the parents of preschool children, most of whom had been blind since birth. The parents were asked about the incidence, frequency, and nature of their child's stereotypic behaviors, and further about the situations in which these behaviors tended to occur. A wide variety of stereotypic behaviors occurred in four primary situations: boredom, arousal, demand, and eating. Different behaviors were observed in these different situations. For example, eye poking occurred in all situations, whereas lamenting/whimpering and finger sucking tended to occur when the child was bored, and repetitive hand and finger movements often appeared under conditions of arousal. These results clearly show the danger of overcategorizing stereotypic behaviors.

Thurrell and Rice (1970) studied the incidence of eye rubbing in relation to the degree of visual loss. The children, aged 6 to 20, were in a school for the blind. Eye rubbing occurred more frequently in the younger children. The children were divided into three groups based on the degree of loss: no measurable visual function, LP or movement perception, and some useful vision (counting fingers). The LP group showed significantly more eye rubbing than the groups with either less or more vision. Thurrell and Rice suggested that the visual system of the LP children was sufficiently functional to allow transmission of phosphenes produced by pressure on the eyes. Dekaban (1972), on the other hand, suggested that eye rubbing may be a result of photophobia rather than a search for addition stimulation of the visual system.

It is difficult to separate the sensory stimulation factor from the social stimulation factor. Webster (1983) cited both in his discussion of the relative absence of mannerisms in black South African blind children, noting that parents who provide an environment rich in social stimulation also in effect provide an enriched environment with respect to vestibular and somatosensory stimulation. Abang (1985), comparing the incidence of mannerisms in African and European samples, reached similar conclusions.

The report by Jan, Freeman, and Scott (1977) is especially informative and shows the incidence of mannerisms to be related to a complex set of interacting variables. Stereotyped behaviors were overrepresented in ROP and optic atrophy etiology groups. Totally blind children also showed a higher incidence than children with partial vision. The two factors are related because total blindness is relatively overrepresented in these two etiology groups. Almost all of the totally blind group showed stereotypic behaviors, compared with just a third of the partially sighted group. Age also interacted with the extent of the impairment: partially sighted children showed a decreasing frequency of mannerisms with increasing age, whereas no such decrease occurred for blind children. In younger children up to five years, eye-related mannerisms were predominant, whereas making noises and head turning were more frequent in the intermediate age range, and rocking and hand flapping in older children. Rocking and hand mannerisms were also more frequent in blind than in partially sighted children, reflecting the persistence of mannerisms in older blind children.

The occurrence of stereotyped behaviors was inversely related to IQ: the higher the intelligence, the fewer the mannerisms. Children with multiple handicaps (particularly cognitive deficits) showed a higher incidence of mannerisms, presumably because of reduced opportunities and/or capabilities for learning alternative behaviors. Finally, and also related to the occurrence of multiple handicaps, the incidence of mannerisms was positively predicted by the duration of hospitalization in the first year. This relationship may stem either from the restriction of learning opportunities or from the greater incidence of multiple handicaps in these children.

In sum, the incidence of stereotyped behaviors was related to several variables. The occurrence of serious mannerisms was positively predictable from the severity of visual loss and duration of hospitalization in the first year, and negatively predictable from age, IQ, and age of visual loss.

Stereotypic behaviors are also sensitive to environmental factors. Sandler (1963) cited the case of a very active blind child who did not show excessive mannerisms, whose mother had responded to early indications of eye rubbing by placing objects in the infant's hands to divert his activity. Various more systematic interventions to decrease stereotypic behaviors have been reported, particularly behavior modification techniques (e.g., Blasch, 1975; Miller & Miller, 1976; Williams, 1978). Hayes and Weinhouse (1978) discussed several behavior modification techniques and the advantages and disadvantages of their use in various situations. They stressed in particular the need for a careful analysis of the nature of the behaviors, their causes, the nature of the reinforcements that sustain the behaviors, and the appropriate choice of a behavior modification approach to suit these factors.

Age. The evidence generally points to a decrease in the incidence of stereotypic behaviors with increasing age. We have already mentioned the data of Thurrell and Rice (1970). Troester et al. (1991) found in their cross-sectional study that the frequency of the most prevalent types of mannerisms, such as eye poking and body rocking, remained relatively stable from one to six years of age, whereas the frequency of less prevalent mannerisms decreased over this age range. Brambring and Troester (1992) corroborated this finding using a longitudinal research design.

Longer-term evidence about the decrease of stereotypic behaviors with age comes from the report by Freeman et al. (1989) of the 14-year-later outcomes of 61 of the 92 children originally studied by Jan et al. (1977). These findings were further corroborated by a subsequent study of 69 of the original 92 (Freeman, Goetz, Richards, & Groenveld, 1991). In the original sample, 85% of the blind and 32% of the partially sighted children showed a significant incidence of mannerisms. In the follow-up studies, mannerisms had largely disappeared in most of the subjects with the exception of a few who were severely multihandicapped. Some reported engaging in mannerisms when alone, but many realized that these behaviors interfered with social acceptance and suppressed them in social contexts. Interestingly, not a single subject reported that the present absence of mannerisms was a result of a systematic treatment program:

social factors (e.g., reminders by parents or others) were far more potent in the reduction of stereotypic behaviors.

If stereotypic behaviors will eventually decrease as the years pass, then we may question whether efforts to reduce them in earlier years are necessary or appropriate. The question may be restated: are there adverse consequences of mannerisms in young children that make it desirable to reduce their frequency? The possibilities fall into three areas. First, of course, there is the possibility of physical injury. Mannerisms such as head banging and serious eye poking are potentially injurious and in the extreme clearly must be controlled by effective means.

Second, there may be consequences in the relationship of the child to his or her social, educational, and physical environments. Mannerisms may be repulsive to a partner in social interaction, and the result may be disengagement of the partner and curtailment of the opportunities for social interaction. This situation may be most potent in the early school years when children are especially sensitive to the social–interactive characteristics of their peers. Several writers (e.g., Caetano & Kauffman, 1975; Hoshmand, 1975) have noted the degree to which stereotypic behaviors may interfere with the blind child's attention in educational settings.

Most obviously, to the extent that the child engages in sensory self-stimulation, his or her attention to the external physical environment is reduced. The reciprocal relationship has been documented by Guess (1966), as noted above. To the extent that the child turns his or her attention inward to sources of self-stimulation, attention is less available to process sources of external stimulation. The consequences for the curtailment of learning opportunities are clear.

Summary. Although there is far from complete agreement about the causes of stereotypic behaviors in children with visual impairments, a reasonable formulation is that certain motor habits are acquired, just as they are in sighted children. There may be a tendency for children to engage in specific types of motor behavior (such as rocking) because of the vestibular or other sensory stimulation that they provide. Further, this tendency may be stronger for children with visual impairments because of the need for a higher level of sensory stimulation than is generally available with decreased visual function. In both blind and sighted children, stressful situations produce a tendency to regress to familiar behavior patterns, but these patterns are fewer and better practiced in children with visual impairments, so that they are more obvious and more interpretable as stereotypic behaviors. Furthermore, their continuation may be explained by their selective reinforcement (e.g., increased attention) by other people, and eventually by the behaviors' becoming self-reinforcing and therefore self-sustaining (Eichel, 1979).

However, it does not follow that every effort should be bent to reducing the incidence of mannerisms in young children with visual impairments. There is good evidence that children are effective in regulating the effective amount of sensory stimulation, and particularly in avoiding overstimulation. Two examples will suffice. First, White (1971) showed that perceptual overloads produce adverse developmental consequences; this point is well supported by experimental interventions with a variety of animal species. Second, the ability of sighted infants to choose a level of visual complexity appropriate to their developmental level, preferring an optimal level of complexity to either less or more complex stimuli, has been documented (e.g., Brennan, Ames, & Moore, 1966). To the extent that the blind infant or child's regression to stereotypic behaviors is a means of avoiding excessively complex perceptual stimulation, intentional reduction of these behaviors may interfere with important self-regulatory processes. This is clearly an area where sensitivity on the part of parents and professionals is required.

3

Understanding the physical world

In order to get along in the physical world, the child must acquire a basic understanding of its characteristics. In adapting to everyday life, it is not vital to understand these characteristics at the level of physical laws or theories, but it is important to understand the basic concepts of physical regularity. For example, when released, objects fall down rather than up, and other things being equal, this is a perfectly reliable property of the physical world. So is the fact that objects tend to retain their characteristics over time and place; and so on.

These varieties of understanding are cognitively adaptive. If the state of the physical world were independent at each moment from that at the previous moment, there would be no regularity over time. There is, of course. But if a child did not, at some level, *understand* these regularities of the physical world, then the cognitive demands of adapting to it would be immeasurably greater. Understanding the basic characteristics of the physical world releases the child from the necessity of attending to its state at each successive moment.

What properties are involved? The list can, of course, be subdivided at will. Our purposes will be best served by a relatively rough division into the following categories:

1. Object permanence: the understanding that objects retain their existence and identity even when they are not stimulating the senses.
2. Properties of matter: the understanding that properties such as mass, number, and volume are retained despite changes in perceptual qualities.
3. Causality: the understanding of cause and effect, that a given action necessarily has a consequence.

4. Time: the understanding of the ordering of events in time, of fixed time periods such as days and weeks, and of the concepts of past, present, and future.

5. Spatial structure: the understanding of space and its structure, its occupation by objects, and the relationships of objects in it. This is a sufficiently large topic that it is treated separately in Chapter 4.

The processes of acquiring these fundamental understandings go on well into childhood (and indeed adulthood), but their seeds begin in infancy. Various theorists have framed the issues in various ways, from William James's notion of the neonate's world as a "blooming, buzzing confusion" to Piaget's view of the infant as a miniature scientist. Regardless of the theoretical basis, it is safe to say that the neonate has no understanding of the laws that govern the physical world, and that the two-year-old has acquired a considerable amount of understanding.

Whereas in childhood and beyond, understanding can result from communication from others, in infancy the vast majority of the information for understanding the physical world arrives directly to the senses. Thus, perceptual capabilities are a fundamental prerequisite for understanding the physical world. We have seen in Chapter 1 that the primary nonvisual modalities, audition and touch, are fully functional in infants with visual impairments. As we proceed to examine the development of understanding, we can thus assume that these infants receive information about the physical world via audition and touch, whereas of course visual information is limited or absent.

The development of object permanence in infancy

The concept of object permanence (or the "object concept") is the understanding that an object continues to exist even if it is not providing current sensory stimulation. If an object that the infant is seeing, hearing, or touching is caused to disappear, silenced, or removed from the grasp, the behavior of the very young infant is interpreted as indicating that in effect, the object simply does not continue to exist. Later, the infant begins to search for the previously perceived object, and finally, when the infant's behaviors with respect to the object are systematic and organized, such that he or she can find the object even when it is hidden, the infant is said to have acquired the concept of object permanence.

We arrive at our consideration of object permanence for the visually impaired infant through two converging paths. Earlier, we reviewed evidence about the development of the blind infant's capabilities to perceive and respond to the various sources of information from objects and events in the physical world. We now move beyond this issue of the immediate processing of sensory information, and to do this, we consider how concepts emerge and allow the infant to deal with objects or events in the physical world even when they are not actually providing sensory information. With the development of concepts the infant moves beyond the constraints of immediate perception into the flexible realm of cognition. The concept of object permanence is one of the first steps along this way.

The second thread that informs our consideration of the development of object permanence is the argument made by several writers (e.g., Fraiberg, 1977) that the development of the blind infant's perceptual-motor interaction with the physical world is restricted by limitations on the development of object permanence. According to this argument, until the infant achieves the concept of object permanence, he or she is not stimulated to engage the external world; thus, lags in the development of reaching and locomotor behaviors are to be expected.

Logical analysis of the task

It is necessary to look carefully at object permanence and what its development entails in the infant without vision. As originally discussed by Piaget, the development of object permanence relies heavily on vision. If an object grasped by the infant is removed or dropped, it no longer provides tactile stimulation, but as long as the infant can see the object, he or she still receives the information on which to base the understanding that the object has not ceased to exist. This same reasoning explains how continued vision of an object that was making a sound but is now silent also facilitates the infant's understanding of the continuing existence of the object.

So the situation for the blind infant might indeed be qualitatively different from that of the infant with sight. If vision is not available to provide continuing information to the infant about a previously heard or touched object's existence, then the concept of object permanence may be more difficult to achieve, and therefore developmentally slower; or it may even follow a different developmental course.

While this scenario seems reasonable on the face of it, we have to examine the alternatives. In particular, considerations of appropriate methodology are important. As was noted earlier, Piaget's account of the development of object permanence was based on the assumption of normal visual functioning. As we consider the corresponding question for the blind infant, we cannot simply borrow the concept and methodology from the literature on sighted children. We have to consider what object permanence means as a concept, taking care not to restrict its definition to the context of a particular sensory modality.

In order to do this, let us consider the difference between perceptual and conceptual behavior. We can adopt a working distinction that perception deals with the world based on information coming immediately to the sensory systems, and that cognition is the ability to deal with the world in the absence of immediate sensory information about it. The key question, then, becomes, What is required to allow the infant to move from the restrictions of perception to the flexibility of cognition?

In a word, the answer is *memory*. Until the infant is capable of remembering events that have been perceived, he or she has no way of bridging one perceptual event to another. Without memory, previous perceptual experience cannot influence current experience, nor can a concept be formed based on previous and current experience of perceptual events.

What is known about the development of memory in the young infant? For sighted infants, evidence suggests that memory begins to mediate perceptual behavior and the development of concepts by the second quarter of the first year. One example is Piaget's (1952) account of the sequence of substages in the period of sensorimotor intelligence. In the stage of "secondary circular reactions," which occurs in the four- to eight-month range, the infant begins to repeat behaviors that produce effects in the external world that are satisfying or interesting. For example, the sighted infant may swipe repeatedly at a hanging object to make it swing back and forth. A single swipe at the object does not signify this stage, but repetition of the behavior does. Clearly at least a fleeting memory is involved; the infant's fragmentary memory of the first encounter stimulates the second, and so on.

In recent decades there has been an explosion of work that bears directly or indirectly on the question of early memory, and this work also tends to show that memory begins to affect behavior significantly by the third or fourth month of life. For example, infants begin in the third month to show a looking preference for a novel stimulus over one that has been seen frequently (Fantz, 1964). The usual explanation is that accumulated exposure to the repeated stimulus causes it to become familiar (i.e., to be remembered), thus causing other stimuli to become relatively more interesting. This preference for novelty is not seen at two months of age, but it occurs at four months, and the change suggests the emergence of memory.

Similar conclusions are drawn from studies in which unusual variations of stimuli are shown. Beginning around four months of age, infants show heightened attention to a face with scrambled features in preference to a standard face (e.g., Kagan, 1970). This heightened attention is attributed to a violation of the infant's expectation of what a face should look like, and thus it carries the implication of a developing memory. In order to have an expectation violated, the infant must have an idea of what the stimulus will look like, and this cannot occur without memory.

Although these lines of evidence converge on the conclusion that memory begins to influence behavior around the third or fourth month, memory does not spring forth all of a sudden. Depending on the nature of the stimuli, the infant's state, and a variety of other factors, evidence of memory may or may not emerge for a given infant in a particular situation. Generally, however, we can think of memory as beginning to emerge around the beginning of the second quarter of the first year.

Unfortunately, there is no direct evidence of this sort that bears fruitfully on the issue with blind infants: early memory has simply not been addressed squarely. However, there are several bits of information that may be gleaned from the material reviewed in the earlier section on perceptual abilities.

Perhaps the clearest evidence has to do with the infant's discriminative behavior with respect to voices. Freedman et al. (1969) reported such differentiation in infants as young as two months: while the mother's voice elicited quieting of motor behavior (i.e., passive attention), there was no discernible response to the voice of a stranger. Fraiberg (1968) noted a similar differentiation at three months, when the infant Toni smiled (though unreliably) in response to the mother's voice but not to other voices. The behavioral evidence becomes reliable by four and five months of age. Memory must be involved: the infant must have learned, and remembered, associations to the parent's voice that mediate the affective reactions to different voices. The positive evidence for memory of objects other than the mother is less clear.

All in all, there is not very satisfying evidence one way or the other about the blind infant's early development of memory. Although memory is an important and interesting topic in its own right, the lack of evidence is especially unfortunate in view of the importance of memory in an evaluation of the development of object permanence.

One thing is clear, however: in the presence of conclusive evidence of memory for the parent's voice, and in the absence of any evidence that memory is *not* following a normal course of development, our best assumption at this point is that the early memory of the blind infant follows the same course of development as that of the sighted infant. Of course, the blind infant will not have memory for visual experiences, but that is trivial – we must look at memory as a cognitive function, not as memory for information that has arrived via a specific sensory modality.

Now let us return to object permanence and its evaluation in infants with visual impairments.

Most research on sighted infants has used a "disappearing object" paradigm that includes the following kinds of tasks: an object in the infant's view is covered so that it is no longer visible; an object is hidden in one place and then visibly moved to another place; or an object is hidden in one place and then invisibly moved to another place. The infant's efforts at retrieval of the object are interpreted to reveal the nature of his or her understanding of the object's continuing existence.

These are obviously inappropriate tasks for evaluating object permanence in blind infants because of the degree to which they involve vision. Nor is it necessarily appropriate simply to substitute auditory and / or tactual information for visual information. The methodology should examine whether the infant continues to remember an object once the object is removed from immediate perceptual experience, and what the nature of that memory is. How can this be done?

Let us say that we present a sounding object at midline, then have the sound cease, and observe the infant's reaction. What may reveal the infant's memory of that event? The developmental progression that would parallel that of the sighted infant with seen objects would proceed from an initial lack of any response, to a fragmentary search, to more systematic search, and finally to systematic search in multiple locations. Identifying the final accomplishment is not difficult: if we see systematic search behavior to an initially sounding but now silent object, we can easily conclude that the blind infant understands object permanence.

The difficulty is in identifying the early and intermediate states. What if we see no manual search activity? It may be that the infant has a perfectly good concept that the object continues to exist but has not acquired the manual search patterns that would serve to attain the object. Alternatively, the infant may simply not be motivated to attain the object. In either case we risk drawing the wrong conclusion about object permanence from the lack of manual search.

Manual search clearly should not be the sole criterion for the infant's demonstration of object permanence. Several investigators (e.g., Burlingham, 1964) have stressed the danger of interpreting the infant's passive motor behavior as lack of interest or attention. In fact, active attention may be *facilitated* by suppression of overt motor activity. It may be that the motorically passive infant understands that the object still exists and is attending in order to hear it when it resumes sounding. Passive attention is difficult to identify and interpret reliably, but this behavior should be fully explored before concluding that the infant is not remembering.

The case of a touched object is a bit different. Consider the situation in which the infant is grasping an object, which is then taken away and placed somewhere within arm's reach. If the infant responds by reaching and retrieving the object, then there is no difficulty in interpreting this as an indicator of object permanence. As before, however, it is risky to interpret lack of reaching as an indication that the infant does not regard the object as continuing to exist. At very least, we should look carefully for any possible evidence of continuing attention before concluding that the infant does not have the concept of object permanence.

In the case in which an object is experienced both tactually and auditorially and is then removed, the situation is more complicated yet. Little is known about the blind infant's organization of the tactual and auditory modalities. One may dominate the other, or both might contribute to the infant's perception of the object; furthermore, the relationship between touch and hearing may change with development.

The point is that methodology is extremely important. We have to be very cautious in making conclusions about the presence of object permanence on the basis of the blind infant's success or failure to exhibit the search behaviors used with the sighted infant to make inferences about object permanence.

Let us prepare for evaluation of the evidence by looking at the sequence of developmental stages that Piaget describes for the sighted infant, adding a translation on the basis of underlying conceptual abilities to the situation of the blind infant. In this, we will focus on the major points in the development of object permanence (see Flavell, 1985, for a more detailed treatment, and Piaget, 1954, for the original).

Several observations are important at the outset. First, the distinctions between adjoining stages are somewhat arbitrary divisions of a continuous process of conceptual development. Second, this means that the behavior at the beginning of a stage is not radically different from that at the end of the preceding stage, and that substantial progress occurs within each stage. Finally, it is also important to note that differences occur between infants; within a normal range of development, not every infant will show the same behavioral or conceptual acquisition at the same time.

Stages 1–2 (through 4 months). The infant shows no evidence of mental representation (memory) of an object in the absence of sight of it.

> *Translation.* For the blind infant, we would expect to find no evidence of mental representation (memory) of an object in the absence of immediate perceptual stimulation by it.

Stage 3 (4–8 months). The infant shows some evidence of fragile visual attention to an object that is removed from sight, but there is no evidence of manual search. Even if the infant is already grasping the object when it is covered, there is no indication that the tactual information serves to inform the infant about the object's continuing existence.

> *Translation.* The blind infant shows briefly sustained attention to the last perceived location of an object that is removed from auditory or tactile experience. No evidence of manual search is expected at Stage 3.

Stage 4 (8–12 months). Manual search begins for an object that has been seen and is then hidden. Even at the end of the stage, the infant does not respond successfully to displacements of the object: if the object is repeatedly covered while in one location and then is *visibly* moved to another location and covered, the infant's search is typically restricted to the location where it was most often hidden.

Translation. For the blind infant, manual reach to a location at which the object was perceived is evidence for attainment of this stage. For example, the infant might reach to the place where a sound-producing object had been heard, but if it were not found there, the infant would not search in other places. Sounding of the object at several locations might not produce search at all locations.

Stage 5 (12–18 months). This stage is somewhat difficult to distinguish from the previous stage, but here the infant may search manually in several locations in which the object has recently been seen, rather than in just one location. Failing to obtain the object in a seen location, however, the infant does not search in other locations in which the object might have been, but was not, seen.

Translation. The blind infant demonstrates attainment of this stage by reaching systematically to the several locations in which an object has been perceived. Systematic search in other locations in which the object has not been perceived does not occur in this stage.

Stage 6 (18–24 months). Here, the infant has the capability of searching the available space systematically, including locations in which the object was not seen. The rule seems to be: "If I don't find it in any of the places where I have seen it, then look in other possible places."

Translation. The blind infant should search for a previously perceived object not only in locations in which it was perceived, but also in other places within reaching range.

The evidence from infants with visual impairments

What evidence is there about the behavior of infants with visual impairments in situations that might show attainment of these various stages?

We can begin with Fraiberg et al. (1966), since a chronological account is provided of the behavior of one infant (Robbie) in response to tasks that are well suited to making inferences about object permanence. Three tasks were given: removal of a touched (and soundless) object; cessation of a sounding (but untouched) object; and removal of an object that was both touched and heard.

The earliest observation occurred at six months, when Robbie was attentive to a bell while it was sounding but made no hand or finger movements upon its cessation. Upon dropping a ball of yarn, he showed fleeting hand responses as if to continue the action of holding the ball. When a held and heard object was removed, he made no hand or arm movement. These behaviors are characteristic of Stage 3, where there should be indications of attention to the place at which the object was last perceived, but no manual response. No evidence of sustained attention was reported for any of the tasks.

At seven and eight months, the picture for Robbie was much the same in response to sound alone: "Robbie appears to recognize the sound [of his musical toy dog], stops what he is doing and attends. He does not reach for the toy; shows no attempt to search" (p. 341). In response to sound alone, "The face shows alertness and attention. There is no gesture of reaching" (p. 342). While these accounts were offered by Fraiberg et al. (1966) as evidence of the lack of object permanence, in fact the behaviors fit exactly the expectations for an infant at the end of Stage 3, where there is expectation of attention but no expectation of search. In response to an object both heard and felt, "Robbie makes a tentative search on the table, makes accidental contact with it [the object] and recovers it . . . after this first success Robbie does not attempt a search" (p. 342). This behavior, at 7:11, parallels almost exactly Piaget's reports of tentative and fragile hand activity to regrasp an object that has escaped the hand.

A more advanced behavior was reported by Als et al. (1980b): an infant at 7:18, while grasping a cookie, dropped it out of her right hand. Noting the beginnings of distress, the mother said: " 'O-ooh, o-ooh, where's your cookie?' The infant . . . pulls her arms in smoothly toward her sides, and begins to search with her right hand in the area next to her leg to find the cookie. . . . As she touches the cookie with her right hand, she lets out a squeal of pleasure, picks it up slowly, . . . " (p. 34). This observation demonstrates not only sustained attention to the disappearance of the object (thus meeting the requirements of Stage 3), but to the extent that sustained manual search activity occurred (that is, intentional search, as contrasted with accidentally successful manual activity), the behavior meets the requirements of Stage 4.

A milestone task assessed by Ferrell et al. (1990, see Table 2), "searches for a dropped toy," may be interpreted as either a Stage 4 or Stage 5 behavior, depending on the fragility of the search. Given that the data were from parents' reports, we should not put too fine a point on the stage. Nevertheless, the median age for attainment of this item among the visually impaired children was 12 months, roughly the normative dividing line between Stages 4 and 5 in Piaget's account. Of more importance, there was considerable variation within the sample, with only half of the sample falling within a 4.5 month range bracketing the median age.

We return to Fraiberg's account. At 8:8, in response to the removal of a touched object, "Robbie withdraws his hand, then makes a sure reach in the direction and the area where he last had contact with the cube" (p. 344). Upon hearing the sound of his musical dog, "Robbie makes groping gestures with both hands" (p. 347). Upon removal of an object both felt and heard: "Robbie reaches directly to the place on the tray where he first encountered it. He does not recover it. He does not conduct a further search" (p. 346). In each of the three situations, Robbie showed exactly the behaviors characteristic of Stage 4.

Thus, up to this point, it is clear that Robbie's development of object permanence is squarely on track, with appropriate behaviors seen at ages that fit nicely within the ranges noted by Piaget.

Fraiberg's account of Robbie's reach to sound ended with a last observation at 1:0:19, but this observation is a key one for our analysis. Robbie is now crawling, and a cardboard box is moved around from one place to another on the rug: "The only sound heard by the investigators was the faint scratching of the lid of the cardboard box as it abraded another surface of the box in coming to rest on the rug. Robbie immediately crawled to the box and retrieved it. . . . The experiment is repeated with two other locations. Robbie retrieves the box each time, using minimal sound cues as the box makes contact with the rug" (p. 355). This is fully appropriate behavior for Stage 5, which Robbie should be just entering at a year of age: on hands and knees, he retrieves the object regardless of which of several locations it is moved to. To be sure, there were evidently acoustic cues available, but Robbie did not persevere in searching at a single location, as would be expected in Stage 4.

Fraiberg et al. (1966) did not speak to Stage 6 behaviors or to the age range (18–24 months) in which they typically emerge. However, Fraiberg (1968) reported that through three years of age, none of the children in the sample had demonstrated the behaviors of Stage 6: "He will track an object only to the place where he last heard it. If a toy that he values is soundlessly moved, he will scream with frustration, or flip over in a tantrum on the floor, or switch his attention to something else – but he will not search. . . . Search is futile, for the child of this age, because he cannot deduce the displacements of an object in space" (p. 287). On the other hand, another of Fraiberg's subjects (Toni) gave strong evidence of Stage 6 behavior in searching for her bottle, which she threw away and then proceeded to search for (Fraiberg & Freedman, 1964).

This last observation aside, and referring now only to the evidence relevant to the first five stages, it is my view that Fraiberg and others have misinterpreted some very provocative observations. Fraiberg et al. (1966) concluded that "for the blind child 'something out there' is a chance encounter for most of his first year. . . . An object lost is an object swallowed up in a void" (p. 357). In fact, the behaviors observed for Robbie (and three other infants who were reported to show much the same sequence of development) on which this conclusion were based are perfectly appropriate to the ages at which they occurred. From this evidence, it would appear that the fundamentals of object permanence develop not only in the same sequence but on the same schedule that they do for sighted infants.

One reason that Fraiberg's infants appear to be developing in a timely way is that the criteria for successful response were relatively permissive. The behaviors that have been noted did not typically occur on each instance of the task; credit for attainment was given if the behavior occurred only once in an extended series of trials that was limited only by the infant's patience. If a more conservative criterion had been used, for example requiring successful performance on half of the trials, the ages of attainment would undoubtedly have been later.

It should also be added that the infants in Fraiberg's program of research benefited from intensive efforts on the part of the project staff to communicate their growing knowledge to the parents of the infants. The result is that these infants may have been more advanced than infants who do not receive such a program of intervention. That is to say, the Fraiberg infants were to some degree an advantaged, rather than a representative, sample of the population of infants born blind.

In any case, the Fraiberg infants constitute too small a sample on which to base a conclusion that contradicts much of the writing on the issue over the past 25 years. Let us turn to other reports of infant behaviors that might either contradict or support this tentative conclusion that blind infants develop object permanence in an age-appropriate manner.

Schwartz (1984) presented the results from two infants who at five (infant A) and seven (infant C) months of age began a weekly intervention program designed, among other things, to elicit responsiveness to sound. Infant C, though showing passive attention and occasional fragmentary arm and finger movements to sounding toys, did not show any evidence of a desire to retrieve a toy that was removed from her grasp. Infant A, in contrast, reached to a sounding toy at five months. By 12 months he clearly searched for a removed object, and by 14 months he searched among several objects to obtain the one that he desired. These are clearly age-appropriate Stage 5 behaviors.

Bigelow (1986) designed a series of tasks employing tactual and auditory stimuli for use with blind infants to evaluate object permanence. Several of these are offered as examples of behaviors that should be attained in Stages 3, 4, and 5. For example, in Task 1b a sounding toy was placed on the infant's body: while not strictly speaking an object permanence task, the behavior of reaching for the toy should emerge during Stage 3.

Tasks 2 (removal of a sounding toy from grasp, with the sound continuing) and 5 (accidental dropping of a sounding or nonsounding toy from the infant's grasp) tap Stage 4 characteristics of object permanence. In each case, the infant would be judged successful on the basis of reaching in the direction of the sounding object, whether or not reaching resulted in retrieving the toy. Task 6 (placing a sounding toy under a cover in front of the infant, with the sound continuing) also is a Stage 4 task, with the infant required to uncover and secure the toy to be judged successful.

Task 9 (removing a sounding toy from the infant's grasp to a location at in front of the infant, then moving it in an arc to a different location) taps Stage 5 abilities in that it involves displacement of the object from one location to another; the infant is judged successful if reach occurs in the direction of the still-sounding object, rather than only toward the location from which the object was initially removed. Finally, Task 10 involved a toy that sounded intermittently at 2-sec intervals while being moved in an arc around the infant's head. Success was judged by the infant's reaching during a silent interval to the location at which the object was last heard.

Table 3. *Age of infants in months at initial testing, at the end of testing, and at the attainment of each task*

S no.	Initial age	Ending age	Task 1b(3)	2(4)	5(4)	6(4)	9(5)	10(5)
1	11	16	12	14	14	**	**	**
2	13	26	13	13	13	16	21	22
3	15	21	20	**	**	**	**	**
4	17	42	23	23	24	25	30	32
5	32	45	32	32	32	32	34	35

Note: The stage that each task represents is shown in parentheses, and the task numbers are described in the text. The symbol ** indicates that the criterion for the task was not met within the duration of testing.
Source: After Bigelow (1986).

The five infants were all blind from birth with a variety of etiologies (but only one with ROP and presumably born prematurely). They were tested on roughly a monthly basis. As Bigelow pointed out, circumstances beyond the control of the investigation interfered with the intended protocol: in particular, two of the infants were tested for six months or less.

Table 3 (after Bigelow, 1986) summarizes for each infant the age at initial testing, the age at the end of testing, and the data for these tasks relevant to the acquisition of stages of object permanence. All ages are given in months. The criterion for attainment was success on at least 50% of the trials in a session, if this was followed by success on at least 50% in the next session.

Several things are important to note about the results. First, to the extent that the data can be brought to bear on the sequentiality of the stages, these infants show the same sequence that occurs in sighted infants. There is not a single instance in which a behavior characteristic of a later stage occurred earlier than one characteristic of a prior stage.

Second, there is not much to be learned from infant 5, who showed the behaviors required for Stages 3 and 4 in the first test session (at age 32 months), quickly followed by acquisition of Stage 5 behaviors. Similarly, infant 3, who was tested for only six months and did not acquire any behavior beyond the Stage 3 level, does not reveal anything beyond an apparently quite late (20 months) acquisition of Stage 3 behavior. Infant 1, the youngest of the five (and therefore potentially the most interesting), unfortunately remained in the study for only five months. Although most Stage 3 and Stage 4 behaviors did appear relatively soon after testing began, the remainder of the sequence is not available for this infant.

This leaves us with infants 2 and 4. Infant 2, begun at 13 months (i.e., at an early Stage 5 age), immediately showed most behaviors required for Stages 3 and 4 and therefore was roughly on schedule with respect to stage norms. Stage 5 behaviors appeared before the end of the second year, thus showing a delay.

Infant 4, begun at 17 months, showed consistent delays, with Stage 3 and 4 behaviors not appearing until the end of the second year, or six to eight months into testing. Stage 5 behaviors emerged correspondingly late, at almost three years of age.

It is clear, even given the necessarily incomplete data, that there are considerable differences among infants – in particular, infants 2 and 4 present a marked contrast in timing (though not in developmental sequence).

An attractive and seemingly straightforward conclusion is that this evidence shows delays in the emergence of object permanence, judged against the typical age ranges for sighted infants. This conclusion runs contrary to the reinterpretation of Fraiberg's results that I offered earlier in this chapter. Two points should be made. The first is that Bigelow's criteria for successful behaviors were considerably more conservative (and also more defensible) than those of Fraiberg, who reported single instances of successful behavior without the requirement that the behavior must also occur on other trials in the same test session.

The second point is that although the stages in question (3, 4, and 5) span the 4- to 18-month range for expectations of sighted infants, the infants in Bigelow's study were not initially tested until well into – and in the case of infant 5 substantially beyond – this age range. It may be a safe assumption that these infants would not have demonstrated the required behaviors had they been tested during the actual age ranges, but this is not certain, since it sometimes happens that a behavior is seen at one age, does not occur at a subsequent age, and then reappears at a still later age.

Bigelow's study has been presented in considerable detail, not because it is perfect (it is not, for reasons well articulated by its author) but because the tasks are a model for how research on object permanence should be conducted with blind infants. Bigelow's tasks were designed specifically to tap directly the *underlying conceptual capabilities* thought to be characteristic of the stages of object permanence. This represents a valuable improvement over much other work with blind infants and children, in which a task involving vision is simply adapted for tactual or auditory use without considering the underlying concepts that are at issue.

Bigelow (1990) added the results of a sixth infant who was initially thought to be blind but who turned out to have enough vision in one eye to mediate reaching for brightly colored objects. Beginning at 14 months, this infant was tested, with the use of his vision, on tasks requiring Stages 4, 5, and 6 of object permanence. The tasks involved the typical hidden objects with visible and invisible displacements. The infant was already capable of the Stage 4 task at 14 months; he achieved the Stage 5 behaviors at 15 and 16 months, and the Stage 6 task at 19 months. These ages are all within normal expectations based on children with full vision.

In another intensive study, Rogers and Puchalski (1988) tested infants repeatedly to chart the achievement of behaviors indicating acquisition of the object concept. The infants ranged in age from 4 to 25 months at the beginning of the study, and they were tested every other month. The initial sample included 20 infants: 11 who had at most LP and 9 who had sufficient visual function to mediate reaching. The results of these two subgroups did not differ, and they were thus consolidated for analysis. Some additional handicaps were present, but all infants had demonstrated bimanual grasp and none had a severe intellectual dysfunction (based on the Reynell–Zinkin Scales). Four infants left the study before demonstrating success on any of the tasks, leaving 16 for analysis.

In contrast to the tasks of Bigelow (1986), most of which used sounding stimuli, the six tasks were for the most part straightforward adaptations of Piagetian tasks, substituting touch for vision. Tasks 1 ("searches in several places for someone or something") and 2 ("searches for partially hidden object") were thought to tap Stage 3 behaviors; Tasks 3 ("searches for a hidden object") and 4 ("searches for a hidden object under a second cover") were thought to represent Stage 4 behaviors; and Tasks 5 ("searches under two covers") and 6 ("searches under two more spatially separated covers") represented Stage 5 behaviors.

Table 4. *Ages of acquisition of Piagetian items by infants with and without visual impairments*

Item	Stage	P age	N	Mean age	St. dev.	Age range
1	3 (4)	4–8	15	16.3	5.4	9–26
2	3 (4)	4–8	16	17.2	5.7	7–25
3	4	8–12	14	19.1	4.9	13–26
4	4	8–12	13	19.0	5.9	9–26
5	5	12–18	10	20.8	5.2	13–26
6	5	12–18	10	21.8	6.8	13–35

Note: For each item is given the stage that the item represents, the age range in which sighted infants achieve the criterion behaviors according to Piaget (P age), the number of infants meeting the criterion (N), the mean age at which criterion was reached, the standard deviation (St. dev.) of the mean, and the age range within which the visually impaired infants reached the criterion.
Source: After Rogers and Puchalski (1988).

Table 4 summarizes the data from 16 infants for each of the six tasks and provides the benchmark age range at which sighted infants typically achieve each stage, according to Piaget (1954). The mean ages of achievement for the Rogers and Puchalski sample are in every case above the top end of the range based on the Piagetian formulation. From this it appears reasonable to conclude that, on the average, infants with visual impairments are slow to achieve the substages of object concept acquisition.

However, this may be too hasty a conclusion. Rogers and Puchalski noted that the ages of achievement may underrepresent the infants' capabilities for two reasons: first, testing occurred only every other month, and second, older infants who entered the study and immediately showed the criterion behavior for a given item were assigned the age at which they were first tested. These factors both tend to lead to an *over*estimate of the mean age of acquisition. Countering this, it should be added that four infants did not achieve any task before leaving the study, which may have tended, in the aggregate, to *under*represent the mean age of acquisition. The effects of these indeterminate age factors make it unwise to base conclusions on the data for mean age.

We can, however, learn more from the results by looking at individual differences and considering variation as well as central tendency. In fact, the standard deviations of the age-of-acquisition means are quite large, indicating that there was considerable variability among individuals. For each item, the top end of the age range exceeded the top of the range noted by Piaget. The top end of the age range need not concern us, however; it is clear that circumstances can conspire to delay the cognitive development of infants with visual impairments.

But what of the low end? In almost every case, the more advanced infants achieved the task within the age range noted by Piaget for infants with vision. That even one infant fell within the age range for sighted infants suggests that visual impairment is not a guarantee that acquisition of the object concept must necessarily be delayed.

Individual differences

At several points in this section individual differences have been mentioned, and we return to this issue now. The observation is that there is substantial variation among infants in the timetable (though not in the sequence) of acquisition of various criterion behaviors. What can be said about the causes of individual variation? Consider first the evidence from the Fraiberg sample. Fraiberg's work was not intended as a normative evaluation of the development of blind infants in the absence of intervention. Instead, her program specifically incorporated intervention, and every opportunity was taken to educate the infants' parents of the need for specific interventions, based on what had already been learned in the project. This means not only that infants entering the project later were presumably the beneficiaries of better advice, but that the group as a whole was potentially advantaged over blind infants developing without such intervention. This may, in fact, be the very reason that their evidence, as I have reinterpreted it above, shows a relatively smooth and age-appropriate progression through the developmental phases of object permanence. It may also account for the apparent differences between Fraiberg's results and those of Bigelow as well as Rogers and Puchalski.

Fraiberg (1968) made the important point that even a small degree of vision may make a great deal of difference in the infant's development. One infant (excluded from the eventual sample of 10 for this reason) began to show some visual function at eight months and brought objects close to the eyes. All of the infants in Fraiberg's group of 10 and all of Bigelow's (1986) infants were described as having at most light perception. However, although "at most LP" is often used as a categorical distinction, it does not necessarily mean that the boundary of visual acuity is the same for all infants so categorized. Furthermore, even if the boundary were the same across studies and infants within studies, it is still the case that acuity differs among infants within the category, ranging from none in some cases to borderline visual functioning in others. Nor is simple acuity necessarily the best indicator of visual function: sensitivity to contrast may be an equally valid measure. The role of visual function within the category of "at most LP" is undoubtedly important in ways that we have yet to realize.

Although functional vision is a difficult variable to evaluate, researchers must be sensitive to it. It is likely that some of the observed individual differences in the development of object permanence, as well as in other areas, are a result of variations in visual functioning. The infant with some residual vision in one eye reported by Bigelow (1990) reinforces the importance of this variable. It is unclear why the groups of partially sighted and blind infants of Rogers and Puchalski (1988) did not differ; unfortunately the visual characteristics of infants who occupied the low and high ends of the ranges of age of acquisition were not reported.

Adelson and Fraiberg (1974) summarized several other possible sources of individual differences:

If the blind child is provided with good mothering and the chance to become familiar with many body positions, and if his hands and ears are given months of varied play experience with toys that unite tactile and auditory qualities, he will have found interest and taken pleasure in the space immediately around him. He will then be ready to move into a larger space. (p. 125)

Two factors are identified here, opportunity (i.e., tactual and auditory experience), and "good mothering." A strikingly effective example of the latter is found in the report by Als et al. (1980b). The mother was reported to have developed an extraordinarily close affective relationship with her blind infant, and Als et al. attributed the infant's excellent development in large part to the quality of this relationship.

The contrast between the two infants reported by Schwartz (1984) suggests another interesting effect of experience. Both infants were blind from retinopathy of prematurity (ROP). Infant C had no additional impairments, but infant A had some cerebral palsy that limited manual activity at midyear and apparently delayed the onset of crawling. Infant C was manually active at the outset of testing at 28 weeks, whereas infant A, due to the cerebral palsy, showed little hand activity at five months or for some months thereafter. However, infant A showed early attentiveness to sound and began to reach for sounding toys during the sixth month, whereas infant C did not reach for sounding objects for the duration of testing, which ended at about 10 months. Schwartz suggested that the active manual activity shown by infant C in examining held objects may have inhibited the development of reaching outward; infant A's lack of manipulative capability may have fostered his use of his hands to reach outward. Schwartz concluded, "The manual behaviors served by tactual perception only too readily become empty perseverative actions rather than purposive actions, and development is hindered rather than advanced" (p. 52).

Thus, there are several variables that might produce the developmental differences among individual infants evident in the literature: quality of interpersonal relationships, opportunity for appropriate experiences, and amount of visual function. No doubt these factors interact with one another as well. The sources of individual differences are complex, but for this reason researchers must attend carefully not only to observed differences in development, but also to the circumstances that produce them.

The object concept and spatial structure

Schwartz's (1984) observations suggest an interesting possibility with respect to the development of object permanence. Mature Stage 6 behavior is characterized by searching external space systematically at all locations where an object might be found. Failure to search is normally taken as indicating immaturity of object permanence. However, this reasoning assumes that the infant has a stable concept of the external space that must be explored to retrieve an object. It is possible that an infant may have a mature concept of object permanence but still fail to search external space because he or she does not understand the structure of that space.

This formulation is consonant with my reinterpretation of the evidence for the development of object permanence in blind infants. Much of the available evidence shows reasonable progression through the stages of object permanence up to Stage 6, but failure at that point. It may be that this failure has not so much to do with a weakness of the concept of object permanence itself, but with an inadequate understanding of the spatial structure of the environment to be searched. We will treat the concepts of spatial structure and spatial relations in Chapter 4. For now, it suffices to suggest that the turning point for the blind infant may be between Stages 5 and 6. According to the reinterpretation of the literature that I have suggested, there is not good evidence for a general slowdown beginning at Stage 3, as has been thought. On the other hand, the blind infant's difficulty with concepts of spatial structure may interfere with the emergence of Stage 6 indications. The advantage of residual vision found by Bigelow (1990) may have its positive influence on the concept of object permanence indirectly by facilitating the understanding of spatial structure.

The object concept and language

Although we will review other aspects of language development in later sections, it is appropriate here to consider the extent to which the development of the object concept may be related to the child's emerging language capabilities. There is not much available evidence on this issue, but Bigelow (1990) presented a valuable approach to the question. On the language side, Bigelow used Nelson's (1973) method of recording and evaluating each child's first 50-word vocabulary (see Chapter 5 for details). To evaluate object permanence, Bigelow used the series of tasks developed for blind infants (see Bigelow, 1986, described earlier). Each of three boys was studied longitudinally over a period of months. Infants 1 and 2 were blind. While infant 3 was initially thought to be totally blind, testing at 17 months revealed 20/400 acuity in one eye.

For the three infants, the ages at the onset of word use and the acquisition of the 50-word vocabulary were as follows: infant 1 (14 months, 19 months), infant 2 (16, 23), infant 3 (17, 21). As we discuss later, these ages place all three within the normal ranges for vocabulary acquisition in sighted children. However, the structure of their 50-word vocabularies was not the same as that reported by Nelson (1973): specifically, they used more specific nominals and more words referring to their own actions (see Mulford, 1988, reviewed in Chapter 5). With respect to the acquisition of object permanence, we will consider Bigelow's report of the acquisition of Stage 5 behaviors, which are characterized by the infant's ability to track several successive displacements of an object and to find it in any of the locations where it has been experienced. The infant with partial vision in one eye attained Stage 5 at 15 months, squarely within the age ranges noted by Piaget and others. The two blind infants attained this stage at 21 and 34 months, the former marginally and the latter seriously delayed.

Bigelow pointed out the disparity between the normal attainment of vocabulary for these two children and their delayed progress toward object permanence. The temptation is to conclude that there is no limitation of vocabulary acquisition by delayed cognitive skills. This is too facile, though, because as Bigelow suggested, the structure of all three children's 50-word vocabularies differed from the normative structure of sighted children. In reference to infant 3, she pointed out that even a very limited amount of vision can facilitate the acquisition of object permanence: "Seeing form even in restricted space helps locate objects, generate search strategies, and develop knowledge of the independent existence of objects" (p. 417). Further, this child's vocabulary structure was not apparently facilitated by partial vision: "Although [even] severely limited vision helps a child to understand objects in space, it does not make it easy for the child to observe others' actions or external events out of the limited visual field. Nor does it greatly facilitate the recognition of multiple referents of a word" (p. 417).

Bigelow suggested that the child's difficulty in escaping an egocentric perspective may create problems both in the acquisition of object permanence and in the development of a vocabulary with general referential properties. In the case of object permanence, this egocentrism takes the form of an inability to understand external spatial structure. In the case of a referential vocabulary, egocentrism implies using words that are tied to one's own self and immediate perceptual experience. We will review evidence about egocentrism with respect to spatial concepts in Chapter 4, and with respect to language in Chapter 5.

In her study of three infants in their second year, Urwin (1983) also studied the relationship between word use and object permanence. In describing the characteristics of the children's early vocabulary, Urwin noted that they did use some overextensions and that during the one-word stage they broadened their references to include external objects: their vocabulary was not limited to reference to self and self-actions. Rapid vocabulary growth occurred in the middle of the second year. As for the relationship of these features of vocabulary growth to cognitive development, Urwin noted that "in each case these developments occurred with the beginnings of pretend play and changes in search behaviour which indicated that the children knew of the continued existence of objects apart from their own actions and independent of specific locations" (p. 150). This, then, is a relatively optimistic picture not only of the versatility of the blind child's early language, but also of the ties between that language and healthy signs of object permanence.

Much more needs to be learned about the relationships between the development of object permanence, as well as other conceptual understandings, and the emergence of language. In particular it will be important to look not just at the correspondence of the age of attainment of various cognitive or language milestones, but at the functional interaction between domains. In the present context, the question is not only whether language and concepts *do* emerge in temporal relationship to one another, but *how* the emergence of language and cognition might facilitate one another in interactive fashion. Bigelow's (1990) work represents a promising start in this difficult area.

Understanding the properties of the physical world

In the case of understanding the properties of the physical world, there has been virtually no research done with children with visual impairments from other than the Piagetian perspective. We will thus take this approach as the basis for our review.

Conservation

Conservation refers in general to the understanding of properties of physical objects such as their shape, mass, and size. Many aspects of conservation have been studied: those that have been most thoroughly studied in children with visual impairments are substance, weight, and volume. Briefly described, the typical tasks used to assess the child's understanding of these properties of the physical world are as follows:

Conservation of substance. After obtaining the child's agreement that the amount of clay in two balls is equal, one of the balls is transformed into another shape or divided into smaller pieces, and the child's evaluation of the continued equivalence of their substance is assessed.

Conservation of weight. The same operation is performed as for conservation of substance, but the child's evaluation of the continued equivalence of weight is assessed.

Conservation of volume. After obtaining the child's agreement that two balls of clay are equal in amount and that two glasses of water are also equal, the shape of one ball of clay is changed and the child is queried about the water levels that would result if one ball of clay were put into one glass and the other ball into the other glass.

For each of these tasks, the usual procedure is to ask the child for a prediction of the result of the transformation, then to perform the transformation and ask for a judgment, then to ask for an explanation of the child's response. If the child is successful up to this point, a further question about the reversibility of the operation is often added. Full credit for a conservation concept is typically given only if the responses are satisfactory at each stage of the procedure; partial conservation scores are sometimes used. The goal of graduated scoring is to allow partial credit to indicate an emerging but immature concept. Overall, the goal of the tasks and their scoring is to capture important elements of the quality of the child's understanding of these properties of the physical world.

With sighted children, these tasks are typically performed with visually presented materials. The usual adaptation for children with visual impairments is to give the child haptic exposure to the stimulus materials; in the case of partially sighted subjects, the available vision is usually occluded (but see Lister, Leach, & Walsh, 1989, for a valuable exception).

Five studies (Gottesman, 1973; Hatwell, 1985; Miller, 1969; Stephens & Simpkins, 1974; Wan-Lin & Tait, 1987) have addressed all three of these conservation concepts with blind children, and two of these (Miller; Wan-Lin & Tait) as well as a sixth study (Swanson, Minifie, & Minifie, 1979) have also studied the three basic conservation tasks with partially sighted children. The study by Lister et al. (1989) with partially sighted children will be considered separately since it involved a different method of assessment.

Before examining the commonalities among these studies, we should note that they employed a variety of methodologies with samples of varying characteristics, and that their results were reported in different formats. The results are therefore only roughly comparable, and the following analysis and summary is intended as a conceptual synthesis rather than as a strict melding of results.

We look first at the five studies of blind children to examine the order of acquisition of these three basic conservation abilities.

All five studies clearly showed conservation of volume to be a later development than conservation of weight or substance. The order of acquisition of weight and substance is less clear: Stephens and Simpkins (1974) and Miller (1969) both found substance to emerge earlier, whereas Wan-Lin and Tait (1987) found the opposite. Gottesman (1973) concluded that conservation of substance emerges earlier, although his results as presented seem to show the opposite. In any case, these two conservation abilities would seem to emerge in close conjunction.

It is more difficult to ascertain a typical age at which the various conservation concepts emerge, in part because data are reported in different ways in different studies and in part because even when similar methods are used, there is still variation, apparently due to other causes. Taking all of this variation into account, the age of conservation appears to be in the range of 8 to 11 years for weight and substance, and perhaps 12 to 14 years for volume. Likely causes of variation within these age ranges will be discussed presently.

Several other studies have assessed one or another, but not all three, of these conservation abilities. Tobin (1972) found conservation of substance in the midrange reported in other studies, while Cromer (1973) found conservation to occur on the early side, with all children aged 7:9 and above reported to be conservers of substance. Davidson, Dunn, Wiles-Kettenmann, and Appelle (1981), on the other hand, found the average 11-year-old to be a nonconserver of substance. The results of conservation of weight by Brekke, Williams, and Tait (1974) are comparable to those of Gottesman (1973) and Wan-Lin and Tait (1987).

Other conservation concepts have also been studied, although not as frequently as substance, weight, and volume. For example, Wan-Lin and Tait (1987) studied the conservation of number and found it to be acquired marginally earlier than the other concepts, with half of the sample showing conservation by 7 years and all by 11 years. Adi and Pulos (1977–1978) studied Lebanese children who ranged in age from 6 to 12 and were blind from birth. Number conservation appeared consistently in the older nine-year-olds but was consistently absent in seven-year-olds. Conservation of liquid was found by Stephens and Simpkins (1974) to be, like substance, a relatively early acquisition, and Canning's (1957) results concurred. Wan-Lin and Tait (1987) found conservation of liquid to be much more difficult, and it is tempting to suspect that the task was quite a different one from those used by the others. Finally, conservation of length was found by both Stephens and Simpkins (1974) and Wan-Lin and Tait (1987) to occur in the same time period as conservation of weight and substance.

Individual differences

A good deal of variation has been reported in the ages of acquisition of these conservation abilities. While part of this variation is undoubtedly due to methodological differences, part of it may also be due to differences among samples. Indeed, comparison of the five studies that evaluated substance, weight, and volume reveals that Gottesman (1973) generally found the earliest acquisition, followed by Miller (1969), Hatwell (1985), and Wan-Lin and Tait (1987), with Stephens and Simpkins (1974) reporting the latest acquisition. Aside from variation in methodological and data reporting procedures, to what can such consistent differences be attributed?

Likely sources of variation include severity of visual loss, age at visual loss, intelligence, school and home characteristics, and cultural differences. Training studies are also designed to effect variation in cognitive skills.

Severity of visual loss. Several studies have evaluated the severity of visual loss. Wan-Lin and Tait (1987), for example, compared groups of partially sighted and blind children and found the partially sighted group to precede the blind group by a year to several years for each conservation concept. Severity of loss was also used as a variable in a discriminate function analysis to predict conservation ability: it was a significant predictor in all areas of conservation except volume.

For Miller's sample of 6- to 10-year-olds, the only evidence of conservation was among the partially sighted group: children with "no usable vision" did not conserve substance, weight, or volume by the age of 10. Although there were not sufficient numbers of cases to allow formal analysis of the effects of this variable, Tobin's (1972) partially sighted children appear to be roughly a year earlier in showing conservation of substance than his blind children. Canning (1957) found conservation of number to emerge somewhat earlier in a partially sighted group.

Lister et al. (1989) tested children who had some useful vision but required educational adaptations and who ranged in age from 5 to 17 years. Conservation of substance, weight, and volume were evaluated, along with several other abilities. The usual practice with partially sighted children has, curiously, been to occlude vision and test with adapted tactual materials. Appropriately, Lister et al. worked within the partially sighted child's perceptual abilities, allowing vision and using materials that were minimally adapted. Using this approach, Lister et al. found their group of children with partial sight to be not only more advanced than blind children, but also more advanced than the partially sighted children tested by other investigators who have used tactual adaptations of conservation tasks. Indeed, Lister et al. found no differences between the developmental acquisition of conservation concepts between this group and an age-matched group of sighted children.

It is impossible to stress heavily enough the importance of evaluating children using methodologies that optimize the expression of their capabilities and that tap as well as possible their everyday perceptual functioning. It simply does not make sense to evaluate the conservation concepts of partially sighted children, who make much use of their limited sight in their daily existence, under blindfolded conditions.

Other researchers have chosen to restrict the vision characteristics of their samples. Stephens and Simpkins (1974) included only children with LP or less, and as noted earlier, they were very late in showing conservation, compared to other studies. On the other hand, Gottesman's (1973) children were similar in their visual status, and in general they showed conservation on the early side. Thus, while partial vision seems to play a part, it is clearly not the only variable affecting the acquisition of conservation concepts.

Age at visual loss. Another potentially important variable is the age at which vision is lost. Of the studies that have reported age at visual loss, virtually all have characterized all or the large majority of the children as "congenitally" blind, although this criterion in some cases included children who lost visual function as late as four years of age. Thus, unfortunately, no analysis may be made of the effects of age of visual loss from the studies reviewed here, and the results can generally be considered to apply to children blind from birth or very early in life. The study of the acquisition of conservation concepts in children with varying amounts of early vision would be of value.

Intelligence. A third candidate is intelligence: since both conservation tasks and IQ tests are thought to tap some aspect(s) of intelligence, a significant relationship should be expected. Miller (1969) and Brekke et al. (1974) addressed the issue, and the evidence is mixed. Miller found significant correlations between IQ and conservation of substance, weight, and volume (these correlations held up even with variation due to visual status taken into account), even though the age range was only 6 to 10 years. Although Dimcovic (1992) did not find a significant correlation of IQ, measured by the verbal parts of the Wechsler Intelligence Scale for Children (WISC) and conservation of substance, she did note significant correlations between the latter and several tests of "vocabulary of relations," which tap children's understanding of spatial, temporal, and physical relational vocabulary. On the negative side, Brekke et al. found no significant correlation between IQ and conservation of weight: children in this study ranged from 6 to 14 years. In the Brekke et al. study, other factors were strongly predictive of the conservation results, and it may be that weaker effects of IQ were overshadowed in the analyses.

In any case, I believe that the issue is not of deep interest, since as I argue elsewhere (Chapter 7), children's performance on tests of intelligence is at best a side issue.

School and home environments. Another cluster of variables that is complex but of potential interest relates to variation in children's school and home environments. Research samples vary in their selection of children from residential and public schools, and from institutional and home environments. This combination of characteristics may affect the acquisition of cognitive skills in complex ways. For example, in Stephens and Simpkins's (1974) study, only 20 of the 75 subjects attended public schools, whereas more than 50% of Gottesman's (1973) sample were from public schools. Gottesman's children tended to show earlier acquisition of conservation than those of Stephens and Simpkins (1974). In fact, in a follow-up analysis Gottesman (1976) found some advantage of the public school children compared to the residential school children; this difference was concentrated in the younger (four- to seven-year old) age group.

Some studies have analyzed the home–school variable directly. For example, Brekke et al. (1974) found a significant advantage of children who were living at home and attending public schools over those in the institutional setting. Although the former group had a higher ratio of large print to braille readers, the home–institution difference held up even with this factor taken into account.

There is no clear theoretical prediction to be made based on the "school setting" variable. On the one hand, residential schools tend to have a greater concentration of professionals specifically trained in the education of children with visual impairments than do public schools; this difference should tend to favor the residential school children. On the other hand, for various reasons the expectations for the cognitive development and educational progress of children in residential schools may be lower, with possible adverse consequences for their actual progress in intellectual development. At the same time, children in the public school setting generally are living in a home family environment, with presumably positive implications for the breadth of their extracurricular experience. Thus, school setting per se is not a simple predictive variable, and our research should focus on other factors that tend to accompany it both directly and indirectly.

Cultural variables. There has been some interest in comparing the cognitive development of U.S. children having visual impairments with those raised in other cultures. The issue is of interest because of the question whether conservation abilities are fundamental cognitive skills that develop in similar manner in all children, or are somehow culturally dependent. Furthermore, studies comparing children across cultural settings can make effective use of cross-cultural variation to examine the factors that may influence the course of cognitive development. The excellent study by Wan-Lin and Tait (1987) of blind and partially sighted children is a case in point.

The children, ranging in age from 6 to 15 years, were drawn from residential and public day schools in Taiwan. Eight conservation tasks were used, and results from most of these have already been cited in relevant sections. Generally the results fit within the range of typical acquisition ages found in research with U.S. samples, and the results also show the typical advantage of partial vision. Of particular interest here are the cultural and educational factors that characterized the difference between day schools and residential schools. The formal Mandarin language is exclusively used in public schools; the Taiwanese dialect is forbidden in the day school setting and may be used only at home. However, children in residential schools *are* allowed to use the Taiwanese dialect. Wan–Lin and Tait (1987) noted that Mandarin, with its written form, is the traditional language of literature and philosophy, and that by contrast, the dialects, in their primarily spoken form, remain on a more concrete level and may not serve as well to mediate the development of abstract thought. Consequently, children with visual impairments in residential schools, who are permitted to maintain their dialect rather than being forced to learn Mandarin, may be at a disadvantage in the acquisition of cognitive capabilities.

A second factor differentiating residential and day schools is the nature of the child's out-of-school experience. Parents and older siblings in the home setting are important parts of the child's overall education: children in the residential school setting do not share this experience to the same degree and may be more likely to pass their spare time in ways that are not cognitively challenging. Of course this depends on the characteristics of the school program as well as on what children actually do when not in school.

Third, Wan–Lin and Tait (1987) noted that in the science curriculum, residential schools tend to substitute verbal description of scientific experiments for direct participation, and they suggested that this lack of opportunity may allow the development and maintenance of incorrect understanding of the properties of the physical world.

The results of Tait (1990) reinforce the importance of direct experience with materials in enhancing the acquisition of conservation concepts. In this study, Tait further analyzed the results of the Wan–Lin and Tait (1987) work and added new data from a sample of children in India. Overall, the Indian and Taiwanese children with visual impairments were similar in showing slower acquisition of conservation concepts than is typical for sighted children. However, there were substantial individual differences within the groups, and in both samples, more advanced cognitive development was related to specific experiences of the more advanced children with concept-relevant materials. For example, the Indian children who showed relatively advanced conservation of liquid volume tended to have had experience with drawing water from public wells, and the relatively advanced Taiwanese children had extensive experience at handling materials such as produce and handicrafts.

Although these factors emerged in studies of children in non-European cultures, none of them is unique to the cultural situation. Encouragement to learn formal language in all its complexity, constructive use of out-of-school time, and opportunity for fully participatory learning are all factors that are, without undue effort, available to children in all educational settings, regardless of cultural context or visual status.

Training studies. Training is a formal intervention in the child's environment, and there are two excellent examples of training studies of conservation abilities with visually impaired children. Stephens and Grube (1982) reported the effects of a training program in which 13 of the children from the previous Stephens and Simpkins (1974) work were enrolled. These included 6- to 10-year-olds, 10- to 14-year-olds, and 14- to 18-year-olds. They were age-matched by a group of blind control children who did not receive the training program. Each group received a pre-test and, after about 18 months, a post-test of various conservation and classification abilities. During the 17-month intervention period, children received an extensive individualized training program that averaged about 95 hours per child. The teachers who administered the training were coached in the use of a "discovery process" method. Compared with the control group, the training group showed general superiority, except in tests of spatial relations and mental imagery.

Lopata and Pasnak (1976) reported a similar training study. The 8- to 13-year-old children varied widely in intelligence, with Slossen scores ranging from 62 to 131 at the beginning of the study. Twenty-eight children were given a pre-test involving weight and substance conservation, then were divided into two groups for training and control conditions. The groups were thus matched on the basis of visual characteristics, age, IQ, and cognitive pre-test. The pre- and post-tests included a battery of weight and substance conservation tasks. Training involved a learning-set approach and included training on measurement to a standard, seriation, classification, and substance conservation. Each child was given one hour per week of training for as long as it took to progress through the training protocol: the average was 10.2 hours. Each child in the control group was given an equivalent amount of exposure to the trainer, but the materials were unrelated to the training program. At the end, both trained and control children received the post-test and the IQ test. Conservation responses were evaluated allowing partial credit. The trained group showed significant improvements in substance and weight conservation, as well as increased IQ scores, whereas the control group did not improve significantly on any of these measures.

Thus, training on cognitive skills improved performance on those skills. The results are important in another respect, however, in that improvement also occurred on the IQ test. The training on cognitive skills apparently generalized to a test that is not designed specifically to evaluate those skills. This result lends some validity to the procedure of evaluation by Piagetian tasks and suggests that training may have a more generalized cognitive effect. There is an important lesson here for training studies: they should evaluate not only the trained abilities, but also other abilities that are related or of which the trained abilities are thought to be representative.

Summary

It may be useful to summarize this section by reviewing the factors associated with more developmentally advanced cognitive abilities. It is convenient to divide these into two categories, "status" variables such as partial vision, which are not readily amenable to manipulation, and "environmental" variables, which may be readily manipulated.

Status variables. The literature is very clear in showing that children with some visual function are at an advantage in cognitive development. Although the existence or amount of partial vision is not under our control, the encouragement of the child with partial vision to use that visual capability is. Barraga (1976) has been persuasive in encouraging the effective use of any residual visual capability, and the present pattern of results bears out her argument forcefully.

There is little evidence available about the effect of early visual experience on the acquisition of conservation abilities, since the research has for the most part tested children who were visually impaired at birth or who lost vision shortly thereafter.

The relationship between IQ and conservation development is not clear, but the issue is not particularly important. IQ is a derivative measure that is, as it has usually been measured, of questionable validity with children with visual impairments (see Warren, 1984, chapter 4; Chapter 7 in this volume), and that is no more amenable to environmental manipulation than is cognitive performance itself as measured by the Piagetian tasks. Said another way, if we knew enough about arranging the environment to promote optimal cognitive development as assessed by tests of conservation and other cognitive abilities, we would have no need to worry about performance on tests of IQ.

Environmental variables. Environmental factors are potentially under the control of parents and professionals. Perhaps the most important general point to be made is that a stimulating learning environment facilitates the acquisition of cognitive abilities. Evidence for this conclusion emerges directly and indirectly from studies that have compared children from various school settings, although it should again be stressed that it is not the school itself that is important but the variables that tend to accompany the child's educational situation. These include the nature of the curriculum and the child's participation in it, the use of out-of-school time, and the expectations held for the child's cognitive growth and educational progress. Finally, training programs that focus on the acquisition of concepts are an obvious manipulation of the environment, and some success has been demonstrated with them.

In sum, while factors such as early visual experience and residual visual function are not amenable to change, other variables under our potential influence have an equally great impact on the course of acquisition of conservation abilities, and optimizing those factors should lead to optimal conceptual development in these areas.

Understanding causality

The concepts of causality are closely related to those of the physical properties of objects, as exemplified in the various conservation concepts. However, simply knowing *that* is not the same as knowing *why;* knowing *why* requires the understanding of causality.

The sighted child's understanding of causality undergoes a long and involved progression that goes well beyond the scope of the present treatment. For example, when already in the sensorimotor period infants begin, by their own physical activity, to create cause–effect relationships; they bang on something, it moves and/or makes a noise, they perceive the effect, and based on the accumulation of such experiences they gradually come to understand cause and effect as it involves their own actions. Later, the child's own actions need not be involved, and cause and effect can be perceived at a distance. It is a long while before concepts of causality are fully mature. Indeed, it is questionable whether most adults really understand such complex questions of causality as gravity. They know that things do fall when dropped, but most people do not really know *why* they fall.

I am not aware of any research on the development of concepts of causality in the infant or child with impaired vision. This is an unfortunate gap in the literature. In many areas of development it might be reasonable, absent empirical evidence, to suppose that the development of the child with impaired vision would be just like that of the child with sight. In the case of causality this is not a good supposition, since the perceptual evidence upon which the acquisition of causal concepts is quite different for the child with impaired vision. The blind infant can hear but cannot see the effect of banging on the crib side. Possibly more constraining is the need for vision to perceive cause and effect at a distance, particularly when the child's own action is not involved. On the other hand, the child with impaired vision may have better evidence on which to understand that objects must ordinarily be in physical contact in order for one to have an effect on the other.

The circumstances are simply different, and partial vision complicates the picture still further. This is an area in which we cannot make a logical supposition, and where empirical evidence is needed.

Understanding time

The development of concepts of time has not been studied a great deal. Piaget (1946, cited by Flavell, 1963) contributed early work on the questions involved, but there has not been much sustained follow-up. In brief, the child's ability to understand temporal intervals and the measurement of time proceeds gradually and intersects heavily with the understanding of spatial events. For example, the concept of age tends to be confused with physical size (a larger tree is judged as being necessarily older than a smaller one). The concept of elapsed time tends to be confused with spatial extent; the young child judges that travel over a greater distance must necessarily take more time than travel over a lesser distance, for example. Time is interpreted as a straightforward correlate of distance, without the understanding that velocity has to be taken into account.

I am not aware of any research on the understanding of time in children with visual impairments. Based on what we know about the development of concepts of time in sighted children, though, this would be an exceptionally interesting topic. If time is confused with spatial extent by children with vision, and if the understanding of spatial extent is different in children without vision, then what of time? Do blind children acquire the concept of time in a different manner altogether? Or is the concept of time still tied to the development of concepts of space? There is important research to be done on these issues.

4

Spatial understanding and spatial behavior

In Chapter 3 we considered evidence about the infant's and child's understanding of the properties of the physical world. The spatial properties of the physical world are properly a subset of this domain. However, we will treat this area in a separate chapter for two reasons. First, this is a relatively large body of work. Second, there may be differences in the acquisition of spatial as opposed to more general concepts. This possibility is well illustrated in a study by Hartlage (1969), who found that young congenitally blind children are not as good at dealing with spatial concepts as they are with nonspatial concepts.

An example of a question that taps spatial concepts is: "Mary is in front of Bill. Bill is in front of John. What is Mary's relationship to John?" A corresponding nonspatial item substitutes "smarter than" for "in front of." Improvement occurred with increasing age as expected. The results suggest that beginning at grade 5, the blind children are just as able to deal with spatial as with nonspatial concepts. Younger children, though, showed considerably worse performance on spatial than on nonspatial items. Unfortunately, no detail was offered about the variation in performance with degree of visual impairment, intelligence, or gender. The inclusion of the nonspatial questions makes it clear that the children did not have a general problem with concepts, but rather that the problem was specific to spatial concepts.

It is difficult to separate the study of spatial concepts from that of spatial behavior. Spatial behaviors are relatively easy to observe, but spatial concepts are not; the approach taken by Hartlage is a rare example in which concepts are tapped relatively directly. Usually the quality of spatial concepts must be inferred from behavior. Often it is unclear whether poor performance on a spatial task is a result of inadequate spatial concepts or of poor motor control. In the face of this kind of difficulty, it is important to examine the issues from different perspectives.

We will begin consideration of this area in infancy, and then move to the preschool and school-age child.

Infancy

An understanding of spatial structure depends on the integration of spatially distributed visual, auditory, and tactual experiences with motor activity. Infants with sight begin to show evidence of this integration early, making swiping movements with the arms in response to objects in near space in the first several months. These actions develop into reaching for and grasping of objects by midyear. By midyear infants also integrate auditory and visual information about location and action (see Spelke, 1976). Locomotion in the physical environment advances as well: typically infants begin to crawl by midyear and to take their first steps by the end of the first year.

Throughout, the infant can often see the sources of sound, can see the hands moving in space, can see the objects that are grasped, and can see the changes in spatial structure that result from movement. Along with visual information, infants can experience changes in auditory information as they locomote or are carried within the spatial environment, and they can see the changing relationships of their own position to the positions of sound-making objects. In short, by the end of the first year, the infant has had a great deal of correlated visual, auditory, tactual, and motor experience of the surrounding spatial environment, and can execute purposeful behavior in relation to objects that occupy that environment.

Vision normally plays an exceedingly important role in the development of concepts of spatial structure, for two reasons. First, vision provides a very precise and extensive source of real-time information about spatial structure. Beyond any question, the human visual system is better equipped for the perception of spatial structure than any other sensory modality.

Vision is important in another way, however. Vision serves to integrate the spatial information that the infant receives from other sources, including tactual and auditory information as well as the visual, auditory, and tactual results of motor and locomotor actions. Given the apparent importance of vision, a logical hypothesis would be that the blind infant may have difficulty conceptualizing spatial relationships.

Evidence about the development of the concept of object permanence, reviewed in the preceding chapter, suggests that this is the case. Although many blind infants progress in a timely manner through the earlier stages of object permanence, the scanty available evidence suggests that they do not move readily from Stage 5 to Stage 6. Recall that for Stage 5 the infant is expected to search those locations in which the object had been perceived. These behaviors can be accomplished on the basis of an ego-centric spatial concept, that is, one that is referenced to the body's location. The requirements of Stage 6 are more demanding, in that the infant is expected to search the surrounding space systematically for a hidden object. An egocentric concept of space does not serve this kind of systematic search effectively. Instead, Stage 6 behavior requires a conception of the surrounding space as a set of locations "out there," independent of the infant's own experience of those locations. In short, the blind infant's difficulty in moving from Stage 5 to Stage 6 suggests a problem in making the transition from egocentrically to externally (or allocentrically) organized space.

It is not surprising that vision should facilitate this transition, since it enables the infant to see several spatial locations and their relationships simultaneously, as well as to see where touched and sounding objects are in relation to other objects. However, why should the combination of sound and touch not suffice to allow the blind infant to make this same transition to an allocentric concept of space? Schwartz (1984) suggested that although sound can specify spatial location for infants (whether blind or sighted), it is not generally an effective cue for the detection of spatial structure. The information that sound carries about spatial location is simply not attended to. Rather, "The infant begins to selectively attend to the sound characteristics of the auditory stimulus, rather than its location" (p. 30).

Nor is touch an effective substitute, in part because it is not effective beyond arm's reach. Schwartz (1984) argued, in addition, that as manual manipulation develops, the hands tend to be used more for the grasping and manipulation of objects than for the exploration of spatial structure.

Schwartz's argument is not that the auditory and tactual systems are incapable of facilitating the perception of spatial structure, but that their typical functional use is not normally directed to the exploration of spatial structure. The ears are more attuned to the sound characteristics of auditory stimuli than to their locations, and the hands are more attuned to the manipulation of objects than to their locations in space.

For the blind infant, then, it is not surprising to find evidence that the spatial world is organized primarily in relation to the self rather than as a system with an external structure that does not depend on the location or orientation of the infant.

Preschool and school-age children

Nor does this change quickly beyond infancy. Many tasks have been used to study spatial concepts and spatial behavior in preschool and school-age children, and in general these show a slow escape from the constraints of egocentrism.

One such task asks the child to construct a straight line to connect two locations on a board. Sighted children show a regular developmental progression from reliance on an egocentric frame of reference to an ability to use appropriate external points of reference such as the edges of the board (see Laurendeau & Pinard, 1970).

Simpkins and Siegel (1979) used a variation of this task to evaluate the ability of blind children to construct a straight line. They were particularly interested in the spatial information that the children used to do this. The materials were a board (either rectangular or circular) with two barns that the child was to connect by constructing a straight fence. On the rectangular board, the barns were set so that the correct fence would parallel a side of the board. On the circular board, the barns were placed such that the correct fence would be horizontal, vertical, or diagonal with respect to the child's location.

Although there was a general improvement in performance with increasing age from 6 to 11 years, age was not a strong predictor of performance. The strategies observed suggested that the children did not consistently use an external frame of reference (e.g., the edge of the board) to guide their performance at any age. Their constructions indicated an awareness of relationships between neighboring posts but not an overall concept of a straight-line relationship between the two barns. Thus, they tended to focus on internal detail rather than external relationships, and they did not use the spatial reference structure that was available.

In a similar task, Birns (1986) used children 6 to 13 years of age. Some were blind from birth, while the others had lost vision at ages ranging from two months to eight years. The child was given a board with two barns and was asked to construct a straight-line fence connecting them using a set of magnetized "fence posts." No difference was found between subgroups divided by age or age of visual loss, and again, none of the children attempted to use the edges of the base as a referent for construction.

Using a more complex spatial task, Hermelin and O'Connor (1971b) designed a learning situation to reveal the frame of reference that school-age children use to learn a spatial array. During a training session, the child's first two fingers of both hands were placed on four adjoining spatial locations. The child learned four words, one corresponding to each of the finger locations. The situation was intended to be ambiguous, in that the child was not instructed whether the word was to be learned in relation to the finger or to the spatial location. The test session evaluated which association had in fact been made. The children associated the words with their fingers about 75% of the time (in contrast, sighted children do so only about 40% of the time). Thus, this finding indicates egocentric referencing of spatial information.

However, 3 of the 10 congenitally blind children did make predominantly location rather than finger responses, and Hermelin and O'Connor concluded that for these children, "spatial representations were constructed on the basis of kinesthetic and motor cues, such as distance from the body and amount and direction movement required" (p. 131). No discussion was offered about what these three children may have had in common that influenced their choice of an external frame of reference for response rather than the egocentric frame adopted by the others. In particular, it was not reported whether the three might have been among the older children in the 6- to 14-year age range, or among the four who had some light perception. In any case, it is clear that egocentric responding is not a necessary concomitant of congenital visual impairment.

These three studies suggest that children with visual impairments do not show a strong tendency to use external spatial referents. Additional illustrations of the ego- or allocentricity of spatial concepts are given throughout the ensuing sections. Although we are attuned to changes in performance related to age, we examine the evidence for variation with other individual differences factors as well.

The near-space versus far-space distinction

A useful distinction can be made between near space and far space. *Near space* refers to the space that surrounds the child within arm's reach, whereas *far space* refers to the spatial environment beyond that. The distinction is more than just a convenience for several reasons. An egocentric spatial organization may often suffice for near-space tasks, since the hand–arm system provides a means of proximal contact with locations and objects in near space, referring them to the child's own fixed location. The hand–arm system is insufficient for far-space tasks unless it is used in conjunction with locomotion. Distal auditory information may be useful for both near-space and far-space tasks, but auditory information about spatial location is fundamentally egocentric, particularly if the perceiver is not moving. Vision is of course useful for both near- and far-space tasks, and among the three senses it is best at conveying information that naturally mediates an understanding of spatial relationships independent of the child's own location.

In all, it seems reasonable to hypothesize that visual impairment may interfere with the development of allocentric spatial concepts and behavior, and that this interference should be revealed more in far-space than in near-space tasks. At the same time, factors related to the child's visual history as well as other individual differences variables may play a significant part.

Near-space concepts and behavior

Laterality. We might expect important developments in the child's understanding of the concepts of laterality, and several revealing studies are of interest. The work of Cratty and Sams (1968) on the development of body image in children with visual impairments is discussed more thoroughly in Chapter 11. The test tapped the child's ability to identify various parts of his or her own body, including distinguishing the left and right sides. Identification of body parts was generally very good over the age range of 5 to 16 years. But when left–right distinctions were involved, performance was considerably worse, with correct use of laterality with respect to the child's own body appearing at an average age of about nine years.

Discrimination of spatial relations related to external objects was more difficult than discrimination of the laterality relationships of the child's own body. Even at age 16 the children "seemed totally incapable of projecting themselves into the tester's left–right reference system" (p. 33). In sum, there was a general progression from acquisition of laterality concepts for the child's own body to the ability to handle spatial relationships among external objects; the ability to take another person's perspective with respect to laterality was a more difficult task. Watemberg, Cermak, and Henderson (1986) used similar tasks with congenitally blind children, ranging in age from 7 to 14 years, and found very similar results to those of Cratty and Sams.

This pattern of results makes good sense with respect to the issue of egocentrism/allocentrism. The understanding of one's own laterality is by definition an egocentric task, and it is not surprising that this ability appeared earlier than the ability to deal with external spatial relationships, which requires an externally referenced system.

Encoding of spatial information. Linear spatial extent is a relatively simple spatial feature. Jones (1972) had the child move his or her hand along a track to a preset stop, then replicate the same path with the stop removed. Performance was reasonably good, with errors averaging only 18% of the path distance for 5-year-olds and decreasing to 8% for 12-year-olds. It should be noted that this task can be performed by simply reproducing the kinesthetic sensation of the sample trial (a very "egocentric" event): it does not require the concept of an extent in external space.

A slight variation on the task changes it so that it does require an external concept. Shagan and Goodnow (1973) had adolescent subjects, who had lost sight by age two, move a lever through a predetermined spatial extent, and then reproduce the same spatial extent starting from a different location. Reproduction occurred either immediately or after a 20-sec delay. Performance did not deteriorate as a result of the delay, suggesting that the spatial extent must have been encoded effectively.

However, in a condition in which the child performed a task of classifying numbers during the delay, performance was worse. Such an effect might be a result of verbal encoding, with which the verbal task would interfere. Shagan and Goodnow favored this explanation, although the specific manner in which verbal encoding of spatial extent occurs is not clear. Alternatively, it seems as likely that whatever encoding of the spatial extent did occur, its maintenance required active attention; when attention was diverted to the verbal task, performance deteriorated.

Subsequent research was directed to the question of the child's ability to encode similar spatial information allocentrically. Hermelin and O'Connor (1975) used three variations of the task. The child first moved a pointer vertically from a fixed starting point to a fixed stop three times. In the *reproduction* task, the child then started at the same point and attempted to reproduce the same extent without the fixed stop. This task, like that of Jones (1972), can be performed using only kinesthetic cues and does not require any concept of an external spatial extent. In the *location* task, the child was to arrive at the same end point but from a different starting point. This task cannot be done purely by reproducing the same extent of movement, but it does not require the representation of a goal point in external space: the child can perform correctly using (egocentric) proprioceptive cues by reproducing the arm's position at the end of the movement. In the *distance* task, the child had to move the hand over the original distance, but from a different starting point and thus with a different end point. This task requires a spatial extent to be reproduced with no point in common with the original, and thus it demands a more sophisticated spatial concept than either of the other tasks.

The children ranged in age from 10 to 15 years and had been blind from birth or the first few months of life. On both reproduction and location tasks, they performed reasonably well, with performance deteriorating mildly as the distances increased. On the distance task, however, the children's performance deteriorated markedly as distances increased. Hermelin and O'Connor (1975) concluded that the children did not have a reliable metric for distance in external space, whereas their performance was adequate when it could be referenced to body-centered kinesthetic or proprioceptive cues.

Millar (1985) evaluated encoding alternatives in a different way. She reasoned that oblique movements should not suffer (compared to horizontal or vertical movements) if kinesthetic cues are encoded, whereas if encoding is of location cues, performance with oblique movements should suffer because of the greater difficulty that children generally have with oblique versus horizontal or vertical directions and locations.

The children were congenitally blind, ranged in age from 7 to 12 years, and were divided into two age groups averaging 9 and 11 years. The task involved having the child move a stylus in a straight-line path from a start location to a goal, then find the same goal either from the same start (repeated movement) or from a different start (changed movement). The movements required for correct response were horizontal, vertical, or oblique in relation to the child's body. For the older children, movements when the child was at the front–middle of the display were about as accurate as those when the child was at the side of the display, and repeated movements were more accurate than changed movements. For the younger children, responses were worse when they were at the side of the display. Oblique movements were not generally worse than horizontal or vertical movements.

The results were thus consonant with the hypothesis that blind children generally use an egocentric (kinesthetic) strategy rather than an external spatial strategy to perform the task, but that the ability to use an external strategy effectively increases with age. In addition, the poor performance by the younger children when they were not at the front of the display suggests that they were less able to use the external spatial cues, such as the straight edges contained in the display itself.

Millar's (1975c) results shed more light on the strategies that are employed in spatial learning tasks. The children had all lost vision before 20 months and had no more than LP. They were divided into three age groups with means of 6:11, 8:2, and 10:4. The child traced a stylus through a simple five-sided path and encountered a block either early or late in the path. The block was then removed and the child traced the path to completion. In recall, the child had to trace the path, starting either from the original starting point (forward condition) or from the end point (backward condition), and was instructed to stop at the point where the block had been in the original path. Generally, performance improved with increasing age. Performance was better in the forward than in the backward direction (in contrast to sighted children who show the reverse effect). One other variable is important. The stop was placed either near the original starting location (early) or far away from it (late). The near stop was thus close to the start for the forward direction, whereas the far stop was far from the start (and therefore had more path turns intervening). In contrast, when the path was traced in the backward direction, the "near" stop was relatively far from the point at which recall was begun. The design thus allowed a "primacy versus recency" effect to be evaluated.

The results were very clear. Performance on near and far points was about equal for the forward recall condition. On the backward recall condition, the worst performance occurred for the "near" point. This pattern of results clearly supports the interpretation that the children encoded the path kinesthetically as an egocentric sequence of motor movements rather than as an allocentric spatial layout. In the forward condition, where the recall movements corresponded to the learned sequence, performance was relatively good. But in the backward condition, the recall movements had to be performed in the reverse order. By the time the child got to the "near" target (which was in fact far from the starting point on recall), the discrepancy between the remembered sequence of movements and the sequence actually being performed led to a serious impairment of performance.

The role of early or partial vision. The samples of children used in the foregoing experiments were all relatively homogeneous (LP at most, blind from within the first year or so), and it is unknown from this work whether some residual visual function or a period of early vision might facilitate the acquisition of allocentric concepts. Millar has provided some valuable information about these variables.

Millar (1979) tested children from 5 to 15 years who were congenitally blind, who had had some early visual experience, or who currently had some residual visual function. In the first experiment, the child was presented with two boards, both square in one task and both diamond-shaped in another, and was asked to transfer a set of objects from one board to the corresponding locations on the other. The children with residual vision or visual experience performed better using the horizontal board, with its orthogonal orientation, and they were relatively better at horizontal than vertical movements. The congenitally blind children did not benefit from either the horizontal board orientation or horizontal movements. This pattern of results supports Millar's hypothesis that children with residual vision or visual experience are more likely to be able to use external spatial cues to guide their performance.

In a second experiment, an attempt was made to enhance the salience of the spatial qualities of the board by placing a raised vertical line on it. This had no effect for the children with no visual experience but tended to enhance the use of the external reference for those with early or current visual experience. Millar concluded that the children with and without visual experience were using entirely different approaches to the tasks; those without visual experience simply did not realize that external spatial cues were available or were potentially valuable in performing the task.

Several results from the older maze-learning literature also bear on the question of visual experience. Knotts and Miles (1929) and Berg and Worchel (1956) found better maze performance by children who had a period of early vision. More recently, Dodds and Carter (1983) found a similar outcome with a task that required the child to reconstruct a simple spatial array with magnetized elements. Furthermore, the performance gap between children with and without early vision widened with age.

It is clear from this research that children with visual impairments have difficulty in making the transition from an egocentric to an allocentric spatial frame of reference. In encoding spatial information, they tend to persist in using strategies that involve self-reference and are slow to develop the use of an external frame of reference to encode spatial information. Millar suggested that this may be not so much a matter of incapability, but of preference based on experience: "Blind children thus have little reason to believe that external relations can serve as useful references. By contrast, encoding relative to the body provides consistent feedback in many blind tasks" (1981b, p. 263). We will discuss strategies of information processing in Chapter 6.

In this literature on near-space tasks, three factors emerge as important in determining the level of performance. First, age is generally a positive predictor in studies that include a substantial age range. The use of an external frame of reference facilitates performance, and the tendency to use an external rather than an egocentric frame of reference increases with age. Second, children with some partial vision perform better, probably because partial vision facilitates the child's attention to external spatial factors. Third, the evidence generally suggests that children with a period of early visual experience do better on such tasks than children who have been blind since birth.

Mental rotation. Certain tasks tap the ability to deal with spatial layout information in a different orientation from that in which it was initially experienced. The term "mental rotation" is used because of the underlying assumption that what must be done in such a task is encode the spatial information into an image, rotate that image mentally, and then access the image in its new orientation.

The classic mental rotation paradigm used with sighted subjects was reported by Shepard and Metzler (1971). A letter of the alphabet is presented, either correctly or in its mirror image form, in an orientation that is rotated by some amount from the upright. When asked to judge as quickly as possible whether the letter is normal or a mirror image, reaction times increase as the amount of rotation increases up to 180 degrees in either direction. This sort of reaction-time function is taken as evidence that the mental image of the visually perceived letter is rotated into an upright orientation before a judgment is made.

The question naturally arises whether this evidence for mental rotation is specific to visual stimuli, or whether it would occur with tactual stimuli. Carpenter and Eisenberg (1978) tested adolescents ranging in age from 15 to 18 years on a tactual version of this task. Some had varying degrees of very limited visual experience whereas others had none, and all were visually impaired since birth. The typical mental rotation function was found, with reaction times increasing regularly from upright to a 180-degree rotation. There was no difference between subjects with and without previous visual experience. The results suggest that cognitive operations on tactually encoded information about orientation are similar to those used by sighted subjects for visually encoded information.

Several variations of the mental rotation task have been used with children with visual impairments. Stephens, Simpkins, and Wexler (1976) used a task called Rotation of Squares to evaluate the mental rotation abilities of 6- to 18-year-old congenitally blind children. In this task, two squares are presented, and while one stays fixed, the other can be rotated into different relationships to the fixed square. The child's task is to imagine where one corner of the rotated square is in relation to its original location and to select the correct alternative from a set of choices. Children were grouped into three age ranges, 6 to 10, 10 to 14, and 14 to 18 years. Overall, performance was poor. The middle age group was not better than the youngest, but the oldest group performed better than the younger groups. Unfortunately, no other individual differences variables were reported. However, using a similar task involving rotation of a pattern of pegs, Drever (1955) found that adolescents who had had sight for longer than four years performed much better than those who had lost vision before the age of four.

Millar (1976) used similar tasks with younger children. The 6- to 11-year-old children had at most LP. In one experiment, a headed matchstick was glued onto a cardboard square. The child's task was to feel the matchstick, then select from an array of choices what the orientation of the matchstick would be to an observer at a location different from the child's. Performance improved somewhat with increasing age, and it was clear that mental rotation was a source of difficulty since performance was significantly better on a comparable task that did not require it. Subgroups divided on the basis of the age of visual loss did not differ on the test of simple matching, but the subgroup with some visual experience performed much better on the mental rotation task. In a second task that required recall in addition to mental rotation, clear differences emerged in favor of the older children.

Ittyerah and Samarapungavan (1989) tested congenitally blind 4- to 11-year-olds in tasks similar to those used by Millar (1976). The figures were more complex arrays involving eight spokes radiating from a center point, with one spoke marked by an arrowhead. In a matching task, the child felt the array and then attempted to rotate a second array into the same orientation. There was considerable age-related improvement in performance: the younger children performed almost at chance, whereas the older children performed significantly better. An element of memory was involved in this task: as in the case of Millar's (1976) second task, the poor performance of the younger children may have been due to poor memory for the standard.

In a second task, the same array was used but a second spoke was marked by a lump of clay. The comparison array was presented for tactual examination with the arrowhead in a different direction. Then the standard was removed and the child's task was to indicate where the clay would be on the comparison array in relation to the spoke with the (rotated) arrowhead. This is a very difficult task of mental rotation, since it requires not only rotation of a spatial element but retention of relational information within the array. It is not surprising, therefore, that the performance of even the older children was virtually random. (By contrast, Millar's older children did show some measure of success on the mental rotation tasks.)

It is evident from this literature that children with visual impairments can perform tasks requiring mental rotation; furthermore, some of the work shows evidence that these tasks can be accomplished by forming and manipulating a topological mental image. Experiments with totally blind children have clearly shown that such images can be based on tactual information, although this is a more difficult task than performance with vision. Variations in performance due to factors related to visual experiance have not been reported frequently, although the results of several studies suggest that a period of early vision facilitates mental rotation ability. Generally performance on tasks requiring mental rotation improves with increasing age. Finally, and not surprisingly, performance deteriorates with increasing complexity of the task.

Far-space concepts and behavior

We turn now to spatial concepts of the larger spatial environment. It is useful to distinguish between concepts of environments that are known from natural experience and those that are learned experimentally. We examine first concepts of familiar environments, that is, those in which the child has had extensive experience and has learned naturally. There is surprisingly little work available on this topic with children with visual impairments.

Familiar environments. Kephart, Kephart, and Schwarz (1974) asked five-to seven-year-old blind children questions about their surroundings, including the rooms within their houses and the overall layout of their houses, neighborhoods, and towns. There was an expected improvement in the quality of the children's knowledge with increasing age, and generally there was an age-related tendency to broaden the scope of knowledge from the room to the house to the neighborhood. Other evidence about individual differences was unfortunately not reported. Generally the children were not as advanced in their spatial knowledge as sighted children of comparable age. Kephart et al. argued, reasonably, that the nature and quality of the blind children's spatial knowledge was closely related to the extent of their experience, and they suggested that carefully constructed experiential intervention might succeed in creating a broader base of spatial knowledge.

In a similar study, Bigelow (1991) compared two partially sighted with two blind children in their ability to point to places in their immediate and more extended environments. The children ranged from five to eight years at the beginning of the study. Each child was tested until the tasks had been mastered or until he or she had been in the study for 15 months.

The child's task, while sitting in a familiar place in the home, was to point to locations in the house on the same level, in the house but on a different floor, in the surrounding yard, and in the neighborhood. The partially sighted children performed with sight (none of the locations was visible from the testing point).

The performance of the partially sighted and blind children differed dramatically. The younger child with partial vision mastered all tasks in the very first session, and the older progressively mastered the locations on the same floor, then those in the yard, then those in the home on a different floor. On the other hand, in 15 months of testing, one blind child did not master any of the tasks, and the other succeeded only with the locations on the same floor and in the yard.

However, this does not mean that these children did not have spatial knowledge. The instruction was to "point to *x*" and did not specify whether to point to the location of *x* or to the direction that one would walk to get to *x*. In fact, many of the "errors" were of this sort; the child pointed to the direction of the correct route. The conclusion seems warranted that the knowledge of familiar spatial environments is organized differently when partial vision is available and when it is not.

McReynolds and Worchel (1954) studied a similar issue of spatial layout knowledge, but with a greatly expanded scope. The children were asked to point to places on their school campus, in the city, to other cities, and to compass directions. Although the children varied in age, IQ, age of visual loss, and degree of impairment, no significant effects of any of these variables emerged, although the raw data suggest a relationship of performance to chronological age (the older the better), to intelligence (the higher the better), and to age at visual loss (the later the better). Possible effects may have been masked by the nature of the statistical analysis, in which each of these variables was treated as a binary (low vs. high) rather than as a continuous variable.

All of these studies show that knowledge is best for more local spatial locations and deteriorates as locations become more distant. It is reasonable to suppose that this trend is a function of the child's greater experience with nearby locations. Although the evidence is not extensive, it is evident that either former or current visual experience is facilitative. It is likely that the visual experience factor is related to performance because children with some visual experience have an expanded scope of experience in the spatial environment.

Casey (1978) evaluated adolescents' knowledge of the spatial layout of their residential school grounds. Ten children were blind since birth and 10 had partial vision, and all had lived in the school for at least a year. Each child constructed a model of the school by arranging labeled blocks representing buildings, and adhesive strips representing roadways and paths. The result was evaluated on the basis of organizational accuracy as well as correct placement of individual elements.

The children with partial vision, who constructed the model while blindfolded, scored higher in organizational accuracy and included more elements than the blind subjects. The latter group tended to cluster groups of items together rather than using an overall organizational framework. These are not at all surprising results given the differences that Bigelow (1991) found between younger blind and partially sighted children, and they support the view that residual vision facilitates the acquisition of well-organized concepts of far space.

The surprise was that Casey found that several totally blind children did relatively well on overall organization. These tended to be the ones whose independent travel ability was highly rated, whereas the blind children who constructed poorer models tended to be more restricted in their mobility both on and off the school campus. Although it is tempting to suppose that more extensive mobility on the school grounds would lead to a greater degree of exposure to the setting and therefore to a better concept of its spatial layout, conclusions about causality are risky from this research design. At least the results suggest that there are important relationships between experience in an environment and the quality of the child's concept of the spatial layout of that environment.

Reasonable though Casey's results seem, a word of methodological caution is in order. The procedure required the child to construct a model. This is a complex activity regardless of the quality of the child's concept of the spatial environment itself, and it is possible that the observed variation was in model-making ability rather than in the quality of concept of the spatial environment. It is a risky proposition to make inferences about cognitive capabilities, and we have to be especially careful when the response process itself involves complexity. The multidimensional scaling technique, used by Lockman, Rieser, and Pick (1981) to evaluate blind adults' knowledge of a familiar spatial environment, holds great promise. The technique involves asking the subject very simple questions about relationships among elements in the environment, such as their distances. From the collection of a subject's responses, a map is generated by computer to represent the subject's spatial concept of the environment. The technique is potentially useful with children because of its simplicity.

There is a great gap in our knowledge about the quality of spatial concepts that are acquired as a result of natural experience in environments, and there is an even greater lack of information about what the process of that acquisition might be. Research attention to these issues should yield useful knowledge.

Learning novel environments. Children are often exposed to new environments and have to learn about them. From a research standpoint, it should be easier to study this situation because the nature of the child's exposure to the environment can be controlled, and at least in principle, concepts can be studied as they are acquired.

One of the most impressive examples of the ability of a blind child to learn novel spatial environments was reported by Landau, Gleitman, and Spelke (1981). Kelli had lost sight as a result of ROP. At two years of age, she was active motorically and was familiar with the spatial layout of some areas of her home, although she was not generally able to find her way from room to room. The experimental work began at 31 months (all ages are uncorrected for prematurity) and was designed to evaluate how she learned novel spatial patterns.

Four landmarks (table, basket, pillows, and the child's mother) were arranged in a diamond pattern in an unfamiliar room. In the exposure phase, Kelli began at her mother's location and was led to each of the other landmarks and back twice, accompanied by verbal identification of the items. Then in the test phase she was placed at each of the landmarks in turn and was asked to walk to each of the other items. She was successful in moving to the correct segment of the room on 8 of 12 trials. When the array of objects was rotated 90 degrees within the room, still retaining the relationships within the array, she succeeded on five of eight trials. Her performance was apparently based on her concept of the relationships among the objects, that is to say, an allocentric concept, rather than on her own location. In subsequent experiments the possibility that she was using acoustic cues or echodetection was ruled out.

Landau, Spelke, and Gleitman (1984) tested Kelli again at age 43 months in a similar task, although in this case they evaluated her ability to deal with distance as well as direction. While her distance performance was not as good as her direction performance, it was far from random, with an average error of 27% of the correct distance.

In these experiments Kelli's paths were generally not straight, and in some cases, even when eventually successful, she made several turns in her path. This was reported to be more a matter of faulty locomotor control (reminiscent of the "veering" tendency that characterizes the straight-line locomotion of blind adults, e.g., Cratty, 1967), rather than of inadequate conceptualization of the spatial layout.

In another series of tests (Landau, 1986) conducted when she was about five years old, Kelli demonstrated remarkably good ability to use map representations of relationships between spatial locations. These included using a map presented flat in front of her, to one side or the other, or in front but tilted up at an angle of 60 degrees. In all conditions, her performance was clearly much better than chance.

In summary, the results of Landau and her colleagues (1981, 1984, 1986) are impressive in what they suggest about the spatial conceptual abilities of a blind preschooler. It is of course inappropriate to make inferences about a population based on the results of one individual, and indeed many more cases must be examined before the nature of the population distribution can be inferred. Given the difficulties that older children have in learning novel spatial layouts (see following studies), it is tempting to suppose that Kelli will prove to be an exceptional case, perhaps representing the limits on the positive end of the distribution. If so, this might well be a result of effective experiential structuring on the part of her parents. Whether Kelli proves to be representative or an unusually positive example, her demonstrated capabilities provide optimism in this area. Clearly research on spatial concepts in the preschool period deserves much more extensive attention.

There are several excellent studies of spatial learning in school-age children. A example is the comprehensive study of Fletcher (1980; 1981a,b). The children ranged in age from 7 to 18 years and had lost vision by the age of 3. The procedure involved the exploration of a full-size room that contained items of furniture, or a scale model of the same room. Each wall in the room had a distinguishing feature such as a door, and during exposure the child's attention was drawn to this feature in relation to the items of furniture that were placed near that wall. Two kinds of exposure were used. In the *guided exploration* condition the experimenter led the child around the room counterclockwise. In the *free exploration* condition the child explored in the room in any fashion that he or she desired.

After exploring the room, the child was asked questions of two types. *Route questions* asked for relationships among items, based on the child's actual sequence of exploration, whereas *map questions* required the child to synthesize the relationships among the several items (such as asking for the location of an item that was across the room from another item).

Route questions were answered more successfully than map questions. Since route questions asked for information in the sequence in which it was experienced, a strategy of remembering the items in relation to the child's own actions was sufficient. However, the map questions could be answered only if the relationships among the items were known. That performance was worse on these questions suggests that the children did not place the items into an external framework. This finding is analogous to the conclusion from near-space tasks, in that children tend to view objects in a spatial array in reference to their own bodies rather than to one another in an allocentric spatial framework.

No overall difference in performance was found as a result of guided versus free exploration. In the free exploration condition, there was some indication that systematic exploration led to better performance than irregular exploration, but the relationship was not strong.

There was considerable variation among the children (Fletcher, 1981b). On the positive side, some children answered all 16 questions correctly, but on the other hand, 12 of the 34 children did not answer even half of the map questions correctly, and 8 of the 34 failed to answer half of the route questions. For the map questions, teacher-rated intelligence was a significant positive predictor, as was the history of some functional vision during the first three years. ROP children generally performed worse than those of other etiologies. Together, these three factors accounted for 70% of the variance in performance. For the route questions, only early visual history was a significant factor; those who had some functional vision during the first three years performed better than those who did not.

Fletcher's study clearly shows that children with visual impairments can have a great deal of difficulty learning about novel spatial environments. Indeed, there is much similarity to the results for near-space tasks, reviewed earlier, particularly in the tendency to encode spatial information in relation to the child's own location and movements rather than to an external structure. At the same time that many children showed difficulties, however, some performed very well.

The spatial array used by Fletcher was artificial and relatively small. Do children experience the same difficulties when learning about a larger and less artificial array? Dodds, Howarth, and Carter (1982) used an outdoor environment considerably larger than the arrays used by Fletcher, but the procedure was similar to Fletcher's in that children were exposed to the environment by walking through it and then indicated their knowledge of the layout in various ways.

Four congenitally blind and four later blind 11.5-year-olds were tested, all of whom had at least one year of formal mobility training and could travel independently with the long cane. As if playing a game, each child was started from a "home" location and was taken along the route to his or her "friend's house," with instructions to learn the route so that he could later guide the experimenter on it. Turns were pointed out verbally to the child as they were made. After the initial traverse of the route, which was about four city blocks in length, the child drew a map of the route using a raised-line kit. After each of four successive trials, a new map was drawn, and at each turning point on the route the child was required to point to the home and the goal. Thus, although the child traversed a specific route in the environment, knowledge was requested about the relative locations of points (that is, layout information of the kind that Fletcher tapped by "map" questions).

There was a dramatic difference between the congenitally blind and later blind children, with the latter showing smaller average errors of pointing to the home and the goal at each response location on the route. Both groups made larger errors when the target was farther away from them, and this tendency was stronger for the congenitally blind than the adventitiously blind children.

Later, the child was told that he or she would learn a new route to the friend's house. An alternate route to the same goal was then traversed for four trials, after which the child was again taken on the alternate route and was asked to point to locations on the morning's route. This constituted a more demanding task of spatial inference, since information from the two routes had to be synthesized. Again, the later blind subjects were more accurate in performance.

Each child's overall response pattern was analyzed as falling into either self-referent (egocentric) or externally referent (allocentric) categories. The responses of all of the later blind children, but only one of the congenitally blind, were externally referenced. The response patterns of the other congenitally blind children fell in the self-referent categories.

The study by Dodds et al. provides some of the clearest evidence to date of the advantages of early visual experience in spatial representation and spatial behavior. Although the children who were blind from birth could learn routes involving several turns in a novel environment, they generally showed little evidence of acquiring a representation of the layout of that environment. By contrast, the children with a history of early vision acquired reasonable knowledge of spatial layout, in addition to route knowledge.

Herman, Chatman, and Roth (1983) conducted a very similar study with subjects ranging in age from 12 to 24 years. In all significant respects the outcomes were the same, including substantially better performance by subjects with a history of early vision. Two subjects with partial vision were also tested, and they also performed relatively well. Tanaka, Sato, and Matsui (1987) also found partially sighted children to perform better in a similar task.

Summary. Performance on tasks involving concepts of extended space varies a great deal, and much of this variation can be attributed to the variables that we have been considering throughout this section. There is clear evidence that a period of early vision and residual visual function both facilitate performance, and intelligence is also apparently a factor. The most serious gap in our knowledge in this area is the *process* of acquisition of concepts of extended space, particularly as concepts are acquired as a result of everyday experience. We know a good deal about the nature of concepts once they are acquired, but very little about the process of acquisition.

Formal intervention

Formal intervention programs offer a way of structuring experience with spatial relationships. In this section, two kinds of intervention are considered: traditional training techniques and electronic sensory aids.

Traditional spatial training. In training programs, it is difficult to separate spatial concepts from spatial behaviors. That is, we must generally study children's overt behaviors in order to make inferences about their underlying spatial concepts, and if their behaviors are inadequate, it is often difficult to say whether this is because of inadequate concepts or inadequate behavioral control. Of course, the simpler the behaviors are, the more we can be confident that performance is not getting in the way of the concepts.

Hill (1970, 1971) assessed the effectiveness of a training approach for spatial concepts. Children with visual impairments since birth, aged seven to nine and varying in intelligence and degree of residual vision, were divided into a control and a training group. The training group received training sessions several times a week for three months. The training included segments on verbalization, identification, manipulation, and recognition of changing relationships.

All children were pre- and post-tested on the Hill (1971) test of the use of positional terminology, which requires response to verbally presented items in three categories: relationship of body parts, relationship of body to external objects, and relationships among external objects. The training group improved significantly from pre- to post-test, while the non-trained group did not show significant gains. Hill discussed several variables, aside from the training itself, that may have contributed to improved performance. Nonetheless, the conclusion seems justified that the training program produced improvement in the use of spatial concepts. Hill and Hill (1980) refined a version of the test, now called the Hill Performance Test of Selected Positional Concepts (Hill, 1981). Test norms were developed on a large sample that included children varying on several important characteristics. Both boys and girls ranged in age from 6 to 11 years, were with or without additional handicaps, and were from residential or public school settings. There were no significant performance differences related to school setting. As expected, children with additional handicaps did not score as well as those who had just a visual impairment; additionally, the variability in the multihandicapped group was much greater. Curiously, the relationship of test scores to CA was not strong; the data were not given separately for the group with just a visual impairment, and it may be that the inclusion of the group with additional handicaps, with its greater variability, masked age trends that would otherwise have emerged.

Hill, Guth, and Hill (1985) further analyzed the Hill and Hill (1980) data with special attention to the role of partial vision. Of the original sample, nearly half were classified as "low vision," with a variety of reduced acuity and visual field deficits. No difference was found between the overall test score or the subtest scores of this group and those of the remaining children, who had at most LP.

A methodological point may be interjected here, with this study as an example. The children in the overall sample varied along several dimensions that might be expected to influence their spatial concept performance, including presence or absence of additional handicaps, CA, amount of visual function, gender, and intelligence. When the overall sample is divided into subgroups on any of these variables (e.g., visual function in Hill et al., 1985), the group is indeed divided on the basis of that variable, but each resulting subgroup contains a great deal of variability that is caused by other factors (e.g., CA, intelligence, or additional handicaps). The result is that it is very unlikely for any effect of the target variable to emerge as statistically significant because of the large within-subgroup variability that is generated by other variables. Multivariate analysis, in which the relationships of each of a number of variables to the dependent variable can be simultaneously examined, is an appropriate procedure in such a case if there are sufficient numbers of subjects to satisfy the assumptions of the statistical procedures.

A different approach to training spatial concepts and awareness was taken by Chin (1988), who evaluated the effects of instruction in dance movement on the acquisition of spatial concepts. The Hill (1981) test was used as a pre- and post-test measure. The children were of normal intelligence, ranged in age from 6 to 10 years, and varied widely in visual function. All were visually impaired since birth. Two groups were formed, one of which received a 20-hour program of dance training spread over a 10-week period. This group showed a significantly greater improvement from pre- to post-test than the untrained control group. Earlier, Duehl (1979) had demonstrated a positive effect of dance training on movement and body control. The work by Chin (1988), by examining the quality of spatial concepts on which movement and body control are partly based, suggests that both concepts and body movement itself are amenable to intervention.

Many reports of training programs appear in the literature, and various claims are made for their effectiveness. In the vast majority of cases, though, little basis for these claims is offered. The studies cited above are valuable, though unfortunately unusual, in providing objective evaluation of progress based on pre- and post-test measures. Because of the evidence of difficulties that children with visual impairments show in acquiring allocentric spatial concepts, training is an important issue that has to be taken seriously and evaluated with careful research procedures.

Electronic sensory aids. Although the concern with electronic sensory aids during the 1970s and 1980s was primarily related to mobility in the physical environment, some attention was given to the possibility that such aids might be of benefit in training spatial concepts. In fact, much of the research relevant to spatial concepts is also concerned with mobility, and indeed it is often impossible to separate the two issues.

The Optacon (Linvill & Bliss, 1971) is an electronic device that scans printed material and transduces the pattern of light–dark contrast to a pattern of vibrotactile stimulation that can be sensed by the fingertip. Miletic, Hughes, and Bach-y-Rita (1988) modified an Optacon device to allow detection of the spatial environment, rather than the printed page, and they conducted a program of training with children from 8 to 14 years old, who were for the most part congenitally blind. The training program consisted of a series of lessons ranging from the logistics of scanning with the device to recognition of patterns, movement, and three-dimensional space.

Individual children took from 15 to 25 hours to complete the self-paced program, with older children generally requiring less time than younger. Tasks varied in difficulty, three-dimensional tasks generally being the most demanding. The children improved considerably in their ability to deal with external spatial relations, including the ability to understand the visual concept of interposition. There is much work yet to be done with this sort of device, but the preliminary indications are positive for facilitating the understanding of spatial concepts. Given the differences that have been found among individuals in other training work with electronic sensory aids, attention should be devoted to exploration of individual differences in such work.

We discussed the Sonicguide in Chapter 2 in other contexts. The Trisensor is a refined version of the Sonicguide that has a central channel added to facilitate the discrimination of spatial detail (Kay & Kay, 1983).

It has been used in several programs of spatial training with school-age children.

Strelow and Warren (1985) assumed that pretraining on selected components of spatial perception in near space, such as object discrimination, would facilitate the acquisition of spatial concepts and thus the child's subsequent learning to use the Trisensor in mobility performance. They proceeded in a relatively clinical manner from tabletop exercises for the seated child to mobility exercises in the larger environment, using the Trisensor for training sessions. The near-space pretraining showed mixed success, and transfer to far space was unimpressive: other training activities may give better results (e.g., see Hornby et al., 1985, discussed in the next paragraph). Trisensor-mediated performance of far-space tasks was better when training was directly on components of those tasks, rather than on near-space components. Thus, Strelow and Warren did not produce evidence of generalizable spatial concept training.

Hornby, Kay, Satherley, and Kay (1985) took a more intensive and systematic approach to a similar issue. Although their primary concern was to evaluate the effectiveness of the Trisensor in perceiving spatial relationships, generalization to locomotor and nondevice tasks was evaluated as well. The exercises were designed for tabletop administration and emphasized object discrimination as well as direction and distance information. Subsequent activities included distance and direction discrimination in larger space, and finally walking among obstacles. There was some evidence of transfer of distance experience from the near- to the far-space setting, and the children's ability to negotiate moderately cluttered environments using the Trisensor was evident.

What effect, though, does such experience have on spatial concepts and behavior when the device is no longer worn? Improvements in spatial behavior may be specific to the device, or it may be that improvements in device-assisted spatial behavior carry over to nonassisted behavior. Hornby et al. (1985) used a pre-test of spatial orientation involving a series of spatial-orientation and travel tasks; the same test was then given as a post-test within a month of completion of the program. The clear improvements on this test, for which the device was not worn, show generalization of device-assisted acquisition to nondevice behaviors. Thus, the results of Hornby et al. (1985) are promising about the potential of sensory devices to aid in the spatial conceptual development of blind children, including those blind from birth.

One problem with the Hornby et al. (1985) study is that all children received the same intervention, and therefore it is impossible to know whether the demonstrated improvements might also have occurred with another kind of intervention. That is, were the effects specific to the Trisensor intervention?

Easton (1985) resolved this problem in a similar study: a Trisensor-trained group was compared with another group that received an alternative form of training. All children were congenitally blind, of varying etiology, and all were pre-tested on a series of perceptual-motor tests and the Hill Performance Test of Selected Positional Concepts (Hill, 1981). The two subgroups then received a six-week series of training sessions designed to facilitate such skills as spatial discrimination, pattern recognition, and mental rotation. The groups differed only in that one perceived the spatial stimuli with the Trisensor, whereas the other did not use the Trisensor but received haptic–proprioceptive information. After six weeks, the children were again given the original battery of tests, and then the Trisensor subgroup continued with haptic–proprioceptive training and the haptic–proprioceptive group switched to Trisensor training for a second six-week period, followed again by the test battery.

The Trisensor group began at a lower level of performance but caught up to the haptic–proprioceptive group midway through the first six-week period. When the groups switched training procedures, the group now receiving the Trisensor training initially became worse, but after several weeks this group reached the same level as the haptic–proprioceptive training group. With regard to the pre- and post-tests, as a total group the children improved on some tasks, but notably not on the test of mental rotation despite specific attempts to train this capability. (As we have seen earlier, this is typically one of the most challenging tests of spatial concepts for children with visual impairments.) Localization of auditory targets improved as a result of Trisensor training, whereas localization of haptic targets improved as a result of haptic–proprioceptive training. Thus both training modes produced modality-specific improvements; neither produced an improvement that generalized across modalities.

Both groups improved in their performance on the Hill Test. However, the improvement was significantly greater in the group that was initially trained with the Trisensor, and this group maintained its gains through the second phase of haptic training.

Easton's work clearly shows that school-age blind children can learn to use the Trisensor to mediate near-space spatial tasks to a level of performance equivalent to their performance using haptic-proprioceptive cues. However, the results were disappointing in two respects. First, Trisensor training apparently did not produce a generalized improvement in spatial concepts, but rather an effect specific to Trisensor use. (Generalization might, of course, emerge with more extended training.) Second, the level of performance resulting from Trisensor training was not better than that resulting from haptic-proprioceptive training. To be sure, Easton noted that the Trisensor does extend the field of perceptual availability beyond the reach of the hands, and that this may be a considerable potential benefit.

In Chapter 2 we considered the evidence about the possible beneficial effects of electronic sensory aids in facilitating the development of reaching and locomotion in infants, and our general conclusion was that there is not cause for great optimism that these devices can serve the broad role that vision would otherwise perform. In the case of spatial concept training, the evidence is similarly guarded. On the positive side, there is no question that children with visual impairments can, with extensive practice, come to interpret the signals of devices such as the Trisensor – that is, to *perceive* with it. However, this does not mean that such devices facilitate the acquisition and solidification of spatial *concepts*. The weight of the limited evidence is that the effect of training is specific rather than general, and that the acquisition of general spatial concepts is not facilitated.

Individual differences in spatial concepts and spatial behavior

Many of the studies reviewed in this chapter have sought not to explore individual differences within the population of children with visual impairments, but to characterize the typical performance of that population (and often to compare it with a comparable sighted population). Thus, the subject selection strategy in many studies has been to limit the sample to children who lost vision at birth or very early in life, and/or to children who have at most LP. Relatively few studies have compared children with early and later visual loss or evaluated the effects of partial vision. Among other potentially relevant factors of subject selection, CA has often been systematically varied, IQ has usually been constrained to a normal range (e.g., 85 and above), and gender has often been balanced but rarely analyzed. Etiology of impairment has occasionally been noted as part of the description of the sample. The purpose of this section is to summarize the information that is available about these individual differences variables.

Etiology. Of all the studies reviewed in this chapter, only Fletcher (1981b) reported variation in performance related to etiology: ROP-caused blindness was associated with poor performance. (On the other hand, the single child studied by Landau and her colleagues had lost vision due to ROP and performed very well.)

Chronological age. Variation with age has been noted wherever it has been reported, and a brief summary will suffice. Not surprisingly, as a general matter, studies that have tested children over a substantial range of ages tend to find age-related improvements in abilities and performance, whereas studies that limit the sample to a narrow age range typically do not.

We should not expect all forms of behavior that depend on spatial concepts to show the same age-related changes, since different behaviors require more sophisticated spatial concepts or cognitive operations than others. For example, one task used by Ittyerah and Samarapungavan (1989) involved the relatively simple matching of spatial orientation, and there was significant improvement over the 4- to 11-year age range. Their second task required the mental rotation of a more complex relational stimulus; on this task there was little age-related improvement and even the 11-year-olds performed very poorly. It is possible that an upward extension of the age range would have revealed age-related improvement on this task as well.

A word of caution should be made about interpreting age trends (or the lack thereof). Consider Millar's (1981b) rotation task, which was designed to identify the use of self-referential strategies in rotating a stimulus display. Based on results from sighted children (e.g., Laurendeau & Pinard, 1970), we would expect a decrease with age in self-referential strategies. Even over the 6- to 14-year range, Millar found no reduction in this tendency. Millar cautioned that the failure to find strategy shifts with age does not necessarily mean that older children (or younger, for that matter) are incapable of using these strategies. They may indeed be capable of the strategies but do not use them because of their experience-based preference for other strategies.

Intelligence. Although many of the studies reviewed here are careful to report the IQ characteristics of their subjects, relatively few record whether performance varies with IQ. Positive relationships of IQ to performance have been reported by Knotts and Miles (1929) for maze learning tasks, by McReynolds and Worchel (1954) for pointing to geographic directions, and by Fletcher (1981b) for learning a novel environment. On the other side, Drever (1955) found no relationship between IQ and performance on a mental rotation task.

In dealing with a relatively small and heterogeneous population, researchers rarely can, even if they want to, work with a narrowly constrained IQ range. If the sample is limited to a narrow range of IQ, correlations with performance are unlikely to emerge because the statistic depends on variation in both correlated variables.

As I have stated elsewhere, I regard IQ as a derivative measure that has little inherent theoretical value. However, it is widely used, and if it is used as a means of sample selection, the results should certainly be reported, whether they are positive or negative.

Gender. Gender is a source of variation within the population. Indeed, gender differences have not infrequently been found in research on spatial concepts and spatial behavior with sighted adults and children. In view of this, it is surprising that little attention has been paid to possible gender differences in studies of children with visual impairments. In fact, of all the studies reviewed in this chapter, gender analyses have been reported in only four studies, and of these, only the study by McReynolds and Worchel (1954) reported even a hint of difference: in that study, boys performed marginally better on all six measures.

This is not to say that researchers have been wholly inattentive to gender. In fact, many of the studies have been conducted with comparison of visually impaired and sighted samples as the primary goal, and in most of those, care has been taken to match sighted and visually impaired subjects on the basis of gender (as well as other factors such as CA and IQ). Clearly gender is seen as a potential source of variation:

given this, it is remarkable that gender analyses have typically not been done within the samples with visual impairments. This is, if not a primary goal, certainly a secondary one for future research: analyses should be done, and they should be reported even if they yield negative results.

Early visual experience. Perhaps the most interesting area of individual differences is early visual experience. The issue is theoretically provocative, since it is not clear on the face of it why, for example, two nine-year-olds, one of them blind since birth and the other having had vision until age three, should differ in their spatial conceptual abilities. The literature indeed does tend to show an advantage of early visual experience in many types of spatial behavior, and we will return to the possible reasons for this after a brief summary of the results.

The advantages of early visual experience have been found in many task paradigms. On near-space tasks, Millar (1979) found better performance by later blind children: she attributed this to their ability to use the spatial reference cues (e.g., a border or a reference line) that were available. On the other hand, Birns (1986) found no differences as a function of visual experience on a similar task. Working with finger mazes, Knotts and Miles (1929) found that subjects who had sight until age five years or later performed better than those who lost sight earlier. Berg and Worchel (1956) found similar effects with maze tasks, even though their criterion for early blindness, at a cutoff of one year, was more conservative than that of Knotts and Miles. Millar (1976) found no performance differences on a simpler task between children who lost their vision early or later, but the introduction of a mental rotation component into the task produced a significant performance difference in favor of the group with early vision. Drever (1955) found similar differences in a mental rotation task.

Moving to performance in extended space, Fletcher (1981b) found that children who had lost vision within the first three years were less able to answer either route or layout questions about a spatial environment than those who lost vision after age three. Similarly, Dodds et al. (1982) and Herman et al. (1983) found generally better performance in spatial tasks in children who had lost vision later.

Thus age at visual loss is perhaps the most robust individual differences variable in the literature. The effect is found in a wide variety of tasks. A useful review of the early literature was provided by Warren,

Anooshian, and Bollinger (1973), who reported that task complexity is a factor, with the advantages of early vision increasing as the complexity of the spatial task increases. An excellent and more recent review, using formal meta-analytic procedures, is provided by McLinden (1988).

Methodologically, different researchers have handled the variable in very different ways. Often the approach is to divide the sample at some age, and to compare "early" with "later" blind subgroups. The dividing line may be as early as a year (e.g., Berg & Worchel, 1956) or as late as four years (e.g., Knotts & Miles, 1929). The choice of a dividing line is often arbitrary, and the rationale for division is rarely offered. The appropriate approach is not to dichotomize the variable, but to treat early vision as a continuous variable and to examine correlations between the age of visual loss and performance.

Nor is there agreement about why early vision confers a lasting beneficial effect on spatial concepts and spatial behavior. Warren (1974) suggested a "visual organization" hypothesis. He reasoned that the periods when the child is organizing near space (the middle of the first year, when the hand normally comes under visual control) and extended space (the period of crawling into walking) may be particularly important. If the child can see during these periods, the spatial information that is received not only from vision, but from hearing, touch, and motor activity as well, may be organized in reference to a stable visual framework. Even if vision is later lost, the organizational benefits of early visual experience remain.

Jones (1975) offered an alternative hypothesis, that it is motor activity, not vision, that accounts for the differences between early- and later-blind children. The typical disadvantage of the child who is blind from birth is a result of his or her curtailed motor activity as an infant and young child. The lower level of motor activity is, of course, at least indirectly a result of the lack of vision, but Jones argued that the direct cause of poor spatial behavior is lack of motor activity, not lack of vision.

Millar (1982) provided an insightful view of this issue: vision "promotes attention to external cues, and it provides information about directional relations between external cues" (p. 116). The availability of vision tends to induce children to adopt information-processing strategies that lead them to attend to external spatial relationships, and even a small amount of visual function can serve this purpose. It follows that any nonvisual stimulus that serves effectively to draw the child's attention to external spatial relationships should serve the same purpose. Thus Millar suggested that it is not vision, but the attentional and information-processing strategies that normally accompany vision, that produce the differences so prevalent in the literature.

Residual visual function. Relatively few of these studies have examined the effects of the amount of visual function: more often, samples have been limited to children with LP or less. The exceptions, however, are very interesting.

Generally, children with partial vision show a performance advantage. For example, Casey (1978) found superior performance in modeling the familiar school environment by children with partial vision, and Herman et al. (1983) found better learning of spatial layout based on route experience in two individuals with partial vision than in the remaining blind sample. On the other hand, Knotts and Miles (1929) found that the maze-learning performance of a group with partial vision was not different on the average from that of a blind group.

It is not surprising to find that certain spatial behaviors are performed better by children with some useful vision, since the acuity required to detect or even identify large features of the environment is not great. However, it is less clear why partial vision should aid in the formulation of spatial *concepts*. In fact, Hill et al. (1985) analyzed data from a previous study (Hill & Hill, 1980), comparing the spatial concepts of low vision and blind children ranging in age from 6 to 11 years, using the Hill Test of Positional Concepts. The scores of the blind group were comparable to those of the low vision group. This finding suggests that the differences found in other work may be a result of disparities in motor or locomotor skills rather than in the quality of spatial concepts.

The question remains about concepts of extended space. Is there, for example, a relationship between the amount of useful vision and the magnitude of the spatial environment that can be adequately conceptualized, such that more visual function is required to formulate adequate concepts of "far" than "near" space? It seems logical to expect so, but in the absence of solid empirical evidence, no firm statements can be made. These are empirical questions with interesting theoretical as well as practical implications, and research attention in this area should be very fruitful.

Perspective. While early visual loss and severe visual loss are highly predictive of poor performance on a variety of spatial tasks, there are several interesting counterinstances that contain an important lesson. Four examples should suffice to make the point. First, Casey (1978) found generally better performance in modeling a spatial layout by partially sighted than by blind adolescents, but several blind children with high independent travel ratings did very well on the task. Second, Hermelin and O'Connor (1971b) found that given the choice, most of their congenitally blind children associated words with their fingers rather than with the external locations that their fingers occupied, thus showing the typical "egocentric" organization of space. However, several children did associate the words with external spatial locations; they had apparently overcome the restrictions of egocentric space. Third, Dodds et al. (1982) found one congenitally blind child who, like the later blind children and unlike the other congenitally blind children, used an externally referenced spatial organization. Fourth, Kelli, the young ROP-blind girl studied by Landau et al. (1981, 1984, 1986), showed a set of remarkably well-developed abilities to perform in a room-sized spatial environment.

All of these examples of individual cases run counter to the general rule. What do they tell us? They prove that early and complete visual loss does not unalterably dictate that spatial concepts and behaviors must be poor. In Millar's (1982) terms, these children have escaped the limitations of the attentional and information-processing strategies that normally accompany blindness from birth and have adopted strategies conducive to the development of external spatial relationships.

What permits these exceptional children to do better? The existing literature is not sufficiently detailed to reveal the answer. Nevertheless, surely the difference must lie in large part in the early experiences of these children. The prospect of finding effective ways of intervening with blind infants and structuring their experiences so that they acquire good spatial concepts should surely motivate researchers to discover the characteristics of effective early experience; and they can accomplish this only by attending to individual differences.

Part II

The acquisition of cognitive skills

Our immediate contact with the physical and social environment comes through the senses. However, we are not restricted to the information available at any one moment. We remember events in prior experience, we learn about situations by experiencing them, we can reason about possible situations, and so on. Humans rely on cognitive skills to deal with the world conceptually. In order to be guided by prior experience, we have to have the ability to learn, to accumulate the implications of that experience, and to bring it to bear on our immediate situation. The cognitive skills involved may be organized in various ways, but we will use the following division.

Language, concept formation, and classification. These cognitive skills are closely related to one another, and any division is somewhat arbitrary. Besides being a means of social communication, language is a cognitive skill. It can serve to guide us through a complex set of operations and help to keep them straight (for example, most people covertly talk to themselves while doing long division). Language can serve to arrange concepts in relation to one another, and to mediate reasoning. This is not to say that all reasoning is done using language as a mediator, but that language is often a part of the reasoning process and should be considered as part of the child's armament of cognitive skills.

Concepts are the stuff of thought. At one level, "concept" implies that the limitations of perception have been escaped. If the child has a concept of an object, then he or she need not have that object physically present in order to think about it. Abstract concepts do not refer to perceivable items or events: the concept of "truth" is an example. Qualities such as "red" or "heavy" are also conceptualized.

Classification is a subset of concept formation that is typically studied using tasks that present a variety of stimuli and ask children to classify them – to put together those that belong together. Such tasks reveal children's "decision rules," that is, their bases for organizing experiences.

Executive functions: memory, attention, and cognitive strategies. In recent decades emphasis has been placed increasingly on the so-called executive functions, such as memory, attention, and cognitive strategies. Any division among these topics is also no more than an organizational convenience, since the interactions are complex and it is almost impossible to isolate one function from the others.

Obviously experience cannot be accumulated without some system of storage, and that is what we call memory. Memory is not adult-like in the human infant, but rather develops over the course of months and years. Thus the limitations of memory place at least a theoretical limit on the quality of conceptual thought at any developmental level.

Young infants seem to have little choice about what they attend to. Their attention is "captured" by physical features such as loud sounds, bright lights, and figural properties of form. Gradually, attention comes to be largely under internal control, rather than dictated by the physical stimulation, and the child can voluntarily shift eye position on a stimulus array, selectively attend to competing auditory signals, and so on. Attention, particularly as it becomes internally directed, is an important cognitive skill.

Many of the components of attention can also be conceptualized as cognitive strategies of acquiring and processing information. On the acquisition side, what is learned is dictated to a great extent by what is attended. In processing, the manner in which information is encoded has a great influence on its subsequent utility.

The creation of images can be thought of as a strategy of information processing, but the issue of imagery is broader and warrants a separate section.

Cognitive style, creativity, and intelligence. These three topics represent areas of cognitive functioning in which dramatic differences among individuals within populations occur.

Cognitive style refers to the degree of analytic orientation that an individual brings to a cognitive task. Creativity is one of the most elusive psychological concepts to define or measure, in large part because of the variety of ways in which the term is used. As a basic form of cognitive adaptation, intelligence has been largely subsumed in the preceding sections. In this summary section we will review briefly the more important aspects of the intelligence testing literature.

5

Language, concept formation, and classification

Language

In the literature on child development, language development is usually treated as a single body of evidence. We will consider language development in two parts. On the one hand, language serves as one of several avenues of communication with other people. We will treat this topic in Chapter 10 on social interaction. Language also develops as a skill that facilitates the child's developing conceptual abilities. This aspect of language is at issue here.

Vocabulary: the first words

As difficult as it is to identify the infant's first words, various reports in the literature purport to fix the earliest use of words. These reports present a mixed picture of the emergence of early words. Some studies show first-word use among blind infants to be like that of the general population, but other studies show evidence of lags.

Evidence of timely word-use onset comes from studies of both groups and individuals. Maxfield and Fjeld (1942), using the Vineland Social Maturity Scale, found that on the item "uses names of familiar objects," their heterogeneous group of children with visual impairments scored marginally better than sighted norms. More recently, Ferrell et al. (1990) included "first word" as a milestone item in the VIIRC study (see Table 2). The median age for this item was 10 months, with fully half of the children falling into a five-month period encompassing the median. Also in the mainstream, and citing individual cases rather than group data, Andersen, Dunlea, and Kekelis (1984) reported first words appearing at

11 and 15 months, Mills (1983) at 12, 13, and 16 months, and Bigelow (1990) at 14 months. Equally on the positive side, Haspiel (1965) noted that even in a group of emotionally disturbed blind children, a few words are usually produced by 18 months or so, a figure comparable to that for sighted children; and in their study of a single blind child, Wilson and Halverson (1947) found the first few words to be achieved at just the normative ages for sighted children, despite lags in other areas of development.

Not all of the evidence is so positive. Landau (1983) reported first-word use in two infants at 23 and 26 months of age, considerably later than any norms for sighted children. Correspondingly, Landau and Gleitman (1985) noted delays in two-morpheme combinations. Burlingham (1961) cited reports by mothers of congenitally blind children that during the 16- to 18-month period, when sighted children are typically showing a spurt of vocabulary growth, the blind children were slower in adding words to their vocabulary, and often showed regression from points once reached. Burlingham suggested that this slowness may be due to the mother's perception of the child's "helplessness," which may cause her to anticipate his or her needs more than she would for a "nonhelpless" child; consequently, fewer demands are placed on the blind child for language use. Burlingham noted, though, that while the early stages of vocabulary acquisition proceed somewhat more slowly in blind children, there is typically a spurt following the toddler stage, such that by the time the children are of nursery school age they approximate sighted children in vocabulary and fluency.

Norris et al. (1957) reported several items from the Cattell Scale that also tend to indicate delays in early language. At least half of their intensive sample showed the first word at 15 months (Cattell norm 11 months), two words at 18 months (norm 12 months), and five words at 24 months (norm 16 months). These items show an apparent lag compared to standardized CA norms, although if a three-month correction for prematurity is applied to the Norris et al. results because a high proportion of their sample was of ROP etiology, the differences diminish.

In addition, Norris et al. made two very important points. First, on each item there was a considerable range of individual differences, with some children achieving the item well before the normative age and others later. Second, most cases of retarded speech were associated with the parents' unrealistic expectations for the child: "In no case did problems in the area of speech appear to be a direct result of blindness. They seemed, rather, to be related to problems of disturbed relationships and to unrealistic expectations of performance" (p. 36).

Thus, in general, wherever reports of slower acquisition of vocabulary have occurred, they have been accompanied by commentary that addresses the experiential or other circumstances of the child's situation: any delay noted is not generally attributed to the lack of vision itself. For example, Norris et al. (1957) spoke of the blind infant's curtailed experiences, Keeler (1958) discussed lags in the context of a larger pattern of "autistic-like" symptoms, and Burlingham (1961, 1965) discussed slow vocabulary growth in the context of the sometimes inappropriate linguistic context provided by the parents. These early reports thus presage the later development of methodologies that directly evaluate the infant's language acquisition explicitly within the social-interactive context.

Vocabulary: early word sets

Another approach to early vocabulary involves looking at the timing and content of initial vocabularies, such as the first 50 words. This approach avoids the tricky issue of identifying the first word or two, which are often perceptible only to the eager parent and which in any case are hard to distinguish from imitation of sounds without meaning. Looking at the first 50 words, not only can we be more confident of analyzing words that carry meaning for the child but we can, in addition, evaluate how this early vocabulary set is distributed into various word types and therefore what it shows about the development of lexical meaning.

Nelson (1973) established the framework for this type of analysis in her study of the early vocabulary of sighted children. Words in the 50-word vocabulary were classified as belonging to the following categories: specific nominals (names of people, toys, or pets), general nominals (names of classes of objects, e.g., "dog"), action words (showing a manner or direction of action, e.g., "up"), modifiers (qualities of objects, e.g., "hot"), personal-social words (used in social interaction, e.g., "thank you"), and function words (e.g., "what's this?"). Based on Nelson's data, the distributions of the 50-word vocabulary into these categories is given in Table 5.

Several investigators (e.g., Andersen et al., 1984; Bigelow, 1987; Landau, 1983) have analyzed the 50-word vocabularies of small numbers

Table 5. *Percentages of 50-word vocabulary that fall into the word-type categories of Nelson for sighted and blind infants*

	Nelson (1973) (sighted)	Mulford (1988) (blind)
Specific nominals	14	22
General nominals	52	38
Action words	13	24
Modifiers	11	6
Personal-social	9	13
Function words	5	3

Note: Data are for a composite of infants in several studies, summarized by Mulford (1988). Totals do not sum to 100% due to rounding based on relatively small numbers of subjects ($n = 9$ for blind, 18 for sighted sample).

of blind children with respect to these categories. Mulford (1988) presented an integration and comparison of these data with those of Nelson, and the pattern is shown in Table 5. Mulford noted several difficulties in making classifications of some utterances in the blind children's repertoire, and the resulting distributions must be taken as indicative rather than definitive.

An interesting pattern of differences appears in the three most frequently used categories. Note that for the two distributions, the overall total of nominals is roughly equal, but that blind children produce more specific nominals and fewer general nominals than sighted children.

The category of action words in Table 5 also deserves some comment. Mulford noted that several investigators (e.g., Dunlea, 1984; Urwin, 1978) found that children with visual impairments tend to use action words mainly to describe their own actions. While this is also a characteristic of the sighted child's earliest use of such words, the indications are that the self-referred action persists longer as a characteristic of blind children: they do not refer as frequently to actions that other agents (e.g., parents) perform. This difference should not be surprising: without vision, the blind child is less likely to perceive the actions of other people, unless those actions are directed to him- or herself.

Nelson (1973, 1981) suggested that individual children may be characterized as having a referential or an expressive language style, or something in between, based on their patterns of word frequency. The referential style is characterized by a high proportion of general nominals and can be thought of as having more a cognitive than a social-interactive use. In contrast, the expressive style reflects a more social-interactive functional usage; it is characterized by fewer general and more specific nominals, and by more multiword phrases.

What about children with visual impairments? The pattern of relationship between general and specific nominals that appears in Table 5 suggests that they have a tendency to fall toward the expressive end of the expressive–referential dimension, and indeed several investigators have noted this (e.g., Andersen et al., 1984; Bigelow, 1987; Landau, 1983; Mulford, 1988).

Bigelow (1987) suggested that the more limited experience of children with visual impairments tends to give their language characteristics of the expressive style. In the scoring procedure, if a word is used to refer to only one instance of a category, then it is classified as a specific nominal, whereas if it is used to refer to two or more instances of the category, it is classified as a general nominal. If the experience of blind children has been restricted to a single instance, their language tends to show more specific nominals, and thus may be classified as having an expressive style.

On the other hand, Andersen et al. (1984) suggested that the fundamental problem is not restricted experience on which to base vocabulary learning, but rather limited ability to form concepts to which words are attached as labels. They argued that the infrequency of general language labels reflects a lack of general concepts. Of course, limitations in concept formation may not be a necessary consequence of restricted visual experience, but instead may result from a limitation in the overall experience of the blind infant and young child. As Landau (1983) aptly put it, "Where relevant experience is lacking, concepts cannot develop; and where concepts are lacking, word meanings cannot be learned" (p. 63).

Whether the cause lies in restricted concept-formation ability (Andersen et al., 1984) or in a limited set of referents (Bigelow, 1987), it is clear that the ultimate cause is the restriction of experience. The phenomenon has nothing necessarily to do with visual impairment, except that visual impairment tends to restrict experience in such a way that terms classified as specific nominals often occur in the child's 50-word vocabulary. Presumably, if the experience of sighted children were similarly restricted, they too would tend to fall toward the expressive end of the dimension. The balance of experience may indeed shift the norm for visually impaired children as a group. Nevertheless, it is not only inappropriate to generalize too far; it is also inappropriate to implicate lack of vision as a direct causal factor.

Language and concept formation

Although there is legitimate argument about the primacy of language and thought, there is no doubt that word meaning is an important aspect of concept formation. Consideration of this relationship has taken several directions in the literature, but underlying all of them is the notion that somehow the adequacy of word meaning is critical to the quality of concepts. We will consider first the notion of "verbalism" as it has been discussed in the literature on visual impairment, and then move to broader issues of word meaning.

The verbalism issue

Cutsforth (1932) published a study in which he noted the tendency of blind children to use words for which they could not have had firsthand sensory experience. His discussion of the implications of the use of such words, which he called "verbalisms," sparked a continuing debate about the desirability of such usage in blind children.

Cutsforth's procedure involved telling the child an object name and asking him or her to state a quality of that object. He found that 48% of the responses of congenitally blind children were visual qualities, while adventitiously blind children produced 65% visual responses. In a later discussion of these results, Cutsforth (1951) argued that such verbalisms must lead to "incoherent and loose thinking" on the part of the blind child, since the words (and implicitly the concepts) used by the blind child are farther removed from their sensory referents than those of the sighted child. As a result, some educational programs for children with visual impairments were structured to avoid the use of visually based vocabulary and concepts.

Several writers in the psychoanalytic literature have discussed a very similar language phenomenon, generally characterizing the behavior as "parroting." Burlingham (1961) noted that the blind child's speech is "less firmly connected with his sensory experience" (p. 137). She pointed out that the blind child receives a great deal of praise for imitation of the parent's speech, thus encouraging the use of words from the sighted parent's vocabulary for which the child has less concrete sensory referents. Burlingham (1965) elaborated this argument in noting that the blind child develops a mixture of words, some of which refer (perhaps idiosyncratically) to his or her own sensory experience and some of which are verbalisms that parrot the usage of sighted persons. Nagera and Colonna (1965) noted a similar tendency and echoed Cutsforth's concern that the use of such words may restrict the symbolic or cognitive capacities of the blind child. On a more positive note, they pointed out that "in spite of the absence of the visual contribution to many of these 'word symbols,' alternative compensatory means are finally found so that these symbols become useful elements in the performance of the complex mental processes for which these basic units are required" (p. 280).

The view that repetitive speech (echolalia) serves a functional purpose was articulated by Prizant (1984), who suggested that by imitating and parroting words and phrases heard from others, the child stores these uncomprehended terms without lexical meaning. Later, as the terms are heard more frequently and in other contexts, the child can develop their meaning and add the words and phrases to his or her own lexicon.

Research on verbalism has taken two directions. One issue is whether Cutsforth's estimates of verbalism in children with visual impairments were too high. Based on a replication and extension of Cutsforth's study, Nolan (1960b) concluded that the incidence is much lower. The children, ranging in age from 9 to 20 years, were mostly blind from birth. The frequency of associations that represented "visual" responses was significantly lower than that reported by Cutsforth, and Nolan concluded that any problem associated with verbalism is much less serious than Cutsforth had thought.

The second issue is whether the use of verbalism by children with visual impairments, with whatever frequency, has undesirable consequences, such as the development of "incoherent and loose thinking" as Cutsforth assumed, or perhaps in the role of language in social communication. Harley (1963) evaluated the relation of verbalism to IQ, age, experience, and personal adjustment. The children ranged in age from 7 to 14 and were drawn from residential schools. All had become blind very early, and none had more than LP. The verbalism score was the number of appropriate definitions minus the number of correct identifications. In addition, a visual verbalism score was determined by counting the number of items for which the child used visual terminology in the definition part of the procedure. Experience was scored by counting the number of objects with which the child said that he or she had had direct contact.

There were significant negative correlations between verbalism scores and age, IQ, and experience. Thus younger, lower-IQ, and less-experienced children showed higher incidence of verbalism. Scores on the visual verbalism index did not show significant correlations with any of the other measures. This negative finding should be viewed in the context of the relatively low visual verbalism scores and correspondingly low variability among subjects.

It is clear that Harley offered a quite different view from Cutsforth about the dynamics of verbalism. Cutsforth considered verbalism to be a cause of "incoherent and loose thinking"; in contrast, Harley suggested that "since verbalism may be caused by inaccurate and vague concepts resulting from insufficient sensory experience, verbalism may also vary with intelligence" (p. 12). If there is in fact a relationship between cognitive abilities and verbalism, Harley's perspective is an important one. That is, the lack of sensory experience may be a cause both of verbalism and of cognitive difficulties, rather than being a cause of verbalism, which in turn causes cognitive difficulties. The implication for intervention is that concentration should be on providing appropriate kinds of experience at the right times, rather than on discouraging the use of visual terminology. Summarizing, Harley suggested that "the key to the reduction of verbalism among blind children is the increasing of interaction with their environments" (p. 32).

Tufenkjian's (1971) conclusion was similar: the "relevant question to ask is not the meaningfulness or meaninglessness of words to congenitally blind persons but rather to ask the nature of the meaningfulness of words in specific contexts. . . . The point is not that these subjects' understanding of these concepts are meaningless but that they demonstrate a different mode of experiencing some aspect of their world" (pp. 40–41).

Thus, it is clearly not valid simply to assume that the use of visual words is indicative of "loose thinking" on the part of blind children. Dokecki (1966) provided an insightful review of the arguments and research on the verbalism issue, including the logical argument that many words used by sighted people cannot possibly have sensory referents, and that there is no indication that the concepts these words represent are meaningless or involve loose thinking. Dokecki concluded that "it still remains to be demonstrated that associative and word–thing meanings are functionally different for the blind or for any other group" (p. 528).

It is important to separate the question of the frequency of verbalisms from the issue of meaning and utility. There is ample evidence that verbalisms are not words used without meaning by the blind, and the educational implications seem very clear: the use of visually related vocabulary should not, contrary to the advice of Cutsforth, be discouraged in the blind child. It seems likely, as Dokecki has suggested, that the sheltering of the blind child from language that is visually based "might be producing a detrimental effect, since the scope of language is being curtailed" (p. 527), and its social–interactive utility may be impaired.

Word meaning

The verbalism debate focused on a subset of the question of word meaning. Other research has concentrated on broader aspects of the issue. Simply put, the question is whether visual impairment is somehow associated with differences in word meaning, and whether concepts might differ as a consequence.

One approach to this question is illustrated by the study of Dershowitz (1975), who used the semantic differential test to evaluate the connotative meaning of emotional terms (pride, sadness, or anger). The semantic differential is a test in which a word is presented and the subject selects adjectives that fit it. Analysis of the responses produces clusters of features that characterize various words, thus producing an index of meaning (Osgood, Suci, & Tannenbaum, 1957). The children ranged in age from 9 to 17 years and had lost vision early in life. Their patterns of response to the emotional terms were fully appropriate and in fact were quite similar to the patterns shown by a group of sighted adults. Based on this first indication, then, there is no reason to suspect differences in word meaning associated with visual impairment.

DeMott (1972) also used the semantic differential to evaluate the affective meaning of words that varied in concreteness and visual connotations. The subjects, all from a residential school, ranged from 6 to 20 years of age. They were divided into two groups. The group with at most

LP had all lost vision within the first year of age. The other group had vision ranging from "movement perception" to an acuity of 20/200 (their age of visual loss was unfortunately not reported). The factor structure was nearly identical for the two groups, and DeMott concluded that there is no variation in the affective meaning of these words as a function of degree of visual loss.

Another way to approach the issue of meaning is to evaluate the appropriateness of adjective–noun combinations. Millar (1983) studied children's ability to differentiate between appropriate (e.g., "round ball") and inappropriate ("barking cat") adjective–noun pairs. The children were congenitally blind and ranged in age from 8 to 13 years. The older children performed better than the younger, who showed particular difficulties with adjectives having spatial or visual meanings. The improvement with age is not surprising, since the task reflects accumulating verbal experience and general knowledge. Performance was in general very good, though, and Millar rejected the notion that the word meanings of blind children are inadequate in any significant sense.

Millar's finding that younger children had difficulty with words having spatial or visual meanings raises the obvious possibility that word meaning is tied to perceptual experience, and particularly to visual experience in the case of children with visual impairments. Anderson (1979; and Anderson & Olson, 1981) pursued this issue by assessing the definitions and descriptions of "more tangible" and "less tangible" objects. More tangible items were those that could be encompassed within the hand, whereas less tangible ones were touchable though not graspable (e.g., house or tree). The congenitally blind children ranged in age from three to nine years. Their responses to each item were classified as egocentric, functional, or perceptual. Responses to the more tangible items tended to be egocentric rather than perceptual or functional; this was especially true of the younger children. Sighted children of comparable ages were generally more responsive than the blind children to the less tangible items and made fewer references to tactual qualities. The blind children's functional attributes tended to be somewhat more concrete and less abstract than those of the sighted children, but there was no evidence of difference in the meaning of the objects for the blind and sighted children.

Anderson (1984) introduced a memory task in a similar experiment. In this study, the child was first asked to describe each object, based on memory. Then the child was given the object and asked to identify and describe it. In both tasks, attributes were again classified as egocentric, functional, or perceptual. As expected, in the tactual task the children tended to give more perceptual than egocentric or functional attributes. The pattern was reversed for the memory task, showing that the children were not captured by the immediate tactual features of the objects. Unfortunately there was no mention of any possible variation in this pattern as a function of age.

Based on this work, Anderson and his colleagues argued that the response patterns of blind children demonstrate that their language does not simply reflect the usage of the surrounding language environment. Instead, it appropriately reflects the experience-specific conceptualizations of objects that the children obtain via touch and other nonvisual senses.

Gleitman (1981; and again Landau, 1983, and Landau & Gleitman, 1985) used a more intensive case study approach to a similar issue. They examined the early vocabularies of two ROP children who began using language relatively late, at 23 and 26 months of age. The qualities of their vocabularies acquired over the course of the following several months were compared with Nelson's (1973) reports for sighted children. Both children used all of the categories reported by Nelson, with only minor differences in the distribution of word types.

Concluding that there were no substantial differences between blind and sighted children in the vocabulary patterns, Landau (1983) went on to look for any evidence of "empty meaning" in the words used by the blind children. Do they simply repeat some words heard from others without understanding them? Based on a detailed examination of one child, Landau concluded that there was no such evidence. Her conclusion was based in part on the blind child's interesting use of the verb "look" to refer to the active perceptual activities of the hands, in contrast to the verb "feel" to denote passive hand contact. The term "look" was clearly meaningful and not devoid of content: it meant something specific to the child that could not have been simply borrowed from the language of the child's sighted conversational partners.

The foregoing results demonstrate that the language usage of children with visual impairments is grounded in their perceptual experience rather than in the vocabulary of sight. Their words are not devoid of content or based on an unexperienced set of perceptual referents. Landau

(1983) provided a positive summary: "These data suggest that knowledge of language is not diminished by blindness. Blind children do talk about objects and their locations in space, actions, and events, and do so in just the same way as sighted children at the same linguistic level" (p. 66).

The breadth of meaning. Meaning is usually taken to imply more than just the association of a word with a referent. It implies, in addition, appropriate generalization and a network of semantic relationships to other words. This is a difficult issue to attack, but Andersen and her colleagues have made a promising start. In general, the results suggest that there are, after all, some important aspects of the relationships between words and concepts that may suffer as a result of visual impairment.

Andersen et al. (1984) studied children at roughly the 100-word vocabulary stage. Their basic data, like those of Landau (1983), show similar distributions of word types for blind and sighted children. However, they also found several differences that bear on the larger issue of meaning and its underlying concepts.

First, there were very few idiosyncratic word inventions by the blind children. Generally children invent words, and these inventions are taken as evidence of lexical creativity. Andersen et al. argued that the scarcity of such inventions in the blind child's vocabulary suggests that they are simply mimicking terms that they hear.

Second, Andersen and her colleagues found far fewer extensions of meaning in the vocabulary of their blind children. It is normal for children to overextend referents, as when they use the term *dog* to refer to all four-legged animals before they refine the concept and recognize that dogs are but a subcategory of animals. The finding that children with visual impairments overextend less supports the notion that they may tend to accept limited meanings for words rather than actively operating on them within a larger cognitive framework. Andersen et al. (1984) concluded that "the process which enables young sighted children to abstract criterial features of a referent and to extend the domain of early words is not functioning at the same level for blind children at the onset of language" (p. 656). In other words, they argued that differences in language meaning reflect differences in the richness of the underlying concepts that the words represent. In a sense, this is a very much refined version of the verbalism issue.

Dunlea (1982) extended the question of the concreteness of referents from single words to multiword constructions. Based on the evidence from single words, Dunlea expected that similar limitations would be found in two- and three-word combinations: "The fact that blind children do not discuss the qualities of objects in the early multi-word period parallels the limited process of extension observed in their corpora during the single word period" (p. 26). Dunlea clearly interpreted this language usage as an indicator of cognitive processing: "Both developments are rooted in the ability to recognize and extract salient attributes from encounters with entities and events" (p. 26).

Summary. The issue of word meaning is complex, and the literature contains important contradictions that will need further study for resolution. On the one hand, several studies of the meanings of individual words (DeMott, 1972; Dershowitz, 1975) and word usage (Millar, 1983) show the word meanings of children with visual impairments to be very similar to those of children with vision. The differences that do occur (e.g., Anderson, 1979) appear linked to the child's perceptual experiences, and specifically to the role of visual experience, but there is little evidence from these studies that the underlying concepts that words represent are impaired in any significant way.

On the other hand, the evidence of Andersen and her colleagues suggests more fundamental differences when we look at the interrelationships among words and their underlying concepts: these may be less elaborated for children with visual impairments.

From a methodological standpoint, Andersen's work is the best we have since it provides the closest analysis of the relationship among individual words and their meanings, as well as their relationships to other words and related concepts. However, this work to date is based on very few cases and must be expanded before general conclusions are warranted. The issue will not be significantly advanced by additional studies of the surface characteristics of vocabulary, such as word counts; a close analysis of individual cases is necessary, and it should be undertaken in the context of the functional use of language.

Referential language

Pronouns are an example of referential language: the word "she" is potentially ambiguous and may refer to any of several people depending on the identity of the speaker and who is being spoken to. "She" can correctly refer to the child when spoken by another person, but not when the child refers to herself. Because of the utility of vision in resolving this ambiguity, this is an area in which we might expect children with visual impairments to experience difficulty. Indeed, there is such evidence.

McGuire and Meyers (1971) reported a long-term study of 27 blind children of mixed age and etiology. A substantial subset (46%) of the children were found to refer to themselves in the third person, as "he" or "she" rather than "I." Ferrell et al. (1990, see Table 2) included an item, "uses first-person pronouns appropriately," in their set of developmental milestones. The median age for attainment was 36 months (as opposed to a norm of 24 months for sighted children). The variation within the sample was considerable, and we can estimate that only about a quarter of the sample showed appropriate first-person pronoun use by about 30 months of age. Thus this is clearly an area of language difficulty.

Fraiberg and Adelson (1976) differentiated two uses of the pronoun "I." The syncretic "I" is used with verbs such as "want" or "need" to express straightforward statements, whereas "I" is also used inventively in new combinations. This second use, "which is freed from syncretic forms, requires a high level of inference" (p. 137). The (congenitally) blind children showed appropriate use of the syncretic "I," but use of the inventive "I" did not emerge in their usage as early as it does in sighted children.

According to Fraiberg and Adelson's analysis, the difficulty in the use of personal pronouns is cognitively based: the same word, such as "I" or "he," may be applied to different people, depending on who the speaker is, and a degree of "cognitive relativity" is required to resolve this ambiguity. It is reasonable to expect that vision might be useful in providing the child with an extralinguistic source of referential information. Indeed, Fraiberg and Adelson noted that three children who developed use of the inventive "I" between 2:11 and 3:6 had some light perception, while one totally blind child showed usage at age 4:9 and another had not shown it by age six. Fraiberg and Adelson discussed the delayed use of the inventive "I," as well as other misuse of personal pronouns, in terms of difficulties with self-representation. For example, they observed a delay in the child's ability to represent him- or herself in play, citing Piaget's observation that levels of representation may be inferred from play in that objects may be used as symbolic representations of the self. The same blind children who had difficulty with the use of personal pronouns apparently did not have any trouble with the concept of self as represented by their proper names: this serves as an example of the successful use of specific nominals as opposed to general nominals, as discussed earlier.

Pronouns are one form of referential vocabulary, but there are other kinds as well. An example is spatial terms such as "here" and "there," which take different meanings depending on the location and identity of the speaker. Bernstein (1978) evaluated the use of self-referent and external-referent locatives in congenitally blind children between the ages of two and four years, and compared their pattern with that of sighted children of comparable age. For both blind and sighted children, the self-referent locatives were easier. The usage of the blind children was less advanced for a given age than that of sighted children. Bernstein attributed this result primarily to spatial cognitive difficulties (see Chapter 4), although at the same time allowing that there might be a causal relationship such that the acquisition of an appropriate language label might aid in the development and refinement of an emerging concept.

Mulford (1980) proposed a linguistic uncertainty hypothesis as an alternative to the cognitive hypothesis. Mulford's approach involved the study of five-year-old blind children interacting with an adult in a naturalistic setting. Spatial deictic terms (those that refer to location concepts such as "this," "that," "here," and "there") have in common that their meaning is situational. That is, "here" has a different referent in an absolute sense than it does if the listener can take the relative viewpoint of the speaker. Mulford found the children's use of such situational terms to be immature in relation to other aspects of their language usage.

Summary. It is quite clear that children with visual impairments can experience developmental difficulties in the acquisition of referential vocabulary; the examples are evident both for personal pronouns and for spatial-relational terms. Unfortunately, with the exception of partial vision, there has been very little study of the individual differences in this area. It would be especially rewarding to examine the relationships between referential difficulties and the features of the language environments to which the children are exposed.

Classification and concept formation

Much of human conceptual behavior involves the creation of and interaction among classes of events and information. As development proceeds, children acquire the ability to form conceptual classes, to add new experiences appropriately to them, and to modify them as necessary to accommodate new experiences and information. They come to recognize that while the members of a given conceptual class share some attributes in common, they also differ on other attributes, and that therefore alternative classifications are possible and important. They understand that various concepts may be subordinate or superordinate to one another. In short, the development of mature thought requires adequate ability to deal with classification.

Classification

An excellent general study of the development of classification skills in blind children is that of Higgins (1973), who studied children of average IQ ages 5 to 11. Use of the Modified Kofsky Battery (MKB) allowed the developmental evaluation of aspects of classification such as subordination and multiple inclusion, while additional use of the Verbal Test of Class Inclusion (VCI) allowed the relationship between abstract and concrete concepts to be assessed. Two key conclusions emerged.

First, the development of aspects of classification emerged with age in much the same way that Piaget and others have found for sighted children: the general principle of cognitive growth, that preoperational skills precede the emergence of operational skills, clearly applies to children with visual impairments. Second, although the results from the VCI were much like those from the MKB, the VCI showed a pattern of divergence between concrete and abstract concepts, with the former preceding the latter developmentally, as expected. Higgins concluded that this did not represent a general conceptual problem, but rather "reflected a child's previous activity with the elements about which he had to reason. The likelihood of a correct response was significantly greater if the child had performed perceptual or motor actions in relation to the elements specified in the class inclusion questions" (p. 33). Said another way, experience, not visual status, is the primary factor influencing the course of cognitive development.

Beyond this, what other factors influence the emergence of classification skills? The age at onset of visual loss is a likely candidate. Hatwell (1966, 1985) compared children who had lost vision within the first year to those who had had vision for at least four years. She found a significant advantage of the latter group on tasks that involved finding an odd attribute and using multiple bases for classification.

Partial vision is another candidate. Friedman and Pasnak (1973a) evaluated children from 6 to 14 years of age on verbal and tactual tests of seriation and classification, comparing blind children with those who could read large print. The younger groups with some functional vision generally made fewer errors than the blind children on the tactual tasks, but this difference did not occur on the verbal tasks. The oldest group (14 years) did not differ as a function of either vision or task modality.

The difference in the patterns of tactual and verbal test results for the blind and partially sighted younger children is curious. It is hard to imagine that a concept adequately expressed using one method should suddenly be a less adequate concept using another method, and it is tempting to conclude that this is not a real conceptual difference but rather a matter of differing task demands.

Intelligence is another possible factor that might affect classification abilities. Dimcovic (1992) found a significant correlation between IQ (verbal WISC) and a test of verbal classification, but IQ was not correlated with a traditional test of physical classification based on multiple attributes. Both classification tests were significantly related to several subtests of "vocabulary of relations," tapping spatial, temporal, or physical relationships. No relationship was found between classification and the judged propensity of the family to stimulate the child's cognitive growth.

Summary. In brief summary, these studies show that the acquisition of classification abilities in children with visual impairments generally proceeds along a normal developmental path. Variations are evident as a function of visual experience (both the age of visual loss and partial vision), intelligence, and most important, the child's range of experience with materials related to those used in the test.

In the work discussed up to this point, the youngest children have been five years of age. Gerhardt (1982) reported a classification study of a single infant at the ages of 14, 16, and 18 months. A free-play technique was used in which the experimenter handed the child various sets of objects to play with and observed the manner in which the infant handled and grouped them. Over the four-month span, the infant showed the predicted progress from grouping dissimilar items to making similarity-based classifications. Although research with infants is difficult, full understanding of the development of classification skills in older children will depend on more study of the preschool child, particularly examining classification behavior in relation to the child's accumulating experiences.

Training studies. Training studies have a firm place in the developmental evaluation of cognitive skills, and of classification in particular. An illustration of such studies is the simple, one-session training study reported by Adkins (1965), who compared blind with partially sighted children in the age range of 6 to 16 regarding the effects of a series of classification training tasks. The older children tended to show more training gain, perhaps because of greater readiness for the concepts involved. The children with partial vision showed more regular gain over the graded series of tasks, while the blind children showed less gain from the earlier series involving two stimulus dimensions, but more gain from the later series in which three stimulus dimensions were involved.

Though Adkins's study did show benefits from training, it would be more satisfying to know what happened to the trained abilities over a longer term. Friedman and Pasnak (1973b) illustrated this approach. They evaluated the effects of the training of classification skills in blind children ranging from 6 to 12 years of age, all of whom had lost vision by two years of age. They were divided into two matched groups based on age, IQ, degree of visual loss, and age at onset. One group received a classification training program based on a learning-set approach. Each child's progress was self-paced; the number of 30-minute sessions ranged from 3 to 26 and covered from 2 to 13 weeks. A pre- and post-test design showed significant improvement for the classification training group but not for the control group. Friedman and Pasnak stressed that their study did not attempt to train a cognitive skill prematurely: "Rather, children who were chronologically mature were aided in acquiring a concept that they had failed to master because of a sensory handicap" (p. 337).

In a similar study, Lebron-Rodriguez and Pasnak (1977) used three groups of children. One received seriation and then classification training, another received only seriation training, and a control group received neither. This last group showed negligible gains from pre- to posttest on seriation and classification, whereas the other groups showed significant gains specific to the areas of their training.

Summary. Thus training of classification skills may be successful, although as in the sighted training literature, one may be more confident of training gains in the neighborhood of the child's capabilities than those that seem to pull the child along exceptionally rapidly. In the case of children with visual impairments, in particular, the relationships among the skills to be trained, the training materials, and the individual child's general level of accomplishment and specific experiential history deserve careful study, as does the training outcome in relation to its practical function in the child's educational and everyday experience.

Abstractness of concepts

The issue of the abstractness or concreteness of concepts has also received research attention. The issue has been studied largely in terms of the comparison between sighted children and those with visual impairments. We noted earlier that Anderson (1979) found that blind children tended to be somewhat more concrete and less abstract than sighted children in their descriptions of objects, and for children with visual impairments, Higgins (1973) also found concrete classification concepts to precede abstract concepts developmentally.

Tillman (1967) approached the issue by submitting children's responses on the WISC verbal scales to factor analysis. The children with visual impairments ranged in age from 6 to 13, and most had been blind since birth. Children with significant residual vision were excluded from the sample. On the similarities scale, two factors emerged for the sighted group, representing relatively concrete and relatively more abstract items. For the group with visual impairments, only one factor emerged, and it was similar to the concrete factor for the sighted children. Zweibelson and Barg (1967) also evaluated the abstractness of the responses of blind and sighted children on the similarities and vocabulary scales of the WISC. The children were 11 to 13 years old, were for the most part blind since birth, and ranged widely in IQ. The blind children showed significantly more concrete and functional scores and fewer abstract scores than the sighted children.

Thus, these studies suggest a difference between sighted and blind children in abstractness versus concreteness. On the other hand, Schwartz (1972) compared congenitally blind with sighted children from the lower grades on an aurally administered abstraction test and found no differences between the groups.

In all of these studies, the comparisons are clouded by differences in IQ and CA distribution between the visually impaired and sighted samples. The relationships between these variables and abstract reasoning are not well understood, and thus the ways that the group differences on these variables might have affected the abstract reasoning scores are not clear.

In any case, the issue would be better advanced by examining the relationship between measures of abstract reasoning and other variables within the population of children with visual impairments. For example, Hammill and Powell (1967) provided some evidence about the relationships between abstract reasoning and IQ and age in children ranging from 5 to 10 years of age, of normal intelligence (test not specified), who had varying amounts of visual function. Scores on the aurally administered abstraction test successfully discriminated the high and low extremes of both age and IQ, indicating that, at least for this test of abstract reasoning, abstraction ability is positively related to both variables.

Counting

Counting can be regarded as a form of classification, since it involves the concept of drawing a match between numbers and members of a set of objects to be counted. As children learn to count items in a group, they bring various strategies to bear, and these strategies vary with age. For example, pointing to and touching items begins to facilitate counting around four years of age, and shortly thereafter, grouping items into similar sets facilitates counting. Generally, strategies become more sophisticated with age, and counting becomes more accurate. There is little evidence about the development of counting in children with visual impairments, but the study by Sicilian (1988) is useful. He studied the development of these strategies in congenitally blind children in the 3- to 14-year age range, looking in particular at how tactually based strategies emerge as an adaptive basis for counting. In some tasks the objects to be counted could be moved around, whereas in others the objects were fixed in various configurations.

Three successful strategies were identified: "scanning," in which the array is scanned to determine whether there are organizing features that may be used; "count organizing," in which similarity characteristics of items within the array are noted; and "partitioning," in which items are physically grouped in order to simplify the counting process. Sicilian identified three developmental levels within each of these strategies, progressing from no use, to inefficient use, to efficient use of the strategy. More efficient use of each strategy emerged as age increased. Furthermore, counting accuracy was highly correlated with the level of efficiency for each type of strategy. Successful counting requires the understanding and use of the concept of one-to-one correspondence between numbers and items: Sicilian concluded that it is the refinement of this concept that motivates the child to develop progressively more efficient strategies.

6

Executive functions: memory, attention, and cognitive strategies

We consider now a set of interrelated cognitive processes that includes memory, attention, and cognitive strategies. These "executive functions" have not received much direct research attention in the visual impairment literature, particularly that with infants and children. However, many studies, some of which we have already mentioned in previous sections, bear at least indirectly on these issues.

Infancy

Several lines of innovative research with sighted infants have revealed that the neonate's attention is "captured" by certain perceptual events, and that the neonate has little if any volitional choice about which stimuli are actually attended. Initially involuntary, attention gradually comes under a degree of voluntary control. For example, early eye fixations are entirely determined by stimulus features but become largely volitional during the first year.

Among the visual events that are particularly attention-commanding are moving stimuli, facelike stimuli, and areas within the visual field that contain a moderate degree of complexity. Moving stimuli are especially effective in eliciting visual attention. Complexity is an intriguing dimension of visual attention: the evidence supports the notion that as the infant's visual information-processing capacities develop, the infant prefers to look at progressively more complex stimulus arrays. The other sensory modalities have been far less completely studied, and the existence of analogs to these visual-developmental principles in other modalities is for the most part a hypothetical question at present.

One of the most interesting lines of recent research in early perceptual and cognitive development has been in the area of memory. The use of ingenious research methods has revealed that by at least four months, infants begin to recognize and remember perceptual stimuli that they have encountered before. The implications of this development are clear: it is only when recognition and memory begin that conceptual representation and an understanding of the physical world can begin. Caution is in order, however: to say that the first evidence of recognition and memory occurs around four months of age is not to say that memory is mature at that point or that the capacity to represent aspects of the physical world conceptually springs forth fully formed.

Without research on perceptual development and executive functions such as attention and memory, our knowledge about the human infant's cognitive understanding of the physical world would be incomplete. Impressive strides have been made in research on these issues with sighted infants. There is as yet little such work with visually impaired infants. Some inferences about memory can be made, and we reviewed the evidence for these in connection with our discussion of the development of object permanence in Chapter 3.

We turn now to consideration of these issues in preschool and school-age children.

Memory span

The digit span subscale of the WISC can be taken as a measure of simple memory. Tillman and Osborne (1969) evaluated WISC verbal scale scores for groups of blind and sighted children, ages 7 to 11, for whom overall WISC scores were equated. Analysis revealed a significant interaction of scale (the six verbal scales) and group (blind and sighted). This was produced by superior performance of sighted children on the similarities scale, offset by superior performance of blind children on the digit span scale. This pattern of superiority of the blind children's memory, relative to their performance on the other scales, did not change with age. Print readers were excluded from the sample of blind children, and thus the results can be taken as applying to children with severe visual loss.

Smits and Mommers (1976), studying children in the Netherlands, reported a similar finding with children ranging from 7 to 13 years of age.

The pattern was exactly the same, with digit span performance relatively stronger for the children with visual impairments than performance on other scales. When the group was divided into blind and partially sighted subgroups, the overall WISC verbal IQ was higher for the blind subgroup. This difference appeared in each of the six scales and was apparently no stronger for the digit span than for the other scales.

From this evidence, then, there is clearly nothing wrong with the simple memory capabilities of children with visual impairments, and indeed this may be an area of relatively high function.

Encoding of tactual information

How is tactual information encoded in memory by children with visual impairments? Although it seems evident that the nature of coding must be tactual, the issue is not that simple, since it is possible that aspects of verbal or visual encoding may also be involved.

Davidson, Barnes, and Mullen (1974) varied the memory demand in a task involving matching of three-dimensional shape stimuli. The child explored the standard stimulus, then felt each of the comparison stimuli in succession and chose the one that matched the standard. Memory demand was varied by including either three or five items in the comparison set: since the incorrect members of the set were similar to the standard, exploration of them constituted tactual interference. Increasing the size of the comparison set increased the error frequency significantly. The results thus support the hypothesis that features of tactually experienced stimuli are encoded in a specifically tactual form.

A useful paradigm for studying the nature of encoding involves inserting a delay between the experience of the standard and the choice of the comparison, during which various activities are interposed. The logic is that different kinds of intervening activity should interfere selectively with memory, depending on the nature of the encoding. For example, tactual intervening activity should interfere if the standard stimulus is tactually encoded, but not if it is encoded in some other form.

Following this logic, Millar (1974) used three-dimensional nonsense shapes designed to be easily discriminated but not easily labeled. The subjects were 9- and 10-year-olds who were blind from very early in life. The procedure was to present a standard stimulus for a 2-sec inspection, then after a delay to present a comparison stimulus for the child's same–

different judgment. The delay was either unfilled (no activity) or involved rehearsal (finger tracing of the shape of the standard on the flat floor of the apparatus), verbal distractor (counting backward by threes), or tactual distractor (a tactual manipulation activity). If memory of the standard is tactual, then rehearsal should facilitate performance, whereas the tactual distractor should interfere with it. The verbal distractor should presumably be neutral in its effect if the standard stimulus is encoded tactually.

Errors were were infrequent in all conditions, but response latencies varied with the nature of the delay activity. Responses were slow in the tactual distractor condition, a result that supports the tactual encoding hypothesis. However, rehearsal did not facilitate performance; furthermore, the verbal distractor did interfere with performance. These results do not conform to the hypothesis of tactual encoding.

Since the tasks did not produce differential error rates, a second experiment was conducted with five- to seven-year-old children, using basically the same procedures. More errors occurred in the verbal distractor and movement distractor conditions than in the unfilled delay or rehearsal conditions.

The hypothesis that encoding is specifically tactual predicts that the tactual distractor should interfere most with performance, and specifically should interfere more than the verbal distractor. That the verbal and movement distractors both had interfering effects suggests that the interference was not a modality-specific effect that interferes with encoding, but rather was a matter of distraction of the child's attention.

Pursuing the attention versus modality issue, Kool and Rana (1980) hypothesized that a verbal distractor would interfere by distracting attention, whereas a tactual distractor would interfere specifically with the retention of tactual information. They used conditions like those of Millar (1974) with congenitally blind children ages 9 to 11, and ages 13 to 16 years in a second experiment. There was a decay of tactual memory with increasing delay in the unfilled delay condition. The verbal distractor interfered with performance, thus corroborating Millar's (1974) results. It was assumed that the older children would have more tactual experience and would therefore be more inclined to encode tactually. With these children, both verbal and tactual distractor conditions were effective. The effect of the tactual distractor was greater than that of the verbal distractor at every delay interval. This result supports the notion that the stimuli were tactually encoded. The significant effect of the verbal distractor suggests that there is also a general effect on attention, thus supporting Millar's (1974) conclusion.

These three studies support the hypothesis that tactual stimuli are indeed encoded in a tactual manner, but that the retention of tactually encoded information is affected by attentional factors that are not specific to sensory modality.

It is known that phonologically similar items can interfere with one another in memory and cause lower recall. Millar (1975a) asked whether a similar process might occur with tactual features encoded in memory. Such interference would be evidence for the encoding of tactual features.

The blind children ranged in age from 4 to 10 years, and all had lost vision by the age of 18 months. The procedure required the recall of the position of an item in a series, with series length ranging from two to six items. The objects were presented sequentially, then one test object was given to the child with the request to replace it in its correct position in the series. Three types of series were used. One contained phonologically similar (but tactually distinct, e.g., rat, bag, man) items, another contained items that were tactually similar (but phonologically distinct, e.g., ruler, knife, comb), and the third was heterogeneous, containing items that were tactually and phonologically distinct (e.g., ball, watch, chair).

As expected, recall performance was worse for the phonologically similar series than for the heterogenous series. This finding shows the well-known phonological interference effect. The question of interest was whether a similar effect would be found for tactually similar series. Overall recall of the tactually similar items was indeed worse than for items in the heterogeneous series, thus indicating that tactual features must have been stored in memory. Interestingly, the tactual interference effect was strongest for the smaller series and decreased as series length increased. No variation with age or other individual differences variables was reported.

Summary. This literature on the nature of encoding of tactual experience is small but interesting. Studies that show adverse effects of tactual distractors during a delay before recall suggest that tactually experienced information is encoded in a specifically tactual form. However, the issue is not that simple, since performance also deteriorates, though typically to a lesser degree, as a result of verbal distractors. This may be largely an effect of attention, but the relationship between initial encoding and retention variables is not completely clear. Finally, it is surprising that not more has been done to explore the possibilities that children with early visual experience encode tactual information in a different way that is somehow affected by that experience.

Strategies of tactual information processing

Performance in many perceptual and cognitive tasks is found to vary significantly as a function of the information-processing strategy that the subject adopts. There is a small but exemplary literature on this regarding children with visual impairments.

Using a very basic paradigm, Simpkins (1979) examined children's ability to recognize geometric shapes tactually. The child first felt a standard stimulus, then subsequently chose a match from a set of four sequentially presented alternatives. The children were four to seven years of age and varied in the amount of visual function.

There was little variation due to gender or visual status, but the older children performed better than the younger ones. Simpkins reported that in touching the stimuli, the younger children tended to attend to a peculiar topological property of a form (e.g., a hole in it) whereas the older children tended to hold the shape in one hand and trace its contour with the other hand. This shift in exploration strategy parallels that found with sighted children (Gliner, 1966), and it is not surprising that strategy shifts are related to performance in a similar way. Berlá (1974) used irregular geometric stimuli varying in complexity from three to five sides. The child felt a shape in one orientation, then the shape was quickly rotated by 90, 180, or 270 degrees without the child touching it. The child's task was to return the shape to its original orientation. The accuracy of performance improved with grade level from grades two through eight. Increasing complexity did not decrease accuracy but did increase the time required for performance. Berlá noted that the grade-related performance differences seemed to be connected to the strategy of choosing a distinctive feature of the shape to concentrate on: the older children appeared to attend more to the distinctive features (e.g., sharp angles) of the shapes. Berlá suggested that a consistent information-processing strategy was the basis for their better performance.

Berlá's analysis of shape discrimination in terms of distinctive features is reminiscent of Gibson's (1969) formulation: attention to peculiar distinguishing features, or areas of high information content, improves the efficiency and effectiveness of shape perception. In a similar vein, Solntseva (1966) suggested that the difficulties that the blind child experiences in the formation of tactual images of the external environment are caused by problems in the ability to differentiate distinctive features of tactual experience. Tactual qualities such as texture and hardness are relatively attention commanding (Klatzky, Lederman, & Reed, 1987) and easy to discriminate, but the discrimination of shape requires a more systematic approach for the detection of critical features.

Davidson (1972), studying adolescents, used haptic judgments of curvature as a vehicle for studying the relationship of tactual scanning strategies and task success. The task was to judge whether an edge was convex, concave, or straight. Hand movement patterns were videotaped. The most frequently used strategy was the "grip," in which all four fingers are spread out along the curve, followed by the "top sweep," which involved running the forefinger along the length of the curve. It is interesting that the blind subjects used the grip strategy much more frequently than a comparable group of blindfolded sighted subjects, and that the judgments of the blind group were more accurate. (When sighted subjects were instructed to use the grip strategy, their performance improved.)

The relationship of strategies and performance under variations in task difficulty is also of interest. Davidson and Whitson (1974) varied task difficulty by changing the number of items in the comparison set. That is, a standard curve was presented and felt, and then the subject had to find the standard when it was part of a comparison set of one, three, or five curves. (In the case of the single curve comparison, a simple same–different judgment was required.) The congenitally blind subjects averaged 19 years of age.

When search strategy was unrestricted, errors increased regularly with the number of comparison alternatives, showing a basic effect of task difficulty. The question of interest, though, is whether strategies are differentially effective for various difficulty levels. The "grip" strategy was most frequently used regardless of difficulty level, but there was a tendency for the "top sweep" strategy to increase and the "grip" to decrease at the highest difficulty level.

Instructed strategies

In a second part of the same experiment, subjects were instructed to use a single strategy. There was a tendency for better performance when strategies were used in which more of the curved stimulus was simultaneously apprehended (e.g., the "grip," in which the subject's four fingers are spread along a substantial portion of the edge).

Berlá and Butterfield (1977) examined the effectiveness of training procedures in improving tactual search performance. The subjects were braille readers in kindergarten through fifth grade, age range 6 to 17 years. The test stimuli were outline tracings of various states and countries. The child felt the stimulus for 30 sec, then attempted to find the same stimulus in a set of four shapes. Based on a pre-test, children were divided into a training and a control group. The training group received three training sessions in which the child's attention was drawn to distinctive features of the shapes (e.g., "parts that stick out"). Following training, a post-test was given, and the trained group, which was matched to the control group on the basis of pre-test scores, performed very much better than the control group, with 84% of the training group showing an improvement.

In a second experiment, the test materials were changed to involve searching for a shape in a complex array of shapes. Training was similar to that in the first experiment but involved shapes embedded in more complex arrays. On the post-test, the trained group again performed significantly better and faster than the untrained control group. Thus training improved performance, apparently not only by drawing the child's attention to distinctive features but also by encouraging a more systematic search process as well.

Berlá and Murr (1974) also instructed subjects in the use of specific search strategies while searching for features on a tactual map. The subjects were drawn from grades 4 through 12 and ranged in age from 11 to 19 years. All of the children were braille readers. Following a pre-test requiring the location of tactual symbols without strategy instructions, three groups were instructed to use either a vertical, a one-handed horizontal, or a two-handed horizontal scanning strategy. The children practiced the strategy for 4 min. Children in a fourth condition were free to scan as they wished. The task then involved finding as many target symbols on the map as possible. There was a modest general increase with grade level in the number of symbols located. Of more importance, the scanning strategies produced different rates of success: each of the three instructed strategies produced significant improvement compared to the pre-test, with the vertical strategy producing the greatest improvement. The uninstructed control group did not improve over the pre-test performance. The benefit of the instructed strategies in general seemed to stem from the more systematic coverage of the map that resulted.

Berlá (1981) further explored the effectiveness of training scanning strategies as a function of age. The children, all braille readers, were divided into group that averaged 11, 15, and 19 years. Each age group was divided into a control and a training group. Early in the test procedure, children in the training group were briefly instructed in the use of a systematic vertical scanning strategy. The task required the child to feel the parts of a nine-item "puzzle" and remember their locations, and then to recreate the puzzle on a blank board using the nine individual elements.

There were no obvious effects of the training on vertical location errors. For horizontal errors, however, the effect of training varied with age group. Specifically, the youngest group benefited from training, while the performance of the oldest group suffered from training. The performance of the middle group was not affected. Berlá reasoned that the youngest children benefited from training because they had not yet established habitual search patterns, whereas the instructed search strategy may have interfered with search patterns that the older children had already established.

Summary. Davidson (1976) argued that the better search strategies facilitate the representation of the stimulus in memory, with attention as the mediating process: as attention is more organized, so is search, the result being more effective encoding of tactually perceived information. Whatever the exact mechanism, it is clear from the work of Berlá and Davidson that more systematic strategies lead to better performance, and that furthermore, strategies can benefit from training.

Integration of information from different sensory modalities

There is extensive literature on sighted children regarding issues of intermodality relations, and particularly on what happens when information about events is received simultaneously from two or more sensory modalities. The literature on the visually impaired population is more limited, but several interesting studies illustrate important points, particularly about the perception of spatial structure.

One issue is the relative effectiveness of the perception of spatial and temporal structure. O'Connor and Hermelin (1972a) addressed this question using auditory stimuli that were distributed both temporally and spatially. A sequence of three spoken digits was heard from an array of three spatially separated speakers. The sequences were designed so that when asked for the "middle" digit, the child would have to choose between the digit that had occurred at the *spatially middle* speaker and the digit that had occurred in the *temporal middle* of the sequence. The children were 13-year-olds who had been blind since birth.

The results were very clear: the overwhelming choice was of the temporally middle digit, rather than of the digit that sounded from the spatially middle speaker. This pattern was strikingly different from that found with sighted children who saw the sequence of three digits at different spatial locations rather than hearing them. In this condition, the sighted subjects overwhelmingly reported the digit from the middle spatial location, rather than the digit in the middle of the temporal sequence. Children with hearing impairments responded in much the same manner as did the sighted children in this condition. O'Connor and Hermelin argued that blind children do not naturally encode spatially distributed auditory information in terms of its spatial distribution (and that hearing-impaired children, correspondingly, do not naturally encode spatially distributed visual information in terms of its temporal distribution).

Battacchi, Franza, and Pani (1981) similarly evaluated children's ability to process the spatial structure of auditory events. They used a semicircular array of six loudspeakers that were separated by at least 25 degrees and therefore highly spatially discriminable from one another. A sequence of six names was heard, one from each speaker, at a rate of one per second. In the *congruent* condition, the sequence started at one end and proceeded regularly to the other end of the set of speakers, while in the *incongruent* condition the order of the names did not correspond to the spatial sequence of the speakers. After the presentation, the child was asked to say the names that had been heard at two of the speakers, chosen at random.

Sighted children perform this task better in the congruent condition than they do on the incongruent condition: apparently the spatial structure of the speaker array facilitates their processing of the auditory information. In contrast, neither partially sighted nor blind children (ages 8 to 10) performed better in the congruent than in the incongruent condition: the regularity of the spatial sequence in the congruent condition did not facilitate their processing of the auditory information. In fact, the performance of the blind children was not above chance. The performance of the partially sighted children, however, was better than that of the blind. (A group of blind young adults did show a performance advantage in the congruent condition, suggesting that this ability develops, albeit slowly, with age.)

We should stress that in these experiments, the task is to process auditory spatial information. On the face of it, there is no reason to expect that impairment of vision should interfere with this ability. However, the empirical evidence is clear.

In another approach to the concept of "middleness," O'Connor and Hermelin (1972b) assessed the encoding strategies of seven- to nine-year-old blind children in a three-term series problem. Two types of sentences were constructed, each expressing a relationship among three items. In one type, the sequential order of presentation corresponded to their logical relationship, and in the other the sequential and logical orders did not correspond. The child was asked two types of question, one dealing with the logically middle member of the triad and the other dealing with one of the two logically extreme members. There was a tendency to report the sequentially middle item when it was incorrect. O'Connor and Hermelin suggested that the blind children did not have a readily available spatial code for use when it was appropriate, and instead tended to rely on a temporal code even when it was inappropriate.

Axelrod (1968) used still another method to approach the same issue: an oddity problem, in which the child is required to identify a characteristic that distinguishes one member of a triad from the others. Children who had lost vision earlier than 18 months had greater difficulty than children who had lost vision later than two years in learning such problems when the key characteristic was that the item occupied the temporal or spatial "middle" of a triad. Axelrod also evaluated the formation of intermodality learning sets, which have to do with the ability to transfer a solution from a problem learned in one sensory modality to a similar problem presented in another modality. When the problem was initially learned tactually or auditorially and then presented in the other modality, children with early visual loss were again worse than those with later visual loss.

With respect to the question of information-processing strategies applied to spatial and other tasks, Millar (1981a, 1982) argued that there is nothing inherently different in the information-processing capabilities of blind children, but rather that preferred strategies develop as a result of the typical ways that children gain their primary information. Thus, with respect to spatial perception, "If blindness leads subjects to neglect external cues, they will learn less, and know less about directional connections between external cues. This, in turn, strengthens the preference for strategies derived from the remaining modalities" (1982, p. 119).

This is not to say that the strategies actually chosen for spatial (and presumably other) tasks are necessarily the optimal ones: a visualization strategy may not be optimal for a given task, but the child with residual vision may use it nonetheless because of the effectiveness of visualization in many prior experiences. Similarly, the blind child may have external spatial-referential strategies available but tend not to use them because the primary source of spatial information (touch) tends to elicit internally referenced strategies. Similar conclusions were reached by Robin and Pecheux (1976), working with tasks requiring reproduction of two- and three-dimensional spatial models.

Summary. It is clear that the processing of even nonvisual information about spatial structure is hampered by impaired vision. These results again underscore the important role of vision as a vehicle for the organization of spatial structure, regardless of modality. However, the issue is complicated by the issue of information-processing strategies: strategies tend to be selected based on the particular sensory modality through which information is received. Although this association of strategy and sensory modality may be natural, Millar suggests that it is not inviolable. The implication is that training studies designed to help children select appropriate strategies of information processing may prove useful.

Verbal and phonological issues in encoding and memory

We turn now from spatial issues to those related to the encoding of verbal and phonological information. Much of this research uses braille characters as stimuli: these are especially interesting as research stimuli because they have both tactual and verbal–phonological properties. Our intent here is not to review how braille characters are learned or how braille reading is acquired, but rather to examine the nature of encoding and memory of verbal and phonological information, particularly as it is obtained via touch. The issue, in short, is the nature of encoding of information in memory.

Tactual versus phonological encoding

As we noted earlier, Millar (1975a) demonstrated that tactual information is stored in memory in a specifically tactual form, since interpolated activity of a tactual nature during a delay interfered specifically with the recall of tactually experienced information. Millar (1975b) examined the corresponding question with braille stimuli. That is, would braille stimuli, with both tactual and phonological properties, be stored phonologically, tactually, or perhaps in both forms?

Three sets of stimuli were used, one consisting of items that were tactually dissimilar but phonologically similar, another of items that were tactually similar but phonologically dissimilar, and the third of items that were dissimilar both tactually and phonologically. Set size ranged from two to six items. The blind children ranged in age from 4 to 12 years and had lost vision within the first 18 months of life. They were screened by pre-test to ensure their ability to discriminate the letters tactually, and in the case of the older children, to identify the letters. The child felt each letter of a sequence in succession, then was given one of the letters and asked to indicate where it had occurred in the series.

Evidence for both phonological and tactual interference was found for all ages, indicating that both the phonological and the tactual properties of the stimuli were encoded. However, the younger children tended to show stronger evidence of tactual than phonological encoding. It was also clear that different processes were involved for tactual and phonological information, since there were different relationships of tactual and phonological interference effects in relation to overall memory demand. Additionally, there was a tendency for children with higher IQ generally to perform better than those with lower IQ.

Overall, Millar's (1975b) results for braille stimuli corroborated her (1975a) results for purely tactual stimuli in confirming that tactual encoding does occur. However, the addition of phonological properties added a specifically phonological form of encoding as well.

It is well known that the grouping of items within a serial string of verbal material facilitates memory of that material. Presumably such a grouping effect should also occur with tactual material that has phonological correlates. Indeed, Millar (1978) used strings of braille letters and found that grouping facilitates recall. This result further corroborates the evidence of phonological influence on the tactual encoding of verbal material. However, would similar facilitatory effects of grouping occur with tactual material without verbal association? The answer was a clear no: when the stimulus strings were nonsense shapes without phonological correlates, grouping actually interfered with recall. The results supported the hypothesis that tactual encoding is significantly different when the stimuli have verbal associations than when they do not. Overall performance improved with increasing age over the 7- to 11-year range, but the difference between associative and nonassociative stimuli did not change with age. Mental age (as well as digit span) was similarly related to overall performance but also did not interact with stimulus type effects.

These findings constitute further evidence for the existence of different memory processes for verbal and tactual information, and particularly for the interaction of these processes when verbal–phonological information is involved.

At another level of phonological–tactual interaction, pronounceability may facilitate braille letter recognition. Such a study was reported by Pick, Thomas, and Pick (1966). The subjects were braille readers ranging in age from 9 to 21. They varied in age at visual loss, amount of residual vision, and braille reading experience. The stimuli were letter groups containing from three to six characters. In one condition the stimuli were pronounceable, whereas in another condition, the letters of each group were rearranged to render it unpronounceable. The child's task was to scan the letters tactually and name each letter as quickly as possible. It was hypothesized that for the pronounceable stimuli, the sound sequence would facilitate discrimination of the letters. Indeed, there was a dramatic speed difference in favor of the letters occurring in pronounceable groups, and fewer errors occurred for letters in these groups, again showing the facilitative role of phonological context. The results did not differ as a function of either age or braille reading experience; variation with age at visual loss or amount of residual vision was not reported.

Summary. In sum, the evidence about tactual and phonological encoding supports the view that when stimuli have both tactual and phonological properties, these are both encoded. The two kinds of encoding follow somewhat different processes. However, these processes operate interdependently, particularly in the encoding of braille.

The role of touch in semantic coding

In the case of print reading, if letter sounds are encoded one-by-one, as novice readers may be inclined to do, reading suffers. This is particularly so if the sound of the word is not congruent with the sequential sounds of the letters. (For example, it is difficult to arrive at the sound of the word *eat* by combining the sequence of sounds of the letters *e-a-t*.)

Does such an effect also occur for braille? In fact, the effect might be *stronger* because of the sequential nature of encountering braille characters. Pring (1982) asked whether a phonological code is generated as the braille letters are contacted tactually, or whether touch simply serves as a channel, with phonological encoding occurring at some higher level. If individual letters are phonologically encoded, a phonological–lexical conflict would be generated in an incongruent condition where the sounds of individual letters do not match their role in the sound of the word (e.g., in the pair *steak–leak*) and reading should be slower. In contrast, in the congruent case (e.g., *stake–leak*) no conflict is present and reading should be faster.

Pring studied children who were congenitally blind, were rated as good braille readers, and ranged in age from 11 to 13. Relatively few errors were made in reading the word-pair lists, and the primary analysis was of response latency. The time required to read the target word was longer in the incongruent than in the congruent condition. This result supports the notion that phonological encoding occurs at the tactual level, and thus that pronunciation is constructed by assigning phonological properties to individual letters and generating the sound of the word (and thus eventually its meaning) by combining the individual sounds.

However, if the children used only this form of tactual–phonological encoding, then errors of pronunciation would be expected for words with irregular spelling. That such errors were not generally found supports the notion of direct access via touch to the known meaning of the word, rather than a constructive process from individual letters. In short, the results yield evidence for both processes.

In a second experiment with the same children, Pring tested the hypothesis that this process is mediated specifically by grapheme–phoneme (letter–sound) correspondence. This was done by having the children read lists of words that were either regular (words whose pronunciation corresponds to their spelling, such as *wood* and *dance*) or irregular (those whose pronunciation does not correspond to their spelling, such as *pint* and *talk*). Errors were again few, and latency data showed that regular words were pronounced more quickly than irregular words. This suggests that extra processing is required for irregular words, or that an alternative processing route is used for them.

Overall, these results show interesting parallels to the processes involved in reading print visually, but they do not yet yield a clear picture of how the processes work.

Attention to features of braille stimuli

In earlier sections we addressed the question of the relative effectiveness of different information-processing strategies in mediating performance in tactual perception, and the issue arises here as well for the perception of braille stimuli. Millar (1984) investigated children's attention to various features of braille characters, exploring in particular the relative attention to phonological and tactual properties of the characters in relation to the children's level of skill in braille reading. The children were congenitally blind and ranged in age from 7 to 12 years. They were divided into three reading groups based on reading rate: these groups overlapped substantially in age and were moderately differentiated by IQ score.

The test was a multidimensional oddity problem. Three stimuli were presented on each trial, and the child had to choose which of the three stimuli was the "odd one." The child was instructed that a stimulus could be "odd" by differing in meaning, sound, shape, or number of dots from the others. From the child's choice it is possible to discern which of the dimensions governed the child's choices.

Differences were found between the reading groups. Faster readers based their choices more on semantic features and less on shape features. This choice pattern was even more highly related to mental age than to reading level. Each child was additionally classified as a normal or a retarded reader, based on whether or not his or her reading proficiency score was within a year of chronological age. The normal readers did not show predominance of any of the dimensions, whereas the retarded readers tended to focus on phonological features. This indicates that their reading strategy was to construct the sound of the word by combining the sounds of the individual letters, which also characterizes poorer sighted readers.

In a second experiment, children were instructed to use specific features for judgment. Faster readers were better able to respond to different features in accordance with the instructions, whereas slower readers were less able to escape their own spontaneous strategies.

Thus, Millar's work shows that there are relationships between attentional propensities and reading capability. The direction of causality, of course, is elusive.

Pring (1984) used a word-recognition task to explore a similar issue at the semantic level. The question at issue was the degree to which semantic or tactual information would govern children's ability to recognize words. Word pairs were constructed to contain semantically related (e.g., *bread–butter*) or unrelated (*nurse–butter*) members. Nonword combinations were also included. The child's task was to determine, as quickly as possible, whether or not the stimulus was an English word. Words in semantically related pairs were correctly recognized faster than those in unrelated pairs. This semantic facilitation effect is evidence that the children attend to the semantic context while processing information about an individual word.

However, when the braille stimuli were tactually degraded by physically reducing the height of the braille dots, the semantic facilitation effect did not occur. Apparently reducing the legibility of the braille dots redirected the child's attention from the semantic to the perceptual characteristics of the stimuli. The children were congenitally blind, were of normal to high intelligence, were relatively experienced braille readers, and averaged 10:6 years of age.

Summary. The implication of the Millar and Pring studies is that there are indeed individual differences in children's attentional propensities, and furthermore that these are related to reading level. Pring's results in particular support the view that the child's attention is limited and that its allocation is flexible, depending on the balance of cognitive and perceptual task demands.

The relationship between verbal and pictorial information

When sighted children look at pictures, their recognition and memory can be facilitated by accompanying verbal information: this is an example of verbal mediation. The question arises whether a similar phenomenon occurs when the verbal information is experienced via braille. Pring (1987) examined the role of verbal mediation in the recognition of pictures by congenitally blind children ranging in age from 7 to 16, all of whom were braille readers. The picture stimuli were raised-line drawings of objects with which familiarity could be expected (e.g., *shoe, hand,* or *sofa*). In a matching task, each picture was paired with a word and printed in braille; the child's task was to report whether the word went with the picture ("same") or not ("different"). Following this, a recognition test was performed in which a series of pictures and words was presented. Some of the words and the pictures had been experienced in the matching task and some had not. The child's task was to judge whether each item had or had not been encountered in the matching task.

Performance was in general very good. For recognition of pictures, performance was best for pictures that had been encountered together with the matching word, and specifically better than for those with a mismatched word. Pring suggested that the results may reflect not verbal mediation in the true sense, but rather a dual encoding of the stimuli such that the picture and the verbal information are encoded in parallel. Whatever the exact mechanism, association of verbal material and pictures clearly occurred. In fact, this association also operated in a negative way in the results. Having encountered a word in the matching phase increased the likelihood that an erroneous "yes" recognition response would be given to the picture corresponding to that word. That is, false positive picture recognition responses were made as a result of previous exposure to the word.

Although it is not strictly an example of verbal mediation, the question also occurs whether there might be a reciprocal effect, such that picture information aids in the recall of verbal information. Pring and Rusted (1985) found positive evidence. A short prose passage containing specific facts corresponded to each of six raised-line pictures of animals or plants that were explored tactually. Each of the passages contained information represented in the picture, as well as other information not depicted. The child heard the prose text twice, once with and once without the picture available. When the picture was available, the child was encouraged to explore the picture and identify features as they were mentioned in the text. Immediately after each text, the child was asked to describe the subject of the text (and picture). After completing the trials, an interpolated task of braille letter naming was used for 15 min, after which a delayed recall task was given.

Immediate recall for pictured information was, not surprisingly, better than delayed recall. When the text was accompanied by the picture, immediate recall of the depicted information was better than when there was no picture. Thus, there was a positive effect of depicted information, indicating that an effective association was being made between the verbal and the pictorial information.

When recall was delayed, the results were more complex. Two groups were tested, one of congenitally blind 13- to 15-year-olds, and another that had lost visual function after age two. Two-thirds of the latter group had some residual pattern vision, although it was not sufficient to discriminate the pictures. On delayed recall, the group that lost vision later showed the same pattern of facilitation by pictured information as in the immediate recall task. The pattern of the congenitally blind children showed that pictured information was recalled better in the illustrated condition, but that nonpictured information was better recalled in the unillustrated condition. Pring and Rusted suggested that this was a result of attention: the availability of a picture draws the child's attention to the textual information pictured, at the expense of information not pictured. Further, when a picture is not available, the child devotes less attention to information that is picturable. This is a provocative pattern of results, since it suggests that strategies of attention and information encoding differ as a function of early vision.

Summary

Several major summary points emerge from this body of research. First, it is clear that when stimuli have both tactual and phonological properties, as in the case of braille characters, separate processes of tactual and phonological encoding occur. However, these forms of encoding can have reciprocal effects on one another, and thus they are not completely independent. Second, the evidence shows that the child does not operate with a limitless reservoir of attention, but instead allocates attention variously to tactual, phonological, and semantic features of letters and words as the demands of the task vary. Third, in the case of tactually perceived pictorial stimuli, there are clear effects of related verbal information, and the reciprocal influence also occurs.

This body of evidence has been primarily directed to demonstrating the operation of basic processes of information encoding and to elucidating the variables that affect their operation. This is certainly a valid and valuable pursuit. However, the literature has generally not addressed issues of individual differences, aside from some interesting evidence of strategy variations in relation to reading.

Imagery

For decades there has been interest in the nature of the mental images that blind adults and children have, and in how their imagery may vary as a function of such variables as partial vision or an early period of visual experience.

For example, Fernald (1913) reported a study of imagery in two university students, one blind from birth and the other partially sighted. Reportedly, the latter used visual imagery abundantly whereas the totally blind student never used visual imagery. Schlaegel (1953) reported interesting variations between children with differing amounts of vision in the imagery characteristics that words evoke. Test words and phrases were presented orally to the child, who was asked to report the sensory experience evoked by the "first mental image." The predominant image reported by visually impaired children, as by sighted children, was visual. The visually impaired group was divided into three subgroups. The predominance of visual imagery varied regularly with the amount of residual vision: those with the least vision reported the fewest visual images, and those with the most visual capability reported the most. It may be that children with partial vision did indeed experience a greater frequency of visual images, but an equally plausible explanation is that there was a response artifact, such that children in this subgroup were more inclined to report visual images.

As a procedural matter, the difficulty of studying imagery should be noted. Two approaches are possible, and each involves its own assumptions. On the one hand, the child may be asked, as in the work by Fernald and Schlaegel, to describe the nature of his or her images. This procedure is open to the question of whether habits of language use are artifactually biasing the outcome: are reported variations in imagery really that, or just differences in the use of particular words to report images? Generally, this approach cannot generate unequivocal results.

The second approach involves the functional aspects of imagery: tasks can be designed on which performance should differ in predictable ways depending on the images hypothesized to be involved. The work on mental rotation, discussed in an earlier section, serves to illustrate this point. For example, when Carpenter and Eisenberg (1978) found longer reaction times to make judgments about letters that were rotated from the upright, they reasonably concluded that imagery must have been the mediating mechanism, and specifically that cognitive rotation of a mental image had occurred. As sound as this reasoning may be, it is good to remember that images are being examined not directly, but indirectly by inference based on the nature of their mediation of behavior.

Imagery in spatial tasks

The imagery work may be broadly divided into that which involves the use of imagery in performing spatial tasks and that which involves imagery in other learning tasks. We have considered much of the work on spatial behavior in earlier sections, and a brief mention of the imagery aspects of that work should suffice here. Both Knotts and Miles (1929) and Duncan (1934) asked their subjects to report the nature of their imagery in solving maze problems: in both cases, subjects who reported using a verbal approach performed better than those who reported using visual images or kinesthetic–motor images. Worchel (1951) used tasks involving various tactually perceived shapes and solicited reports of the subjects of the nature of their imagery. The responses of the congenitally blind subjects tended to refer to the "feel" of the shapes, whereas the adventitiously blind subjects tended to refer to "mental pictures." Worchel interpreted this result as indicating that visual imagery results from early vision. Interestingly, the performance of the later blind subjects was better than that of the congenitally blind, thus suggesting that visual imagery can effectively mediate performance.

Imagery in verbal tasks

We turn now to the issue of imagery in learning tasks, which have involved primarily verbal material. It is known that words that evoke images are easier to learn, for example in a paired-associate task, than those which do not. (The typical paired-associate task involves the presentation of a list in which both words appear, then testing for the recall of one word with the other as a cue.) This paradigm has been used to assess the imagery of children with visual impairments. Kenmore (1965) studied third and sixth graders from schools for the blind. About half of the children were blind, while visual function in the remainder ranged from object perception to 2/200: age of visual loss was not reported. The speed of paired-associate learning was assessed in conditions involving verbally and tactually presented material of varying familiarity.

Overall, the sixth graders learned more quickly than the third graders, and children with higher IQ scores performed better than those with lower scores. No variation in results as a function of residual vision was reported. More substantively, Kenmore hypothesized that since the school experience of visually impaired children is highly verbally structured, it should lead to stronger verbal imagery in older children because of their longer experience in the environment. The older children were indeed better than the younger in learning verbally presented pairs. Conversely, the older children were worse at learning tactually presented material. Kenmore suggested that this may be a result of the relative neglect of tactual learning strategies in schools for the blind, which should in turn lead to less tactual imagery. (The inferential dangers of imagery work are evident here: since imagery was not measured directly, its role as a mediating mechanism is uncertain even though the results are consonant with that formulation.)

Paivio and Okovita (1971) studied visual and auditory imagery using a paired-associate learning paradigm. The congenitally blind children, whose ages were 14 to 18 years, were all "above average" in IQ. Lists of word pairs were constructed to be high in both visual and auditory imagery (e.g., *ocean–clock*), or high in visual but low in auditory imagery (e.g., *green–palace*). Performance was significantly better throughout for words with high auditory imagery, although the children did learn both the high- and low-auditory imagery lists.

In a second experiment, pair lists were created to contain words with high visual and low auditory (and tactual) imagery, or with high auditory and low visual (and tactual) imagery. Again, performance was better with the lists that contained words high in auditory imagery, although the differences decreased over the course of the experimental session. Both experiments clearly showed the ability of the children to benefit from auditory imagery, and a relative lack of ability to benefit from visual imagery. No variation in results was reported as a function of age or IQ, but this is not surprising given the limited range of these variables in the sample.

On the other hand, Zimler and Keenan (1983) studied younger children, 7 to 12 years of age, who had lost sight within the first six months of life. Word-pair lists of four types were created: high visual and low auditory imagery in both (V–V), high auditory and low visual imagery in both (A–A), and mixed imagery (V–A, A–V). The children's performance did not differ as a function of list type. The lack of an advantage for the lists with high auditory imagery stands in contrast to the results of Paivio and Okovita (1971). Although the children were younger than those of Paivio and Okovita, it is not clear how this variable may have affected the results.

Again we can turn to the issue of cognitive strategies in paired-associate learning, with a study by Martin and Herndon (1971). The words were not chosen for their modality-specific imagery; rather, the purpose of the study was to investigate the nature of verbal strategies in remembering word pairs. One member of each pair was a real word (and therefore presumably "imageable"), while the other was either a pronounceable nonword or a very low-frequency word (presumably less imageable). In a control condition, children were not instructed as to strategy, whereas in an "aided" condition they were instructed in the use of associative strategies such as recognizing superordinate relationships between the two members of a pair. Learning performance was significantly better in the aided condition.

The children's reports of their strategies were classified according to the type and complexity of cues used (after Martin, Boersma, & Cox, 1965). There was a significant correlation between performance and the level of associative strategy. This result, coupled with the overall superiority of the aided group, suggests that learning is better when associative strategies are used, and that such strategies can be effectively instructed.

The results of studies using the paired-associate learning task suggest a facilitory role of auditory imagery in paired-associate learning, although the relationship to CA is uncertain. Furthermore, there are variations in performance with associative strategy.

Serial learning tasks have also been used to investigate the role of imagery in learning. In this paradigm, the subject's task is to learn items presented in a serial list. After each run-through of a list, the subject is asked to remember as many of the items as possible, either in order or not (free recall). Craig (1973) used this method with adolescents whose IQ scores were in the normal range. Age at visual loss ranged from birth (70%) to six years, and all were braille users. Lists of high- and low-imagery words were created (the imagery characteristics of the words were not further specified). More items were recalled from the high- than from the low-imagery lists. In serial learning tasks there is a general tendency to find higher recall of items both early and late in the list than in the middle; this effect was found for both high- and low-imagery lists.

Groups of hearing-impaired, visually impaired, and sighted subjects were tested. The subjects with both sight and hearing performed better than either the visually impaired or the hearing impaired (who experienced the lists visually rather than auditorially). Following the reasoning of Paivio and Okovita (1971), Craig concluded that sighted subjects have two codes (visual and auditory) potentially available for mediating the task, whereas the visually impaired and the hearing-impaired subjects do not perform as well because in each case one of the codes is unavailable. Although there was apparently some range of visual function in the visually impaired group as well as variation in the age of visual loss, the possible relationship of these variables to performance was unfortunately not reported.

In the research noted above, Zimler and Keenan (1983) studied the free recall of serial word lists that differed in their common attributes. Three attributes were used, "redness," "loudness," and "roundness." The rationale for this choice was that the visual attribute "redness" should facilitate recall by sighted children, the auditory attribute "loudness" should facilitate recall by blind children, and the attribute "roundness," which is accessible both visually and tactually, should facilitate the two groups equally.

Four words of one category were presented seriatim, then four of the next, and four of the third. The blind children were indeed better at recalling the "loud" words, but they were also better at recalling the "round" words than the sighted children, and contrary to expectations, they were equal to the sighted in recalling the "red" words. These results do not correspond to expectations based on a modality-specific coding hypothesis.

Summary. There is no doubt, based on this work, that imagery facilitates verbal learning. More specific questions arise about the specific form of imagery and how it exerts its effect. On the one hand, some results (e.g., Craig, as well as Paivio & Okovita) support the notion of modality-specific imagery, and specifically that visual imagery is not facilitative of learning by children with visual impairments, while auditory imagery is. However, other results (e.g., Zimler & Keenan) cast doubt on the modality-specific formulation. It is possible that this varies with individual differences characteristics such as visual experience, but for the most part the research has unfortunately not explored this issue. Kenmore's work raised an important issue in finding age-related shifts in imagery and in questioning whether these are experience related. There are obviously many unanswered questions in this area.

Developmental shifts in imagery

According to Bruner (1966), experience is encoded in a series of stages that proceeds developmentally from actions to images to symbols. *Enactive* representation refers to an action; *ikonic* representation refers to an image that is pictorial (and free of action); and *symbolic* refers to an arbitrary or more conceptual form of representation, as in the case of language labels. Hall (1981a,b) used Bruner's framework for representation as a starting point. Based on a review of the literature on imagery in relation to the performance of various tasks by children with visual impairments, Hall suggested that these forms of representation may not be tapped in the same ways as in sighted children, and specifically that because of their experiential structure, children with visual impairments may not use ikonic representation as much but may rely more on symbolic and enactive modes of representation.

Hall designed a series of tasks to explore the use of representational modes in blind children who had lost vision within the first year. Three tasks were used: a concrete task, a verbal task with high-imagery words, and a verbal task with low-imagery words. Questions were designed to tap classification strategies, and specifically to show whether grouping would be done on the basis of perceptible (sensory), functional (referring to the function of an object), or nominal (name) attributes. It was expected that the children's classifications would be based primarily on perceptible attributes in the early years, with functional and nominal groupings more frequent with increasing age. In addition, the formation of equivalence groupings was expected to vary with the degree of concreteness and imagery level of the task.

In the concrete task, children tended to classify based primarily on perceptible attributes over the entire age range from 7 to 17. As expected, nominal and functional strategies increased slightly over age for both of the imagery tasks, although the use of perceptible strategies in these tasks remained high. Surprisingly, perceptible attributes did not diminish in use with age. Based on this result, Hall (1983) suggested that the use of concrete tasks in the educational setting may not promote cognitive growth and higher-level thinking skills. The relationship is evident between this possibility and Kenmore's (1965) suggestion of shifts in imagery tendencies as a result of school experience.

Summary

We should reiterate the difficulty of studying imagery, and particularly the danger of relying on subjects' reports of the nature of their imagery. Nonetheless, some studies that obtain performance indicators along with self-reports (e.g., Worchel, 1951) tend to support the validity of self-reports. Other studies use performance indicators such as the paired-associate or serial learning task as a basis on which to infer the nature of imagery. Much of this work has been done with children who lost vision at birth or early in life and who have at most LP, and consequently information about visual experience variables is unfortunately lacking. However, there is a body of evidence that suggests, though not unequivocally, that performance varies as a function of the imagery characteristics of the stimulus words; blind children's performance using words with visual imagery characteristics is not facilitated, whereas auditory imagery characteristics are facilitative. All in all, though, the literature on imagery is not very satisfying.

7

Cognitive style, creativity, and intelligence

Cognitive style, creativity, and intelligence are not properly cognitive executive functions, but they are nevertheless important to consider for a full picture of the cognitive capabilities and functioning of children with visual impairments. In each area there is important evidence of individual differences.

Cognitive style

The term *cognitive style* refers to the fact that children differ in their approaches to cognitive tasks. Although there are different ways of defining cognitive style, one of the most useful is the global–articulated dimension. An articulated style refers to the ability to impose structure on an inherently unstructured situation, or to recognize structure that exists. In contrast, global style refers to the tendency to deal with events in a diffuse and unstructured manner. The dimension thus has to do with cognitive organization.

This aspect of cognitive functioning is of interest in children with visual impairments because of the role that vision is hypothesized to play in the developing cognitive abilities of sighted children. In studies of sighted children, Witkin and his colleagues have generally found a developmental progression from global to articulated cognitive style; that is, with increasing age children become more able to differentiate structure within a field and more able to impose structure when little exists (Witkin, Birnbaum, Lomonaco, Lehr, & Herman, 1968). Vision is thought to play a major role not only in the developing articulation of visual perception itself, but also as an aid to articulation of experience gained through other sensory modalities. Witkin et al. thus hypothesized that congenitally blind children would show individual consistencies of cognitive style, but that in general they would be relatively more global in their cognitive functioning than sighted children of comparable age.

The children were all blind from birth, and 20 of 25 had lost vision due to ROP. The age range was from 12 to 19, and boys and girls were equally represented. IQ scores ranged from 92 to 153, with a mean of 115. A sighted group, matched for age and school grade, was also studied. A series of cognitive tests, administered to each child, included two tests of analytic ability in problem solving (tactile block design and tactile matchsticks), a test of body concept, and two tests of analytic ability in perception (a tactile and an auditory embedded-figures test). An embedded-figures test requires the child to perceive a simple pattern against a more complex background. The tactile version of this is self-evident, and the auditory version involved discerning a short tune within a longer and more complex tune.

For the blind group as a whole, there was strong evidence for consistency of results across the various analytic tests: with the exception of the auditory embedded-figures test, the correlations between pairs of tests were significant. The blind children showed less articulation than the sighted children on the tactile embedded-figures test, but the blind children showed higher articulation scores on the auditory embedded-figures test.

Overall, although there was some support for the notion that blind children show more global cognitive styles, the pattern of group results was complex and does not allow ready generalization. Even more important, there was substantial variation among individuals in the blind group. However, possible correlates of cognitive style, such as gender and age, were not evident. The degree of articulation was not significantly correlated with measures of verbal IQ (nor was it in the group of sighted children). We should note, however, that the IQ range was skewed toward the higher end: it is possible that a relationship might be found in the lower and middle portion of the IQ range. Additionally, the IQ scores were only verbal scores, and since the articulation tasks were more closely related to abilities typically tapped by measures of performance IQ, it may be that relationships would indeed be found between articulation and performance IQ.

Witkin, Oltman, Chase, and Friedman (1971) used the same battery of tests with subjects who had lost vision due to retinoblastoma. They ranged in age from 11 to 24 years, and their mean verbal IQ was 122. Generally the pattern of results was similar to that of the previous group, although on the general global–articulation measure, the retinoblastoma subjects scored nearer the articulation end of the dimension than the previous group, which had a high proportion of ROP-blind children.

It is tempting to conclude that the differences between groups are due to the differences in their visual experience, since the retinoblastoma subjects tested by Witkin et al. (1971) had generally had vision for some time before visual loss, whereas the predominantly ROP subjects had lost vision very early. Huckabee and Ferrell (1971) also studied adolescents who varied in their degree of visual function. The subjects with partial vision generally showed more articulated cognitive style than the blind group.

Thus, it seems likely, as Witkin hypothesized, that variations in cognitive style are associated with early visual experience and/or residual visual capability, with vision facilitating the acquisition of a more articulated cognitive style. However, other differences between the ROP and retinoblastoma etiologies must be ruled out before vision itself can be accepted as the major causal factor.

Although Witkin et al. (1968) found a generally low level of articulation in their sample of early blind subjects, they did note that several of the children showed a high degree of articulation. They suggested that "at least in some children, blindness may actually serve as an impetus to the development of differentiation. The special effort the blind child must make to achieve an articulated concept of the world, precisely because vision is lacking, may conceivably encourage greater investment in articulation and so actually foster the development of differentiation" (p. 779). It is not clear, if this greater investment and effort is involved, why blind children in general do not show greater articulation. Although Witkin et al. (1968) suggested that "parents, teachers, and others may go to great lengths to help the blind child achieve an articulated impression," this does not identify the factors that may lead to articulation. The evidence of individual differences is provocative, but an explanation of their causes remains to be clarified. In particular, the possible role of experience in these differences is unclear.

Summary. Cognitive style is an interesting dimension of individual variation, but whether it is important in any significant sense is another issue.

The possibility that cognitive style is related to variations in educational approaches has received increasing attention. On the basis of the research currently available, however, the determinants of cognitive style in children with visual impairments are not at all clear, and thus the functional relationship of cognitive style to educational practice remains to be clarified.

Creativity

Creativity is a dimension of cognitive function that has received some research attention with blind children. The same problems plague the study of creativity in blind as in sighted children, not the least of which are the design of appropriate tests, the evaluation of responses, and the relationships between cognitive and artistic aspects of creativity.

Standardized tests of creativity

As in the case of sighted children, one approach to creativity in children with visual impairments has used standardized tests. Halpin (1972) used the Torrance Tests of Creative Ability to make various comparisons between visually impaired residential and day school students, as well as between visually impaired and sighted children, and to evaluate the relationship of such factors as age, gender, and race to creativity. The children ranged in age from 6 to 12 years. They were all braille users, but degree of residual vision varied considerably. Most had lost vision by a year of age, and none had additional handicapping conditions. Sixty-one children attended residential schools; 20 attended regular classes in public schools and received additional instruction from an itinerant teacher.

Four activities from the Torrance tests were used: product improvement, unusual uses, unusual questions, and "just suppose." The scores from these were rated on verbal fluency, verbal flexibility, and verbal originality. The visually impaired group as a whole scored higher on these measures than the sighted comparison group. Halpin suggested that visually impaired children show this superiority because they are more dependent on verbal communication, are forced by their handicap to be more flexible and imaginative in dealing with the environment, and are not as pressured to conform to behavioral norms as their sighted counterparts.

Of more interest to us here are the factors that might differentiate within the group of children with visual impairments. Neither type of school, gender, nor race differentiated within this group. On the measure of verbal flexibility, there was a significant advantage of the older (9 to 12 years) children over the younger (6 to 8 years). The lack of a difference between residential and day school children bears comment. If, as some have argued, the residential school setting is more constraining and less challenging, then lower creativity scores might be expected. Halpin's data belie this notion. She noted that the curriculum of these schools paralleled that of the public schools and included special emphasis on music, physical education, and arts and crafts. Additionally, parent visitation at the school and involvement in the children's education were encouraged, and the children visited home as often as possible. Thus, in this case there is little reason to expect that educational setting would foster differences in creativity.

Using roughly the same samples, Halpin, Halpin, and Tillman (1973) evaluated the relationships between the creativity scores of residential and day school children and teacher-rated mobility, adjustment to blindness, social acceptance, dependence/independence, conformity, rigidity, curiosity, and academic achievement. A five-point scale was used for each of these teacher-rated variables. Of these, only the curiosity rating showed an across-the-board correlation with the three measures of creativity as well as IQ (Hayes–Binet or WISC).

Blackhurst, Marks, and Tisdall (1969) hypothesized that highly mobile blind children are more willing to engage in risk-taking behavior and should therefore show more evidence of divergent thinking. Numerous measures of creativity were taken, including word fluency, product improvement, unusual uses, ideational fluency, and recognizing problems. In general, the hypothesized relationship between mobility and creativity was not found. The children were mostly congenitally blind 10- to 12-year-olds from residential and day-school settings, and their IQs averaged slightly above 100 with a roughly normal distribution. The only evidence of significant individual differences was a weak pattern of positive correlation between creativity and mobility for the day-school group.

Summary. It is clear that we have a great deal to learn about the evaluation of creativity in children with visual impairments by the use of standardized tests. Substantial variation is evident in most of the available studies, but patterns are not obvious. It may well be that progress in this area will depend to great extent on an improved definition of creativity and on the development of credible ways of evaluating it. These problems are as difficult in the study of children with visual impairments as they are in studying sighted children.

Creativity in art

The popular idea that the blind are unusually creative musically is not generally supported by the scanty empirical evidence. Pitman (1965) used the Wing Test of Musical Intelligence to address this issue. The musical abilities of comparable groups of visually impaired and sighted children were compared in the age range of 8 to 11 years. No remarkable differences were found, although the visually impaired group tended to excel on subtests in which aural perception was of particular importance. Unfortunately, the overall thrust of the research was to compare visually impaired and sighted groups, and no report was made of possible differences within the visually impaired group related to variables such as age, IQ, or visual characteristics.

There has been little study of the sculptural creations of children with visual impairments, although again there is some comparative work available. The work of Revesz (1950) is the most detailed, although the developmental aspects of the work are not strong. Revesz maintained that all aesthetic insight, and thus all artistic creation, depends on vision, and therefore anyone born blind could not possibly develop more than a rudimentary aesthetic sense. Revesz's approach clearly rested on a sighted framework, and his conclusions were based on the responses of sighted judges to the artistic creations of blind persons.

Both Witkin et al. (1968) and Kinsbourne and Lempert (1980) used tasks involving clay modeling of the human figure, and both found that children with visual impairments created models that were less representational than those of sighted comparison subjects. Although both studies found variation within the groups of subjects with visual impairments, neither study reported lawful variation of performance with any individual differences variables. Nor did either study adequately distinguish between the possibilities that the visually impaired child may not have an adequate internal representation of the human form, or may have one but may not be able to model it in acceptable form.

Millar (1975d) addressed this issue, although using drawings rather than models. Millar's subjects were 6- to 11-year-old (early) blind children and sighted children matched for age, gender, and digit span. Each child was asked to draw the human figure and to name each body part as it was drawn. The child was then asked to indicate the position of the floor on the picture and its relation to the human figure. The Sewell Raised Line Drawing Kit was used, in which the child draws on a plastic sheet with a ball-point pen, producing a raised line. Scoring was based on the general body scheme, the appropriate connection of body parts, details such as fingers and toes, and the alignment of the body with the floor.

The six- and eight-year-old blind children tended to produce drawings inferior to those of their sighted peers, but those of the older children did not differ in the depiction of the human form. There was a dramatic difference at all ages between the blind and sighted children in the relationship of the body figure to the floor, with the blind children making significantly more errors. In Millar's terminology, the blind children were not aware of the "translation rules" by which such things as floors and walls are represented in drawings. Millar pointed out that artists took centuries to develop effective ways of representing spatial relationships in pictures, and that it is unreasonable to expect that the blind child should accomplish this naturally in just a few years. Millar concluded that the blind child has the basic abilities for pictorial representation at a relatively early age and can acquire an understanding of the conventional translation rules with experience.

Kennedy (1980, 1982, 1983; Kennedy & Domander, 1981) offered a nativist view of the representational abilities of the blind, in contrast to the empiricist view of Millar. Kennedy's work has been mostly with adults, although some has been with children, and has been directed at the nature of pictorial representation. The blind, particularly those without any history of visual experience, offer potentially important evidence, since if they were to show similarities to the sighted in depiction, some sort of universal principles must be operating rather than a strictly learned ability. Indeed, this is Kennedy's basic conclusion.

One important question is whether blind individuals can recognize tactual depictions of objects. Kennedy's (1980) answer was an emphatic yes: although blind subjects who had lost vision early were initially not as good as those who lost vision later, they performed relatively well with minor hints about the identity of objects. A second question concerns the blind subjects' own drawings. Although some of the pictures shown by Kennedy (1980) are scarcely discernible, most are easily recognizable and differ from pictures that sighted subjects produce only in technical aspects such as the precision of the attachment of related elements within the picture.

Kennedy (1983) further argued that the pictures made by the blind show perspective, evidently without direct visual experience of it. In support of the argument that perspective is meaningful even to the blind child, Kennedy (1982) noted that 5- to 15-year-old blind children, when pointing simultaneously to two corners of a room from various locations, open their arms at a wider angle when they are close to the corners than when they are farther away: this difference parallels the change in visual angle as one moves away from a wall.

Kennedy and Domander (1981) asked blind children and adults to depict events such as the wind, a shout, and pain. They found that the blind, much as the sighted, spontaneously use representations such as wavy lines to represent the wind. Further, both adults and children used acceptable ways of depicting movement, as for example depicting the spokes of a moving wheel as curved. The subjects' comments demonstrated that they realized that such representations should be taken metaphorically rather than literally.

Summary. It is clear that many blind children, as well as adults, understand what it means to represent a scene pictorially. Whether this ability is innate or learned is unclear, since there is evidence on both sides of the issue. This area is open to much interpretation, and Millar and Kennedy differ on this point. With any set of drawings by the blind, one can see elements of configuration and of detail that are impressively mature. On the other hand, one can also see many aspects that are immature. In part, one can find evidence to support either argument, since there is little agreement on any objective method for evaluating artistic representation. This area awaits definitive research.

Creativity in play

Although it can be regarded as an aspect of social interaction, play is also a major expression of creativity in children.

Subjective reports. There are many subjective reports, chiefly from case histories, about the creative play of children with visual impairments. Many of these reports indicate that such children exhibit little creativity and imagination in their play (e.g., Burlingham, 1965, 1967; Rothschild, 1960; Sandler, 1963; Sandler & Wills, 1965; Tait, 1972c,d; Wills, 1968). Children with visual impairments are also said to be less interested in play. According to Rothschild, "the blind child may not be accustomed to express and to involve himself in play. Play may be a less frequently pursued endeavor and considerably less important in the blind child's life than in the life of the child with full vision" (1960, p. 330). Tait (1972d) suggested that "the blind child must actually be taught to engage actively, creatively and independently in spontaneous play activities" (p. 368). However, Wills (1968) noted that as soon as adult stimulation is withdrawn, they quickly regress into "simple, primitive activities." She noted that much of the play that blind children engage in is repetitive. They practice well-learned activities such as opening and closing doors, or they relive certain experiences over and over through play.

Some authors claim that the blind child is particularly prone to fantasy. Avery (1968) stated, "The intriguing aspect of play therapy with a blind child is the original fashion in which play materials can be used" (p. 42). It was not clear whether the originality of the blind children was spontaneously present or a result of the play therapy. Morrissey (1950) reported that blind children, because of their loneliness, frequently indulge in fantasies, but he stressed that this is not necessarily a sign that the blind are "mentally abnormal"(!). Deutsch (1940) observed blind children playing with wooden blocks and noted their reactions to and fantasies over the loss of one or more blocks. According to Deutsch, the blind children showed "a striking readiness to give up reality and escape into fantasy" (p. 140).

Wills (1968) offered two reasons for the development of these "aberrant" play patterns. First, people are cathected more heavily by the blind child, resulting in relative lack of interest in toys: people offer more stimulation to the blind child than objects do. In support of this point, Tait (1972b) noted a high frequency among blind children of attempts to interact with the adult observer in the play context. Similarly, Schneekloth (1989), examining the nature of children's free play within an environmental context, found that when dealing with other people, sighted children most often interacted with other children and rarely did so with adults, whereas children with visual impairments spent about one-third of their interactive time with adults.

Second, Wills suggested that the excessive anxiety to which blind children are prone "narrows the field of the blind child's play" (p. 218). Wills cited the example of a young boy who was afraid of a teddy bear because he could not decide if it was alive or not. Personification of inanimate objects, important in fantasy play, was lacking in his because of the anxiety it provoked.

Objective evidence. As engaging as these subjective reports are, there is little credible data to support their conclusions, and in general these reports read more like advertisements for sympathy than dispassionate evaluation. Happily, there is more objective, balanced evidence available.

Singer and Streiner (1966) evaluated the imaginative content of the fantasy play of blind and sighted children. The former scored significantly lower than the latter on "imaginativeness of play" and "imaginativeness of spontaneous fantasy" and were described as less imaginative, less flexible, and more concrete. However, the blind children showed a greater predilection for fantasy in the occurrence of imaginary companions. Fantasy playmates are a frequent occurrence in younger seeing children, but in blind children they may persist to a later age. According to Singer and Streiner, the fantasy companions are "generally of a clearly wishful or compensatory character" (p. 480) in that they are generally sighted companions who can do things that the blind child cannot.

Tait (1972a) evaluated a number of aspects of the play of visually impaired and sighted children ranging in age from four to nine years. The children were free to play with several common objects. Play activity was scored in three categories: *dramatic play* involved assigning roles to the play objects, the observer, or the subject him- or herself; in *manipulative play*, the children handled the objects but assigned no roles to them; and *other play* was a residual category. Manipulative play was more frequent in the visually impaired children than in the sighted children; still, this was not a predominating mode of play for the former. The fact that over half of the children with visual impairments engaged in dramatic play suggests a high degree of creativity and imagination.

Tait explored several aspects of individual differences but did not find any notable results. The children were divided into a group with at most LP and another group with object perception or travel vision. No differences were found between the two groups on any of the play indices. The children were drawn from residential schools for the blind or from public schools, and there were no differences between these two groups in any of the play indices.

Olson (1983) studied the exploratory behaviors of preschool children, from two to six years of age, in interaction with toys. The children were rated as showing normal development aside from the visual loss. Four of the children had LP or less, while the remaining 11 had varying degrees of visual capability and were prospectively large print readers. Each child was given a novel toy (a set of stacked wheels with notches that, when aligned, allowed a metal rod to drop through to the base and activate a buzzer), as well as other toys. For each toy, the child was asked to "find out how it works." The child's behavior was videotaped. Compared to a sighted group, the children with visual impairments differed only in their greater tendency to examine the toys tactually. Within the group with visual impairments, the older children were more likely to sustain interest in the toys, to "solve" their functions, and to verbalize about the toys. Children who showed more initiative and aggressiveness in approaching the toy were, not surprisingly, more likely to "solve" it.

Parsons (1986a,b) reviewed the previous literature on play behavior and conducted a study of two- to four-year-old low-vision (and sighted) children in a free-play situation with a variety of toys. Ratings were made of total play behaviors, functional behaviors (use of toys according to their "adult-intended purposes"), stereotypical play, relational play (interactions between two or more toys), undifferentiated play, generating ideas, and number of different appropriate uses.

Comparison of the groups yielded differences only in the indices of functional play (where the low-vision children were marginally lower than the sighted) and stereotypical play (where the low-vision children were higher). Within the low-vision group, stereotypical play decreased with age and functional play increased with age. Total active play increased steadily with age (as it did for the sighted group as well).

Summary. The studies that have used objective evaluations of play have, in contrast to the subjective reports, tended to find negligible differences between blind and sighted children. On the other hand, while there are typically dramatic differences within groups of children with visual impairments, there has been little success in identifying variables associated with greater or lesser creativity in play.

Humor

The child's appreciation of humor is also of interest, since it can be thought of as a form of "cognitive play." Tait and Ward (1982) evaluated the comprehension of verbal humor in visually impaired (and sighted) children ranging in age from 7 to 15 years and in IQ from about 70 to 140. Each child was given a series of jokes and was asked to label them as jokes or nonjokes. Age, IQ, and visual status were examined as predictors of appropriate judgments in a multivariate analysis. Age and IQ accounted for significant proportions of the variance (i.e., the older and the higher the IQ, the better the performance), while the degree of visual loss did not. Nor was the joke comprehension of children with visual impairments different from that of comparably aged sighted children.

Rogow (1981) reached a similar conclusion about the appreciation of riddles by children with visual impairments, ages seven and eight years. Each child was given a set of 20 riddles, and the answers were scored with respect to how the incongruity of the riddle was addressed. This task requires a level of cognitive development that escapes the immediate information (concrete operational thinking, in Piagetian terms). The children with visual impairments all showed a basic appreciation of riddles and could in fact generate their own riddles. They scored somewhat higher on the language-based than the concept-based riddles, and in fact two of the children were "riddle collectors." There were no differences between the four totally blind and the eight partially sighted children. Riddle comprehension was clearly within their capabilities.

Summary

It is difficult to summarize the literature on the question of creativity as it is expressed in play behavior. The subjective reports tend to rate children with visual impairments as lacking in creativity, while the objective evidence tends to show a much more balanced picture. The results depend to a great deal on the individual investigator's definitions of play and its categories, and there is little consistency in this. Factors that might produce consistent differences between subgroups of visually impaired children have not been systematically examined. In the absence of compelling evidence to the contrary, the conclusion seems warranted that visual impairment itself is not a determining factor.

Aspects of intelligence

There is a long history of debate about intelligence. Some of it has been directed at what intelligence is, and indeed whether there is a psychological entity that should be called intelligence. Another part of the debate, assuming that there *is* such an entity, has centered on appropriate means of evaluating it. The latter question has a special construction for the issue of visual impairment because of the questionability of testing children with visual impairments using instruments designed for sighted children and the difficulty of designing valid tests specifically for children with visual impairments.

Much of the literature has focused on the comparative intelligence of sighted and visually impaired children. Lest the reader think it an oversight, I intend to ignore this issue, which I believe to be wholly irrelevant and in any case methodologically impossible.

I will also not treat the issue of the relationships among the tests themselves – the extent, for example, to which scores on the verbal scales of the WISC may show correlations with outcomes on the Binet tests. While these are legitimate concerns for test makers, they do not for the most part give us relevant information about intelligence in children with visual impairments and the factors that influence it.

Indeed, for the near-term goals of constructing a knowledge base about children with visual impairments, I am not convinced of the fundamental value of the construct called intelligence. This construct refers to the individual's potential for adapting to the cognitive demands of existence, and in turn the intelligence test is a way of measuring and representing those cognitive skills, typically expressing them as a score called IQ. I would far rather see our research attention devoted to investigation of the adaptive cognitive skills themselves than to the investigation of performance on instruments called intelligence tests. These tests are worthless if they are not highly valid indicators of some area of adaptive functioning. Why not study the adaptive functioning directly, whether it be success in school, ability to discern spatial relationships in the en vironment, or capacity to remember telephone numbers, rather than studying a secondary indicator?

Nevertheless, there is a substantial tradition of accepting performance on intelligence tests as a summary indicator of some or all of these more practical adaptive abilities, and it is worthwhile to review the individual differences variables associated with variation in intelligence test scores.

Intelligence tests used with visually impaired children

Perhaps the most naive, yet the most prevalent, approach to testing the intelligence of visually impaired children is the use of the verbal scales of the Wechsler Intelligence Scale for Children. The reasoning behind exclusion of the performance scales is that they require vision for their execution. The verbal scales are used, since they can be administered verbally. This approach ignores the reason for the presence of the performance scales in the first place, which is that some aspects of intelligence cannot be tapped by purely verbal means. Goldman (1970) cogently summarized the problems inherent in this approach.

A second and more valid approach is exemplified by the various adaptations of the Stanford–Binet tests created for children with visual impairments. The reasoning is that some items in traditional tests are not appropriate because of their reference to vision or to content that can only be experienced visually. Thus, items are selected for their appropriateness for children with visual impairments. For example, Hayes selected the verbal content from forms L and M of the Stanford–Binet and created the Hayes–Binet test (Hayes, 1929, 1930), which was extensively used. A later version of this test, the Interim Hayes–Binet (Hayes, 1942), was based on a later revision of the Stanford test. The Perkins–Binet (Davis, 1980) is the most recent offspring of this genealogy.

A third approach addresses the gap left in the prior approach by the omission of the performance tests by focusing on evaluation of the performance aspects of intelligence. Wattron (1956) investigated the possibility of using a tactual adaptation of the Kohs Blocks tests with visually impaired children. Instead of the colors used for visual patterns, Wattron used textures embossed on wood blocks. Another example of this approach is represented by Ohwaki and his colleagues (Ohwaki et al., 1960), who produced a test called the Ohwaki–Kohs Tactile Block Design Intelligence Test for the Blind.

A fourth approach is exemplified by the work of Newland (1964, 1979), who developed the Blind Learning Aptitude Test (BLAT). Newland's fundamental premise is the same as that of many critics of intelligence tests for sighted children, who argue that while billed as tests of *aptitude*, they in fact rely so heavily on content that they should more appropriately be termed tests of *achievement*. Newland sought to differentiate between product (which reflects achievement) and process (which reflects fundamental psychological operations). Focusing on process, the BLAT is designed to test the child's ability to discover differences, identify commonalities, and extrapolate relationships among items.

The results of the BLAT show a substantial correlation with results of the WISC-V and Hayes–Binet tests, and Newland argued that the test is "in the same 'ball park' as the other two, but it is doing a somewhat different kind of sampling" (Newland, 1979, p. 137). Generally the BLAT shows lower, though very significant, correlations with scales of the Stanford Achievement Test. Newland does not argue that the BLAT should replace the other tests, but that it does a better job of evaluating process, whereas the others tap primarily product.

A fifth approach is perhaps the most comprehensive, and it is exemplified by the work of Dekker and her colleagues (Dekker, Drenth, Zaal, & Koole, 1990; Dekker, Drenth, & Zaal, 1991; Dekker & Koole, 1992). They reported the development and initial evaluation of the Intelligence Test for Visually Impaired Children (ITVIC). Scales involving both verbal and tactual performance were either borrowed from existing intelligence tests or were created to represent the various Thurstone primary factors of intelligence (Thurstone, 1938). The virtue of this eclectic approach is that it seeks to represent the range of components of intelligence within an established theoretical framework for approaching the concept of intelligence. This does not, however, absolve the test creator from the requirements of validity, and Dekker and her colleagues have attended to this requirement as well.

The initial testing involved 155 children in the age range 6 to 15 years. The sample varied in several ways, including amount of useful vision, age of visual loss, etiology, and educational setting. Both boys and girls were included. A major division was made into groups of children with and without useful vision. Scores were linearly related to age for both groups, and there was no interaction of visual status with age.

More complete data are given for children without useful vision, since this subgroup was considerably larger ($n = 106$) than the group with some useful vision. From the 13 scales, factor analysis produced four factors. These were called *orientation* (tests that require subjects to orient themselves in space), *reasoning* (analogies, as well as attention and memory), *spatial ability* (block design), and *verbal ability* (vocabulary and comprehension). Tests tapping primarily spatial abilities differentiated between the vision groups, with the "useful vision" group performing better, as expected; the differences increased as the complexity of the tasks increased. On the other hand, performance on the memory scales was better for the group without useful vision.

Dekker made the important point that certain executive functions such as memory and concentration contribute to the performance of children on various components of the test. Correlations between test scores and indices of school achievement were calculated. Generally, the tests involving spatial abilities were least related to achievement, whereas high correlations were found between achievement and the scales tapping reasoning and verbal abilities.

Dekker's approach is important in several respects. First, it is grounded in a theory of the structure of intelligence (Thurstone, 1938). One might, of course, select one as well as another of the existing theories as a starting place, but the important point is that the approach is grounded in theory. Second, guided by this theoretical approach, Dekker et al. appropriately include a broad range of tests designed to tap various facets of intelligence. Third, there is attention to validity. As befits the original purpose of intelligence testing, the primary orientation is to the prediction of measures of school achievement. The scales of spatial abilities were not found to be highly predictive of school achievement, but presumably these abilities are related to other general measures of adaptiveness. Fourth, very careful attention is devoted to technical issues of reliability.

Only the most basic results have been presented here. The interested reader should refer to the original articles, which contain a great deal of additional detail.

Individual differences

In this section we focus on several variables that may differentiate subgroups of children with visual impairments and that might be expected to bear on the nature of their performance on tests of intelligence. Such individual differences factors include visual capability, age and etiology of visual loss, and the various environmental circumstances that may affect the level of children's intellectual functioning. Vander Kolk (1977) provided an excellent review of the early literature on intelligence testing and the variation of performance on IQ tests with a variety of individual differences variables. We will consider each of these categories very briefly.

Partial vision. Although several studies have found some differences between groups of children divided by residual vision, there is no convincing evidence one way or the other. For example, Smits and Mommers (1976), studying children in Dutch schools for the blind, found a slight difference in favor of children with less visual function, but they advised caution because of selection factors that influence the school placement of children with visual impairments and that may therefore have affected the composition of their samples. Jordan and Felty (1968) found no relationship of IQ to the degree of visual loss in 6- to 18-year-old residential school children. Using a measure of social quotient (SQ), which is widely regarded as a downward developmental extension of the IQ test, Maxfield and Fjeld (1942) found marginal differences between blind and partially sighted children, in a direction favoring the latter.

An excellent study of this issue is reported by Groenveld and Jan (1992). The Wechsler Preschool and Primary Scale of Intelligence (WP-PSI) and the Wechsler Intelligence Scale for Children (revised version) were used with children ranging in age from 4 to 17 years, and they were divided into three groups based on their degree of partial vision. The lowest vision group ranged from "finger counting at 1 meter" downward to no sight at all, and the highest group had acuity measures ranging from 20/60 to 20/200 (note that these children are not legally blind).

There were no consistent differences between groups on the verbal tests (although some subscale differences did emerge). Scores on the performance test (performed using the child's available vision) were consistently better in the highest vision group than in the intermediate group (these scales were not administered in the lowest vision group). In the intermediate vision group, division of the age range into two subgroups broken at nine years revealed an interesting pattern. There was no consistent age-related variation on the verbal subtests, but on the performance scales, the older subgroup performed less well than the younger on all five subscales.

Dekker and Koole (1992) also generally found few subscale differences related to the amount of visual loss, although performance on the digit-span scale was best in children with least vision. In this study, as in that of Groenveld and Jan, children with more visual function showed better performance on scales that tapped spatial abilities.

Thus, with respect to verbal components of intelligence there is no clear effect of partial vision, while in the performance area the evidence is, not surprisingly, in favor of children with partial vision.

Age of visual loss. One might also expect outcomes on performance tests of intelligence to show differences as a function of age of visual loss, since performance tests tap primarily spatially based abilities and since, as we have seen, a period of early vision is a generally positive predictor of spatial concepts and spatial behavior. However, differences have not generally been reported in the literature.

Using primarily verbal tests of IQ, Jordan and Felty (1968) found no relationship of IQ to age of visual loss. Vander Kolk (1977), using the Wechsler Adult Intelligence Scale, reported no IQ differences between large samples of adults who had been blind from birth and those who had lost vision later. Other investigators using verbal tests have generally not reported comparisons of children with early and later visual loss.

Etiology. Aside from conditions of multiple handicap (including cortical visual impairment), two categories of etiology stand out in relation to intelligence, retinoblastoma and retinopathy of prematurity.

Retinoblastoma is a tumor of the eye that causes blindness. The condition is typically diagnosed within the first couple of years of life and is progressive, so that children with retinoblastoma blindness have typically had vision for a year or more. Retinoblastoma may affect one eye or both. Upon diagnosis, the condition is typically treated by radiation or chemotherapy. The treatment has a high probability of success if diagnosis is sufficiently early, but if it is not successful, then removal of the eye (or eyes) is necessitated to prevent spread of the tumor to the brain via the optic nerves.

Thus a sample of children with visual loss due to retinoblastoma is likely to be heterogeneous with respect to the age of visual loss as well as unilateral versus bilateral loss. In addition, the periods of hospitalization required for surgery and / or treatment vary. To make matters even more complicated, there is evidence that retinoblastoma may be familial (i.e., hereditary) or sporadic (a euphemism for unknown cause).

In most areas of development, there is no evidence that children blind from retinoblastoma are different from those who have lost vision from other causes. The major exception to this is in intelligence, where there are some remarkable results. In particular, there are reports of both unusually high and low intelligence. At least two studies have found samples of retinoblastoma children to be markedly superior in IQ. Thurrell and Josephson (1966) reported an archival study of 15 retinoblastoma children whose ages were not included. They had been enrolled at a school for the blind, and all were totally blind. A group of blind children, with no more than LP, was used for comparison. Each retinoblastoma child was matched within two years with a non-retinoblastoma partner. Mean (Hayes–Binet) IQ for the retinoblastoma group was 120, while that of the comparison group was 99. The difference was highly significant. Although the issue was not discussed extensively, the authors mentioned the possibility of a genetic linkage of retinoblastoma and intelligence.

Williams (1968) found similar evidence of the IQ superiority of retinoblastoma children. Fifty retinoblastoma children were drawn from a wide range of schools for the blind in England and Wales. Their age range was from 5 to 16 years. A comparison group of 74 non-retinoblastoma children was drawn from the same schools. A range of etiologies was included in this sample, and as in the case of Thurrell and Josephson (1966), children with additional handicaps were excluded. The Williams Intelligence Test Scale (a primarily verbal, Binet-type test, standardized on blind and partially sighted children) was used. The mean IQ of the retinoblastoma group was 120, significantly higher than the mean of 103 for the non-retinoblastoma group.

Not all reports of the IQ of retinoblastoma children are so positive: Taktikos (1964) found a higher than normal frequency of retardation than in the general population. Taktikos suggested a genetic linkage, a point also made by Thurrell and Josephson (1966) and Williams (1968), though the latter discussed the genetic possibility in relation to high rather than low IQ. Some cases of retinoblastoma are nonhereditary, but a substantial proportion can be identified as having familial precursors. While intelligence is complexly determined, there is by most accounts a strong thread of hereditary predisposition. One must be cautious in concluding from this association that intelligence and a predisposition for retinoblastoma are therefore genetically linked, if for no other reason than that the determinants of intelligence are so elusive.

In an attempt to evaluate the genetic and environmental contributions to the superior intelligence of retinoblastoma children, Levitt, Rosenbaum, Willerman, and Levitt (1972) studied a group of 44 retinoblastoma children, along with a comparison group composed of sighted siblings of the children. The 44 retinoblastoma children ranged in age from 2 to 23 years and included 16 with unilateral blindness, 19 with bilateral retinoblastoma blindness, and 9 with bilateral retinoblastoma but with sight preserved in one eye due to successful radiation or chemotherapy. Intelligence tests were chosen as appropriate to the subjects' ages. It is risky to compare the IQ scores of blind and sighted groups because of serious problems of validity, but in any case there was not a significant difference between the retinoblastoma group as a whole and their sighted siblings. An interesting pattern emerged among the subgroups of retinoblastoma children, however. The bilaterally blind group had significantly higher IQ scores than the unilaterally blind group. The superiority of the bilaterally blind group was concentrated in the information, arithmetic, and digit span subscales of the Wechsler tests.

The complexity of these results suggests that any relationships between intelligence and retinoblastoma blindness are complex indeed. In particular, the difference between the group with bilateral blindness and that with bilateral retinoblastoma but remaining unilateral vision suggests that there are strong experiential effects at work, since in terms of the etiology of the retinoblastoma, these subgroups presumably had a similar genetic predisposition to retinoblastoma. Furthermore, the great heterogeneity within the retinoblastoma etiology category signals the need for caution in drawing conclusions about retinoblastoma from any given sample, since the probability of making a sampling error increases as the variance within a population increases.

In a study reviewed earlier, Witkin et al. (1971) examined a group of retinoblastoma subjects, ranging in age from 11 to 24 years, on a battery of tests designed to evaluate cognitive patterning. All subjects were blind: enucleation had occurred at ages ranging from within the first two years to as late as 15 years. A comparison group of children who were congenitally blind from other causes was also tested. The mean verbal IQ of the retinoblastoma group was 122, as compared to the mean of 115 for the other group. Of more interest is performance on the set of cognitive tasks, which yielded three dimensions of cognitive functioning. There were no differences between groups on the verbal-comprehension and attention-concentration dimensions, but the retinoblastoma group had significantly more articulated scores on the global-articulation dimension. The tasks involved in generating this dimension were tactile matchsticks, tactile embedded figures, and tactile block design, all tasks involving tactile discrimination and some elements of spatial understanding. Children with retinoblastoma virtually all have vision for some period of time, and this early visual experience is a possible candidate to explain their superiority on tasks involving spatial understanding. However, performance was superior even in retinoblastoma children who had lost their sight during the first year of life. Witkin et al. also cautioned that the parents, aware of their children's impending loss of sight, may have treated them differently than they would have otherwise, thus fostering the development of cognitive articulation. This is an intriguing possibility because of its potential generalizability to parental intervention in all conditions of early visual loss.

It is risky from these results to conclude a necessary relationship between the retinoblastoma etiology and cognitive structure. However, the Witkin et al. (1971) results, together with those of Levitt et al. (1972), show a provocative pattern of complex differences associated with the retinoblastoma etiology. At very least, it is clearly dangerous to ignore etiological variation in research samples.

Retinopathy of prematurity is the other etiology category that has received attention in relation to intelligence scores. Here, the general notion is that the range of intelligence may be lower than in the population of children who have lost vision from other causes, but the evidence is not at all convincing. Gore (1966) studied records of children who were blind from ROP and comparable children who had lost vision early in life from other causes. They found no evidence of differences in IQ. In the several follow-ups to the Norris et al. (1957) study by Cohen and his colleagues (see Chapter 12), a low distribution of IQ scores was indeed evident, but in view of the other factors involved (such as emerging evidence of brain damage), it is not likely that ROP is itself the culprit. Parmalee, Fiske, and Right (1959) did find three cases of sub-80 IQ in their sample of 10 ROP children, but they noted that these may have been cases in which normal intellectual capability was "functionally suppressed because of severe emotional problems" (p. 203). Hallenbeck (1954b) also noted that "pseudoretardation" in ROP-blind children may be a consequence of adjustment problems attributable to adverse maternal reactions to the child's blindness.

In a larger-scale study, Parmalee, Cutsforth, and Jackson (1958) assessed IQ in samples of children who lost vision from ROP and other causes. Again, a significant frequency of emotional disturbances was noted for the ROP group, but although several such children showed low IQ scores, it was also clear that emotional disturbance was not necessarily associated with low IQ. Finally, Genn and Silverman (1964) studied children born prematurely with and without ensuing ROP blindness. At age seven, there was a slight normative tendency for the ROP-blind children to show lower IQ scores than nonblind but prematurely born children; but at the same time there were several ROP-blind children who scored in the "bright to superior" range.

On balance, then, it is clear from the evidence that blindness caused by ROP does not by any means necessarily predict a low level of IQ test performance, let alone low levels of cognitive adaptiveness.

Environmental factors. Researchers studying performance by visually impaired children on IQ tests have in general been much more concerned with relationships among various measures of IQ than they have with relationships of test performance to determinants of cognitive functioning. However, Norris et al. (1957) argued persuasively that environmental factors are implicated in IQ test performance. They administered the Cattell Infant Intelligence Scale, the Kuhlmann Tests of Mental Development, and the Interim Hayes–Binet Intelligence Scales for the Blind, as appropriate to the ages of the children. In discussing the variability of outcomes for each of these tests, they stressed the importance of the child's experiences: for example, "The Kuhlmann data serve to support the hypothesis that, when opportunities for learning are adequate, blind children develop at essentially the same rate as sighted children" (p. 26).

Summary

Not to belabor the point unduly, the research on intelligence test performance is generally unsatisfying, but in my view the issue is not one of great importance. There are indeed some variations in IQ test performance that are associated with major individual differences variables; but IQ is a secondary indicator of cognitive adaptiveness, and it would be far more productive to devote research attention to primary indicators of the child's ability to deal with the cognitive demands of his or her various adaptive tasks.

Part III

Adapting to the social world

The newborn human infant does not exhibit behaviors that can be considered truly "social." Gradually, the infant becomes responsive to specific people and develops emotional bonds to them. These are the beginnings of social and emotional relationships that will develop and mature throughout the individual's lifetime. As the infant develops, parents and others begin to impose the demands of "socialization"; that is, they expect the child to modify his or her behavior in response to their expectations and to assume increasing responsibility for self-care.

Of course, language is a significant medium of social interaction; we will examine its development as a tool of communication. The roots of language lie in infancy, though, and it is necessary to look at prelanguage communicative behaviors. Increasingly, the child faces requirements to monitor his or her own behavior without being continuously directed by others. At some point in the first few years, the child enters into social relationships that extend beyond the family, and whether this is in child care, preschool, or a school setting, additional demands are placed on the child's capacities for interaction and adaptation to the social situation.

As the child progressively adapts to the demands of socialization and independence, stable characteristics of self emerge. These are seen in the consistencies in behavioral and attitudinal traits that affect the nature and quality of the child's interaction with other people as well as his or her pattern of self-conceptualization and self-regard.

8

Social–emotional and communicative development in infancy

At birth, the human infant shows no evidence of true social responsiveness. Physical states such as hunger and pain elicit crying or other signs of distress, and these indications are reduced or eliminated by food or removal of the aversive stimulus. It makes little difference who or what causes the change in stimulus; one breast or bottle is as good as another, as long as it contains the right stuff. The neonate is nondiscriminatory as to the identity of the agent. By the age of six months, however, the typical infant has begun to discriminate among persons and respond selectively to them emotionally and socially; and well before a year of age, the infant has a well-refined system of response to individual people, including aversions as well as attractions.

Attachment

The term *attachment* refers to the development in the first year of selective social–emotional responsiveness to individual people, with positive responses to a small number of people (typically including one or both parents) and negative responses to other people (the phenomenon called "stranger fear"). This progression is typically described as a narrowing of the objects of attachment that begins to be apparent around six months of age, together with the development of an aversion to other individuals. Indices of positive attachment include smiling and vocalizing, and indices of aversion include distress not only when the attachment objects *are not* present but also when "strangers" *are* present. The development of specific attachments shows not only discrimination among people, but also the beginnings of emotional responsiveness upon which subsequent emotional ties will be based.

One view is that the fundamental purpose of the infant's behaviors that eventually lead to attachment is to maintain the proximity of other people (such as a parent)[1] so that the infant's needs for nutrition, warmth, and protection from danger are met. This view can be put in evolutionary-adaptive terms: infant behaviors that achieve the proximity of other people are adaptive in a survival sense, and therefore selection has worked to support those behaviors in the species. Alternatively, it is possible to take a social learning view of the same phenomena. Whatever the theoretical orientation, infant behaviors occur that tend to elicit a certain pattern of parental responsiveness.

However, the infant's behaviors alone are not sufficient either to ensure survival or to cause attachment: the parent's behaviors are also critical. In this interaction, the infant's behaviors are important in eliciting the parent's attention and reciprocal behaviors, and the parent's reciprocal behaviors are in turn important to sustain the infant's role in the relationship. Obviously perception is critically involved: the parent must be able to perceive, understand the significance of, and respond appropriately to the infant's behaviors. The infant in turn must be able to perceive the parent's reciprocal behaviors.

What infant and parent behaviors are involved? The key behaviors of the infant that elicit parental response are crying, smiling, and clinging. It is interesting that this array of behaviors engages several of the parent's sensory modalities for their perception: crying is heard, smiling is seen, clinging is felt. To the extent that the parent is insensitive to these, the infant's behaviors will be ineffective. On the other side, the parent may respond in ways that the infant can hear (vocalizing), feel (touching, holding), taste (food), and see (proximity, smiling). To the extent that the infant may be incapable of perceiving any of these, there is potential for disruption of the attachment process.

For the true attachment of midyear to occur, the infant's conceptual as well as perceptual abilities are involved. The infant variously hears, sees, and feels (as well as tastes and smells) the parent. It is not until the infant

---

[1] In the classical literature, the mother is typically presented as that individual to whom the infant becomes attached. However, there is strong evidence that the father, as well as other individuals who interact frequently and intensively with the infant, can also become objects of attachment. For the sake of economy, I will use the term "parent" in this treatment. The term is to be understood to include either parent, or for that matter other people who become objects of attachment.

can begin to unite these various sources of perceptual information into a single "parent concept" that the infant can begin to discriminate between the parent and other people, and it is only then that a selective attachment to the parent (and the accompanying aversion to nonparent) can begin.

In recent years much productive use has been made of the "strange situation" method developed by Ainsworth and her colleagues (e.g., Ainsworth & Wittig, 1969) to study attachment. This procedure involves a sequence of segments in which the infant is variously with the parent, with a stranger, with both parent and stranger, or alone. The infant's responses in the various situations are evaluated, including the response to the parent's departure, the stranger's arrival, the parent's rearrival, and so on.

At about a year of age, half or more of the infant population shows a set of behaviors that is labeled "securely attached." They are distressed upon the parent's departure and happy upon the parent's rearrival, they explore the environment when the parent is present, and they show distress in the presence of a stranger, particularly if the parent is absent. Almost a third of the infant population is called "anxious." They are not distressed by the parent's absence or the stranger's presence, they resist being held, and they seem more responsive to the physical environment than to the social. A small fraction of infants are classified as "ambivalent." They exhibit a tantalizing mixture of both positive and negative reactions to the parent as well as to the stranger, seeming on the one hand to want closeness but on the other hand to reject closeness when it is offered.

What causes these differences? Observations of the parent's and infant's behaviors in unstructured situations reveal that parents of securely attached infants tend to provide a good deal of physical contact and are warm, responsive, and playful in their interactions with their infants. Parents of anxious infants tend to show irritation and anger in reaction to the infants and are described as cold, rejecting, or rigid. Parents of ambivalent infants are harder to characterize, but they tend to be less responsive to the infant's behaviors (crying, smiling, etc.). They may be well motivated but seem to lack a sense of timing with respect to their interactions with the infant, as if they do not perceive the infant's behaviors appropriately. (I am indebted to Tomlinson-Keasey, 1985, on whose summary of the attachment syndromes and the parental behavior characteristics this synopsis is based.)

Various factors can adversely affect the development of these parent–infant relationships. First, characteristics that lead parents inherently to be angry or irritated with their infants, or to be rigid or rejecting, are obvious candidates to produce adverse development. Second, various situational factors are also involved. If the parent is absent because of other circumstances (e.g., work) or distracted when present (e.g., by other children), then the infant may not receive the amount or quality of interaction that contributes to strong attachment. Third, we noted earlier that the parent–infant interactions on which attachment is based are dependent on the perceptual abilities of both parent and infant. The parent must be able to perceive the infant's communicative behaviors such as smiling and crying; in turn, the infant must be able to perceive the parent's reciprocal responses. This last point is particularly relevant to the situation of the blind infant, and we will return to it presently.

Another factor that has received more attention in recent years is the infant's "temperament." Thomas and Chess and their colleagues (e.g., Thomas & Chess 1981) have charted variations in the infant's behaviors and conclude that infants may be roughly classified as "easy," "difficult," or "slow to warm up." For our purposes it is not important to delve beyond the labels: each label captures intuitively the characteristics of the infant. It *is* important for our purposes to recognize that these tendencies are evident virtually from birth, that they show a strong thread of developmental consistency, and that they persist relatively independently of the parent's patterns of reactive behaviors.

Attachment in infants with visual impairments

Now let us look at the situation of the infant with a visual impairment. Consider first the condition of visual impairment itself and the difficulties that might occur as a specific result of the lack of vision. We noted that crying, smiling, and clinging are key behaviors of the infant that elicit parental attention. On the face of it, none of these requires vision for its production, although smiling becomes an important vehicle for social interaction (as opposed to a simple elicitor of parental response) early in the first year, and the role of vision in this development is probably very important.

With regard to the parent's response to the behaviors of the infant, the situation is different. The occurrence of parental response is not by itself sufficient to sustain and develop the interaction: the parent's response must also be perceived by the infant. Information reviewed in Chapter 1 makes it clear that auditory and tactual stimuli do not present a problem, but if the parent's responses can be perceived only visually, there is potential for lack of effective interaction.

To the extent that the development of attachment depends on the infant's construction of an integrated concept of the parent as differing from other persons, a potential problem exists in the blind infant's ability to integrate the information about the parent's identity that arrives via the auditory, tactual, and other nonvisual modalities.

The potential problems are not restricted to those that are a direct result of visual loss itself, however; there are potential secondary problems as well. It is well established for visual impairment as well as for other disabilities that a parent's emotional responsiveness to the infant may be tempered by his or her realization of the "imperfection" of the infant. To put it bluntly, a parent who expects a fully normal infant, and receives instead one with a significant handicap, is vulnerable to a range of reactions that may adversely affect the quality of his or her emotional responsiveness to the infant. In addition, situational factors such as the extended hospitalization necessitated by premature birth, the extra efforts needed to adapt to the needs of a handicapped infant (and later, child), the added financial strain, and the disruption of normal family life make this a difficult situation for even the most well-adapted parents.

In short, a number of ancillary pitfalls exist for the parent of a blind infant that can potentially affect the nature and quality of the parent's participation in the social–emotional interaction with the infant. There are all kinds of factors, both directly and indirectly related to the infant's blindness, that we might expect to affect the development of social attachment. Let us see what the literature shows.

The empirical evidence. We start with evidence about the infant's ability to discriminate among different people: this is certainly a key prerequisite to establishing emotional bonds with a select few. One basis for discrimination is voice, and there is evidence that blind infants make such discriminations very early. Fraiberg (1968), Als et al. (1980a), and Freedman et al. (1969) all reported various attentive reactions to the parent's voice at two months, and Fraiberg and Freedman (1964) observed that infant behaviors in response to the parent's voice differed from those to the voices of other people. By four months, there are numerous reports of responses to the parent's voice that seem to imply positive affect (e.g., smiling). In short, there is every evidence that voice discrimination occurs early and that different meanings are associated with different voices.

Touch is another avenue of information on which the infant's discrimination among people can be based. Fraiberg (1968) observed a progressive increase over the two- to five-month period in the blind infant's seeking of tactile contact with the mother. This was accompanied by occasional smiling, indicating that positive affect was involved. Further, Fraiberg reported a progressive increase over the five- to eight-month range in the infant's manual exploration of the parent's face; she suggested a pattern in this activity of increasing familiarity and discrimination. Even more directly, Fraiberg noted distinct evidence of discrimination at seven months: the manual exploration of the parent's face contrasted with the squirming, whimpering, and crying that occurred when the infant was held by a stranger.

Thus the perceptual bases for person discrimination are present in both the auditory and tactile modalities. Furthermore, there is evidence that the blind infant does make use of both sources of information to make such discriminations. We now turn to the question of whether these behaviors serve the process of attachment.

There are several key indicators of attachment we can examine, including selective smiling and vocalization, response to strangers, and response to separation.

Smiling. Smiling has received much attention, and appropriately so, since while it may be important as an indicator of the discriminative and affective behaviors of the infant, it also is an important stimulus in eliciting interactive responses from the parent. Because smiling becomes more selective as other indices of attachment are emerging, the smile is often interpreted as an indicator of the strength of the developing attachment bond.

For sighted infants, smiling is not very discriminative early in the first year: although they give other evidence of being able to tell one person from another, infants tend to smile indiscriminately for the first few months. Toward the middle of the first year, the smile gradually becomes more selective, and in the second half of the year there is a marked decrease in the occurrence of smiling to people other than the objects of attachment.

Fraiberg (1970) suggested that this parallel may not hold for blind infants. Observing that smiling in blind infants is more selective for the parent's voice during the three- to six-month period than it is for sighted infants, she suggested that smiling should not be taken as a comparable indicator of attachment, and that indices such as vocal interactions may be more reliable. Whether or not this reasoning is valid, it is important to remember that smiling is just one of several indicators that show infant attachment. Commenting on the blind infant's smile during the same period (second quarter of the first year), Freedman (1964) argued that the smiles of blind infants are not entirely normal but consist of a series of reflexive movements.

Freedman's approach was very subjective. On the other hand, Rogers and Puchalski (1986) presented objective evidence about the course of smiling during the first year. We will return to other findings of this study later, but for now it is sufficient to note that Rogers and Puchalski observed smiling throughout the age range from 4 to 12 months. It was clear that the infants' smiles were not random or unstimulated occurrences: the vast majority of instances occurred in response to "a familiar environmental sound, a parental vocalization, or a parental auditory/kinesthetic/tactile game" (p. 865).

Response to strangers. The typical pattern is for infants to begin to respond adversely, with crying, withdrawal, or other signs of fear, to strangers during the second six months. We have seen evidence of this in Fraiberg and Freedman's (1964) reports of a blind infant's fear reaction to a stranger's voice and also to being held by a stranger at age seven months. It is interesting that although the general trend in the age range of 4 to 12 months was a progressive increase in the frequency of smiling, Rogers and Puchalski (1986) found a decrease in frequency during the eight- to nine-month period, in comparison to earlier periods. Occurring at the same time that stranger fear normally emerges, this finding may be another indication of the normal unfolding of attachment and its sequelae in blind infants. Indeed, Fraiberg (1970) found that stranger fear, as evidenced by negative reactions such as squirming and crying, appeared in the 7- to 15-month range for 9 of the 10 infants in her sample.

Separation anxiety. Separation anxiety refers to negative affect shown in response to withdrawal of the attachment object, and it typically appears in the second six months along with stranger fear. Despite her observation of signs of stranger fear in the 7- to 15-month range, Fraiberg (1970) saw no instances of separation anxiety within the first year in any of the 10 blind infants. Why should this be?

One possibility is that without vision to unite the perceptual experiences of the parent that come to the blind infant via sound and touch, the blind infant is slower to form a concept of the parent as a continuously existing entity. It is, after all, only after the infant has formed a concept of the parent's existence that the notion of the parent's leaving makes any sense. This is an unsatisfactory hypothesis, however, because the other evidence, including positive attachment behaviors and stranger anxiety, shows that the developmental course of attachment in the blind infant proceeds along a normal path. How could this happen without the infant's having a basic concept of the parent as a person who exists?

I suggest that there may be a viable alternative hypothesis. Even when the attached parent is present, the blind infant does not have a continuous stream of sensory information about the parent's presence. This presence may be signaled by auditory, tactile, or other nonvisual information, but these are discontinuous sources of information. In effect, the blind infant experiences separations almost continuously, at times due to the physical absence of the parent but at other times due to the absence of a continuous information source to denote the parent's presence. It may be that the blind infant is much more accustomed to these periods of effective separation, so that real physical separation, when it does occur and is perceived, is not distressing.

(This does not mean that the blind infant does not have adverse reactions to prolonged periods of separation. The present discussion of separation anxiety as an indicator of attachment is restricted to very brief periods of separation. We will deal with the case of prolonged separation in a later section.)

In short, there are reasons to argue that separation anxiety is not a valid indicator of attachment for the blind infant. Not the least of these reasons is that the other two major indicators, positive attachment behaviors and stranger anxiety, show a normal developmental course of attachment. It seems reasonable to conclude that there is nothing about the absence of visual function that necessarily interferes with the development of social attachment.

That is not to say that attachment occurs normally under all circumstances; in fact, there are not infrequent reports of lack of strong attachment in blind infants, as there are in sighted infants – recall the minority of sighted infants who show the pattern called "anxious attachment." In order to identify the possible pitfalls in the development of attachment, let us examine the process of the development of attachment and its dynamics.

The dynamics of attachment. We noted at the outset that the development of attachment depends not just on the behavior of the infant or the parent, but on patterns of interaction between them. The study by Rogers and Puchalski (1984a) is an excellent example of the empirical study of these patterns. Their sample of infants with visual impairments ranged in age from 4 to 25 months at the beginning of study; about half of the sample had no more than LP, while the other half showed some visually directed reaching. There were no significant differences between the two groups, and thus they can be discussed together. A comparable sample of sighted infants was also tested. The mother and infant were filmed in a series of 10-min play periods, in which the mother was simply instructed to interact normally with the infant. The records were scored for infant behaviors including general affect, vocal quality, smiles, responses to parent-initiated interaction, and self-initiated interaction. The parent behaviors scored were looking at the infant, vocal quality, initiation of interactions, response to infant-initiated interactions, and response to child's distress.

The visually impaired infants showed, on the whole, less positive and more negative vocalization, and more negative affect, than the sighted group. The mothers of the visually impaired infants looked at the infants less and showed less positive vocalization than mothers of the sighted group. Turning to the issue of how mother and infant interacted, Rogers and Puchalski found less response by the visually impaired infants to the mother's initiations and fewer initiations by the infant. On the mother's part, there were fewer positive responses to the infant's initiations than in the case of mothers of sighted infants. But close analysis of a subset of ten of these same infants in the play situation revealed that every instance of an infant's smile was followed by a positive parental response (Rogers & Puchalski, 1984a).

Rogers and Puchalski (1984a) commented not only that the visually impaired infant is less responsive and less demanding of the mother's attention, but that since the mother looks less at the infant, she may miss some of the cues that the infant does send. They conclude: "Both partners in the visually-impaired dyads are deprived. The infants are obviously deprived of all visual information, but also lack affective information from the mothers. The mothers are deprived of positive, responsive cues from their babies that would communicate, 'That's what I like. You're doing a good job, Mom'" (p. 55).

Stone and Chesney (1978) reported a similar study, although based on maternal reports buttressed by observation. They evaluated the occurrence of several kinds of "disturbances" in infant behaviors, such as "tense when handled, unresponsive, not demanding of attention, seldom smiled, seldom vocalized." Three blind infants were evaluated, along with several infants with other difficulties (e.g., Down's). In general, the blind infants showed more normal patterns of interactive behaviors than infants with other problems; the single notable exception was that the blind infants were reported to vocalize infrequently.

These are indeed factors that can potentially interfere with the dynamics of the attachment process and that can lead to insecure or anxious attachment. Few of these, though, are necessitated by the condition of visual impairment. Rogers and Puchalski (1984a) noted several areas in which the infant's behaviors are potentially counterproductive, for example expression of negative affect, infrequent vocalization, and infrequent initiation of interaction. None of these, though, is unique to blindness or necessarily disruptive of the attachment process; the outcome depends on how the parent participates in the interaction. The parent has it in his or her power to respond positively to the infant's initiations and to maintain vocal behavior as well as tactile and auditory communication with the infant – in short, to participate actively in the social–emotional interaction. To the extent of their perceptual limitations, infants respond: the observation by Rogers and Puchalski (1984a) that a high majority of infant smiles were in response to parent-initiated communication is evidence of this.

Of course, if the parent responds to the infant's lesser frequency of vocalization and initiation of interaction by decreasing his or her own interactive behaviors, then there is less for the infant to respond to, less in turn for the parent to respond to, and a vicious cycle may result. This need not be the case, however.

Other characteristics of the parent may also cause him or her to fail to participate effectively in the interaction. There are countless examples in the research and clinical literature of parents who are emotionally depressed by the infant's handicap, who are distracted from the blind infant by other things (such as other children), who are not present in the home as a result of work or other demands, and the like.

Summary. There is no question whether the visually impaired infant is at risk for inadequate attachment. Nevertheless, the risks are not necessary consequences of the infant's visual impairment. They can be avoided in a social-interactive environment in which the infant's interactive behaviors are encouraged and are responded to. Perhaps the most encouraging case study is that reported by Als et al. (1980b), in which the mother created a relationship of "affective reciprocity" with the blind infant by initiating a long-lasting set of highly interactive relationships. The infant was not only securely attached, but was developmentally normal in many areas and even precocious on some cognitive and locomotor indices. Even this mother had to grapple, sometimes more successfully than at others, with her own adverse reactions to the infant's situation and sometimes negative behaviors, but the net result was an exceedingly well-adjusted and developmentally normal infant.

Separation

Infants with visual impairments are sometimes subject to longer-term separation from the parent(s) for a variety of reasons. These include conditions specific to blindness (e.g., retinoblastoma, which often requires periods of hospitalization) as well as conditions that can also occur for sighted infants, such as prolonged parental absence. In these situations, the experience of separation from the parent(s) may be accompanied by other alterations in the infant's experiences.

Several interesting case reports deal with the reactions of blind children to separations. Colonna (1968) described in detail the case of a retinoblastoma child who was hospitalized for surgery several times during the period from 14 months to five years, in addition to frequent brief periods of hospitalization for radiation treatment. The situation was further complicated by the birth of a sister when the subject was about three. The subject showed various psychiatric difficulties, characterized generally by the fear of being rejected or discarded. Perhaps the most significant aspect of the case was the extent to which the mother's reactions to the developing situation exacerbated the child's problem. The mother became depressed at the child's visual problems, and she changed her response from her previous warmth and acceptance of a "normal" child to a relative rejection of a "damaged" child who had, at 14 months, lost one eye by operation. Thus the parents' response may be critical. The child is faced with much difficulty even given the best of emotional interactions with others. The progression may become worse when negative parental response to the discovery of the visual problem is followed by hospitalization or other separation, since these factors may add to the child's perception of rejection. The spiral may then continue when the parent, perhaps already feeling guilty, perceives the child's response to the rejection.

Fraiberg (1968) described the case of a 17-month-old infant that illustrates that even a short separation, unaccompanied by the trauma of an operation, may lead to problems. The mother was away for only three days; shortly after she returned, the child began to regress in several areas. He rejected his food, engaged in screaming fits lasting for hours, and craved physical contact with his mother. In another case, the mother was not physically separated from the child but was effectively absent for periods of time because of severe depression. Before the onset of maternal depression, the child's developmental progress was quite adequate, but at 13 months, when the mother began to fail to control her withdrawal and depression, he showed an abrupt change in developmental progress, losing his social responsiveness and cognitive progress, and showing increased rocking behavior.

Separation occurs for various reasons, many of them unavoidable. Children have to be hospitalized, parents have to leave the home for periods of time, and emotional withdrawal by the parent may occur for various reasons. These situations have potentially serious consequences for the social development of children, whether they can see or not. But as Fraiberg (1972) pointed out, separation may have more serious implications for the blind than for the sighted child, since "(1) We have a child whose own adaptive capacity to sustain loss is diminished by blindness. (2) We have a mother who must deal with a developmental crisis in her blind child's experience without anything in her own experience which can help her understand the extraordinary significance of loss to a blind child" (p. 359).

Communication in infancy

The infant communicates from the moment of birth, if by communication we mean that the infant produces signals that may be perceived by and elicit a response from other people. To be sure, these signals initially are neither intentional nor language-like, but they need not be either in order to communicate. The neonate's initial cry means something to the delivering physician; subsequently the cry means other things in other situations to other people. Other vocal communication develops: the infant's early babbling is not communication in the strict sense, but its refinement into a set of specific phonemes and then into the earliest words signals the beginning of verbal communication, the development of which continues well beyond the infancy period. Nor is communication just oral; body movements and facial expressions are part of the infant's communicative equipment, even though they may not be as intentionally communicative as verbal language.

These are examples of the infant's production of communicative signals. The infant's reception of communication is equally important, including the gradual acquisition of the ability to understand spoken language as well as the perception of body and facial expressions.

Nor should we neglect tactual communication, either in its productive or its receptive modes. On the productive side, the clench of the infant's fingers in her father's hair can be just as meaningful as any verbal production; on the receptive side, the soothing qualities of rocking and vocalization are known to every parent.

All of these seemingly disparate examples have in common the fact that they are forms of productive or receptive communication. It is too simple to think about communication just in terms of spoken language produced by the diaphragm, lungs, vocal cords, and mouth and heard by the auditory system. In order to understand the development of communication, we must consider, in addition, the gestures and the expressions of the body, the face, and the hands. Human communication includes every means that humans use to exchange information.

Infants with visual impairments

To the extent that any of this depends on vision, we might expect the visually impaired infant to be forced to find alternative modes of adaptation. Communication is a developmental continuum that begins in infancy and proceeds well into childhood, and there is no dividing line to tell us where to stop the story in this general treatment of infancy and where to take it up in other sections. In the present section, we take the infant through the establishment of various forms of preverbal communication.

For the sighted infant, a variety of behaviors establish a communicative relationship with others: eye contact and smiling are good examples. These behaviors do not serve so much to convey specific information as to establish and maintain a communicative link. In infancy, eye contact probably is not specific in its communicative intent, but it still serves to engage the parent in an interaction, if in no other way than to let the parent know that the infant is attending. In the beginning, smiling no doubt plays a similar role: it is not until after several months that positive affect becomes involved on the part of the infant.

In order to be effective, these behaviors must be perceived by the parent. If the parent is not looking, then neither eye contact nor smiling serves the purpose of establishing the communicative link.

Other behaviors require, in addition, parental discrimination of the infant's behavior. For example, a relaxed and compliant body posture when the infant is held denotes comfort and security, whereas stiffening and awkward posture denotes the opposite; but this communication is not effective unless the parent can discriminate between the infant's behaviors.

Eye contact. It is known (e.g., Klaus & Kennell, 1976) that parent–infant eye contact is an important event in the establishment of very early bonding by the parent. It is not surprising, then, that the lack of eye contact by blind neonates and infants can have a depressive impact on the parent's state: it can connote "no interest" or "not friendly" (Fraiberg, 1977, p. 97) and can add an emotional burden to the parent's existing concern about the blind infant's normalcy. The fragile state of the parent's emotions at this point must be recognized: it is critical for parents to have the guidance that they may need to keep the lack of eye contact, among other phenomena, in perspective.

Body posture. It seems logical to expect that neither the infant's ability to communicate via body posture nor the parent's ability to perceive such communication should be affected by the presence or absence of visual function. Indeed, Rowland (1984) noted that her sample of five infants showed a variety of postural behaviors (e.g., throwing the body back, waving the arms) that were appropriately interpreted as being expressive of such affective states as aversion and excitement.

Still, there is a danger. We have mentioned the issue of temperament in an earlier section, and individual differences in infant temperament are expressed in body posture. Quite aside from their momentary level of comfort or discomfort, some infants are more relaxed and posturally compliant than others. The danger is that the parent of a blind infant will interpret postural noncompliance as an indication of rejection and will, accordingly, tend to withdraw emotionally from the relationship. The dynamics of this situation are no different for the parent of a sighted infant, but the parent of a blind infant may be inclined to couple this with the infant's visual condition and thus to assume that it is hopeless to continue to try to engage the infant in an emotional bond. This inclination may be especially strong in the case of prematurity, where the necessity of extended hospitalization tends to exacerbate the difficulties of early parent–infant bonding. Clearly, wise guidance is necessary to combat this possibility.

Smiling. We have already discussed the infant's smiling as a social–emotional response in the context of attachment, and we discussed not only the infant's smile but the parent's perception of and response to it as an important facilitator of the parent–infant bond. Speaking of blind infants, Fraiberg noted that up to midyear and beyond, the sound of the parent's voice is only a fragile elicitor of infant smiling, and that a more effective elicitor is "gross tactile or kinesthetic stimulation, noticeably greater than that observed among parents of sighted babies" (Fraiberg, 1977, p. 99). If the parent of a blind infant is unaware of this different "perceptual ecology" of elicitors of the infant's smiling, then the parent may be inclined, as in the case of postural communication, to conclude that the infant is rejecting of the parent's social–emotional overtures and may tend to withdraw from the relationship as a result.

Nevertheless, the data of Rogers and Puchalski (1984a) suggest that the smile can be an effective mediator of social interaction between parent and infant. As noted earlier, not only did infants' smiles tend strongly to occur in response to instances of parental vocalization or tactile contact, but the infants' smiles were invariably followed by positive parental interactive behavior. The observations of Rogers and Puchalski were, to be sure, taken from 10-min play segments during which the parent could have been expected to be particularly responsive to the infant's signals; observations taken during any random 10 min of the day might show a less interactive pattern. Nonetheless, the lesson should not be lost: these data show that the smiles of blind infants can serve as the basis for social behavior in the parent–infant dyad.

Fraiberg (1977) also expressed concern with facial signs other than the smile. With reference to several examples of parental interpretation of infant expressions (attention, longing, quizzical, doubting, boredom), Fraiberg argued that the blind infant's repertoire of facial expression is impoverished. Although the tendency for the parent of a blind infant may be to infer unresponsiveness from this pattern of relatively un-differentiated behavior, Fraiberg argued that this is a mistaken interpre-tation, and that the blind infant in fact communicates many of these characteristics manually. However, there has been no systematic attempt to evaluate the ability of parents to "read" the facial expressions of their blind infants in the early months of life.

Manual signs. Based on intensive analysis of film records of blind infants, Fraiberg concluded that the blind infant's hand activity shows an expres-sive language, beginning in the second month, and becoming increas-ingly differentiated over the ensuing months. "The hands, not engaged, seek engagement with the mother's hand or her body. The hands linger, lightly finger or grasp, withdraw, return. Sometimes we catch on film a kind of ballet in which the baby's hands seek and find the mother's hand, and the mother's hand sustains or responds to the signal" (Fraiberg, 1974, p. 228). Fraiberg did not suggest that these hand "signals" do not occur in sighted infants, but that for blind infants, this means of potential communication is far more important because of the unavailability of the nonverbal communicative system based on eye contact and facial expressions.

This form of communication has not been studied in detail as to its developmental course, the degree of its differentiation, the infant's intent, or for that matter the part that the parent plays not only in understanding it but in actively participating in the exchange. The individual differences are undoubtedly immense. This is not to say that it is unimportant, however; it is essential for the parent to explore and develop every means of communication with the blind infant, including this hand language. This is an excellent illustration of the need for the exploitation of alternative paths of adaptation, in this case to the need for communication.

Prelinguistic vocalization. Before they can talk, infants babble. That is, they produce sounds using the vocal apparatus that sound vaguely like language but that do not make any sense. These sounds show a gradual refinement during the first year: initially the infant produces a set of sounds that is not restricted to the phonemes of the surrounding language environment; sounds that are not heard there, however, gradually drop out. This refinement is a consequence of maturation of the vocal apparatus and of perceptual learning. It involves a process of matching two sets of sounds, those the infant hears from other people and those the infant perceives in his or her own vocal production. Although the issue has not been systematically studied, the available evidence (Burlingham, 1961; Haspiel, 1965; Maxfield & Fjeld, 1942; Norris et al., 1957; Wilson & Halverson, 1947) suggests on balance that there are no notable differences between blind and sighted infants in the development and refinement of babbling. This should not be surprising: the perceptual apparatus involved is largely auditory rather than visual.

Prelinguistic vocalization is more than just a practice period for the eventual production of language, however. It is potentially another means of establishing a communicative link with other people. Babbling is a stimulus for parental response, and as a response by the infant to parental stimulation, it can further serve the development of social interaction and communication. It is this function of prelinguistic vocalization to which we now turn.

We noted earlier that Rogers and Puchalski (1984a) found that the frequency of vocalization in blind infants was less than in a comparison sample of sighted infants, and that the vocalizations of blind infants were more often negative and less often positive in tone than those of sighted infants. Rowland (1984) evaluated five children, three of whom ranged in age from 11 to 16 months at the beginning of study. All three were developmentally delayed on a variety of criteria, although there were substantial individual differences. Rowland recorded the occurrence of several varieties of potentially communicative behaviors, including gestures, smiling, and vocalization. In seeming contrast to the results of Rogers and Puchalski (1984a), Rowland's data from a smaller number of infants indicated that neither the vocalization rates nor the facial expression rates of the infants were low, with vocalization occurring in 24% of the recording intervals. Neither were the mother's vocalizations low: the observed rate was 40% of the intervals, comparable to the 43% rate reported by Ling and Ling (1976) for sighted infants.

Of particular interest to the current section, Rowland assessed the contingencies linking infant and parent behaviors. The infants were studied for six months. The probability that an infant's vocalization followed a maternal behavior was relatively low: "A mother talking to her infant or rattling a toy did not often prompt the infant into any observable change in behavior . . . the infants' vocalizations were less likely than were their smiles or gestures to increase after their mothers vocalized" (1984, p. 301). The mothers, on the other hand, were more likely to respond to the infant's communicative behaviors. Maternal responses to infant smiles tended to occur more reliably than to the infant's gestures or vocalizations, but mothers tended to respond to infant vocalizations more by a touch or a nonvocal sound than by speech.

Furthermore, Rowland found that mothers produced more noncontingent vocalization. That is, they tended to talk to the infant frequently, but not in response to the infant's vocalizations. Rowland noted that "this [maternal] behavior was a natural consequence of their desire to prod their infants to respond. The result, however, was that a natural conversational pattern was impossible" (p. 301). Thus, the picture we see from Rowland's small sample is of a relative lack of infant vocalization in response to the mother's communicative signals. Moreover, although a great deal of maternal vocalization occurred, it tended to be unrelated to the infant's pattern of vocalization and perhaps even counterproductive to the goal of encouraging infant vocalization in the interactive context.

Dote-Kwan (1991) found more positive relationships in her study of 18 preschoolers and their mothers. Based on observations of the mother–child dyad in naturally occurring interactions, she found that the mothers seldom ignored the child's verbalizations. The maternal responses to the child's communications were characterized by acknowledgment and rephrasing or repeating. Furthermore, there was some evidence of a relationship between frequency of maternal response and various developmental indices of the child.

It is likely that the apparent discrepancy between Rowland's and Dote-Kwan's results about maternal responsiveness is related to the younger age of the Rowland sample. In addition, Dote-Kwan suggested that the mothers in her sample may have been positively affected by their participation in home- or center-based intervention programs.

Summary

There are various vehicles for the communicative link necessary for later developments; these are mediated by the vocal, tactual, and visual modalities. The specific use of one or another of these vehicles is probably less important than the fact that a communicative link is established. Urwin's (1978) evidence, in fact, shows that different infant–parent relationships can serve the purpose. Urwin studied two infants (one totally blind, one with partial vision in one eye) from the preverbal through the one-word stage. During this period, each mother was sensitive to variations in her infant's facial expressions and body movements, and each found ways to communicate in response. Once they discovered particular acts that elicited the infant's response, both used them repeatedly, creating routines for social interaction. As vocal communication began to develop, in each case it was clearly based on the idiosyncratic form of preverbal communication that had been established.

This brings us to consideration of the development of communication via verbal language.

9

Language as a social skill

In Chapter 5 we considered the development of language in relation to the child's emerging cognitive capabilities. In the present chapter, we turn to the developing role of language as a means of social communication.

The bridge from preverbal to verbal communication

Although spoken language may be defined as beginning with the utterance of the first word that carries meaning for the infant, this is an arbitrary milestone. In fact, there is a good deal of continuity from prelanguage communication to language proper, particularly in what we may call the communicative channel. Before the onset of spoken language, parent–infant communication takes place via a variety of activities we have already discussed, including eye contact, smiling, touching, and nonverbal sound. Later, communication may still occur via these nonverbal channels, at the same time that language proper emerges as another channel through which parent–infant communication can take place. In suggesting a framework for the development of early language in multi-handicapped children, Rogow (1980) emphasized the importance of the establishment of a prelanguage "signal system": this is no less important for blind infants.

Wills (1979) noted that in the period of prelanguage vocalization infants "vocalize to get an *unspecific* response from the mother – the mother vocalizes back, touches a cheek, and so on" (p. 87). But language must become capable of eliciting *specific* responses from parents and others. Wills noted that this transition is difficult for some blind infants: she suggested that they are slow to understand that "they could use their

mothers as agents" (p. 86). Vision is certainly important for such understanding to develop: the sighted infant can see distal objects, point to
them, and say something that elicits parental response, such as fetching
the object. For the blind infant, there is simply less effective mutually
shared perception of the world (the "shared frame of reference" mentioned by Urwin, 1983), and thus there is less grist for the mill and
consequently slower development of the understanding of the ability to
act on the environment via language. As Wills put it, "Blind children
appear to take longer to understand that they can *act on the environment*
by the use of words alone" (p. 86).

Thus, the blind infant may be at risk in the establishment and refinement of this preverbal communication system, since such key behaviors
as smiling and eye contact involve vision on one side of the dyad or both.
(We reviewed the evidence on these preverbal activities earlier.) Urwin
(1983) argued that in its late stages, this preverbal communication system
comes to involve more refined activities that require vision for their full
use, such as gestures, mutual attention to external events, and a shared
frame of reference. Since the development of language itself will depend
on this channel of shared communication, there is reason to expect that
blind infants may encounter difficulties at the outset of language
acquisition.

Urwin (1978) showed that motivated parents of blind infants can
establish effective channels of prelanguage communication. The two infants had different characteristics and activity patterns, and in fact the
system of specific communicative activities that each infant–parent dyad
developed was highly idiosyncratic, not only in the events around which
communicative activity occurred but also in the nature of the communicative behaviors themselves. Jerry, although totally blind, showed
relatively rapid development of prelocomotor behaviors such as rolling
over and crawling. Many of the parent's communicative interactions were
built around these behaviors: for example, the mother said "bye-bye" in
reaction to Jerry's movements away from her and "hello" in reaction to
his turning back toward her. Steven had some limited vision, and his
mother made use of this channel of information to gain his attention and
to initiate interactive behaviors.

Furthermore, Urwin gave convincing examples of how the early language emerged from, and as a function of, the preverbal communication
system. For example, during the first six months, Steven's mother used

the expression "arr" to gain his attention and to calm his distress. By 11 months of age, Steven produced this sound himself and continued to use it well into the second year to initiate interactions. Early in the second year, Jerry used the now-familiar "hello" and "bye-bye" to open communicative interactions and to end such encounters. Thus, in the earliest stages of language proper, both children used expressions that the parent had frequently employed in the prelanguage interactive play. Summarizing, Urwin (1983) stated that "each of the children's early words used in communication were initially accompanied by pre-existing vocal and / or action procedures which conveyed particular communicative intentions" (p. 149).

Some investigators (e.g., Andersen et al., 1984; Wills, 1979) have noted a seemingly high incidence of echolalia in blind infants at this transitional period. Wills, however, added that many blind infants who show such imitative or "parroting" verbalizations go on to develop effective language. The examples offered above (e.g., the children's early production of "bye-bye" or "arr") from Urwin's (1978) work are also instances of simple imitation. Urwin noted that "ritualized forms of vocal interchange set apart from ongoing actions remained a dominant feature of their interactive repertoire" (p. 99). Even when his mother was in another room, Jerry and his mother carried on extended "conversations" involving these ritualized exchanges, lasting up to 15 min at a time. The exchanges may not have referred to shared experience of events in the world; nevertheless, it maintained the social interaction even from a distance.

In the extreme, there is the possibility that maintaining this ritualized and imitative form of vocal exchange, as valuable as it may be for sustaining the early vehicle of social interaction, might actually interfere with the development of content-based language. Jerry's parents avoided this by requiring progressively more explicit communication from him, gradually requiring a more differentiated response.

Although some aspects of the shared signal system are based on tactual and auditory information, and although auditory and / or tactual interchange may substitute for some visual aspects of it, the absence of vision may still present a significant impediment to the development of this shared communication. In particular, the role of vision in the perception of distal objects is key, as is vision as a way of monitoring another person's attention. Consider the advantage conveyed by the parent's vision of what the infant is looking at, or vice versa, or of being able to point at a distal object to identify it as an object of shared attention.

For the infant to develop spoken language as a means of social communication, there must be a body of experience shared by the infant and the parents, or by others who provide the infant's language environment. To the extent that the prelanguage signal system is restricted, and specifically so in its ability to make reference to or draw attention to distal events, the body of experience shared by infant and parent is also restricted. It makes sense to suppose that the blind infant's earliest language may be different from that of the sighted infant as a consequence of the lack of visual components of the prelanguage signal system and the resulting curtailment of the body of shared experience.

Perspective. Infants and their parents develop a variety of ways of establishing and maintaining communication, from vocal and other sounds to touching, and to visually based means such as eye contact and mutual attention to objects and events. Many of these forms of communication are available to the blind infant and his or her parent, but shared attention to objects and events may be much more limited and difficult without vision. Consequently, the experience that the blind infant shares with others at the end of the first year may be restricted. Since the development of communicative language is based on shared experience, the blind infant's early language may be different from that of sighted infants, and indeed there is evidence that this is so.

The question remains, To what extent is this scenario unique to – and an unavoidable consequence of – infant blindness?

A constrained body of shared experience is certainly not caused only by blindness. An infant that for *any* reason is restricted in interaction with others is at risk for this kind of constraint, and consequently for the differences in early language that may result. Although the nature of shared experiential constraint may vary depending on whether it results from lack of vision, parental neglect, or some other factor that restricts the degree of involvement by the parent with the infant, all of these factors can underlie variations in early language development. Thus, we should not consider this scenario unique to blindness.

Nevertheless, is the scenario avoidable under conditions of infant blindness? It is certainly not entirely avoidable, since other sensory modalities can provide only limited distal information about the environment upon which part of the signal system depends. Insightful use of tactual and auditory experience can help. The parent's goal should not simply be to increase the amount of the infant's tactual and auditory experience, but to enlarge the experience that the infant shares with the parent. Full exploitation of both of these sensory modalities undoubtedly still results in a situation different from the natural way in which vision can mediate the development of a shared body of experience, but it can go a long way toward avoiding serious problems.

Urwin's (1978) two case studies give us a valuable illustration of the extent to which inspired and attentive parents can establish alternative bases for communication with their blind infants:

In establishing interchange with their babies, the parents capitalized on potential substitutability of communicative channels. . . . As the babies showed increasingly evident control, the parents exploited alternatives and encouraged their children to take more active roles . . . throughout the process is dialectical. While the parent must adjust her mode of participation to developmental change in the baby, the child takes over and transforms procedures first consolidated in social interaction to extend them to a wider range of situations. (p. 107)

In short, the insightful parent can do much to avoid the potentially adverse consequences of the infant's lack of vision in the area of the prelanguage signal system.

The social context for language development

In Chapter 5, we discussed evidence about the child's achievement of the various milestones of productive language such as the age of first word use, two-word utterances, and 50-word vocabularies. While this approach gives a good description of language acquisition, it does not necessarily tell us about the functional role that language plays for the child. Nor does it tell us whether the child can understand the language of others, or whether the child's utterances are appropriate to the linguistic environment – in short, whether the child's language is serving him or her in an adaptive capacity for the purpose of functional social communication.

To address these questions, we need research on the dynamics of the development of language as a vehicle of communication, as a means of participating in the social world. This is a distinct issue that generates a discrete set of questions and requires a different set of methodologies.

Thus, we turn to the development of language as a form of social communication.

Earlier work

Although detailed study of the sociolinguistic context of blind children is a phenomenon primarily of the past decade, there are hints in the earlier literature that point to the importance of this factor.

For example, Keeler (1958) discussed the cases of several blind children for whom development of social communication was seriously retarded. Although there were other developmental complications as well, Keeler particularly noted the impoverished language environment provided by the mother in accounting for language delays.

In her educational program, Fraiberg (1977) encouraged vocal interchange between parent and child in order to "maximize the language environment," pointing out that in some of her cases, the idea of talking to the baby was alien to the parenting style of the parents. As Fraiberg pointed out, even sighted children would have difficulty with language development in such an environment!

More recent work

More detailed and systematic study of the social context of the blind child's language began in the early 1980s. Although her study was largely of the prelinguistic period, Rowland's (1983, 1984) results are worth noting here because of their implications for the development of the social interactive context. In essence, Rowland found that the mothers of blind infants were neither more nor less inclined to vocalize to their infants than mothers of comparable sighted infants. On the question of the contingency between the infant's and the mother's vocalizations, however, Rowland found that mothers of blind infants were somewhat less likely to respond to their infants' vocalizations than to their smiles. Reporting more closely on individual cases, Rowland (1983) noted that the two infants (ages 17 and 22 months) who showed the least adequate language development had mothers who were least responsive to their vocalizations. Further, as noted earlier, some of the mothers talked a great deal to their infants. These well-meaning mothers, responding naturally, probably decreased their infants' learning about the contingencies of interactive vocalization. More is not necessarily better!

Urwin (1983) described three infants whose overall development, including that of language, was generally very good. The parents were described as attentive, concerned, and highly involved with their infants, creating many opportunities for social interaction and exploration of the environment. Specifically with respect to the linguistic environment, one mother (Suzanne's) created a speech context much like that provided by mothers when they speak with their sighted children. In particular, she recognized the danger that dialogue can flag without the communicative "carrier" function that shared visual contact often serves, and she incorporated into her own usage verbal constructions that served to sustain the dialogue.

All three mothers tended to refer more to the child and less to external objects do mothers of sighted children. It would be surprising if this were not so, since the shared experiential base is restricted without vision. As a consequence, though, it is not surprising to see the evidence for more self-referential and less object-referential word usage by blind children. It seems likely that if the parents of a sighted child were to provide the same kind of child-centered language environment, that child would also tend to use self-referential language. In short, it may be argued that it is the language environment, not the blindness, that creates the characteristics of blind children's usage, at least in the early vocabulary stages.

Kekelis and Andersen (1984) have provided the best close analysis of the language environment provided by the mothers of blind children. Only a synopsis of the main findings is presented here; the full account is rich and detailed. There were four visually impaired children, two with sufficient vision to mediate reaching, one with LP, and one totally blind. The primary data were presented for the age range 16 to 22 months, but data were available for some children up to 33 months. Two sighted cases were analyzed as well. The families were part of a larger project that provided an ongoing intervention program, so that the sample is relatively advantaged in that respect.

Parent–child interactions were video- and audiotaped, and detailed analyses were made of the parents' language behavior with the child (hereafter called the child's language *input*, to distinguish it from the child's own language *output*). Four categories were coded: sentence types (declaratives, imperatives, etc.); speech acts (description, statement, request for action, etc.); labels (i.e., names) versus attributions (i.e., qualities); and the focus of the topic (child-centered, environment-related, etc.). Besides coding the language input in this way, Kekelis and Andersen also examined the social-interactive context for particular utterances – for example, what was going on in the social interaction that preceded a verbal exchange, and what was the consequence of the exchange?

The distribution of sentence types in the input to children with visual impairments was not dramatically different from that of sighted children, although there was a greater frequency of imperatives in the visually impaired children's input, particularly in the 19- to 22-month period. (Landau & Gleitman, 1985, similarly noted a high proportion of imperatives.) This difference was produced by the failure of imperatives to decrease with age in the language input of visually impaired children as they did in the input of sighted children. There were also not dramatic differences in speech acts between the inputs of visually impaired and sighted children, although requests for action were somewhat more frequent in the input to the visually impaired children.

Labels and attributes occurred with roughly equal frequency in the input to sighted children through age two, but in the visually impaired children's input, labels were much more prevalent than attributes. By age three, the input to the visually impaired child was composed of about equal proportions of labels and attributes, thus matching the input to sighted children at earlier ages; by age three, however, the input to sighted children consisted of only about one-sixth labels. This is a major difference in the language experience of visually impaired and sighted children, and with a dramatically lower prevalence of attributes in their language input, it is not surprising to find evidence that the vocabulary usage of visually impaired children tends to be more specific to particular instances (e.g., greater prevalence of specific than general nominals; Mulford, 1988) and less extended to related references (Andersen et al., 1984). Again, the question arises whether the differences that occur in the visually impaired child's language are a result of absence of vision or variations in the language input to the child.

Besides these differences in the child's language input, Kekelis and Andersen (1984) also noted a number of interesting differences in the nature of the discourse between child and parent. Generally, topics of discussion were more frequently initiated by the mother than by the child, and this tendency was somewhat stronger in the case of visually impaired than sighted children. Furthermore, the topics themselves were more likely to be child-related in the input to the visually impaired child and less likely to be environment-related, and this balance did not shift in the direction of environment-related topics with increasing age, as it did for sighted children.

All in all, the data of Kekelis and Andersen do not support the idea that the language environment of the visually impaired child is completely different from that of the sighted child, but there are a number of areas where significant differences do occur. Why should this be? Kekelis and Andersen (1984) provided an insightful discussion of the dynamics that lead to such differences. In large part, these dynamics are exactly what one might expect from a parent who is concerned about the child, who is motivated to provide a lively language environment to foster the child's language development, and who recognizes the limitations that the child's visual loss creates. However, as well-motivated as such parents may be, the product of their concern – the language input to the child – may be logical and reasonable, but it may not be the environment to best facilitate the child's acquisition of language. For example, providing a high frequency of labels is a natural tendency for the parent of a visually impaired child, who recognizes that the child needs to know the names of things before being able to attach attributes to them; but this is exactly the sort of input that will not facilitate the child's acquisition of understanding of object attributes and that leads to the kinds of usage limitations summarized by Mulford (1988) and others.

Workman (1986) extended consideration of the child's language environment to the preschool setting. The language behaviors of four-year-old boys – three blind and one with minimal sight in only one eye – and their teachers were studied with an eye to the forms of teacher communication that might foster or hinder the social interaction of the children with their sighted preschool peers. It was clear from videotaped records of interactions that encouragement by the teacher of interactions between visually impaired and sighted children were facilitative both in initiating and in sustaining such interactions.

Perspective. Language development in sighted children has been studied increasingly as a form of social interaction rather than just a mode of expression on the part of the child, and this change in focus has resulted in consideration of the nature of the language environment to which the child is exposed. The result has been a much fuller and richer understanding of language development. This same reorientation of focus has begun to occur in the study of the language development of children with visual impairments, and consequently there has been a significant shift in our understanding of the problems that the child encounters. This research is as yet limited, however. In part because of the level of detail required in analysis of the language behavior of the child as well as of the language partner, and in part because of the small numbers of visually impaired children available for study, the existing data base is quite limited. The most extensive study available is that of Kekelis and Andersen (1984), and it includes only four visually impaired children. The smaller the sample is, the greater the likelihood is that the results will not be representative of the population as a whole. Indeed, Kekelis and Andersen noted that because of the intervention program accompanying their larger study, their children were probably relatively advantaged in their language environment. Thus, these children are probably not representative; that does not detract from the value of the study, however. There is no reason to think that the dynamics of language interaction that Kekelis and Andersen found would not be found in other cases even if the specifics of the language content are different. The caution lies not in characterizing the nature of the dynamics, but in generalizing the specifics to the larger population.

For a full understanding of the range of language development in social-interactive context, we must have additional studies of children who are exposed to a variety of different language environments, with the same kind of careful analysis that Kekelis and Andersen have modeled. Furthermore, such studies will no doubt continue to use small samples. This is not inherently bad; indeed, it is probably good, since the level of analysis can be more penetrating with smaller samples. Nevertheless, what is needed, in addition, is integration across studies of the sort that Mulford (1988) has exemplified.

Many of the characteristics of the language development of visually impaired children that differ from those of sighted children can be attributed to the sociolinguistic environment that the children are exposed to. Let us recall two examples from the preceding material. First, Rowland (1983) found some mothers to provide an "almost constant vocal stimulation" to their children, but at the same time to be relatively unresponsive in a contingent way to their child's vocalizations. Second, Urwin (1983) reported the mothers of blind children to use more self-referential and less object-referential language in talking with their children. In both of these examples, it may be argued that such parental language behavior would stimulate different language behavior on the part of children, whether visually impaired or not.

The question is not whether visually impaired children show these resulting characteristics in their own language; the evidence is that they do. The question is whether these differences are a necessary consequence of visual impairment or a result of the kind of parental language behavior that tends to be used with visually impaired children. The extent of individual differences found even in small samples of visually impaired children suggests that there are indeed other factors besides the visual loss that are implicated in language development, and that visual loss itself is not a direct causal factor. In short, it seems likely that it is primarily the social language environment, not the visual impairment, that produces the characteristics of visually impaired children's language usage.

Effectiveness of communication

In accordance with our orientation to language as a functional vehicle for social interaction, it is reasonable to inquire about the child's effectiveness in using language to engage other people.

Referential abilities

One of the abilities required for communicative effectiveness is referential ability. This is the ability to identify for the listener what the referent of conversation is – what is being talked about. According to Mulford (1983), referential ability involves several components including assessing whether the listener is paying attention to the child, assessing the listener's focus of attention, and directing the listener's attention to appropriate external referents. Without these abilities, it is likely that there will not be a shared focus of communication, and that communication will therefore fail.

Mulford illustrated the exercise of these abilities in three five- and six-year-old congenitally blind boys who showed generally successful progress in all developmental areas. It sometimes occurs that the individual with a visual impairment does not know whether an intended listener is even physically present. It was clear that Mulford's children sometimes failed in this, but they also sometimes used creative ways to ascertain this fact. When the intended listener clearly is present but with his or her attention otherwise directed, such means may include verbal interjection, nonverbal sounds (e.g., the fake cough), or physical contact. Drawing mutual attention to a referent is also critical. While pointing to other visually directed and visually perceived gestures sometimes plays this role for sighted children, some of the same effect can be achieved by various devices such as verbal reference based on other than visual cues. In the case of nonperceivable referents, such as abstract concepts, of course, the blind child may be on a more even footing.

Mulford (1983) did not attempt a quantitative evaluation of the blind child's behaviors in these various areas, but rather an outline of what the issues are that should be examined. Generally speaking, she concluded that these five- and six-year-old children had established several kinds of verbal as well as nonverbal devices for accomplishing the various components of referential communication. In addition, though, the listening adult's participation was critical in effectively inferring the intent of the child's interactive verbal and nonverbal behaviors. The listener to a sighted child is similarly obligated to engage in inference, of course, but the burden may rest more heavily on the listener to a blind child.

Shifting perspectives

Andersen et al. (1984) discussed various characteristics of children's verbal role play that bear on the issue of communicative effectiveness. It was apparent from their data that one of the impediments to effective role play is the child's understanding of shifting perspectives in defining meaning. We have discussed this issue earlier in relation to pronoun use, but it extends to other referential terms such as *this* and *that*, which may take different meanings depending on the relationship of the speaker and listener to the referent. Andersen et al. invoked the notion of cognitive reversibility to explain the visually impaired children's difficulties. Reversibility refers to the child's understanding of both the self-referential aspect (when used by others) and the other-referential aspect of the same word when used by the child. More fundamentally, Andersen et al. argued that the child who has not yet achieved mature use is handicapped by the lack of perspective-taking ability – the failure to recognize that in general, other people have different perspectives in their perception of the world's events, and that in particular, these different perspectives have different situational expressions in language.

Matsuda (1984) reported a study that was designed specifically to evaluate the blind child's ability to perceive the communication-relevant characteristics of the listener and to structure his or her communications to take such characteristics into account in speech acts. Generally, the ability to accomplish these things improves with age, with dramatic improvement in the elementary school years.

The subjects ranged in age from 5 to 12 years. All had lost sight before the onset of language. Each child was presented with a series of 12 messages that varied in the communicative characteristics of the speaker. The child was asked to describe the speaker; these descriptions were analyzed for evidence of comprehension of the communication-relevant characteristics of the speaker. In a second task, the child heard the same set of 12 messages, this time preceded by a description of the context in which the message occurred. The child was asked to make a response to the speaker; the response was evaluated with respect to its appropriateness to the communication-relevant characteristics of the speaker.

The children's detection of communication-relevant characteristics of the speaker improved over the 5- to 12-year age range, parallel to the development of sighted children in the same task. Thus, blind children evidently improve their ability to perceive characteristics of speakers over the elementary school years, and might be expected to show an age-related increase in their ability to tailor their own responses to those speakers' perceived characteristics. This ability was assessed by means of the "construction of messages" task. Contrary to expectation, the children did not show an age-related improvement in their ability to adapt their responses to the speakers' characteristics. (However, the sighted children studied for comparison also did not show such an age-related increase.)

This study illustrates the inherent flaws of the comparative approach. In previous work (Delia & Clark, 1977), sighted children performing with vision did show an improvement over the same age range in the ability to adapt their own responses to the perceived communication-relevant characteristics of the speaker. In contrast, Matsuda (1984) found no such age-related improvement in sighted children. In this study, though, the sighted children responded to tape-recorded messages without benefit of vision. The vision-present and vision-absent performance of the sighted children was clearly different, and although the vision-absent condition is obviously more comparable to the situation of the child without vision, it also does not represent a typical language-interactive situation for sighted children.

Still, considering just the blind children of Matsuda (1984), it is noteworthy that there was a developmental discrepancy between the children's ability to perceive the communication-relevant characteristics of the speaker and their ability to adapt their own responses to those characteristics.

Summary. Summarizing several sources of evidence, McGurk (1983) concluded that

although he takes longer to traverse the route, the visually-impaired child follows the same path to communicative competence as his sighted peers, and the level of competence he eventually achieves is well within the range of reaction we accept as normality. Visual impairment, rather than having specific, determinate effects, thus seems to have general moderating or modulating influences upon the development of communicative competence. (p. 110)

McGurk further concluded that the scanty evidence about differences between blind and partially sighted children is inconclusive.

Articulation and sound quality

Part of the effectiveness of language in social interaction lies in the child's ability to articulate speech so that it is comprehensible, without putting undue strain on the listener that may detract from attention to the speaker's content. Several studies over the decades have treated speech articulation and related questions of sound quality, and overall the picture is a mixed one.

Brieland (1950) studied children from schools for the blind, ranging in age from 12 to 18 years. Each child was given a story to memorize, and then production of the story was filmed and tape-recorded. Speech teachers rated the performance on several factors, including vocal variety, pitch modulation, use of loudness, and degree of lip movement. On the whole there were no unusual deviations, although in comparison with a group of sighted students, the visually impaired children were marginally better on pitch modulation and the sighted marginally better on lip movement. There were no differences between subgroups with some partial vision and without. Most strikingly, on the basis of vocal cues alone, judges could not successfully tell the visually impaired children from the sighted! Finally, Brieland reported generally that gender differences favored the girls in the sample. Using a similar procedure, Eisenstadt (1955) found a mixed pattern, with visually impaired boys better than girls on measures of voice, language, and projection, but with girls better in diction, self-projection, and "visible elements" rated from films.

Although early data from Stinchfield-Hawk (1944) are almost as positive as those of Brieland with respect to problems of articulation, Miner's (1963) conclusions were much more negative. A speech therapist conversed with each of 293 visually impaired children from schools for the blind and evaluated the presence or absence of speech deviations. Articulatory problems were judged to occur in fully 25% of the sample. This is a stark contrast with the picture presented by Brieland (1950); and although the grade range of Miner's sample was somewhat lower (kindergarten through sixth grade) and the presence of additional handicaps somewhat higher than in the Brieland sample, a ready reconciliation of the differences is not evident. Miner also found no difference between partially sighted (in "sight-saving" classes) and braille-using children.

More recently, Lucas (1984) studied a group of "prelingually blind" five- to seven-year-olds, with more positive results. In a speech-imitation task, the child repeated nonsense words, chosen so that the basis for performance would be sound properties rather than semantic familiarity. Performance was very good and did not differ from that of a similar group of sighted children. (In an accompanying task, in which the child was to identify articulatory errors in words spoken by another person, the same blind group performed better than the sighted group.)

Jan et al. (1977) examined a very large sample of children with respect to many aspects of development (we will describe the study in more detail in a later section). With respect the development of language, however, Jan et al. found in general a reasonably smooth process, although their general impression was that the incidence of articulation problems among children with visual impairments was higher (at 27%) than in the general developmental population. Within this, 6% exhibited echolalia and 5% stuttered.

We might not expect all speech sounds to be equally well articulated, and in particular, it seems possible that even partial vision might play a role in the refinement of articulation. Mills (1983) studied two-year-olds at the stage of two-word utterances with respect to their articulation of consonant–vowel (CV) syllables. As expected, sighted children produced better articulation of sounds whose production movements are external and therefore visible (e.g., /b/, /m/) than of those whose production movements are not visible (e.g., /d/, /t/). This finding suggests that vision plays a role in the refinement of articulation of the former category, and furthermore that visually impaired children of comparable development should not show the difference. Mills's results showed just this pattern of interaction between visual status and visibility of articulatory movements.

In all, on the issue of articulation, while there are some interesting results in the literature, it does not seem that visual loss has any overwhelming effect on articulation. Even though vision facilitates the early differentiation of sounds with visible articulatory movements (Mills, 1983), this is apparently a transitory rather than a lasting effect and in any case does not seem to interfere with the visually impaired child's ability to communicate using language.

Stuttering is a specific form of articulatory problem that surely *can* interfere with the effectiveness of interpersonal communication. There is no empirical evidence that stuttering is abnormally present in visually impaired children, and there is no theoretical reason to expect it to be. In his sample that showed many other articulatory problems, Miner (1963) found only one case of stuttering; Stinchfield-Hawk (1944) found about a 3% incidence, and Weinberg (1964) estimated the incidence in schools for the blind at around 2%. The evidence from Stinchfield-Hawk (1944) and Weinberg (1964) is that stuttering is somewhat more frequent in boys than girls, a difference that is found in the sighted population as well. It is clear that stuttering, while an occasional problem, is not highly associated with visual loss.

Complicating conditions

For the most part, we have been discussing language development in the child with a visual impairment but no other complicating conditions. However, a number of other conditions affect language acquisition, and we turn to these now.

If the child with a visual impairment must find alternative adaptive routes to the acquisition of language and other communicative behaviors, then the child with an additional handicap is even more challenged, as are those who work with the child. For example, Rogow (1980) cited the case of an eight-year-old girl, totally blind and severely retarded, with some hearing loss as well as physical anomalies that impeded speech production. Through their sensitivity to the variations in her behavior, the personnel were able to "read" her desires, respond to them, and gradually foster the establishment of a fundamental communicative system.

Rogow (1982) elaborated the varieties of alternative modes of communication with young multihandicapped blind children. Ten children ranged in age from 1:3 to 7:0; all had varyingly severe additional problems, such as various brain damage and physical handicaps, in addition to visual loss ranging from partial to complete. Social interactive behaviors were analyzed from videotape, audiotape, and checklist, with respect to the categories of intentionality, imitation, and spontaneous use of social signals. Rogow hypothesized that structured social routines would be conducive to the evocation of communicative behaviors. The basis of the interactions was nursery rhymes, which were used flexibly in frequent interactive settings either in the home or in school.

Children with different capabilities used different social signals to indicate readiness to participate in social interactions, including language signals, nonverbal vocalizations, motor or body position indicators, and eye contact in the case of one partially sighted child. Most children did not show imitative behaviors at the outset but began to imitate within the first few sessions. Again, the means of imitation varied a good deal, depending on the individual child's behavioral capabilities. Social behavior was apparently facilitated by the process: "The cooperation involved in the social routines seemed to make it possible for the most resistant children to enter into a reciprocal relationship with an adult" (p. 256). Additionally, progress in language development was seen in most children, in both the receptive and expressive aspects, and some children began to show signs of visual attentiveness as well.

Rogow concluded that the key to success lay in the structured nature of the routines, with the rhythmic nature of nursery rhymes as the communicative vehicle. Clearly, though, no consistent behavioral expectation can be applied to children with such diverse characteristics, and an additional feature of the program's success was sensitivity on the part of staff and parents to each child's means of expression.

Hearing impairment. The most obvious additional condition that we might expect to have an impact on language acquisition is hearing impairment, and indeed much of the published work with children with visual and hearing impairments has centered on language and communication.

The problem is clear. As we have seen, difficulties of language acquisition for the child with a visual impairment are generally not severe, and under normal conditions language comes to serve a variety of communicative and other functions. Children with a hearing impairment experience a great deal more difficulty than those with a visual impairment in acquiring language, but considerable success has been reported by the advocates of both oral and manual language approaches. However, both approaches generally depend heavily on the use of visual materials, so the problem for the visually and hearing-impaired child is that the separate handicaps are not additive but multiplicative. It is a positive note that very few children are both totally blind and totally deaf, but even for children with partial impairments the problems are serious.

Much of the published work has focused on the child's readiness for language instruction and on various approaches to such instruction. Elioseff (1971) discussed guidelines for the expectation that a deaf–blind child may be responsive to language instruction. Rather than relying on a base IQ level, Elioseff suggested that a more appropriate index may be the attainment of a minimal mental age, such as 18 months. Even within the range identified by Elioseff and others as "language educable," there is evidence that different instruction methods may be optimal for different children. For example, Umezu (1972) reported, though without further elaboration, that children who are unresponsive to one method respond more favorably to another technique. Schein, Kates, Wolf, and Theil (1983) reported that the results of use of the Assessment–Intervention Model for Deaf-Blind Students (AIM) were mixed, with better performance on some scales and worse on other scales, compared with another group that was exposed to alternative teaching strategies. The overall equivalence of various programs, together with the variation in subscale performance, suggests strongly that different children respond optimally to different approaches. It is likely that individual variation in cognitive ability patterns accounts for some of the variation.

Beyond the availability of various methods, however, it is important to have an effective way of matching an appropriate method to the individual child's characteristics. Although the technology of this matching process is not well developed, Robbins (1971) discussed its fundamental components:

We should then be able to predict level of communication and/or language learning participation possible at a given time for a child by evaluating his physical and cognitive development. . . . There are prerequisite cognitive levels for certain stages of language. . . . If, in addition to cognitive adequacy, the basic components related to language acquisition are present . . . language acquisition may take place with a general "naturalness" and the help of sensory aids and teacher-communication. (p. 77)

The evaluation of cognitive readiness is not a simple task. Salmon and Rusalem (1966) discussed the problems involved in the evaluation of the cognitive abilities of deaf–blind adults. The problems with children are if anything greater than for adults. The importance of the issue is immense, not just for diagnostic purposes related to language acquisition but for making sure that falsely pessimistic diagnoses are not prescriptions for inappropriate institutionalization of the child.

Motor problems. Egland (1955) discussed the possibility of various speech-related difficulties in the blind child with cerebral palsy (CP). CP imposes primarily motor difficulties, particularly with respect to the speech apparatus. In addition, locomotor problems may compound the troubles of the visually impaired child with CP, since locomotion is important in the acquisition of the experiential base for language.

Mental retardation. Several studies have addressed problems of language development in the mentally retarded child with a visual impairment. Rogow (1972) suggested that the adequacy of social interaction may play a part in determining the language development of retarded blind children, cautioning that "clinical evaluations of nonspeaking blind children tend to ignore the fact of social isolation and associated experiential deprivation" (p. 40). Elonen and Zwarensteyn (1964) noted that part of the speech difficulty in the retarded blind child may be attributed to the fact that "this type of child has always been able to indicate his needs satisfactorily through nonverbal methods which have been accepted by others and allowed to persist. Often the parents jump to the conclusion that the child is unable to speak and continue to respond to his nonverbal communication" (p. 606).

The dangers of overprotection or oversolicitousness are apparent. Elonen and Zwarensteyn noted that the retarded blind child is generally slow in language development, and they pointed to an interesting dilemma that the therapist often encounters. On the one hand, the child should not be pushed too hard beyond his or her developmental level. On the other hand, there is considerable evidence that, perhaps more than in other areas of development, language development is characterized by critical periods. That is, if the child does not develop language appropriately within a certain period of chronological age, development will be more difficult later.

Several lines of research are needed to resolve these issues. Critical periods in language development are not well understood in either sighted or nonretarded blind children. Mental retardation may also slow the course of critical periods in language development. Finally, of course, better and more detailed information is needed about the possible disadvantages, as well as benefits, of pushing the retarded child faster than his or her spontaneous rate of development in any area, including language.

Emotional disturbance. Emotional disturbance is used loosely to refer to a wide variety of behaviors, but a common theme is the child's failure to engage in normal social–emotional relationships. A number of observations in the literature link emotional disturbance particularly to blindness caused by ROP. We will address the issue of emotional disturbance, as well as its possible relationship to ROP, more broadly in Chapter 10. For now, we consider the implications for language development of a failure to engage social relationships.

Keeler (1958) reported the cases of five ROP children. All had been born prematurely and had been placed in an incubator. Their social behavior included resistance to physical contact, lack of verbal response to speech by others, difficulties in toilet training and other social skills such as eating, and, notably, a pattern of rejection by the mother. Their auditory and language behavior showed adequate understanding of spoken language but no verbal response to it, an exceptional liking for auditory stimuli including music, excessive echolalia, and an impressive ability to hum and sing songs. Thus, there was apparently no auditory dysfunction that prevented the intake or understanding of speech information, and no motor dysfunction that prevented the child from speaking adequately. Rather, the difficulty was in the appropriate use of speech in social contexts: the children simply did not produce the speech that was needed to maintain their end of a social interchange. Haspiel (1965) made similar points in discussing auditory and speech functions in emotionally disturbed blind children.

It seems reasonable to suggest that the language and communication dysfunction in these children is not fundamentally an aspect of language itself, but rather a symptom of a larger syndrome, the primary characteristics of which involve aversion to and difficulties in social–emotional interactions. Keeler (1958) implicated maternal response as a causal factor; the mothers of his subjects had been distressed to discover that their children were blind, and they tended to neglect their children, leaving them in a crib or playpen for long periods. Whether or not the adverse parental reaction to the child's blindness is the dominant or even the sole causal factor in the child's social-interactive difficulties, the environment thus created for the child is extremely detrimental to language development. The contrast is stark between Keeler's description and Urwin's (1983) report of the highly supportive – and emotionally and linguistically interactive – environment in which her subjects developed so well.

Green and Schecter (1957) also reported three cases of serious lack of communication and autistic-like affect; but in these cases the maternal syndrome was somewhat different. Like the cases described by Keeler, these mothers had been very upset about the child's blindness, but instead of neglect, the predominant pattern was overprotection: the mothers "interfered and did many things for the children, thus preventing them from learning through their own efforts. They were all very lonely, frightened women who found overt comfort in the clinging, infantile behavior of their children" (p. 637). Overprotection, while probably preferable to neglect, still does not create a social–emotional environment conducive to the acquisition of language, or for that matter other developmental achievements.

Again, though, we return to a point that recurs with considerable frequency: it does not seem to be the visual impairment that directly affects the adequacy of communicative development. Rather, the adverse responses of parents and others to the child's impairment lead them in various ways to provide an unsupportive and ineffective environment for the development of language.

Summary

Research on the language development of blind children has progressed tremendously in the past decade as a result of attention to the social-interactive context of language. Clearly there is much yet to be learned about the ways in which language is used by the blind child to engage in effective communicative interaction. As study of these phenomena proceeds, it will be critical for investigators to attend to variations between children and to the factors which cause them.

10

Social development and adjustment

The terms "social development" and "social adjustment" can be distinguished at a technical level. The former refers to the process of development as social characteristics change with age, whereas the latter refers to the quality of the child's adjustment to the demands of the social environment, without necessarily being indexed to age considerations. In practice, however, the literature does not maintain a sharp distinction, and it is not feasible to do so here. As a matter of practical organization, we will consider first the research that has concentrated on the evaluation of the social development and adjustment of children as measured by standardized tests. Then we will move to work that has attempted to identify the dynamics of family-based variation in social characteristics. A third section will cover issues more directly related to variables in the school situation. Finally, we will look at the brief literature on the development of social morality.

Social development and adjustment scales

Several standardized scales have been used to assess the social development and adjustment of children with visual impairments. Although their primary use is diagnosis for individual children, these instruments have also proved to be a rich source of information about the normative characteristics, as well as the variation, of the population of children with visual impairments.

The Vineland Social Maturity Scale, developed by Doll in the 1930s, has been used as an indicator of overall social development in children with visual impairments, although it was originally designed for use with sighted children. The Vineland yields a social quotient (SQ) score that is indexed to CA just as the IQ score is. McKay (1936) reported exploratory use of the Vineland with several visually impaired children and concluded that the test provided an adequate measure of their social competence. McKay suggested that although the blind preschooler may not spontaneously attempt to "dominate" his environment, this may be a matter of lack of motivation, since "if the blind child is stimulated to take an interest in his environment he seems to have the desire to dominate it in much the same manner as a seeing child" (p. 154). Similarly, Bradway (1937) used the Vineland to evaluate social competence of children with visual impairments over the age range of 5 to 20 years. At the youngest level SQ was reasonably age-appropriate but it declined with increasing CA. Based on analysis of individual items, Bradway noted that "blindness alone does not prevent successful performance in any of the items" (p. 66), and thereby implicitly verified the utility of the test for children with visual impairments.

Nonetheless, concern about the validity of the Vineland for evaluation of children with visual impairments led to an adaptation of the test for this population (Maxfield & Fjeld, 1942). Maxfield and Fjeld evaluated children from nine months to seven years of age who varied widely in mental ability and amount of useful vision. The mean SQ for the group was 84. Items that in general were difficult tended to fall into the self-help (eating, dressing) and occupation (play, cutting with scissors, etc.) categories. However, from the range (26 to 163) and standard deviation (29) of the scores, it is clear that there was a great deal of variation within the group.

The sample was divided into blind and partially sighted groups. There was not an overall difference between the groups when age was matched. Item analysis revealed that relatively easy and somewhat difficult items did not tend to differentiate the groups: that is, the former were easy for all and the latter difficult for all. It was in the range of intermediate difficulty that more items favored the group with partial vision. The summary point was offered that the blind children tended to do best on activities "which require less initiative and less out-going behavior" (p. 12). Based on a closer analysis of a subset of the children, factors leading to higher SQ were identified as health, specialized training, and "general environment." Improved vision was a positive indicator and emotional disturbance a negative one in several cases. Referring to the overall pattern of lower SQ, Maxfield and Fjeld suggested, based on study of several cases, that "much of this delay in development could have been avoided by special training at an earlier period in the life of the child. . . . It seems a fair assumption that the visually handicapped child is much more dependent upon training than is the seeing child" (p. 16).

Based on their work, Maxfield and Fjeld proposed a modified Vineland, later referred to as the Maxfield–Fjeld scale (MF), for use with children with visual impairments. Norris et al. (1957) used the MF scale in their extensive study. Despite the fact that all of their intensive sample had lost vision within the first year, and that age was not corrected for prematurity (85% had lost vision as a result of ROP), the overall results showed children scoring higher on the MF scale than had been found by previous investigators, with a mean SQ of 92. The standard deviation was large (27). The general conclusion of Norris et al. (1957) was that "the development of blind children can follow an orderly progression without the serious retardation usually expected as a result of the handicap" (pp. 28, 33). Discussing the generally better profile of their group, they noted that "lowered functioning and limitations in personality development cannot be attributed to the visual handicap alone; other explanations must be sought. . . . The relationship between opportunities and social maturity . . . also casts doubt on the validity of generalizations attributing retarded social functioning to blindness" (pp. 33–34). In addition to noting the large standard deviation of scores within the sample, Norris et al. also found that individual children, tested repeatedly over time, showed a great deal of test-to-test variability. Such variation might be due to an unreliable measure, but based on the profiles of a small number of children who were evaluated as individual cases, Norris et al. concluded that the test-to-test fluctuations were primarily associated with factors in the child's situation that varied from one time to another.

The individually profiled children varied a great deal in social development as well as in other characteristics. A factor commonly noted in children who were developing well was that the family encouraged the child's activities and did not "teach" so much as provide the child with the opportunity to learn.

The successor to the Maxfield–Fjeld scale was the Maxfield-Buchholz (M–B) scale (Maxfield & Buchholz, 1957). The MB scale has seven subscales: general, dressing, eating, communication, socialization, locomotion, and occupation. A norming study was conducted on a group of 484 children, ranging in age from five months to six years, and varying in etiology (60% were blind due to ROP) and visual function. Unfortunately, while Maxfield and Buchholz provided detailed information about the percentage of children passing various items at various age levels, no information was provided about variation in performance as a function of etiology, visual status, gender, or familial variables, and the test is not highly regarded at present. A more recent renorming of the Vineland itself has been carried out (Sparrow, Balla, & Cicchetti, 1984) with a subnorming group of visually impaired children in the 6- to 12-year age range.

Reynell (1978) reported the results of the Reynell–Zinkin Mental Development Scale (which includes a section that evaluates social adaptation) with children who ranged from infants to five-year-olds and varied widely in cognitive ability. A subgroup with partial vision included a higher proportion of children with additional handicaps (particularly CP and hearing impairment) than the blind subgroup. Although there were developmental differences favoring the partially sighted group on the other scales, there were no remarkable differences on the social adaptation scale between blind and partially sighted children. (Both subgroups did, however, show a general lag compared to sighted children, particularly in the 1.5- to 2.5-year-old range, where items related to self-help skills, e.g., eating and dressing, are prevalent.)

As to the factors influencing the dynamics of development, Reynell suggested that blind and partially sighted children alike "tend to be 'babied' by their parents for longer than they need be . . . because the early stages of learning self help are necessarily more messy and clumsy than with sighted children. Many parents did, in fact, confess that they found it hard to tolerate this . . . long drawn out and messy stage" (p. 296). The implication, of course, is that in order to encourage independence in self-help skills to emerge, parents must be able to tolerate the periods of transition and must avoid the temptation to intervene in the interests of expediency.

Brambring (1988; Brambring et al., 1989) has initiated a large-scale project to evaluate the development of preschool children in various areas, including social–emotional development (Scale 3) and daily living skills (Scale 6). Although the longer-range intention is to develop scales that are differentiated for variations in visual functioning and additional handicaps, the initial effort has been directed to children who are blind and who have no additional handicapping conditions.

Initial findings from this project were, not unexpectedly, that pre-schoolers show problems with some categories of self-help skills. Assess-ment of blind children's social behaviors focused on dimensions such as "inactive/active," "outgoing/shy," "tires quickly/persistent," "emo-tionally well-balanced/unsteady," and "self-directed/needing com-pany." In these categories, parents evaluated their blind children as being remarkably like sighted children of corresponding age (Brambring, 1988). Brambring et al. (1989) noted further that the variability of the scores at any given chronological age is great. Clearly some blind children in the sample showed indices of social development comparable to sighted children. The reasons for the within-sample differences, and particularly the environmental conditions associated with fully adequate social behavior, remain to be elucidated.

Summary. Research using standardized tests of social development has yielded much normative information over the decades. Generally, how-ever, these studies have not sought information about the variations in children's environments that might produce variation on scale indicators, although in several cases authors have pointed to variations in the social environment that affected the outcomes. We turn now to a series of studies that have examined social development and adjustment in rela-tion to social environmental factors.

The family setting and social adjustment

The family is a social unit with often complex relationships among and between children and adults. Since young children spend considerable time in this setting, it is logical to expect aspects of their social develop-ment and adjustment to vary with the characteristics of the environment. Several major studies have yielded much useful information about these relationships.

Young children. Imamura (1965) addressed the extent to which the development of the child's social behavior is a product of the social environment and the interactions that it affords between the visually impaired child and other people. The study was primarily comparative, but it provided useful information about the variations among the 10 blind children, who were between three and six years of age. Several categories of the children's behavior were observed, including dominance, nurturance, succorance, submission, sociability, self-reliance, responsibility, and sociable and nonsociable aggression. Imamura also evaluated aspects of the mother's social behavior toward the child, including aggression and dominance, succorance, sociability, and noncompliance. Each child–mother dyad was observed in social interactions in a number of five-minute periods.

Compared to the sighted children, the blind children were less likely to initiate social contacts with the mother and other people. The interactions that the blind children did initiate frequently involved sociability and succorant (help-seeking) contacts. Imamura suggested that the high rate of succorant requests was a result of maternal overprotection: the mothers instigated far more contacts than did the mothers of sighted children. Furthermore, blind children really *do* need help more often than sighted children, so that succorant behaviors are understandable and adaptive. However, Imamura found that the blind children also initiated many succorant acts directed more to seeking attention than to physical assistance. In turn, their mothers showed more frequent responses in the categories "noncompliance," "refusal," and "ignoring": in fact, the rate of these maternal behaviors was about three times that of the mothers of sighted children, who almost never ignored their children's requests for attention. However, the mothers of the blind children were less likely than the mothers of sighted children to refuse a request for real help.

Further analysis showed several additional patterns. Blind children were generally accepting of maternal dominance, whereas they tended to respond to maternal aggressiveness by being less submissive and more socially aggressive in return. In response to maternal compliance, blind children tended to show more sociable and less dominant responses. Thus, somewhat different patterns of social interaction between mother and child occurred for blind and for sighted children.

Imamura's work is useful in several respects. First, behavior was examined in realistic, everyday situations of mother–child interaction. Second, the categories of behavior were carefully defined. Third, the child's social behavior was analyzed within a broader context. Social behavior does not occur in a vacuum, and it is necessary to consider the wider context in interpreting it. However, caution is also in order in making causal conclusions from such work. It is not clear whether, for example, the high incidence of succorant behavior among blind children is a result of or a cause of the mothers' greater tendency to ignore it.

Dote-Kwan (1991) reported a study that was similar in intent to Imamura's (1965) but that used a measure of the quality of the child's home environment. The subjects were 18 children between the ages of 20 and 36 months who had become legally blind before the age of six months. Their mothers were also evaluated. A mother–child interaction rating scale (M–C) was developed to evaluate various aspects of the mother–child interactions. The characteristics of the home environment were assessed by use of the HOME (Home Observation for Measurement of the Environment; Caldwell & Bradley, 1984). The general goal of the study was to evaluate the role of mother-child interactions, the environment, and various child characteristics as determinants of the children's development as measured by the Maxfield–Buchholz and Reynell–Zinkin scales.

Several important conclusions emerged. First, the Maxfield–Buchholz and Reynell–Zinkin scales were highly intercorrelated in their assessment of developmental progress. Second, the HOME scale was generally not predictive of developmental indicators for the sample as a whole, although when the sample was divided into totally blind and partially sighted groups, greater predictiveness was found within each group. Although the HOME has proved to be of value for sighted samples, its utility with visually impaired samples is unclear.

Third, the relationships between CA and developmental indices were only sporadically significant, which is not surprising given the limited age range in the sample. There were apparent gender differences, however, that interacted with the severity of visual loss to make conclusions about either variable risky.

Fourth, the M–C scale revealed a number of interesting correlations with developmental indices. The M–C scale was derived from the observation of mother–child interactions during the course of their daily routines. The pattern of results was complex and in some respects counterintuitive. For example, on the expected side, "complying with the child's request for help or for an object," "encouraging the child to try a task first when he/she requests help," and "repeating or rephrasing the child's communicative behaviors" were positively related to developmental indices. On the less expected side, "encouraging the child's involvement in mobility tasks," "describing the attributes of a new phenomenon," and "attentional cueing" were negative predictors of development. These latter results are not only counterintuitive but generally run contrary to the findings of Imamura (1965).

Dote-Kwan offered two general points of perspective on the unexpected results. First, she noted that since Imamura's study was published in 1965, parental practice may have changed substantially as a result of the introduction of intervention programs. In fact, all of the children in Dote-Kwan's study were involved in such programs. Second, she suggested that in part as a result of Imamura's and other studies, mothers of relatively developmentally delayed children were particularly attuned to the need to provide them with stimulation such as mobility encouragement and attentional cueing, but that despite their efforts, their children were developmentally unable to respond to such efforts.

As Dote-Kwan noted, the M–C scale is in a developmental state and does not at this point have demonstrated validity. However, the goal to which it is directed, assessment of the nature of parent–child relationships, is exceedingly important and should be pursued vigorously.

In another valuable and extensive paper, Lairy and Harrison-Covello (1973) summarized the results of several years of casework with young children having visual impairments. They evaluated the patterns of children's characteristics using a combination of several social development scales in addition to clinical observation. They also studied the characteristics of the parents in interviews and observation sessions designed to provide information about the parents' attitudes toward the children and their handicaps, as well as the nature and quality of the parent–child interaction. Effort was also devoted to reconstructing the history of the parents' reactions to the children's visual loss.

Based on the children's characteristics, the cases were divided into four groups. Group I included children whose developmental patterns were most similar to those of sighted children, with adequate scores in the various areas of evaluation. Fewer than half of the children in this group were totally blind, and the children with some visual function tended to make active use of it. The parents of Group I children tended to show a realistic acceptance of them and their visual impairments. That many of them had had additional children after the subject child was considered an indication of their positive attitude toward the child's visual loss.

In contrast, Group IV included children with a low pattern of developmental indices. Many had additional handicaps and often neurological abnormalities. The developmental prognosis of children in this group was negative, based on organic factors, regardless of the capability of the parents to accept and adjust to the child's handicap.

Groups II and III were intermediate, showing mixed patterns of developmental characteristics. Group II generally had normal scores on the postural and verbal scales, but they were developmentally delayed on the autonomy, sensorimotor, and sociability scales. The low scores were interpreted as simple developmental delays rather than as evidence of pathological development. These children were characterized as being extremely passive, which was apparently encouraged by parental over-protection. The overprotection was often related to an underestimation of the children's abilities. Interestingly, many of the children in this group had been born prematurely, which may have contributed to the parents' underestimates of their abilities. On the positive side, these parents tended to respond well to counseling, and in fact positive changes were often seen in the children's behaviors as a consequence of changes in parental attitudes.

The Group III children also showed a pattern of uneven development, but it differed from that of Group II. The Group III children tended to have good scores on the posture and autonomy scales but low scores on the sociability, language, and sensorimotor scales. Lairy and Harrison-Covello noted the similarity of this group to the children that Fraiberg characterized as having "ego deviations." The developmental abnormalities were attributed largely to the parents' inability to accept the handicap and respond adequately to it. Most of these parents had experienced lengthy periods of depression early in the child's life, and most of them still showed inadequate response to the child and his or her visual loss: "The child seems to be trapped in the maternal falsehood which consists of her apparent wish that he should be 'like a sighted child' and her prohibition of his existence as a blind child" (p. 12).

Thus unlike the Group IV children, whose development was hindered by organic factors, the Group III children had the potential for normal development but were faced with a pattern of parental response that discouraged adequate development. Their low scores were interpreted as being truly pathological, rather than as representing delayed normal development that could be overcome with suitable reparations of the social–emotional environment.

The work of Lairy and Harrison-Covello (1973) is exemplary in several ways. First, it sought not just to characterize the "average" child, but rather to chart the variations within a sample of children with visual impairments. Second, and of equal importance, it sought to differentiate among the existing neurological and environmental conditions and to link patterns of development, both normal and abnormal, with their organic and social antecedents. Group IV children were seen as intractably burdened by neurological conditions that could not, even given the best social–emotional environment, yield normal development. Group II and III children were alike in that they could have shown normal patterns of development, given a suitable social–emotional environment. The prognoses differed, though, in that the parents of Group II children recognized the problems that they faced and were judged capable of adjusting to them, whereas the parents of Group III children were judged as being incapable of adjusting to the degree necessary to provide a suitable social-emotional environment for the child.

Adolescents. Imamura as well as Lairy and Harrison-Covello evaluated child–parent interactive patterns in young children up to the age of six. Sommers (1944) conducted a comparably comprehensive evaluation of a large sample of residential school adolescents with visual impairments. The California Personality Test (CPT) was used, as well as questionnaires designed to evaluate parent and child characteristics and attitudes. Based on this material, parents and children were clustered into several categories.

Five clusters of parental attitudes toward the child were identified:

Acceptance (18%). Parents showed a healthy and genuine acceptance of the child's handicap.

Denial (8%). Parents tended to deny that the child's handicap had an emotional or other impact on them, or indeed that the child had a handicap.

Overprotection (26%). Parents expressed excessive solicitude and overprotectiveness, reflected in doing things for the child and protecting the child from emotional and social hazards.

Disguised rejection (32%). Parents gave the impression of being good parents, but this covered up a fundamental rejection of the child and an overreaction in the direction of oversolicitousness.

Overt rejection (16%). Parents undisguisedly rejected the child, showed no affection and considerable irritation, and generally externalized blame for the child's (and their) situation.

The adolescents' adjustment patterns were characterized as follows:

Compensatory reaction. Children recognized and accepted their limitations and had realistic goals, focusing on their abilities rather than their disabilities.

Denial reaction. Children did not accept their handicap and showed an overcompensatory confidence – for example, "I never worry about anything."

Defensive reactions. Children externalized blame for their situation, attributing a prejudice against the blind to society in general and blaming their lack of success on their handicap.

Withdrawal reaction. Children tended to retreat from situations in which they experienced difficulties of adjustment, and their thoughts and activities centered around their disability. They tended to favor solitary activities and avoid social contacts.

Nonadjustive behavior reactions. While the previous patterns are in some sense adaptive, children in this category are clearly dysfunctional, going "from one unhappy experience to another, . . . and presenting a dysfunctional clinical picture."

Having evaluated children and parents as fitting these typologies, Sommers proceeded to draw relationships among the two sets and other evaluative scores. The data are exceedingly rich and cannot be presented in detail here. However, a synopsis of the more important relationships follows.

The child's general adjustment was highly correlated with the parents' acceptance of the child and with the quality of the emotional environment within the family. The socioeconomic and educational status of the family was positively related to variables such as the emotional atmosphere of the home, the child's social status in the family and his or her general adjustment. Thus, "In stable homes with favorable family relationships the blind child experiences emotional security and feels accepted by his parents, and as a consequence his adjustments to life, to school, and to his handicap are wholesome" (p. 90).

On the other hand, parental overprotectiveness was not related to socioeconomic or educational status, nor was the child's attitude toward his or her handicap related to these variables. A high degree of overprotectiveness was predictive of the child's poor general adjustment and poor adjustment to the handicap.

Finally, Jan et al. (1977) made a comprehensive study of a sample that included all children with visual impairments in British Columbia between birth and the age of 19 years, regardless of the severity of visual loss or the presence of additional handicaps. (Cases of cortical visual impairment were excluded because of the severe mental retardation that is typically a part of this syndrome.) A subsample of 92 was subjected to intensive study. These included 65 children with partial vision and 27 with LP or less. About half had additional handicaps, and the large majority had been visually impaired since birth or early in life.

A very complete evaluation was made of the children and their parents. Parents were interviewed and completed questionnaires about a wide array of child-rearing practices. Information was also gathered about the child's early development, school situation, and health. Finally, home observations were made by the research team. From all of this information, the researchers were able not only to formulate a view of the child's current level of functioning in various areas of development, but also to assess the child's environmental surroundings in great detail, and particularly the parents' initial and continuing reactions to the child's blindness.

Jan et al. assumed that the establishment of emotional bonds (as well as other major features of development) depends on activities of both the child and the parents: in the case of the visually impaired infant, the behavioral mechanisms (such as smiling and eye contact) may be absent or altered, and other events (e.g., hospitalization) or behaviors (e.g., adverse parental emotional reactions) may tend to interfere with the normal developmental processes. Much of the Jan et al. analysis focused on the question: how real are these potential dangers, and how can they be avoided or overcome?

More than one-third of the mothers and fathers had reacted with shock or disbelief upon learning initially of the child's visual impairment; others described themselves as "unable to react." From such rocky beginnings, how did their subsequent adaptation proceed? A variety of difficult reactions were described during the ensuing six-month period, including the parents' own negative emotions and feelings toward the child. About half of the parents did not want to have more children, and of these, about one-third expressed fears about the possibility of having another child with a visual impairment.

When questioned about their later reactions (i.e., after the initial six-month period), about 30% of parents felt that there had been an adverse effect on their lives, whereas 26% reported that there had been an advantage due to the visually impaired child. Two-thirds felt neutral about the child's effect on their marriage, while the reports of positive and negative effects were about evenly balanced.

Mothers also evaluated the behaviors of the sibling(s) of the child. About half felt that the effect of the visually impaired child on the sibling(s) had been neutral, while slightly more thought that there had been a bad rather than a good effect. The reasons offered for adverse sibling reactions included their inability to compete or fight with the visually impaired child, feeling embarrassed about the child in public, overprotection of the child, and having to "take up slack" to make up for the visually impaired sibling's (real or perceived) inability to perform household chores. None of this seems unreasonable or surprising, and none of it should in itself be debilitating for the family structure.

From these various results, Jan et al. concluded that "the presence of a visually impaired child is a relatively weak factor in determining many aspects of family life" (p. 159). The situation need not overwhelm the family structure or personal adaptation of the parents or siblings; when a visually impaired child arrives, some people, including parents and siblings, adapt reasonably, as they do to other situations, and some react adversely. Childhood visual impairment puts pressure on the family, but otherwise well-adjusted and resilient people can adapt.

Jan et al. also provided information about the development of indices of socialization. It should be noted that this evidence on the timing of the accomplishment of various behaviors comes for the most part from parental reports, and thus may be subject to the modulations of memory. Nonetheless, it is evident that some areas of development proceeded more apace than others. For example, no serious problems of toilet training were noted, or differences in onset or completion of independent toileting related to the visual impairment. Similarly, there were no notable differences in sleep patterns.

On the other hand, some difficulties of development were found in such areas as walking, feeding, dressing, and washing. The partially sighted children generally achieved these aspects of independence earlier than those with more severe visual loss. This pattern of difference makes sense in relation to the parental reports of their own degree of "protection" of the child in relation to the severity of the visual impairment. Half of the blind children were reported to have chewing problems, compared with one-fifth of the partially sighted. Weaning and the introduction of solid foods also tended to occur later in the blind than in the partially sighted children. Jan et al. noted, however, that "since some blind children learn to feed normally, deviant patterns are not inevitable" (p. 191). This reflects the conclusion drawn by others, that to a large degree patterns of development are determined by the nature of the environmental stimulation.

Summary. Research that has looked carefully at developmental aspects of socialization in relation to the child's social environment has yielded important and useful information about the degree to which social development is sensitive to family characteristics. It is clear from this work that families that adjust well to the child's visual impairment tend to provide a setting in which the child's social development can thrive; it is just as clear that maladaptive family dynamics make the child's socialization exceedingly difficult. Of course, mere realization of these relationships does not lighten the task for the family, but the results underscore in dramatic fashion the importance of professional services for the families of children with visual impairments.

The special case of retinopathy of prematurity

There are many suggestions in the literature that children who have lost vision as a result of ROP may have special problems of emotional adjustment and social interaction. Chase (1972) provided an excellent and comprehensive review of this work. Blank (1959) reported the case of a young girl who was "unresponsive to teachers and other children. . . . Kicking and screaming were her characteristic responses to stimulation. . . . Her enunciation was defective almost to the point of incomprehensibility and her speech served no function of communication" (pp. 242–243). Three major points are represented in this description: social unresponsiveness, abnormal responsiveness to perceptual stimulation, and language dysfunction. These points have received repeated mention by various authors.

Keeler (1958) particularly stressed similarity of the syndrome to autism. The children showed "self-isolation and . . . lack of the use of language for the purpose of interpersonal communication. . . . When spoken to they would not respond. . . . They appeared to make the same type of contact with complete strangers as they would with their own mothers. . . . These children manifested autistic patterns of activity such as rhythmically rocking back and forth, usually to music" (p. 65). In discussing possible reasons for this behavior syndrome, Keeler noted that the maternal response was quite similar to that of neglect and rejection often associated with parents of sighted autistic children.

Hallenbeck (1954b) also stressed the inadequate emotional relations between parent and child:

Without exception . . . each mother was repeatedly told by professional person-nel and by others who saw her child, that the child was mentally deficient or that the child had brain disease, and would not live long. All factors, a fearful delivery followed by separation, a slowly developing child, the diagnosis of retrolental fibroplasia, and finally a diagnosis of mental deficiency – progressively interfered with the relationship between the mother and child. (p. 302)

Two major questions arise in connection with these observations of a link between ROP and emotional disturbance. First, is emotional distur-bance, particularly in its more severe forms, more prevalent in ROP children than in children who lose vision from other causes? Second, what are the specific causes of emotional disturbance in children with ROP-caused blindness, and are they different in important respects from the causes in other children?

Prevalence. Keeler (1958) compared the communicative abilities and emotional characteristics of children blind from ROP with a group of children who had been blind from birth from other causes. Referring to the non-ROP group, Keeler noted that "one did not see the same degree of autistic patterns of behavior, although some of these children were somewhat withdrawn" (p. 73). Keeler's conclusion should be tempered by the observation that the amount of visual function was generally greater in the non-ROP group than in the ROP group. Reporting on a group that included children blind from ROP as well as other causes, Hallenbeck (1954a) noted that poor emotional adjustment was more prevalent in the former.

Blank (1959) also reported that the incidence of "severe ego defects and autistic and motility disturbances" was higher among children who had lost vision due to ROP than among congenitally blind children who were born at full term. He also noted, however, that brain damage was an important factor: "Severe personality problems among the blind prematurely born with brain damage, but without retrolental fibroplasia, is probably as high as among those with retrolental fibroplasia," and "the incidence of these problems among visually normal children with brain damage, e.g., cerebral palsy, and with a history of two- to three-months premature birth is almost as high as among the blind with retrolental fibroplasia" (p. 237). Blank argued that brain damage and prematurity, coupled with visual loss, may account for the relatively high incidence of emotional disturbance among children who are blind from ROP.

Finally, Parmalee et al. (1958) reported a study of 60 children from 6 to 10 years of age, 38 of whom were blind from ROP and 22 from other causes. For the non-ROP group, the age at visual loss was not specifically noted, although we can infer from the reported etiologies that a large majority were blind from birth. Of the 38 children who were blind from ROP, 7 were reported to be significantly emotionally disturbed, while only 1 of the 22 non-ROP children was so classified. Parmalee et al. suggested that "some special factor is operative, unique either to children of premature birth or to children with blindness due to retrolental fibroplasia or both" (p. 645).

Although based for the most part (Parmalee et al. excepted) on clinical impressions and limited samples, the several sources suggest that there is a somewhat higher incidence of serious emotional disturbance in ROP children than in children who have lost vision early in life from other causes. To what may the greater incidence be attributed?

Possible causes. A number of factors seem potentially important, including prematurity and variables associated with it such as birth weight and duration of gestation, an oxygen-rich atmosphere, and brain damage and mental retardation. The list also includes factors, such as early sensory deprivation and the parent– or caretaker–child relationship, that may or may not occur in conjunction with prematurity.

Two points are obvious from this list. The first is that most of these variables are interdependent and may therefore act in an interactive fashion to affect emotional disturbance. An obvious example is blindness and the parent–child relationship, since it may often be the case that the parent's role in the relationship is adversely affected by his or her reaction to the infant's blindness. The second point is that while one factor may operate as an initial cause, it may have its effect to some degree directly but also indirectly through another factor. For example, brain damage might affect emotional disturbance directly; it might also act indirectly by contributing to mental retardation, which might itself affect emotional disturbance directly. It is difficult if not impossible to separate these complex relationships. Because ROP is apparently increasing again as a cause of infant blindness, it may be useful to review the evidence about these variables in some detail, so that the complexity of the causal relationships will be evident.

Prematurity factors. ROP almost never occurs except with premature birth, and thus prematurity itself must be considered as a possible contributing cause of the emotional disturbance seen in children blind from ROP. However, in her detailed study of a large number of ROP case histories, Chase (1972) found little relationship between the degree of prematurity and the incidence of emotional disturbance. Fraiberg and Freedman (1964) similarly reported a failure to find significant relationships between birth weight or gestational age and degree of "developmental arrest" (a syndrome strongly characterized by emotional disturbance).

It is unlikely that prematurity is a direct cause of emotional disturbance, and more likely that other factors associated with it increase the likelihood of emotional problems. What are these factors?

Oxygen. ROP is understood to result from the oxygen-rich incubator environment that is used with prematurely born infants. Is it oxygen itself that produces the greater incidence of emotional disturbance in ROP children? Parmalee et al. (1958) found no evidence to support this hypothesis, and indeed Chase (1972) found weak evidence that children who had received more intensive oxygen treatment showed *less* rather than more incidence of emotional disturbance. Fraiberg and Freedman (1964) also did not find a relationship between developmental arrest and duration of oxygen treatment. Thus the evidence does not support the suggestion that emotional disturbance is a direct result of the oxygen treatment itself.

Brain damage. Several sources of evidence point to brain damage as a causal factor in the emotional disturbance of children blind from

ROP. Parmalee et al. (1958) and Knobloch, Rider, Harper, and Pasamanick (1956) found that brain damage is more frequent in prematurely born infants regardless of their visual status; Blank (1959) noted that symptoms of emotional disturbance are as likely to occur in premature sighted children with brain damage as in ROP children. In discussing the possibility that brain damage may be implicated in the greater incidence of emotional disturbance in ROP children, Keeler (1958) noted that "such a factor could account for the differences in severity of the condition within the group of children with retrolental fibroplasia, i.e., those with a marked psychiatric syndrome may have marked cerebral involvement and those without much symptomatology may have cerebral involvement either to a very mild degree or perhaps not at all" (p. 75). However, Keeler argued that the clinical picture of emotional disturbance is not typical of that found in other children with brain damage and suggested that brain damage may interact with other factors such as visual loss to produce the specific symptoms seen in some ROP children.

Although it is possible that brain damage may affect emotional disturbance indirectly via mental retardation, it seems quite plausible that brain damage and its effects interact with other situational factors (e.g., inadequate emotional response of parents to a child with physical handicaps) to produce emotional disturbance.

In sum, the evidence suggests that none of the factors related to prematurity causes emotional disturbance directly. However, these factors may conspire with subsequent factors such as sensory deprivation and inadequate parental response to produce emotional disturbance.

Sensory deprivation. Because of the restricted incubator environment and the relative isolation that typically accompanies prematurity, children blind from ROP are more likely to experience a period of early sensory deprivation than those who lose vision from other causes. If early sensory deprivation is a contributing factor in emotional disturbance, then, children blind from ROP might be characterized by more emotional disturbance.

There is abundant research with a wide variety of animal species that indicates early sensory deprivation leads to emotional disturbance. Freedman (1971) suggested that for humans, the coenesthetic (relatively diffuse, including primarily somatosensory and vestibular) stimulation is critical: "In its effect on later physical and psychological development, early coenesthetic deprivation may be more devastating than either congenital blindness or the melange of troubles that affects thalidomide and some rubella babies" (p. 117). The emotional withdrawal syndrome among some emotionally disturbed ROP-blind children has been characterized as an aversion to affection (Keeler, 1958) or an emotional coldness and withdrawal from human contact (Hallenbeck, 1954b).

Granting that the attribution of these tendencies to early somatosensory and vestibular stimulation is based largely on indirect evidence, the formulation does seem reasonable. However, there is one piece of contradictory evidence. Chase (1972) assessed the effects of both duration of incubation and duration of hospitalization. She found that the longer an infant had been in the incubator, the less frequent emotional disturbance was. Similarly, children who had had a longer period of initial hospitalization were less likely to show signs of emotional disturbance. Both relationships argue against sensory deprivation as a simple causal factor, although both may be enmeshed in more complex relationships.

Parent reactions and parent–child interactions. Because experimental manipulation of early deprivation variables is not feasible with human infants, there is some argument in even the literature on sighted children about whether emotional disturbance is a result of sensory deprivation itself or of some more general emotional or social deprivation. These factors are difficult to separate. Spitz (1945, 1946) attributed the problems to maternal deprivation; but others (e.g., Schaffer & Callender, 1959) have suggested that social deprivation does not come into play until the second half of the first year, and that during the first six months, separation has implications for sensory but not for social deprivation.

Parents of sighted autistic children are frequently described as having been emotionally cold and rejecting of their infants. Kaplan and Mason (1960) found less adequate maternal emotional response to premature than to full-term infants. Seashore, Leifer, Barnett, and Leiderman (1973) studied two groups, one of mothers unable to have physical interaction with their sighted premature infants for several weeks after birth and the other of mothers who were allowed such contact. In general, those with low confidence in their mothering skills tended not to increase it when they did not have physical contact with the infant, whereas when they did have physical contact, their confidence increased. In addition, the degree of self-confidence was a moderately good predictor of the quality of mothering a week after the infant was discharged from the hospital. In the case of infants with visual impairments, there may in fact be an interaction between the parent's response to visual impairment and the infant's own predilections: Fraiberg, Smith, and Adelson (1969) noted that the three infants from their sample of 10 that were "noncuddlers" were all prematurely born and had spent several weeks in the hospital before coming home.

Inadequate parental response is not specific to the ROP situation, however. There are published case histories of parents of early blind children who left the blind infant in the crib without attention as much as possible, either because of a fear of damaging the child's eyes further through inappropriate stimulation or because of a more direct emotional rejection of the child. For example, Keeler (1958) cited mothers who "tended literally to put them out of their minds by leaving them in cribs and playpens off in a back room of the house or in the back yard for long periods of time, attending only in a minimal way to the most imperative of their physical needs" (p. 66). The result is sensory as well as social deprivation.

Summary. Many factors accompanying ROP blindness may account for the apparently high incidence of emotional disturbance in this group. However, these are not unique to children with blindness due to ROP. In fact, some factors, such as separation due to hospitalization in cases of retinoblastoma, may operate more strongly in other etiologies. It is unlikely that any of the factors operates independently of the others; indeed, their interdependence is evident. For example, parental neglect may be a response to the blindness itself, to the early separation, to additional physical handicaps, or to some combination of these. Finally, the obvious point should be made that the factors, either in isolation or in combinations, do not necessarily produce emotional disturbance. There are many children with blindness due to ROP whose physical, cognitive, language, and emotional characteristics are fully functional.

Social development and the school setting

When the child enters the preschool or school environment, the factors that affect social development change dramatically. The influence of the parents and family decreases. Other adults and the peer group increasingly influence the child's social development.

These changes present a different set of adaptive demands to the child. Hitherto, the child has been, relatively speaking, a center of attention. Henceforth, the child will become a smaller part of a different and larger social system, with a new set of rules, in which the child's own interests are often subjugated to the demands of the larger social setting. Peer friendship systems are established. Adults other than the parents suddenly have a directive role in the child's life. The child is expected to internalize standards of conduct and thought. Implicitly (if not explicitly), the child is expected to take a broader perspective about his or her role in relation to those of others in the social system.

For the sighted child, these changes are dramatic enough. For the child with a visual impairment, the additional demands of the changed social environment make the adjustment to school even more challenging. The purpose of this section is to chart the development of the visually impaired child in the school years, and to examine the effect of vision-related variables on the quality of the child's adjustment to the social demands of the childhood years, both inside and out of the school setting.

Peer, teacher, and child characteristics

There is a growing literature that explores the impact of integrating handicapped and nonhandicapped preschoolers and school-age children (although little of this work is specifically directed to children with visual impairments). The point generally emerges that simply placing the children together does not lead to effective integration. Structured efforts by means of curriculum design and adult interventions are required, and even when these are effective, their results tend not to generalize or endure (McGlynn & Phillips, 1987).

Specifically with respect to the integration of children with visual impairments, Kekelis and Sacks (1988) provided a conceptual analysis of the requirements for effective social interactions. They began with the premise that social interaction between visually impaired and sighted children is a valuable goal, and that effective interaction does not occur spontaneously but must be encouraged by situational factors. In particular, interaction must be encouraged of both sighted and visually impaired children. The playground setting, for example, must be monitored to insure that the child is not simply isolated from activity. Similar attention must be paid to the classroom, where opportunities for constructive interactions can be found.

Many of the suggestions offered by Kekelis and Sacks are predicated on the assumption, based on the social interaction literature, that the attitudes of sighted children will be improved by engaging in positive interactions with children with visual impairments, and that the latter will benefit in the social structure from their association with sighted peers. The classroom teacher has a great deal of implicit and explicit control over such interactions, and effective exercise of it can lead to the effective social integration of children with visual impairments.

Thus we can roughly divide the issues into three categories, the social skills of the visually impaired child, the reactions of peers, and the role of adults.

Social skills. Although there is evidence that, on the average, social maturity scores of children with visual impairments are lower than those of sighted children of comparable age, it is surprising that there has not been more study of the specific skills critical to peer interactions, and of the extent to which visually impaired children may possess them. Asher, Renshaw, and Hymel (1982) outlined three such skill areas: initiating actions with peers, maintaining relationships, and resolving conflicts in a nonaggressive way. An observational checklist for the evaluation of these skill areas was developed by Read (1989) and was applied to three visually impaired kindergarten children in a public school setting. The three children cannot be taken as a representative sample, and indeed they were quite different from one another. However, they did share the problem of maintaining relationships.

One reason for this is that children with visual impairments may simply not have as much opportunity to engage in peer relationships as sighted children typically do (Kekelis, 1988). This may occur for several reasons. Parents of children with visual impairments may, as a result of their own emotional reactions, not encourage their children's interaction with peers, and such interactions may be stressful to the parents. They may particularly shield the child because of the insensitive comments of strangers. Furthermore, preschool service programs for children with visual impairments that are home-based tend to focus on the development of the parent–child relationship and therefore allow less opportunity for child–peer relationships to occur. Corroborating Kekelis's observations, Jan et al. (1977) found that for their preschool sample, 25% were reported by their parents to have no friends, and an additional 28% were reported to prefer playing alone. This preschool phenomenon persisted into the school-age segments of the sample.

Janson and Merényi (1992) evaluated the characteristics of both the blind child's and the sighted peer's play behavior, as well as the nature of their orientation to adults in the play situation. Their paper was an interim progress report based of half of the eventual sample. Eight congenitally blind children from 3:6 to 6 years of age were age-matched with two sighted peers, one of the same and the other of the opposite gender. Each triad was observed in several play sessions, in which a teacher was also present. The teacher either participated as an active player or was passive, responding only when explicitly addressed by a child. The study was directed to several major issues. Although full analyses must await the completion of the sample, some conclusions are suggested by the preliminary results.

Perhaps the most important point is that while there were differences between the detailed play behaviors of the blind and sighted children, overall the children's behaviors were clearly more alike than different. Two clusters of secondary findings were as follows. First, the blind children were generally more passive in their participation than the sighted children. This was revealed by their greater tendency to ask for and respond to direction from others, and by their relative disinclination to exert their influence on the situation. They were also less likely to show overt affect, especially positive indices such as smiling, or to share play materials. Second, the blind children tended to interact with the teacher in the play situations more than the sighted children did, and to be affected more by the teacher's behavior. When the teacher was active, the blind children tended to orient their behavior to and seek help from the teacher.

Again, it should be stressed that these differences were quantitative rather than qualitative: overall, the blind and sighted children engaged in the same kinds of activities, although their balance of behaviors differed somewhat. We can look forward to the results of the larger study not only to characterize the interactive play behaviors of blind children, but also to see what the effects on blind children's play behaviors are of intentional structuring of the play situation.

Peer responses. How sighted children respond to children with visual impairments in the social situation is equally important. Jan et al. (1977) found that in the school setting, negative reactions of sighted peers were a problem in the form of excessive teasing; only 30% of the mothers reported that teasing was not a problem, and 25% rated it as a major problem. Interestingly, teasing was a far worse problem among the partially sighted than the blind children.

Steinzor (1966) used a projective method of story completion to evaluate the reactions of sighted peers to blind children. Sighted third and fourth grade children were presented with several short stories and were asked to furnish conclusions to them. The stories were either about "a boy," "a girl," "a blind boy," or "a blind girl." Responses were evaluated with respect to cooperation with, and rejection of, blind children. Sighted respondents were drawn from integrated classes or from classes that had not had any blind students in them.

Several major results emerged. First, adverse attitudes were found particularly among children who were in classes with blind peers for the first time. Second, the most positive attitudes were found among children who were not presently in classes with blind peers but who had had blind peers in their classes in previous years. Third, contact with blind children tended to diminish attitudes of overprotectiveness on the part of sighted children. The results were different for junior high school children, where the attitudes of cooperation toward blind peers were higher as the amount of contact increased: cooperation was highest among children who had been in classes with blind peers and lowest among children who had had no contact at all with blind peers.

Do these attitudes translate into interactive behavior? Jones, Lavine, and Shell (1972) studied the acceptance of visually impaired children by their sighted peers in the fourth to sixth grade range. The children were in an integrated setting for at least half of each day. Sighted children answered a sociometric questionnaire that asked the child to name three classmates who fit various classifications, ranging from friendship to popularity to physical abilities. For each item, it was determined whether the visually impaired child fell above or below the median for the item. The results were highly varied, but the tendency was for the visually impaired children to be rated below the median on numerous factors. The extreme negatives tended to be associated with such obvious physical items as "chosen as captain of kickball." Jones et al. also had the children's teachers rate them on various behavioral characteristics and found that "children who were accepted tended to be personally congenial and free from annoying personality and behavior problems; those rejected showed an opposite pattern" (p. 77). It is noteworthy that these same characteristics lead to relative acceptance or rejection of sighted peers.

Jones et al. also examined the social status of sighted children who tended to choose their visually impaired peers as exemplars and found that while there was much variation, the general tendency was for visually impaired children to be chosen by sighted children who were below the median in their own acceptance by other sighted children. Jones et al. speculated that this negative association value may work to the disadvantage of children with visual impairments, and that positive consequences might flow from the intentional pairing of visuallly impaired and popular sighted children on specific tasks.

Although the research of Steinzor and Jones et al. is interesting in what it shows about the attitudes of sighted children, the literature is remarkably devoid of studies of the behaviors of sighted children in actual interactions with visually impaired children, and of how those behaviors vary in relation to the visually impaired children's characteristics.

In Chapter 9 we reviewed the evidence about the development of language as a vehicle of social interaction. Most of this work has been directed to interactions between children with visual impairments and their mothers, but Andersen and Kekelis (1986) evaluated the interactions between children and their older siblings. They found that while the older children's language input to the visually impaired child was much like that of the adult (Kekelis & Andersen, 1984), the older children were less likely than their parents to accommodate to the child's inappropriate or ambiguous speech. For example, they tended to take the literal meaning of an utterance rather than interpreting its intended meaning. However, even if the older sibling did not accommodate to the visually impaired child's utterances, the older child did tend to provide an environment within which the child could learn to correct the utterance.

Corresponding information is not available about linguistic interactions between children with visual impairments and their nonsibling peers. It is likely that such peers may be less willing to accommodate to the difficulties that visually impaired children sometimes have, for example with the correct use of personal pronouns; this may create a dynamic of social rejection of children with visual impairments.

The role of teachers. Adults, and particularly teachers, have potential effects on the interaction between sighted and visually impaired children. Underscoring this point is Janson and Merényi's finding that variations in the teacher's behavior in a triad of children had a larger effect on the visually impaired child's social behaviors than on those of the sighted children.

In the more structured classroom setting, Workman (1986) evaluated the potential of the preschool teacher to affect the peer interactions of four visually impaired boys in an integrated preschool setting. Videotapes were made of interactions among the visually impaired children, their sighted peers, and the teacher; the nature of the teacher's verbal interaction was rated in relation to the presence and quality of interaction between the children. Analysis of periods in which interaction occurred between sighted and visually impaired children showed a pattern of teacher encouragement for such interaction, compared to periods of noninteraction. Furthermore, analysis of the 25-sec periods preceding those of interaction showed that the teachers engaged in verbal behaviors that tended to encourage such interaction. Thus it was clear that the teacher's appropriate verbal behavior could initiate peer interaction, and that it tended to sustain it once initiated.

Summary. The importance of studying issues of social interaction, particularly in the preschool and early school years, can hardly be overstated. Van Hasselt (1983) summarized the various factors that may be involved and noted the paucity of research and training programs. Much of the child's adaptation to the intellectual demands of school will rest on a foundation of adequate social participation in the school setting. The dynamics of interaction among the child, sighted peers, and adults require intensive study. As such research proceeds, it will be extremely important to evaluate the variety of visually impaired children's social skills and manner of interaction and to determine how these variations affect the reactions of sighted peers.

Social cognition

Another factor in this mix is the child's ability to perceive and understand the social behaviors of others. The term "social cognition" refers to the individual's understanding of relationships and the roles of self and others in the social context. The concept is not new, although the terminology reflects the fascination of psychologists in the past decade or so with the role of cognitive processes in a wide variety of areas.

According to Selman and Byrne (1974), children proceed developmentally from an initial inability to assume another person's perspective on social situations, through a gradual set of stages such as realization that different people have different perspectives and that a second person may view the child from a different perspective than the child's own, to a fully relational understanding that a third person could have a different view than either the child or the second person.

Gelber (1980) used several tasks designed to evaluate this progression in elementary school children with visual impairments. The most useful data came from a test in which the child was asked to respond to hypothetical interpersonal dilemmas, from which the child's basis for social–cognitive reasoning could be discerned. Although the children showed a developmental lag compared to sighted children, their progression corresponded to the sequence of stages reported by Selman. Gelber concluded that the sequence of acquisition of levels of social–cognitive understanding is intertwined with the progression, in Piagetian terms, from preoperational to concrete operational thought. The children had at most LP, had lost sight within a year of birth, and were of average IQ. Thus, the sample was relatively homogeneous and did not yield interesting variation aside from the CA progression. There were no gender differences.

There is a related progression in the development of children's perceptions of social behavior, particularly socially abnormal behavior. First graders do not tend to see beyond the immediate consequences of behavior; by the sixth grade, they tend to attribute abnormal behavior to external factors rather than assigning it as an intrinsic quality of the behaver. By the eleventh grade, children are able to use social criteria in evaluating the causes of abnormal behavior (Maas, Marecek, & Travers, 1978). Because the perception of behavior and its situational qualities depends to a large degree on vision, children with visual impairments might be expected to show a different developmental course, both in differentiating normal and abnormal behaviors and in their attitudes toward such behaviors.

Czerwinski and Tait (1981) evaluated this issue with congenitally blind 5- to 17-year-old children from public school settings. Stories describing normal and abnormal behavior were presented, and the child was asked questions designed to evaluate his or her assessment of the behaviors. There was a general age progression in the children's capability to discriminate between normal and abnormal behaviors. However, the blind children did not show a general age progression toward increased attribution of abnormal behaviors to external factors, tending instead to suppose that the behaviors were intrinsic to the child. Some children at each age, however, did believe that the abnormal behaviors could be changed.

The results of Czerwinski and Tait are provocative in suggesting that blind children are less likely to externalize the attribution of abnormal behaviors; this may represent an interesting form of egocentrism. However, the results are not definitive because of the small and heterogeneous sample (e.g., IQ ranged from 83 to 131). The study suggests valuable questions that should be explored with larger samples. In particular, the relationship between the child's perception of behaviors as normal or abnormal, and his or her attributions of both causality and the implications of the behaviors, are of interest.

The child's understanding of sight

Another aspect of social perception and cognition has to do with the child's understanding of the role of vision and of the differences in how people perceive. Flavell (1989), among others, has investigated sighted children's developing awareness of what other people see, as well as their understanding that what other people see does not depend on the child's own perceptual experiences. There is a small body of research on this issue with visually impaired children.

Cratty (1969) suggested that it is around the age of four or five years that blind children begin to recognize that other people may perceive differently than they do. The case in point was a pair of blind twins who had discovered that they could "hide" from one another by being silent, whereas they realized that this would not work with their (sighted) mother.

Bigelow (1988) studied the understanding by two totally blind brothers, ages four and six years, of how people see. Each boy was asked to show an object to three people, a sighted adult, a sighted child, and another blind child (the subject's brother). The child was asked to "Show the ___ to ___." Objects were ones that they could carry, that they could not carry, or that they wore.

Both children "showed" portable or worn objects to sighted others, whether child or adult, by carrying the object to within about five feet of the other person; they did not require the other to feel the object. The two differed in how they treated nonportable objects: the older child believed that the sighted other could not be shown such an object unless there was spatial contiguity, whereas the younger apparently believed that he could show objects from afar, by patting it and saying "look." However, his own position sometimes blocked the necessary line of sight. Both children also gave indication that they were aware that blind and sighted people experience objects in different ways, but understandably, in neither case did the child exhibit understanding of the qualities of vision (e.g., line of sight, viewing from afar). When "showing" a portable object to the blind child, it was clear that "show" was interpreted as requiring the child to feel the object, whereas causing the object to make a sound did not suffice.

Bigelow (1992) studied the same two boys, now six and eight years old, as well as two partially sighted boys, ages six and seven. Each child was studied every two months until a series of tasks was mastered (this period ranged up to 15 months). Various toys were used in several tasks designed to evaluate the child's understanding of what would be visible to the experimenter. The partially sighted children were tested in both blindfolded and nonblindfolded conditions. These children, with or without blindfold, tended to master the tasks more quickly than the blind children. Furthermore, the blind children made different types of errors: it was common in the early stages for them to cover the requested part of the toy with their fingers, thus rendering it invisible to the sighted experimenter. Although based on very few cases, these findings are provocative in suggesting the difficulty that total lack of visual function creates for the development of understanding of visual perception.

There may be a semantic aspect to the problem of the blind child's understanding of sight, in that the blind child may attach different meanings to the terms "look" and "see." Landau and Gleitman (1985) noted that their young blind children consistently distinguished between these words by interpreting "look" to mean "search," and "see" to mean "perceive." "See," therefore, may not be interpreted as being specific to vision (or any other modality).

The school setting

Like the family setting for the preschool child, the school setting is a social environment of major importance for school-age children. Many studies have compared indices of social adjustment and social maturity obtained from children in residential and integrated school settings. The rationale behind such studies typically is that the characteristics of the school setting vary in the opportunities and demands that they present to the child, and that the children's social characteristics may change as a consequence.

However, it should be stressed that school setting is not a simple variable. School environments differ in numerous ways, and it is not the school type but the various factors associated with it that affect the child's social adjustment and development. Within any type of school, the attitudes and social interactive characteristics of teachers and other children create the social environment in which the child with a visual impairment develops and exercises the skills of social adaptation. It is unfortunate that relatively little investigation has been conducted of the dynamics within the school setting.

Social maturity. McGuinness (1970) used the Vineland Social Maturity Scale to compare children in a school for the blind or in regular schools with either resource-room or itinerant-teacher provisions. The children were drawn from the fourth through sixth grades, had at most LP, and for the most part had lost vision very early, a large majority due to ROP. A variation on the Bialer Locus of Control Scale was also administered, and a sociometric questionnaire was used to identify the child's best friends.

Results of the Vineland showed social maturity scores to be higher for both public school groups than for the special school group, but there was no difference between the itinerant-teacher and resource-room situations. McGuinness noted, however, that some individual children in the special-school setting did obtain high scores. Special-school children tended to list other blind children among their friends most frequently, followed by children in the resource room and then the itinerant-teacher setting. Correspondingly, the number of sighted friends was least for the residential school children and greatest for children in the itinerant-teacher setting. Contrary to the hypothesis, there were no differences between groups on the Locus of Control Scale. (See Chapter 11 for discussion of locus of control.)

McGuinness interpreted the results in the context of the different demands and opportunities that characterize school settings: particularly with respect to social integration, he concluded that "the integrated school settings . . . have amply fulfilled the purpose for which they were established, that of facilitating the social integration of blind children with their sighted peers, and of promoting social maturity and independence" (p. 45). McGuinness also argued that independence is fostered in the integrated setting: that these children "have less opportunity to receive special help may force them to learn how to work out problems for themselves. The significantly lower scores of children from the special school setting may perhaps reflect the lowered expectations resulting from lack of competition with sighted children their own age" (p. 40).

Adjustment. A similar question has been posed about social and emotional adjustment by Schindele (1974), who used the Self-Concept Adjustment Score (Cowen, Underberg, Verillo, & Benham, 1961) to evaluate the social adjustment of fifth- and sixth-grade children enrolled in residential or integrated schools. There were no overall differences between the groups, but closer analysis revealed an important distinction. The integrated school children showed growing adjustment with increasing age, whereas in the residential school group the older children were relatively less well adjusted than the younger. Schindele suggested that while the social adjustment of children in regular schools develops in a realistic surrounding, "the social adjustment of the visually handicapped in a residential school is mainly the result of being brought up in a sheltered and unrealistic environment. In this case the good social adjustment of these children might be seriously affected as they grow older and especially when they have to leave the residential school" (p. 141).

For the integrated school group there was a strong positive correlation between social adjustment and intelligence. Schindele proposed that visually impaired students in integrated schools have to make extra efforts to achieve a high level of social adjustment, and that more intelligent children are more likely to be successful in doing so.

Bauman (1964) compared residential and integrated school adolescents using the Adolescent Emotional Factors Inventory (AEFI). She found that many of the items that differentiated the groups revealed a

poorer overall adjustment by the integrated school children. This outcome is unexpected based on Schindele's results. The explanation is
instructive, however: there was a tendency for the residential schools to
have the children with more severe visual loss, whereas the partially
sighted children tended to be in integrated schools. Coupled with this
difference, the data showed less adequate adjustment to visual loss in
partially sighted children, accompanied by a greater sense of tension and
pressure, and less self-confidence. It is thoroughly unclear from this
pattern of results whether it was the children's experience in an integrated school that led to less adequate adjustment, or whether the
difficulties of adjustment to partial vision are the culprit. Whatever the
truth of the matter is, this pattern of results makes evident the danger of
regarding the type of school setting as a simple independent variable.

Determinants of school selection. The higher proportion of partially sighted
children found in integrated schools by Bauman raises the general question of the selection factors that lead to different school placements.
Lukoff and Whiteman (1970) reported an extensive study of the issues,
including the family characteristics that affect the choice of school.

In general, the earlier the child had lost vision, the more likely it was
that the parents chose a special school for the blind. An interesting and
complex relationship was found between the family's expectations for the
child's independence and their choice of school. The pattern was
different for groups of children with early and later visual loss. For
children who lost vision early, the relationship between the family's
expectations of the child's independence and type of school was very
weak. For children with later loss, though, a high proportion (65%)
attended special schools when there were low family expectations for
independence, an intermediate proportion (55%) when expectations for
independence were intermediate, and a low proportion (36%) went to
special schools when family expectations for independence were high.
The dynamics seem clear enough: the less the parents regard the child's
visual impairment as preventing the acquisition of independence, the
more likely they are to choose an educational setting that will encourage
that independence.

The complexity of this pattern was mirrored in the social role categories into which the children fell. In general, and especially when visual
loss was later, children in special schools were less likely to achieve the

most independent social role category. Lukoff and Whiteman discussed this and other results in reference to the environmental context that the special school provides. Because the child's peers, as well as some of the teachers, have visual impairments, "the entire education of these children in these schools, then, is attuned to their handicap" (p. 92). They also argued that this socialization process affects the pattern of friendships of people with visual impairments, suggesting that "whether blindness serves as a sufficient basis for choosing friends, along with such factors as ethnic group and social class, hinges on the significance that the identification of blindness has for the individual" (p. 99). In fact, like McGuinness (1970), they found that attendance at a special school increased the likelihood that a majority of the person's friends were reported also to be blind.

Two concluding points must be made about this material. One is that to the extent that selection factors operate so that the research samples drawn from different schools are not equivalent, methodological caution must be exercised, for example in interpreting the findings reviewed in the previous sections on social maturity and adjustment. The second is that the findings (e.g., of Lukoff & Whiteman) are of more historical than contemporary interest because of the cumulative impact of the move toward maximum use of the integrated school setting for children with handicaps.

Behavior problems. Children show some incidence of behavioral problems in school, and this is no different for children with visual impairments. Teare (1984) used the Child Behavior Checklist (CBCL), developed by Achenbach (1979), to evaluate the behavioral adjustment of 23 children attending a school for the blind. The checklist is completed by the child's parent or other adult (the dorm parent, in this case), and it is normed on sighted children. Teare's orientation was to the exploration of individual differences, noting that early learning experiences, intelligence, mobility, and environmental opportunities may affect adjustment.

About 50% of the variance in CBCL scores was accounted for by IQ: that is, lower-IQ children tended to be rated as having more behavioral adjustment problems. Degree of visual loss (partially sighted vs. blind), gender, socioeconomic status, and age did not account for significant variance in adjustment scores. Noting that there were not significant departures from the CBCL norms for sighted children, Teare concluded:

"Visual functioning may not be the most salient characteristic contributing to the child's behavioral adjustment. As with sighted children, adjustment is most likely the interaction of the child's cognitive resources, other genetic endowments, and the demands of the environmental context in which the child is placed" (p. 240).

This point is also reflected in the study by Jan et al. (1977), who found that behavior problems were not apparently a consequence of visual impairment itself, but were highly related to situational variables. In particular, when broken homes or marital discord was involved, moderate or severe behavior problems occurred in 84% of the cases, in contrast to 33% of the cases in the rest of the sample. Maternal psychiatric problems were also predictive of behavior problems. Like Teare, Jan et al. found that more behavior problems occurred in lower-IQ children. The incidence of problems was also higher when other handicaps accompanied visual impairment.

Schnittjer and Hirshoren (1981) studied problem behaviors in residential school children using the Behavior Problem Checklist (BPC). The children ranged from 6 to 21 years and were characterized as having "substantial visual dysfunction," average intelligence, and no additional handicaps. Three major factors emerged from a factor analysis: "conduct disorder," "personality problem," and "inadequacy–immaturity." The structure of these factors was very similar to what had been found with other populations, including children with no handicaps and those with hearing impairments; Schnittjer and Hirshoren concluded that there is "no factor . . . that we could attribute to visual handicap" (p. 522).

Heinze, Matson, Helsel, and Kapperman (1987) also used the BPC as well as other behavioral measures to compare children from residential and day school settings. There were no overall relationships of the checklist measures to age, and no differences between residential and day school subsamples were reported. Boys generally tended to show more behavior problems than girls. Generally, Heinze et al. concluded that these evaluative scales are useful with visually impaired children, despite their norming on sighted children. However, they found that the symptom clusters (e.g., "schizophrenia," "somatic complaints," "aggression," or "delinquency") were quite different from those found with sighted children.

Summary. These studies reveal that nothing about visual impairment itself necessarily increases the likelihood of behavior problems; indeed, the environmental circumstances that accompany problem behaviors are the same in children with and without visual impairments. The literature does not reveal the actual dynamics of problem behaviors, so the question remains: given a set of predisposing environmental features, what causes some children to develop behavior problems while others do not?

Moral development

Piaget (1948) and Kohlberg (1981) present major theories of moral development that are quite similar to one another; both maintain that progress in moral development rests upon the development of progressively more mature cognitive skills. Both theories also hold that the child's social interactions with his or her peers are critical in developing the desire to cooperate on which a sense of moral values must rest. Thus, it is appropriate to treat moral development as a topic of social interaction, since moral standards are socially based and because the nature of the child's moral conduct – and expectations of the moral conduct of others – has clear social-interactive implications.

Moral judgment and conduct. Stephens and Simpkins (1974) assessed the moral judgment and moral conduct of blind children ranging in age from 6 to 18 years. Moral judgment was assessed from the child's responses to a series of hypothetical situations. Moral conduct was assessed from the child's behavior in structured test situations, for example whether the child took candy from a dish while unattended in the testing room, or took a nickel that the experimenter "inadvertently" dropped when leaving the room. The major thrust of the research was to compare blind children with sighted peers, and in general there were not remarkable differences.

There was a general tendency for moral judgments to become more mature with increasing age, but less age change occurred between the younger (6 to 10 years) and middle (10 to 14) groups than between the middle and older (14 to 18) groups. There was also a tendency for moral conduct to improve with increasing age, as it does in sighted children.

Moral reasoning and cognitive development. Interested in the cognitive bases for moral development, Markoulis (1988) examined the relationship between moral reasoning and cognitive development within a Piagetian framework. According to this approach, the development of moral reasoning is facilitated by two factors. One is the acquisition of the logical characteristics of concrete operational thought; the other is the opportunity for social interaction with peers that leads the child to understand the necessity of moral reciprocity for effective social functioning. Markoulis hypothesized that the social restrictions visual impairment tends to impose would slow the acquisition of moral reasoning compared to that of sighted children, but that as in sighted children, advances in concrete operational thought would be positively related to advances in moral reasoning.

The children, presumably with severe vision loss, were drawn from a (Greek) school for the blind and were divided into groups for ages 6 to 8, 8 to 10, and 10 to 12 years. Sighted children were also tested. Cognitive level was assessed by tasks of conservation of substance, classification, and class inclusion, all adapted for tactual administration to the children with visual impairments. Tasks of moral reasoning were evaluated with respect to (a) the consideration of intention, (b) the realization of moral obligations as a condition of mutual trust among people, and (c) judgments of appropriate punishment.

As expected, the children with visual impairments tended to move developmentally from *heteronomous* moral reasoning (moral realism; the inability to adjust evaluation of transgression in relation to context) through a transitional phase to *autonomous* reasoning (the ability to take intention and circumstances into account), although they did so on a somewhat later timetable than sighted children. However, the hypothesis that concrete operational functioning is a prerequisite for moral reasoning was not strongly supported. For the children with visual impairments, it was not clear that concrete operational thought was prerequisite to moral reasoning. Instead, the evidence supported the hypothesis that the emergence of moral reasoning was related to the quality and extent of social experiences. While this may be so, caution must be used in interpreting the data in this way. It is not at all clear that tactual adaptations of cognitive-developmental tasks assess those developments in exactly the same way for visually impaired children that the visually administered tasks do for sighted children. It is possible that if tests were used that had demonstrable criterion validity for visually impaired children with respect to the concepts that they purport to test, the same synchrony of cognitive achievement and moral reasoning would emerge.

This is a theoretically and practically rich issue that deserves more intense study, particularly of the precursors and dynamics of the emergence of moral reasoning and behavior. Future emphasis should be placed on the factors and dynamics that lead to more or less mature moral behavior, rather than to comparisons between children with and without vision.

11

Developing a sense of self

The neonate does not have a concept of the self as an entity independent of other people or the physical world. The older child has a well-developed sense of him- or herself, not only as an entity distinct from other people and things, but as an independent person with a unique set of emotions, desires, fears, abilities, and other personal characteristics. The development of the sense of self is the topic of this chapter.

The adaptive tasks begin in infancy, when the neonate must acquire the concept of the distinction of the self from the rest of the world. Subsequently, a concept of body image must be acquired, and the child must be able to represent the self in linguistic usage. The child's realization of the facts and implications of his or her visual impairment are of particular interest.

Gradually, and in large part as a consequence of the process of adapting to the demands of the social world, the child acquires a set of characteristics that are often collectively called "personality." With respect to a sense of self, not least among these is the notion of locus of control, which has to do with the child's perception of the extent to which his or her personal situation is primarily under the control of external as opposed to internal factors.

Self-concept in infancy

The general argument is made that initially the infant, with or without vision, does not have a sense of self as distinct from the physical or social world and thus must acquire the distinction. Ordinarily the development of this concept depends on many sources of information, directly from the physical environment as well as indirectly from interactions with other people. Since vision is a potentially rich source of such information, the absence of vision may mean that the concept of self as distinct from the world develops along alternative paths.

Applied to the blind infant, this formulation is expressed in different ways depending on the writer's theoretical orientation. Writers in the psychoanalytic tradition, for example, use the term "ego development." For the most part this term is not meant in the restrictive sense of a personality construct, but encompasses aspects of perceptual, cognitive, and motor functioning. Broadly speaking, it has to do with the emotional and conceptual separation of the self (the "ego") from the rest of the world. Sandler (1963) hypothesized that lack of vision necessarily alters the course of ego development: "Because of the absence of a major sensory modality, the ego development of the blind child will tend to proceed along different lines from that of the sighted . . . the ego development of the blind child is hindered or distorted by his sensory handicap" (p. 344). Further, "Ego deformation resulting from the blindness occurs in its own right, and is linked with a path of development which basically cannot be reversed by the environment, although its outcome can be modified to a large extent by suitable mothering" (p. 346).

Fraiberg and Freedman (1964), while agreeing that the lack of vision changes the situation, were more positive in their view of the potential outcome: "We must assume from the evidence presented by large numbers of healthy and educable blind children that other sensory modalities can substitute for vision in the process of ego formation. There remain the questions: how are these substitutions made, and how does ego formation take place in the absence of vision?" (p. 114).

Scott (1969) approached the issue from a more cognitive point of view but was just as pessimistic as Sandler (1963): "The differentiation between self and environment begins to emerge at this point [third to fourth month]. By differentiating objects from one another, by manipulating them, and by observing his impact upon them, the [sighted] child is slowly able to distinguish the boundary between self and non-self. This process is greatly frustrated in the blind child" (p. 1030). Scott went on to delineate specific areas of behavior, such as linguistic usage and social interactions, that he argued are necessarily affected adversely by the lack of vision. Scott summarized the problems as three: a restriction in the extent of the environment that the infant can engage, a lesser stimulus value of the part of the environment that *is* encountered, and a lack of appreciation of the infant's impact on the objects manipulated.

A still more cognitively based formulation is also available. According to Piaget's (1954) account of the course of sensorimotor development in the sighted infant, for the first four months the child's activity is tied up with actions related to his or her own body and its sensations: it is only with the substage of secondary circular reactions, beginning around four months of age, that the infant begins to show an effective orientation to the external world and to the perceptual stimulation it provides. This timing squares well with the four- to five-month normative onset of reaching outward to visually perceived objects. Without vision to elicit reaching outward, the blind infant might well prolong the prior substage of primary circular reactions, in which activity is directed to his or her own body.

The problem in trying to make sense of all this is that the available evidence is not good. It may be reasonable to accept on face value the various observations, for example that around mid-year, infants with visual impairments do not orient as much to the external world as sighted infants do, but it is a substantial leap to the conclusion that as a consequence of this, concepts about the distinction between the self and the external world differ between blind and sighted infants. From the evidence that is available, I can see no objective basis for drawing conclusions about the quality of the self-concept of blind infants. Absent direct evidence, inferences can be drawn as easily in one direction as the other.

The development of self-concept after infancy

The issue of self-concept in children is difficult to conceptualize and to evaluate. These difficulties arise because the term is used by different people in very different ways and is, correspondingly, evaluated in very different ways. "Body image" captures one set of perceptual–cognitive meanings, referring to the conception of the body and its relationship to the external world. There is also a cluster of work that interprets language as an indicator of self-concept. Yet another approach regards self-concept as a set of personality variables. We will review each of these in turn.

Body image

At one level, "body image" refers to a child's knowledge of the parts of the body and of the relationships among those parts (e.g., the fingers are connected to the hand). A second level is exemplified by Siegel and Murphy (1970), who defined body image as the mental picture that one has of one's body in space. Combining these, Mills (1970) defined body image as "a knowledge of body parts, how the parts relate to each other, how the parts may be utilized both individually and collectively for purposeful activity, and how the parts relate to the child's spatial environment" (p. 81). Various methods have been used to evaluate the child's body image.

Constructive methods. One approach asks the child to construct the body. For example, Millar (1975d) assessed blind children's ability to draw the human body. The children had lost vision within the first two years of life and ranged in age from 6 to 12 years. They were asked to draw a human figure using the Sewell Raised Line Drawing Kit, and to name each part of the figure as they drew it. The drawings were scored for body scheme (number and recognizability of main body parts), cohesion (correct joining of body parts), detail, and alignment to the floor.

There was a general improvement with age. As in other studies of the drawings of blind children (e.g., Kennedy, 1980), some of the drawings were clearly recognizable while others were unidentifiable. The younger children, if they drew recognizable elements, tended to draw legs, arms, and the head.

Witkin et al. (1968) used a battery of tests designed to evaluate cognitive articulation in children who were blind from birth and ranged from 12 to 19 years of age. Among the tasks was a clay modeling test intended to show body concept. The child was asked simply to make a person. The products were rated on a five-point scale, progressing from unarticulated lumps to refined human figures without major distortions. Performance in clay modeling of the human figure was, like most other measures of cognitive articulation, unrelated to IQ. Unfortunately, no relationship of modeling scores to CA was reported, although it was noted that there were considerable individual differences in performance.

Great caution must be used in interpreting the results of drawing and modeling tasks as bearing on the quality of body image. The primary problem is that failure to draw or sculpt a realistic model may reflect nothing more than the child's lack of physical skill in dealing with the medium. To be sure, Millar (1975d) was concerned strictly with the nature of representation, without reference to an underlying "concept" of body image. On the other hand, the discussion of Witkin et al. (1968) implied, inappropriately, that the quality of the child's body concept may be validly tapped by such constructive techniques.

Though still constructive, the method used by Kephart et al. (1974) was designed to avoid the difficulty of physical skills. They administered a verbal test to evaluate blind children's knowledge of the parts of the body and their relationships. The children were asked to construct an imaginary boy or girl by describing the various necessary components. The children ranged from five to seven years of age; the age of visual loss was not specified. There was a gradual increase with age in the completeness of information offered. Interestingly, although facial features gradually appeared with increasing age, ears and eyes were notably absent, as were fingers.

Formal scales. Cratty and Sams (1968) designed a detailed test of body image development of children with visual impairments and reported the results of the test for a large and diverse group of children in the 5- to 16-year age range. The group was mixed in gender and most had lost sight at birth. The children varied widely in IQ, with scores ranging from 57 to 144. The partially sighted subgroup had an average IQ of 88, in contrast to the average of 107 for the blind subset. While the difference was not statistically significant, it signals the need for caution in interpreting any differences between the blind and partially sighted groups.

The test was divided into five parts, *body planes* (child's identification of their sides, front, or back), *body parts* (identification of specific parts of the child's own body), *body movement* (performing directed movement of parts of the entire body), *laterality* (identification of the body as well as of the body in relation to external objects), and *directionality* (identifying the right and left sides of other people and objects.)

Total test scores generally showed improved performance with increasing age in the 5- to 16-year range. The age differences appeared to be concentrated in the body parts and the directionality items. There were no significant gender differences. There was generally better performance by the blind group than the partially sighted group, although this must be qualified in light of the subsample differences in IQ noted above. Children with an IQ of 80 or greater tended to perform better than those with an IQ below 80. This difference did not appear for the laterality and directionality subscales. In any case, the covariation of IQ and visual status in the sample makes a conclusion about either variable risky, as Cratty and Sams noted.

Some important points about the developmental sequence of the acquisition of body image emerge from the data. Identification of body planes was performed well by even the youngest children. The body parts subscale revealed a general developmental progression of knowledge from the upper to the lower body, and a tendency for more extreme parts (e.g., fingers or hands) to be more readily identified than intermediate parts (e.g., forearm or thigh), particularly when a right–left distinction was involved.

Watemberg, Cernak, and Henderson (1986) assessed the ability of congenitally blind children in the 7- to 14-year age range to identify left–right relationships, with respect both to the child's own body and to external relationships. The children's ability to deal with the left–right relationships of their own body generally improved with age, and it was usually better than their ability to deal with external right–left spatial relationships. (Other aspects of laterality are reviewed in Chapter 4.)

Training. Several programs have been designed to improve body image through training. Cratty and Sams (1968) presented a justification for such efforts, citing the importance of a strong body image as a conceptual basis for structuring external space. The proposed program stressed the importance of several sensory modalities, as well as the need for the child to build "cognitive bridges" to integrate information from various sources. Cratty and Sams identified four phases of body image development: (1) body planes, parts, and movements (two to five years), (2) left–right discrimination (five to seven years), (3) complex judgments of the body and of body–object relationships (six to eight years), and (4) understanding of another person's reference system. A number of exercises were designed to foster adequate progress through these stages.

The program stressed auditory, motor, tactual, and kinesthetic aspects as well as verbal mediation. It emphasized experiences appropriate to the developmental level of the child, and it stressed the necessity of providing a variety of activities to produce adequate generalization of concepts. Finally, it noted the importance of a gradual externalization of body image concepts to build an idea of external space using the body image as a basis.

Based on Cratty's work, Walker (1970, 1971, cited by Walker, 1973) presented a structured set of lessons in body image training to groups of kindergarten and early elementary school children. The body image test of Cratty and Sams (1968) was used for evaluation. The results for the kindergarten children indicated that "the program was effective in improving the body image" (p. 224). The effects were apparently greater for children without than with useful vision. These subgroups apparently differed in intelligence, however, so it is not clear whether more effective training was related to the severity of visual loss or to variation in intellectual skills.

Summary. Age-related improvement is evident from a variety of methods of evaluating body image. Although the available evidence is not completely convincing, good body image also appears to be related to partial vision and to higher intelligence.

Self-concept as expressed in language

Self-concept can also be expressed in language. For the most part, this literature takes as a starting point the fact that children with visual impairments often use personal pronouns differently than do sighted children. We can (albeit with due caution) examine the nature of these phenomena, particularly the nature of the reference to self in the child's language, to make inferences about the child's self-concept.

Several reports of the misuse of personal pronouns were discussed in Chapter 5. For example, Fraiberg and Adelson (1976) discussed the delayed use of the inventive "I," as well as other misuse of personal pronouns such as referring to one's self in the third person, in terms of difficulties with self-representation in the blind child. They also reasoned that such difficulties might emerge in the play situation, in which objects may be used as symbolic representations of the self.

Rogers and Puchalski (1984b) reported an empirical study directed to this issue. The procedure involved having the child perform several "pretend" scenarios involving a breakfast setting, a doll-bathing setting, and a bedtime setting. After the child's modeling of each setting with conventional props, one prop was changed to neutral (neither appropriate nor inappropriate to the setting). In a third phase, the prop was changed to counterconventional (inappropriate). The child's activities were noted, particularly for evidence of engaging in symbolic "pretend" actions. About half of the children did so.

There were some interesting differences, and even more interesting similarities, between the children who showed symbolic activities and those who did not. There was no relationship between age (range 18 to 37 months) and symbolic activities, nor was there any difference associated with the child's degree of vision loss (blind vs. partially sighted). Those who showed symbolic actions tended more than the others to use the word "no" in their language interactions. On the face of it, the use of "no" is taken as an assertion of independence, but its use also signifies that the child conceptualizes him- or herself as separate and independent – the essence of self-representation. The use of the word "no" can be representational in another way, as denoting the opposite of a situation; for example, the relationship between "milk" and "no milk" is a conceptual one. There was also a significant relationship between symbolic actions and the use of two-word combinations in the child's language.

It is not clear what the causal relationships among these developmental indices may be, although it is reasonable to suggest that the conceptual ability to use symbolic representation underlies both the emergence of relational language forms ("no" or two-word combinations) and the ability to represent the self symbolically in play as well as in other conceptual ways.

Self-concept as an aspect of personality

Scott's (1968) words (though with gender-appropriate apologies!) provide a useful introduction to this section: "By 'self-concept' I mean an individual's perception of himself. A man's self-concept consists of the attitudes, feelings and beliefs he has about the kind of person he is, his strengths and weaknesses, his potentials and limitations, his characteristic qualities, and so forth. These things are expressed both in his actions and in his responses to the questions, 'Who am I?', 'What kind of a person am I?'" (pp. 14–15). We will begin our consideration with research that has addressed self-concept directly, then move to related personality variables.

Much of the evidence about self-concept comes from studies whose primary focus has been comparative, but some limited differential information about children with visual impairments can nevertheless be gleaned.

Jervis (1959) used an interview that probed the child's interests, self-evaluations, and expectations for the future, and a modified Q-sort procedure that was designed to evaluate the discrepancy between the child's self-perceived characteristics and traits he or she would have liked to have. The subjects were 20 blind residential school adolescents with visual loss before the third birthday. As a group, they were generally apprehensive about the future and expressed limited goals for themselves. Interestingly, in relation to these relatively low self-expectations, 18 of the 20 felt that not enough was expected of them. Asked to mention their personal strengths, 14 noted their ability to get along with other people.

Jervis concluded that in comparison with sighted adolescents, these subjects tended to have either a strongly positive or a strongly negative attitude about themselves: "It is apparently quite difficult for a blind person to take a middle ground; either he is forced into having a negative self-concept or if he is fortunate enough to find positive attributes in his personality he tends to exaggerate them" (p. 23). Unfortunately, no evidence was presented about which factors might have tended to push an individual in one or the other direction.

Zunich and Ledwith (1965) also noted the tendency of fourth grade children to use highly positive or negative traits to describe themselves, using Lipsitt's (1958) self-concept scale. The girls generally tended to rate themselves higher on the positive traits than did the boys. Unfortunately no relationships were reported between self-evaluations and factors that might be expected to influence them, such as parental acceptance.

On the somewhat more positive side, Coker (1979) found elementary school children in both residential and integrated schools to have a generally positive self-image, as measured by the Piers–Harris Self Concept Test. Coker was also concerned with the relative academic achievement of the children, evaluated by the Stanford Achievement Test. Interestingly, the achievement of children from both types of school were equivalent and age-appropriate at the third grade, but while children from the residential schools maintained their achievement through sixth grade, the achievement of the integrated school children progressively declined. The study provided an ideal opportunity to examine the relationship between self-concept and achievement, but unfortunately no relationship was reported, despite the availability of the data.

The Tennessee Self Concept Scale (TCSC) was used by both Meighan (1971) and Head (1979) to evaluate the self-concept of adolescents. Both samples were heterogeneous with respect to ethnicity, gender, and severity of visual loss, as well as age. Neither study found any remarkable differences in self-concept scores related to these variables, or to school setting or academic achievement, and the appropriateness of the TCSC for this population has to be questioned.

Jan et al. (1977) reported the reactions of children to their visual impairment. According to parental reports, a small number of children (5%) were "quite preoccupied" by their visual condition, whereas 21% denied any adverse feelings about their impairment. In contrast to these relative extremes, 70% of the children were judged to have a "realistic" attitude toward their visual impairment. That is, they realized that the impairment imposed some limitations on their activities, but were not unduly depressed by the recognition. This relatively healthy picture was mirrored in evaluations by the children's teachers. It was also reflected in relatively low incidence of autistic symptoms, as evaluated by this clinically experienced team of researchers. Unfortunately it is not possible to assess any age differences from the data.

Summary. Overall, this body of work is disappointing in its impact. While several studies have evaluated individual differences, there are few findings of interest, and we have to wonder about the adequacy of conceptualization and evaluation of self-concept in this research. Furthermore, self-image has not generally been evaluated in relation to areas for which it might have functional implications, such as school performance or level of aspiration. Cook-Clampert (1981) noted that the research is unsatisfying and raised the questions (which are even now still unanswered): "(1) How does the child's visual impairment influence the family's rearing methods and thus the development of the child's self-concept? (2) Is there a correlation between the extent of visual loss and the growth of a positive self-concept?" (p. 238).

Realization of blindness. Speaking primarily of partially sighted children, Winton (1970) stressed the need for informing the child as early as possible of his or her handicap, so that "he can thus adjust to his difficulties by making appropriate indications to himself. He can answer his questions about why he cannot do all the things that other children can do" (p. 21). In view of the desirability of a stable self-concept, this advice seems wise: if the child's realization of his or her visual impairment is sudden, an abrupt change in self-concept may result, with negative implications for overall adjustment.

On the other hand, there is reason to avoid overemphasizing the fact of visual impairment. In their study of blind adults with respect to vocational success, Bauman and Yoder (1966) found that the more self-sufficient and mobile individuals tended to come from families that had not made an issue of the visual impairment: "The pattern of family relationships is more likely to be the pattern it would have been had the individual had normal vision" (p. 69).

Other aspects of personality

Personality tests have a long history, and they have been used no less avidly to evaluate people with visual impairments than they have with the sighted population. In my view, the result is disappointing; it is not very helpful to know that the average child with a visual impairment is more or less anxious than the average child with vision. It *would* be important to know what the functional implications of such a difference are, but the body of research is remarkably silent on such issues. In brief, the main themes that appear in this literature are the following.

Introversion / extroversion

In his study of 9- to 14-year-old congenitally blind residential school children, Zahran (1965) found no gender differences in extroversion using the Junior Maudsley Personality Inventory. Brown (1938), on the other hand, evaluated introversion and extroversion in residential school adolescents and found a slight difference in gender, with boys tending to be more extroverted than girls. Neither age nor IQ was significantly related to introversion / extroversion, and no relationships were reported with visual experience variables.

Studying partially sighted children, Pintner and Forlano (1943) found that girls were markedly more introverted than boys in the elementary grades, but that no such differences appeared in children above the sixth grade. Unfortunately, no relationships were reported between introversion and adjustment scores. Boys and girls did not tend to differ on the adjustment scales, however, and it is possible to infer cautiously that the relatively higher extroversion of the younger boys was not associated with better adjustment.

Summary. No consistent pattern of relationship of introversion-extroversion to age, gender, or other variables appears in this group of studies, and indeed several internal contradictions characterize the findings. The relationship to visual characteristics has apparently not been examined.

Dominance / submissiveness and aggression

Using the Bernreuter Personality Inventory, Petrucci (1953) found a pattern of submissiveness in the interpersonal relationships of adolescents with visual impairments. Other authors, for example Bauman (1964), have mentioned similar tendencies, and in this case there is some evidence about how dominance / submissiveness is related to other variables. For example, Greenberg, Allison, Fewell, and Rich (1957) found a general tendency to submissiveness in their study of residential school adolescents, and dominance scores generally increased from the sixth to the twelfth grade level. This age progression was considerably stronger for boys than for girls.

Greenberg and Jordan (1957) hypothesized that higher interpersonal dominance would be found in blind than in partially sighted adolescents. Contrary to the hypothesis, no difference was found between the groups using the Bernreuter Personality Inventory, and in fact on the California 'F' scale, which measures authoritarianism, the group with partial vision group scored higher.

In her intensive study of mother–child dyads, Imamura (1965) included several variables related to dominance, including succorance (requesting help), submission, and self-reliance. The children, who were three to six years of age (and therefore younger than those in the foregoing studies), were rated on these characteristics in a series of observational sessions. The blind children tended to be less dominant, though no more submissive, than an archival group of sighted children. Of more interest was Imamura's exploration of the relationships between the blind children's characteristics and the social-interactive characteristics of their mothers in relation to the child. Most striking was the strong positive correlation between the child's submissiveness and the mother's dominance. That is, children may respond to maternal dominance by adopting a submissive role. (The dynamics may be different for sighted children and their mothers, since no such correlation emerged in that group.)

Imamura also evaluated the dimensions of sociable aggression (aggression with the intent of being sociable) and nonsociable aggression (aggression with the intent to harm). There was no consistent pattern of relationships between maternal characteristics and child behaviors, although curiously, child sociable aggression was positively correlated with maternal nonsociable aggression.

Summary. No remarkable findings emerge from this body of work, although some evidence of individual differences has been reported. The research model used by Imamura, in which the child's characteristics are assessed in relation to features of the social environment, offers more promise than the simple assessment of personality variables using standardized tests.

Neuroticism

Petrucci (1953) reported a high incidence of neuroticism in adolescents with visual impairments, but no gender differences were reported. However, Brown (1939), using a variation of the Thurstone Personality Schedule, did find the distribution of neuroticism scores for blind residential school students higher for girls than for boys.

Greenberg and Jordan (1957), also evaluating high school residential students, found no differences between partially sighted and blind children on the neuroticism scale of the Bernreuter inventory. As for the possible relation of neuroticism to age, Greenberg et al. (1957) found a generally high level of neuroticism in residential school children from grades 6 to 12, but no variation with age within this grade range.

Overall scores on neuroticism scales are unsatisfying, since the term covers a range of more specific difficulties. One such aspect is anxiety. Hardy (1968) described the development of the Anxiety Scale for the Blind (ASB) as an alternative to the traditional Taylor Manifest Anxiety Scale (TMAS). Items were intensively screened by clinical experts. The ASB and the TMAS were each administered twice to 122 adolescents ranging in age from 13 to 22 years and varying in intelligence and degree of visual loss. Teacher ratings of students' anxiety were also obtained.

The correlations between teacher ratings of anxiety and ASB outcomes were statistically significant but not impressive. The correlation between the ASB and the TMAS was .74. There were no marked variations in anxiety scores as a function of severity of visual loss, although there was a tendency for the children with intermediate visual loss to score somewhat higher on anxiety. Anxiety scores generally increased with age, but this did not hold for the group with total blindness. Verbal intelligence was generally negatively correlated with anxiety scores; that is, students testing lower in intelligence tended to show higher anxiety scores. This relationship was, however, not found for the totally blind children.

Miller (1970) found similar results using the ASB. There were no overall differences between partially sighted and blind samples of ninth through twelfth graders, or between special class (EMR) and the regular residential school sample. Similarly, Wilhelm (1989) did not find consistent patterns of difference between partially sighted and blind children in the 6- to 17-year age range. Like Hardy (1968), Miller found a general increase in anxiety with increasing grade level. Miller attributed the increased anxiety to the older child's impending departure from the relatively secure residential school environment.

Summary. The literature on these interpersonal characteristics has been reported only briefly, since it is not at all clear in most instances what, if any, significance they might have. From any practical or theoretical point of view, it is of little value to know that children with visual impairments are more or less introverted, neurotic, or aggressive than sighted children, or for that matter that scores on these scales vary with age, intelligence, school placement, gender, or other individual differences variables. To be useful, research must couple the incidence characteristics of such factors with an analysis of their implications. For example, the question may be posed: are older children, with their higher neuroticism and anxiety ratings, more socially or personally dysfunctional? If not, then the knowledge is interesting but not important. If so, then additional questions arise. What factors lead to increased neuroticism and anxiety? How can they be ameliorated? How, in short, can the visually impaired child's situation be adjusted to optimize the characteristic in question, so that the child's capacity to respond adaptively to the demands of his or her existence can be maximized?

I have used the example of neuroticism, but the same points should be made about other personality characteristics as well. Researchers fall short of their obligations if they are content with evaluating characteristics without regard for the variables that influence them, and if they disregard the functional implications of those characteristics.

Knowledge about sex

A seriously understudied area of social development in children with visual impairments concerns knowledge of sex and sexual behavior. Cutsforth (1951), Gendel (1973), and Scholl (1974) discussed the specific problems that visual impairment creates for the child's acquisition of knowledge about physical and behavioral aspects of sex. However, there is very little empirical evidence about what children know about sex and how they acquire their knowledge. There is agreement that the problems of learning about sex are considerable. Perhaps the most important factor is that touch is taboo when the topic of learning is sex. Children with visual impairments are, as sighted children are, generally discouraged from gaining information about sex via tactual experience with others.

Thus the main problem is access to information. Information about sex is usually conveyed verbally by parents, siblings, and peers. Two factors seem relevant. Many parents are hesitant to discuss sex-related matters frankly with their children, and metaphoric explanations (such as "the stork") must be at least as puzzling to the child with a visual impairment as they are to the sighted child. Second, the stimulus for a parent's explanation is often the child's question; the child without vision may ask fewer questions of the parent or other informant.

Foulke and Uhde (1974) characterized the blind child's situation:

He knows about his own body because he can explore it freely. He is fairly well informed about the bodies of playmates of the same sex. He is less well informed about the bodies of playmates of the opposite sex. He is almost completely uninformed about adult bodies of either sex. By the time he reaches adolescence, he has been brought under the control of the taboos of his society, and is no longer free to explore any body but his own. (p. 194)

At the same time, they noted that "in the course of growing up, the blind child becomes aware of the emphasis on sexuality in our culture, and a reasonable consequence of this combination of ignorance and curiosity is the creation of bizarre theories concerning the anatomy and the functions of sex" (p. 194). Presumably this problem can only have become exacerbated during the intervening two decades.

Foulke and Uhde presented preliminary information from a questionnaire distributed to a large number of (mostly male) visually impaired adolescents and their parents and teachers. About half of the children reported having had discussions of sexual matters with their parents, but the reports of a majority of these indicated that they had been given misinformation or had misinterpreted the information given. More children reported having discussed sex with their friends than with their parents. Definitions of various sex terms were requested, and in general the results suggested a great deal of misunderstanding.

Similar work is lacking with younger children. It may be assumed, from the paucity of veridical information that Foulke and Uhde's adolescent informants had, that such study would reveal quite scanty knowledge among younger children as well.

While there are many discussions in the literature about the pros and cons of various approaches to sex education, there is appallingly little empirical information available about the actual knowledge that children and adolescents with visual impairments have about sex. Particularly in view of the heavy emphasis of contemporary popular culture on sexual matters, the need for effective sex education is critical. Nevertheless, the design of effective sex education must be based on knowledge of the actual state of affairs, and this is a significant gap that should be seriously addressed.

Locus of control

The term *locus of control* (LOC) is used to describe a person's perception of the extent to which he or she is in command of the events that affect his or her life. Internal LOC describes individuals who see themselves as exercising substantial control over their lives, while external LOC describes those who see themselves as being influenced by other people or by situational variables over which they have no control. Of course these represent the extremes of a dimension along which people vary continuously.

The question of LOC is interesting for the case of visual impairment.

According to Tait (1972e), the child with a significant visual impairment may have difficulty knowing when he or she has another person's attention and may thus frequently initiate unreciprocated social interactions because the other person is in fact not attending. Tait reasoned that this dynamic may lead to a sense of lack of control in social interactions and thus to a relatively external LOC. Indeed, Imamura (1965), studying three- to six-year-old blind children, found a relatively low frequency of initiation by these children of social contact with the mother and other adults and children. Of the contacts that were initiated, a high proportion were succorant (asking for help). Beyond this, though, the mothers of blind children were more likely to respond to such succorant contacts by "noncompliance," "refusal," and "ignoring." These are indeed the kinds of circumstances which would be expected to lead to relatively external LOC.

Dote-Kwan (1991) drew a somewhat different picture of these relationships. She found evidence of a greater sensitivity on the parts of preschool children to their mother's presence, in that the children tended, appropriately, to initiate fewer interactive behaviors when the mother was absent. This sensitivity may well have been mediated by a relatively high degree of partial vision in her sample. However, Dote-Kwan also found a much higher frequency of responsiveness by the mother to the child's requests for help than Imamura had reported. Dote-Kwan suggested that the more effective interactive relationship between mothers and children that she found may have been due to the fact that all of the children in her sample were participating in an early intervention program.

Land and Vineberg (1965) did find a general skewing of the distribution of LOC scores (as measured by the Bialer–Cromwell Children's Locus of Control Scale) toward the external end of the scale; however, the variability within the group of 6- to 14-year-old children with visual impairments was great, and some showed as strongly internal LOC as their sighted peers.

More important for our interests is the relationship of LOC to several individual differences variables within the population of children with visual impairments.

CA, MA, and IQ. The trend for sighted children is increasing internalization of LOC with increasing CA, and this is generally interpreted as indicating a progressive personal independence as well as a realization that the child can exert control over the events that affect him or her. The evidence for CA is mixed for children with visual impairments. Parsons (1987), studying the age span from 6 to 19 years, did find higher internal LOC in older than younger children, whereas neither Agrawal and Kaur (1985) nor Jones and McGhee (1972) found significant CA effects in samples that were somewhat more limited in age range.

In any case, because of the conceptual component of LOC, mental age may be a more important correlate. Land and Vineberg (1965) evaluated children in the 6- to 14-year age range and found a significant correlation between mental age and LOC: as mental age increased, so did internal LOC. IQ is of course a derivative of mental and chronological age. The only study that has reported a test of the IQ–LOC relationship is that of Parsons (1987). There was not a significant correlation, but the IQ range of 85 to 115 may have been too limited to allow a relationship to emerge.

In sum, the evidence is generally that more internal LOC accompanies a higher intellectual level in children with visual impairments. This is as expected given the generally increasing conceptual understanding of causality and interpersonal relationships.

Age of visual loss. Only Agrawal and Kaur (1985) reported an evaluation of LOC in relation to age of visual loss; the evidence was that the later the loss, the more likely LOC was to be internal.

Severity of visual impairment. Land and Vineberg (1965) evaluated LOC in relation to the severity of visual impairment in their group whose acuity ranged downward from 20/200; the correlation was not significant.

Gender. No study of children with visual impairments has reported variation in LOC with gender. The general pattern for Caucasian children is for boys to show somewhat more internal LOC than girls.

Variations in environment. For the most part the studies of LOC have unfortunately not evaluated variations as a function of aspects of the child's environment. Two studies, Land and Vineberg (1965) and McGuinness (1970), compared children from residential and integrated school settings, and neither found differences. McGuinness observed, "Despite the fact that subjects in the integrated settings have enjoyed significantly greater success in social independence their expectations of success as the result of their own efforts does not differ significantly from that of subjects from the special school setting" (p. 43). Aside from these studies, there are no other evaluations of LOC in relation to environmental characteristics.

Summary. With the exception of the interdependent relationship among chronological and mental age and IQ, the results reported here are of relationships of LOC with a single factor. The general lack of variation of LOC with these factors is noteworthy. It seems likely that LOC is indeed related to such factors as partial vision in complex ways, but univariate analyses are unlikely to reveal these relationships, whereas multivariate analyses are more appropriate.

LOC and functional behavior

A more important question has to do with the significance of LOC for areas of functional behavior. For example, what implications does relatively internal or external LOC have for aspects of adjustment and achievement?

Agrawal and Kaur (1985) evaluated the relationships among LOC and various attributes including anxiety and adjustment. Better adjustment was found in children with internal LOC, and higher anxiety was found in children with external LOC. (Anxiety and adjustment were negatively correlated.)

Parsons (1987) also explored the relationship between LOC and adjustment as measured by the Vineland Adaptive Behavior Scales (Sparrow et al., 1984). LOC was evaluated by use of the Children's Intellectual Achievement Responsibility Questionnaire (IAR) (Crandall, Katkovsky, & Crandall, 1965), which evaluates the child's view of his or her own responsibility for achievement.

On the various subscales of the Vineland, the older children generally showed higher scores, as expected. Moving to the key question of the relationship between LOC and adjustment, a significant relationship was found: higher internal LOC was associated with higher adjustment scores, both for the communication and the daily living subscales. Causality is elusive in such a set of findings: it is not clear whether LOC or adjustment is causal of the other, or indeed whether both variables might be commonly caused by another constellation of variables related to child-rearing practices.

In sighted children, internal LOC has been found to be positively related to motivation and to school achievement (e.g., Lefcourt, 1976). Jones and McGhee (1972) examined the relationship between LOC and academic achievement. As hypothesized, internal LOC was generally associated with good academic achievement. The IAR was also administered, and contrary to the hypothesis, a negative correlation was found between academic achievement and IAR scores. Generally, higher academic achievement was accompanied by lower perception of self-responsibility for that achievement. Jones and McGhee suggested that whatever the individual child's assumptions about self-responsibility for academic success, these may have been subjugated to a belief that for blind children in general, external factors are overriding.

Summary. Broad relationships have been found among LOC, age, adjustment, and achievement in these studies. It remains for future research to establish the causal relationships among variables and to discover other factors that might also be involved in what is undoubtedly a complex causal chain.

Related constructs

Several other constructs, such as expectations and level of aspiration, are similar to LOC in that they are hypothesized to be mediators of performance. One has to do with attribution of blame. Jervis and Haslerud (1950) evaluated early blind adolescents' reactions to having to perform a series of frustrating puzzles. They tended to show a higher frequency of intropunitive (self-blame) reactions than extrapunitive (attributing blame to others) or impunitive (intellectualization of blame) reactions. In that they tended to attribute their failure to their own shortcomings, this finding corresponds roughly to internal LOC.

McAndrew (1948a,b) assessed level of aspiration by having the child make a prediction of the amount of hand pressure that he or she could exert, compared to what had been achieved on a prior trial. The reward situation was structured so as to put a premium on high values, except that if the child did not meet his or her own prediction, points would be taken away. Thus, the assessment was of reactions to success and failure on the hand pressure task. Generally the children were similar in their pattern of predictions to a sighted comparison group, although the children with visual impairments were inclined to react to failure by adjusting their subsequent predictions downward. These children were 10 to 15 years of age, with IQ 80 or above and with varying degrees of visual loss.

Social role expectations. The expectations of other people may be at least as important as the children's self-expectations in affecting behaviors. Mayadas (1972) studied the congruence between the role expectations held by various "significant others" and the actual behavior of adolescents from a school for the blind. The children's self-expectations and their perceptions of the expectations of significant others were assessed. Positive relationships were found between the quality of social behaviors of the children and (1) the expectations of significant others (parents, teachers, etc.), (2) the children's perceptions of the expectations of significant others, and (3) the children's self-expectations. On the other hand, there was no relationship between the children's behavior and the expectations of a group of people who had no particular experience with blind individuals. Thus the results strongly supported the notion of congruence between role expectations, both of children themselves and of those close to them, and actual behavior.

Mayadas and Duehn (1976) presented a further analysis of data from (apparently) the same sample. Performance on a variety of social behaviors (e.g., table etiquette, physical self-management, or personal hygiene) was evaluated and linked to various categories of expectations through multiple regression analyses. The categories included expectations by parents, counselors, teachers, and houseparents, as well as by the child. The child's perceptions of these various expectations were also tabulated and used as predictors of actual performance.

A general result was that a relatively small percentage of the variance in performance was accounted for by the categories of actual expectations or the child's perception of them. That is to say, a great deal of variance in performance is *not* accounted for by these variables.

More specific differences emerged. For example, girls' behaviors were more related to the expectations than were boys' behaviors. Mayadas and Duehn speculated that girls are more sensitive to demands of the social environment than boys are. Interestingly, girls and boys were equally unresponsive to external expectations about their social interactions with the opposite sex.

Generally, Mayadas and Duehn concluded that their results tended to contradict the "overall prevalence of the 'blind role' as the central organizing concept for the personality of children with visual impairments. Despite a marked tendency toward conformity in the total sample, the subsamples suggest that visually impaired adolescents tend to assert themselves on meaningful behaviors" (p. 289). Further, "Blindness is not an all encompassing behavioral trait, . . . sociocultural variables do affect the behaviors of blind people just as they affect the sighted . . . significant others can help to de-emphasize the blind role and help to develop the individualized capabilities of the blind child within the context of his social reality and physical limitations" (p. 289).

Educational and occupational expectations. Bush-LaFrance (1988) evaluated the educational and occupational expectations of 105 visually impaired adolescents, based on their responses to a questionnaire. Questions were designed to distinguish between choices (e.g., "what would you like to do?") and expectations (e.g., "what do you expect to do?"). The responses were analyzed in relation to amount of visual loss, gender, self-reported school performance, socioeconomic status, and friends' educational plans. Visual status was a relatively weak negative predictor of occupational expectations: children with more vision had somewhat lower expectations. Academic performance and socioeconomic status were both positive predictors. Together these three variables accounted for 33% of the variance in occupational expectations. The visually impaired sample showed generally lower occupational expectations than an archival sample of sighted adolescents.

As for educational expectations, academic performance was the major positive predictor; socioeconomic status and friends' educational plans also contributed. These three factors accounted for 37% of the variance. Visual status was a negligible factor. The educational expectations of the visually impaired sample were not substantially different from those of the archival sample of sighted adolescents. Gender was not a predictor of either variable.

Summary. On the whole, adolescents with visual impairments conceptualize their social roles and behaviors in much the same way that sighted children do, and they do or do not respond to significant others' expectations according to the same variables that characterize the social behaviors of sighted children. They do not seem to conform to a set of social expectations that might be thought characteristic of blindness.

Part IV

Summary

The purpose of this concluding section is twofold. In Chapter 12 I review the limited but important literature that has used the longitudinal approach to trace developmental continuity over age. In Chapter 13 I outline the conclusions that can be made about the effects of individual differences factors which are related to developmental variations. A brief conclusion follows.

12

Longitudinal studies

In research with children, a fundamental concern is how abilities and characteristics change over time as age increases and development proceeds. Two basic research models have been used in this quest, the cross-sectional model and the longitudinal model. The cross-sectional model involves taking samples of children at the various ages required by the research design, evaluating each sample, and constructing the developmental picture by charting characteristics as a function of chronological age. In the longitudinal model, one sample of children is selected at the earliest age required, and then the same children are followed as they age and are tested at each subsequent age level. The developmental picture emerges as the children's results are accumulated over time.

Each of these models has significant advantages and disadvantages. The cross-sectional model has the important advantage that the time required to complete the research is relatively short: testing can be completed efficiently because the samples at the various ages are simultaneously available and can be tested in short order. However, the critical shortcoming of the cross-sectional model is that although it reveals the general nature of development, it does not tell us about its continuity within individuals. The longitudinal model reverses these features. It has the major advantage that it reveals the developmental continuity (or lack thereof) within individual children. However, it is inefficient in terms of time and expense and has the additional problem of attrition; for a variety of reasons not under the researcher's control, not all children in the initial sample will be available for evaluation at subsequent test times.

The vast majority of developmental research has been conducted using the cross-sectional model. A great deal of important information has been obtained using this approach. However, the inability of this

model to address the issue of continuity in individual children is a fundamental shortcoming, and without longitudinal research, our knowledge
about child development would be seriously compromised. Happily,
some researchers have endured the additional expense and inefficiency of
the longitudinal model and have provided important information about
developmental continuity.

There is some longitudinal research available in the literature on the
development of children with visual impairments. The work varies in the
size of samples, the length of time over which children are traced, and the
breadth or narrowness of focus. Most of these studies have followed a
relatively small number of children for a period of a few months to a year
or more, and have focused on a limited area of development. Such studies
have for the most part been reviewed in preceding sections, and a sampling of them is mentioned here to illustrate the advantages that they
confer. A very few longitudinal studies have addressed a broad range of
developmental issues; we will turn to these in a subsequent section.

Studies of limited scope

The term "limited" does not carry any negative connotation: these are
studies whose authors have recognized the value of tracking specific
abilities or characteristics over time.

Perceptual and perceptual–motor abilities. Several studies have applied a
short-term longitudinal approach to the evaluation of perceptual–motor
behaviors. For example, Schwartz (1984) studied two infants weekly,
from their entry into the project at 19 and 28 weeks until a year of age.
Their reaching and responsiveness to sound were of particular interest.
The infants were very different in their motor capabilities (one had mild
CP) as well as in their perceptual responsiveness and social characteristics. Their developmental progress in reaching to sounds was also quite
different. For each infant, though, the pattern of relationship among
indices of social, motor, perceptual, and cognitive behavior was understandable. If these two infants had been evaluated at any given cross-
sectional age, their reaching behavior would have looked quite different,
and no generalization would have been possible. Using the longitudinal
approach, though, a clear picture of each infant's development emerged.

Aitken and Bower (1982) studied the responsiveness of infants and young children to the Sonicguide. Some of the children were evaluated over a very short term, but several were followed for periods ranging up to 17 months. They differed remarkably from one another in their patterns of motor and locomotor development and perceptual responsiveness. The major differences were discussed in relation to situational factors, such as the parents' reactions to the child's blindness, and particularly their willingness to let the child encounter novel situations. Aitken and Bower noted that "the long-term studies do not permit such easy generalizations as the short-term sample" (p 321). From another perspective, though, the generalizations that were drawn from the short-term sample may have been inappropriate, since they apparently did not hold up over more extended study. While the longer-term children did not show equivalence with one another (thus generating the authors' criticism), each child revealed a sensible pattern of the relationship of development to situational factors.

Cognitive abilities. Bigelow (1986, 1988) evaluated the development of cognitive (and perceptual–motor) behaviors in five infants over time periods ranging from 5 to 25 months. Despite substantial differences in the ages at which different tasks of object permanence were achieved, it was clear that the sequence of developmental progression was virtually identical for the several children. Cross-sectional evaluation would have revealed a very high variance in capabilities at any given age, and generalization would have been risky. The longitudinal approach revealed the same variability, but this variability can be understood in the context of the consistency of the developmental sequence.

Social characteristics. Rogers and Puchalski (1986) analyzed the development of social smiling in infants. (This work was part of a long-term study that addresses several areas of development.) The development of smiling in a play context was traced over several months, allowing an individual child's behavior to be examined in relation to the social context as well as charting the parental response to the infant's smile. A temporary decrease in the frequency of smiling occurred around eight months of age. With a cross-sectional research design, it would have been risky to conclude that such a phenomenon was anything but a sampling error, but the longitudinal design allowed the investigators to conclude that the decrease was a reliable phenomenon.

Urwin (1983) used a longitudinal approach to the study of communication in three infants, beginning in the prelanguage period and progressing until the children had acquired substantial language communication. Significant differences among the three were observed in the nature of the prelanguage signal system, and these continued into the development of language proper. Again, cross-sectional study would have yielded variability among the three that would have precluded any generalization. The longitudinal approach allowed these differences to be understood in terms of evident developmental continuities and in the context of the sociolinguistic environment provided by the parents.

Studies of broad scope

Fraiberg. The work of Fraiberg and her colleagues, summarized by Fraiberg (1977), has been cited throughout the preceding chapters, and its substance will not be repeated here. Fraiberg's educational program was not intended as a pure research study; indeed, later children in the program no doubt benefited from the application of information gained in the study of earlier children. Furthermore, the sample of 10 children was not, and was not argued to be, broadly representative, and the results should not be taken as normative. Fraiberg's project is a model of careful and intensive observation of children over a prolonged period of time. It is particularly valuable as an example of the desirability of evaluation of the breadth of developmental issues, including aspects of emotional, cognitive, perceptual, and motor development. Fraiberg's observations about the role of cognitive development in other areas are particularly informative (although as I argued in Chapter 3, some of the behaviors are open to alternative interpretation).

Norris, Spaulding, and Brodie. In earlier references to the study by Norris et al. (1957), we have cited primarily the normative data. Besides providing this normative data, however, the project was a major longitudinal study of the development of preschool children with visual impairments. The 66 children were included in the intensive sample on the basis of having diagnosis and referral by 15 months of age, observations at no more than 12-month intervals, availability for testing up to age six, and "educational blindness" without additional handicaps. In addition to the psychological tests (of intelligence, sensorimotor, and social development) that we have discussed earlier, Norris et al. obtained measures of the child's mobility, and a "prognostic rating scale" was designed to "estimate the child's potentialities for optimal development and to predict his future functioning" (p. 55).

Norris et al. were also concerned with the influence of environmental characteristics. A rating was made of various aspects of the child's "opportunities for learning." This measure was composed of factors related to the family's capability to meet the basic needs of the child, and in particular the needs related to the visual impairment, the availability of professional help, the degree of family stability, and the family's reaction to the child's blindness. These factors were chosen because of their potential influence on the child's ability to develop motivation, independence, and active interest in the environment. The "opportunities for learning" assessment was made by the child's caseworker(s), as was the child's rating on the prognostic scale.

Interesting relationships were found among the individual differences variables and the psychological and mobility evaluations. Degree of functional vision was not significantly correlated with any of the outcome measures except mobility. Indeed, Norris et al. concluded that the parents' feeling about the child's visual status is far more important in affecting outcomes than the visual status itself. The summary measure of the "opportunities for learning" scale was highly correlated with both social maturity and intelligence measures, and less highly with mobility. The prognostic rating scale was strongly correlated with the "opportunities for learning" measure as well as with the psychological tests and the mobility rating. It is not clear at what point during the study the prognostic rating scale was applied, or for that matter the degree to which ratings may have been informed by the caseworker's knowledge of the child's characteristics as revealed by the other measures.

The Norris et al. (1957) study provides an exceptionally rich set of data on a substantial sample. It is impossible to summarize all of the results here, but a sampling of phrases from a summary chapter should suffice to give the flavor of the conclusions.

It is possible to identify the conditions under which optimum development . . . takes place. Under these conditions the blind child can develop into an independent, responsible, freely functioning child whose use of his potential compares favorably with that of most sighted children of his age. . . . Favorable opportunities for learning . . . are more important in determining the child's functioning level than such factors as his degree of blindness, his intelligence as measured by psychological tests, or the social, economic, or educational background of his parents. . . . There are no special problems or 'handicaps' which can be attributed directly to the blindness. The tendency to assume that developmental problems which the child may show are caused directly by his blindness obscures an understanding of the nature and treatment of these problems. . . . The earliest months of the blind child's life and the years of the preschool period are of primary importance. . . . The damage that is done by prolonged failure to provide satisfaction of these needs is apt to be permanent. It can be only partially alleviated by later treatment. . . . Helping the parents provide the kinds of appropriate opportunities for learning that are essential to the blind child requires great professional skill and the services of all appropriate agencies in the community that can make a contribution to the family and to the child. (p. 66)

As was noted, a criterion for inclusion in the intensive sample of Norris et al. (1957) was the absence of additional handicaps, and the absence of specific neurological indications in this sample formed part of the basis for the authors' conclusion that variations in capabilities were largely a result of environmental circumstances. Subsequent evaluation of many of these same children by Cohen and his colleagues, however, revealed an increasing pattern of neurological abnormalities. Cohen, Boshes, and Snider (1961) studied 28 of the 66 original children. The distribution of their intelligence scores was substantially lower than the distribution reported by Norris et al. (1957) for the original group of 66. In addition, all 28 were diagnosed as showing various signs of EEG abnormality, particularly occipital spiking. Attenuation or absence of alpha activity was also common. Although these EEG patterns were described as "abnormal," and indeed were abnormal in comparison to normal patterns for children with vision, extreme caution should be advised against the easy tendency to regard this as a sign of brain damage. Indeed, it should be no surprise that brain activity is different under conditions of restricted sensory input. Novikova (1973) has provided much detailed information about brain activity under various conditions of visual impairment, and the results cited by Cohen et al. (1961) do not differ materially from her report.

In a subsequent report, Cohen, Alfano, Boshes, and Palmgren (1964) reported data from a larger subset (43) of the original 66 children. Again, the distribution of IQ scores was lower than for the original group, and although a criterion for inclusion in the original group was no "additional physical handicaps," Cohen et al. (1964) found indications of neurological abnormalities in 35% of the sample, including a number of epilepsy and CP cases.

Cohen (1966) evaluated the intelligence of a still larger subset (57) of the original 66. Of the 57, four were not reliably testable and five were in institutions for the mentally retarded (although caution must be exercised in taking institutionalization as evidence of retardation). Of the remaining 48, 18 (38%) scored below 80; 12 of these scored below 70.

It is difficult to know what to make of these discrepancies. A progressive decline in IQ with increasing age is one possibility, although other evidence shows that if anything, IQ shows a general increase with age in children with visual impairments (Hayes, 1950; Hopkins & McGuire, 1967; Komisar & MacDonnell, 1955). Sampling bias is also an unlikely candidate, since the Cohen studies tested progressively larger subsamples of the original sample of 66. In any case, the weight of the Cohen studies would seem to require a tempering of the optimism expressed by Norris et al., both with respect to IQ range and to the evidence of neurological abnormalities. The longitudinal approach was critical to the tracking of these changes over time.

Gillman and Goddard. A report by Gillman and Goddard (1974) exemplifies an even longer-term approach to longitudinal evaluation. An earlier unpublished study had evaluated 77 legally blind children between the ages of two and seven years. The sample was heterogeneous, with a preponderance of premature birth and consequent ROP etiology, almost exclusive early visual loss, and varied residual vision; 17 of the 77 had some additional handicap. The Maxfield–Buchholz social maturity scale had been administered to 66 children, and 26 of these had additionally taken the WISC (verbal portion). Social quotient scores from the Maxfield test ranged from 44 to 166, and IQ ranged from 27 to 146. Based on other factors, this group of 26 was thought to be representative of the larger group of 77. In the 20-year follow-up, Gillman and Goddard (1974) found just as large a variation in accomplishment. Seven of the higher IQ children were in college or postgraduate programs and four were in various professional or skilled occupations. Of the lower IQ group, several were successful occupationally, but several were at-home dependents or in institutions. Thus, there was reasonable predictiveness in at least some of the cases based on early childhood test scores. However, prediction was far from perfect, and the danger of predicting low functioning from low test scores in childhood is great.

Of interest particularly in relation to Cohen's follow-up studies of the Norris et al. sample, Gillman and Goddard (1974) found a larger incidence of additional handicaps than had been diagnosed in their original sample, and 20% of the known cases were institutionalized 20 years later. It may be that incipient neurological problems can go undiagnosed in children in the midst of concerns about the visual impairment itself. In any case, this kind of question is impervious to cross-sectional research designs and can be answered only with longitudinal data.

Jan, Freeman, and Scott. The final longitudinal study that we review is also one of the most ambitious and longest term. We have reviewed in previous sections various results from the study by Jan et al. (1977). A fuller account of the sample and procedures of the initial study appears in Chapter 10. The sample included 92 children from a broad age range, of whom 65 had some partial vision and many had additional handicaps. Data were collected from many sources, including parent questionnaires and interviews, school and medical records, and home observations.

Fourteen years later, 69 of the 92 subjects were located. For each of these 69, a prognosis was made, based on the original records, of what the individual's level of functioning in various areas would be. They were intensively interviewed with respect to social relationships and a wide range of personal, educational, and vocational factors. The results were reported by Freeman et al. (1991) and provide a wealth of information about the later status of these individuals. In general, the level of functioning was as good as or better than was predicted. This was particularly true of the blind subjects, who exceeded expectations more frequently than those with partial vision.

With respect to social and emotional relationships, half reported having had a romantic relationship and about 20% were partnered (all with a sighted partner). Whereas a large proportion of the initial sample showed a variety of stereotypic behaviors, these were generally absent in the follow-up study.

The educational attainment of the follow-up group was remarkably high: 76% had completed secondary school, and 19% had attended or were attending a university. The subjects generally reported that they had taken longer than the normative time to achieve educational milestones; Freeman et al. suggested that this was no doubt a result of the relative scarcity of special educational services in the time period under question.

The vocational accomplishments were much less impressive, and indeed there seemed to be a significant amount of underemployment. Many seemed to have the requisite motivation and intellectual skills for employment but were receiving disability pensions instead. Only 39% of the sample were employed. On the other hand, a very high proportion (71%) participated in physical activities and few reported having no hobbies or special interests.

Interestingly, abnormal neurological indicators were not a particularly strong predictor of later problems. In fact, excluding those who had earlier been diagnosed as mentally retarded, two-thirds were rated as psychiatrically normal, almost three-quarters had graduated from secondary school, and half were in open employment. The coupling of an additional handicap with visual impairment *was* a significant adverse predictor: more than 70% of those who did not have an additional handicap were rated as psychiatrically normal and 44% were in open employment, in contrast to 24% and 17%, respectively, for those with an additional handicap.

The Freeman et al. (1991) study, together with an earlier report of a smaller subset of 41 subjects (Freeman et al., 1989), is a remarkably rich source of information about the long-term outcomes of individuals tested in childhood, and about the relative value of various predictors of later attainment. In particular, early tests of intelligence were poor predictors compared to less formal clinical evaluations of intelligence, and as noted earlier, the presence of neurological signs was not a successful negative predictor. A distinctly positive factor was the report by many subjects in the follow-up that their relationship with their families had been based on mutual understanding and recognition of emotional needs.

Finally, the outcome of the project provides a strong warning signal about the dangers of negative prognoses. Freeman et al. (1989) found that the long-term outcome was "somewhat" higher than predicted in 34% of the sample, and "much" higher in another 22%. Only 5% had an outcome worse than predicted. It is quite possible that if these predictions had been made in a diagnostic manner upon the initial testing, and if the children had been treated in accordance with these expectations, their eventual attainment would have been much less positive. We are far from knowing enough about long-term outcome prediction to base negative expectations and corresponding treatment on current indicators.

Summary

The longitudinal study is an invaluable source of information about development. While cross-sectional studies of age differences can yield valuable information, they are incapable of yielding definitive evidence about developmental continuity. They can tell us, for example, that at three years of age children have a certain normative level of functioning and that at five years of age the level is different, but they cannot tell us whether the children who are relatively advanced in comparison to their peers at five years were also relatively advanced at three years of age. Particularly if we are concerned, as we should be, about the environmental circumstances that lead to more advanced development, the cross-sectional research design falls short.

The longitudinal research design, while difficult, expensive, and time-consuming, can furnish critical information about developmental continuity. This is true of studies that focus on a limited subset of developmental characteristics, and it is equally true of studies that take a broader approach to a range of interrelated characteristics. Despite its logistical problems, the longitudinal design is critical to a complete understanding of development, and the quality of our knowledge in the future will depend heavily on researchers' willingness to address these issues squarely.

13

Individual differences

In the introduction to this book, I offered several reasons for my conviction that a differential approach to research on visual impairment in children is more suitable than the more traditional comparative approach. There are excellent examples of differential research, and these have been noted. Much of the existing research, however, has used the comparative model, and therefore it is difficult to interpret the impact of this work within a differential framework. Use of the comparative model usually means that investigation and explanation of individual differences within the sample of children with visual impairments is not a high priority in the design, analysis, or reporting of the results. Often such information is hidden within the analyses and therefore completely irretrievable, but sometimes it is possible to glean bits of information about how children's characteristics vary as a result of their age or visual status, or of features of their environments. I have searched for and reported such instances as thoroughly as possible. I have summarized the main features of these outcomes in the course of each chapter, and a detailed review is unnecessary here.

It may, however, be useful to consider these variables in broad overview. We will begin with status variables and then move to factors that vary within the child's environment.

Status variables

Status variables are characteristics related to the condition of visual impairment. They have in common that they are not amenable to intervention. That is, we have no control over the age at which the child loses vision, the severity of the visual loss, the cause of the visual loss, or the presence or absence of additional handicapping conditions. Each of these factors has some bearing on development, however.

Severity of visual loss

Visual impairment is not a categorical condition: children's visual loss lies on a continuum from the defining limits of visual impairment to the total lack of vision. It is logical to suppose that children's ability to adapt to the various tasks of development will vary with the degree of available vision, and indeed there is much evidence for this. However, we should not expect all tasks to be equally affected by residual visual capability.

Not surprisingly, there is no evidence that residual vision affects the fundamental discriminative capabilities of the other senses. However, even a small amount of vision is facilitative of motor behavior. For example, the infant with a small amount of vision attends to the hands before the eyes, and this may facilitate the development of spatial understanding, with positive implications for responsiveness to localized auditory events even in infancy. Later components of motor and locomotor control, such as balance, are also facilitated, and it is not surprising that the school-age child's ability to deal with spatial concepts is better when some vision is available. And although imagery is difficult to study, at least self-reports of imagery indicate a greater prevalence of visual images in partially sighted children.

Spatial abilities are not uniformly performed better by children with partial vision, however. Facilitative effects have not generally been found with maze performance, nor does mental rotation capability differ as a function of residual vision.

Moving to the cognitive realm, it is not surprising that partial vision facilitates the acquisition of object permanence, particularly in the final stages when the understanding of spatial structure is involved. These advantages are also routinely found in the acquisition of the various conservation concepts. All of this has to do with the child's understanding of the physical world. However, when we look at other cognitive skills such as language, memory, and attention, differences are rarely found.

In social development the picture is complex, and it is evident that while residual vision may play a part, other variables are more important. In particular, several studies – which find apparent differences between groups of totally blind and partially sighted children – suffer from serious sampling problems, such that it is impossible to attribute the differences to residual vision. Other variables have to do with the children's social environment, including in particular the nature of other people's reactions to them. This point extends to the small number of studies that have found better social adjustment in totally blind children than in those with some visual function. Moving finally to issues of personality, generally no differences are found, and again other variables are more influential.

Thus, the picture is mixed, and facile conclusions are inappropriate. Even in the areas in which residual vision does confer a potential advantage, other variables interact to determine whether this potential advantage becomes an actual advantage. Much of the research has treated this variable as bipolar, comparing "totally blind" (typically with at most LP) with "partially sighted" groups of children. It is far more desirable to use residual vision as a continuous variable.

Early vision

If a child develops for some period of time with vision intact, it is reasonable to expect that adaptation in some areas will benefit. Of course, barring other handicaps or adverse environmental circumstances, development through the point of visual loss should proceed normally, and this is not our concern here. Instead, our focus is on areas of development that may benefit from a period of early vision, even after vision is lost, compared with the situation in which vision has never been available.

As in the case of partial vision, it is naive to suppose that all areas of development might benefit equally, and indeed, it is particularly in the areas of interaction with the physical world that benefits occur: these include aspects of perceptual and cognitive development.

There is no convincing evidence that early vision affects the quality of sensory discrimination in the nonvisual modalities. With more integrative perceptual abilities, though, there is much evidence that early vision provides a lasting advantage. This is particularly so in the perception of spatially distributed events. For example, localization of auditory events is facilitated by early vision; and performance on near-space tasks, as exemplified by maze learning, tends to be better with early vision, although this evidence is mixed. Aspects of locomotor control show a difference in favor of children who have had a period of early vision. This undoubtedly contributes to the many findings that children who have lost vision early are not as adept at performing tasks in the larger spatial environment. Concepts of extended space are also facilitated by early vision.

The research on the perceptual–cognitive processes that underlie performance is not as clear. The sporadic examples tend to show an advantage of a period of early vision; for example, the tendency to persist in spatial egocentrism is not as strong after a period of early vision, and mental rotation abilities suffer from early visual loss. Generally speaking, though, research on perceptual and cognitive processes has generally neglected both partial vision and early vision. The work on the nature of encoding of tactual information, for example, has tended to study children who have been blind since birth or very early in life. This approach is defensible from the viewpoint of wanting to understand the nature of perceptual processing under conditions of lack of vision, but it unfortunately leaves us with little information about the role that early vision or partial vision might play in the development of these processes.

Although the preponderance of evidence confirms the advantages of early vision in spatial perception and concepts, this generalization must be qualified. Some important positive exceptions have been noted in a previous summary section (Chapter 3). These exceptions, which occur across the span from infancy to adolescence, underscore the complexity of the determination of perceptual-cognitive abilities. When the congenitally blind infant or older child demonstrates excellent spatial capabilities, we must look to environmental factors to explain the exceptions. The exceptions, moreover, should provide us with optimism and research curiosity; for although it is evident from the literature that early visual loss places the child at high risk, it is also clear that the risk is surmountable.

Moving to other aspects of development, the literature is very unsatisfying with respect to the impact of early visual loss. Sporadic reports are available of differences between children with early and later visual loss, generally in favor of those with later loss, but some reports have found no differences. Reports of advantages of early visual loss are, not surprisingly, very rare. In view of the importance of other factors, particularly those related to the social environment of the visually impaired child, the relative lack of research attention to early visual experience is probably not a critical gap in the literature.

Gender

The relative lack of reported gender differences in the visual impairment literature is perhaps not remarkable in view of the weakness of this variable in the general developmental literature. Some sporadic findings of gender differences occur in the research on social and personality characteristics, but there is no general tendency for boys or girls to show more adaptiveness.

Despite the low prevalence of visual impairment and the consequent difficulty of obtaining research samples, in many studies care has been taken to equate the numbers of girls and boys in the sample. It is surprising, in view of this procedural care, that gender effects, or the lack thereof, are so rarely reported. It may be that gender analyses were performed and did not yield differences, and that this was simply not reported. This is unfortunate, since negative results may be just as important and interesting as positive differences.

Etiology

The cause of the child's visual impairment is yet another status variable. The array of causes of visual loss is wide indeed, and any given research sample is likely to be composed of children with various etiologies. Typically there are insufficient numbers of children in the different etiology groups to allow detailed analysis of possible differences. However, two groups stand out as having a constellation of characteristics, retinopathy of prematurity and retinoblastoma.

Retinopathy of prematurity (ROP). The case of ROP (formerly called retrolental fibroplasia, or RLF) is interesting because of the high incidence of ROP-caused blindness in the samples reported in much of the literature, and because it continues to be a frequent cause of early visual loss.

ROP blindness is caused by the oxygen-rich atmosphere of the controlled incubator environment that is used for prematurely born infants in the intensive-care setting. Thus, ROP-blind infants are almost invariably premature, of low birth weight, and have been in the ICU environment and thus, concomitantly, have not been in the usual neonatal environment. Premature infants are also at risk for brain damage caused by anoxia or other conditions associated with prematurity or difficult birth. With this plethora of real and potential problems, it is difficult to attribute any developmental differences that they may show to any one variable.

Indices of early perceptual and motor development demonstrate that ROP-blind infants show less mature capabilities at any given age than infants who are blind from other causes (and without additional handicaps). However, when a correction for prematurity is applied, generally no remarkable differences remain.

It is in social–emotional development that some relatively consistent differences have been found; we reviewed this evidence in Chapter 10. The main theme is a pattern of social–emotional characteristics that has an autistic-like quality.

Retinoblastoma. Retinoblastoma is a tumor of the eye that causes unilateral or bilateral blindness. The condition is progressive, so that children who lose sight as a result of retinoblastoma typically have vision for a year or more.

In most areas of development, there is no evidence that children blind from retinoblastoma are any different from those who have lost vision from other causes. The major exception to this is intelligence, where there are reports of both unusually high and low intelligence; we reviewed the literature on this in Chapter 7. In brief, the intelligence scores of retinoblastoma children may be bimodally distributed, with a small portion of the population in the weak normal range and a larger distribution centered about a mean well above average.

Environmental factors

We turn now to an array of factors that influence the child's adaptation to the various tasks of development and that can be characterized loosely as "environmental" factors. This term is meant to imply that the child, equipped with his or her various perceptual skills and other characteristics, encounters an environment that has certain properties. It is obvious that the features of the physical environment vary, but the issue is more complex than this. Parental reactions to the child's visual impairment have implications for the physical environment to which the child is exposed and to the encouragement offered the child to engage it. The consequences of parental reactions extend well beyond the physical aspects, however: they also affect the nature of the social–emotional environment that the child encounters. In short, parents (and others) react in various ways, and these variations affect the setting in which the child develops.

Training and other specific interventions also fall into the category of environmental factors, since here the characteristics of the child's environment are intentionally and programmatically altered with the expectation of affecting the child's developmental course.

There is an immensely important property of these factors that differentiates them from the status variables discussed above, namely that the environmental factors are amenable to change. For example, the physical environment can be altered, and as difficult as it may be for parents to change their natural disappointment about the child's visual impairment, it should be possible for them to avoid having their reactions affect the child's social–emotional environment adversely.

To the extent that developmental adaptation varies as a consequence of these environmental variations, there is hope that children with visual impairments can adapt successfully and enjoy optimal development. Let us summarize the key points of evidence on these issues.

Perceptual–motor development

Infancy. Although the infancy literature is not rich with analysis of individual variation, some very positive examples emerge. For example, placing the infant in the prone position rather than the preferred supine position may enhance the infant's muscular development, with positive consequences for reaching outward for objects in the physical environment (Hart, 1983). In discussing the large variance in their sample on the acquisition of perceptual–motor skills, Norris et al. (1957) implicated opportunity as a major factor: "Children who did not develop some means of getting about on the floor . . . were typically those who were not given appropriate opportunities for doing so" (p. 39).

Nor are the variations solely in the physical environment: Als et al. (1980b) pointed to the high quality of the social interaction between parent and blind infant as an important factor in the precocious reaching and other perceptual–motor behaviors of their single subject. Further evidence about the effects of variations in the quality of the social–emotional environment on perceptual–motor development is regrettably lacking, but the occurrence of even one very positive instance should not go unmarked.

Postinfancy. It is also clear that the physical environment affects the nature of the older child's perceptual–motor behaviors. This conclusion is supported by the findings of Buell (1982) and Short and Winnick (1986, 1988) that exercise is a major factor in the physical fitness of children with visual impairments. The degree of parental encouragement to engage the physical setting plays an additional part (e.g., Nixon, 1988), interacting with the physical environment itself.

Cognitive development

Infancy. There is regrettably little information about how the quality of cognitive development (e.g., object permanence) in the infancy period may differ with variations in the infant's physical or social–emotional environment. For example, despite the close observation by Fraiberg and her colleagues of the early cognitive development of infants, little is reported about the extent to which variations in the sample may have been related to differences in parental behaviors or other aspects of the infant's environment.

Postinfancy. Happily, there is more evidence on this issue in the postinfancy period. For example, differences are evident in the acquisition of conservation abilities between children in public and special school settings (e.g., Gottesman, 1976; Stephens & Simpkins, 1974). By itself this finding is not very informative, since school settings differ in many ways and since there is substantial variation with each school category. Although their study was primarily cross-cultural, Wan-Lin and Tait (1987) identified several variables that tend to vary across school settings and that in any case have much broader significance. These included the nature of the linguistic demands placed on children, specific experience with educational materials as opposed to verbal descriptions, and the nature of the children's out-of-school experience.

Language and communication

The importance of environmental variables is evident in the development of language, both as a tool of cognitive development and as a critical element in social communication.

Prelinguistic communication. It is clear that parental responsiveness is an important factor in the infant's prelinguistic vocal activity (e.g., Dote-Kwan, 1991; Rowland, 1984). Parents and infants develop patterns of prelinguistic communication that are affected by the parents' behaviors, and these patterns play an important part in determining the nature of the "shared frame of reference" that is critical to subsequent language development. Urwin (1978) has also demonstrated that parents can effectively increase the demands on the infant to progressively refine the quality of this shared system of communication.

Language proper. Although most reports are that, on the whole, infants with visual impairments speak their first words at the expected time, there is much variation, just as there is with sighted infants. At least part of this variation can be attributed to environmental variables. For example, Norris et al. (1957) noted that in cases of retarded speech development, parents' unrealistic expectations or other abnormal reactions were often implicated. Citing another factor, Burlingham suggested that often a lag in the production of early words is due to the parents' perception of the child's helplessness, which leads them to anticipate the child's needs and thereby reduces the need for the child to speak.

The issue of verbalism has been laid to rest, but the question of the relationship of the child's word meanings to his or her experience remains. Some patterns of word meaning and usage seem to be a general function of the lack of visual experience, and specific usages and meanings can be traced to the experiences of the child. It is clear from the literature that the vocabulary of children with visual impairments is heavily grounded in their own perceptual experience and is not simply a parroting of sighted vocabulary. While perhaps not surprising, this underscores the importance of the parents' role in ensuring not only that the child's perceptual experience is adequately rich, but also that it is embedded in a context of shared communication.

This takes us to the sociolinguistic environment provided by parents and others. "Sociolinguistic" refers to the social context within which language develops; children learn language not from a book but from their participation in the social environment. That the quality of this social interaction affects language development is not in doubt: the negative and positive extremes are well represented by the reports of Keeler (1958) and Urwin (1983). It is clear from recent research (e.g., Kekelis & Andersen, 1984) that parents use different speech interactions with their blind children than they do with sighted children, and that the patterns used with the former are logical results of the parents' awareness of the child's condition. However, it is also clear that these logical and well-motivated adjustments of the sociolinguistic environment may not optimally facilitate the child's acquisition of language.

Early social development

Infancy. We discussed the dynamics of social–emotional responsiveness in infants at some length in Chapter 8. Perhaps the critical point to be reiterated here is the extent to which the patterns of interaction are critical, with communication proceeding in both directions. If the parent is imperceptive of or unresponsive to the infant's communicative activities, then the emotional environment the parent provides will not encourage the infant's responsiveness. This is a cyclical, interactive pattern in which the parent and infant both shape the other's social–emotional environment. It is very clear from the positive instances that strong and healthy attachment can occur in blind infants. It is just as clear that a parent who has adverse reactions to the infant's visual loss (or for that matter to other characteristics of the infant) is ill-prepared to provide a healthy emotional environment. Further alteration of the social–emotional environment by hospitalization can exacerbate the situation.

Preschool development. Social development as assessed by instruments such as the Vineland Social Maturity Scale shows a great deal of variability in preschool children, with some children showing age-appropriate characteristics and others lagging behind. Several investigators have traced such differences to the child's social environment, such as someone encouraging the child to learn as opposed to "teaching" social skills (Norris et al., 1957) and excessive babying of the preschool child (Reynell, 1978).

There are several excellent studies of the range of parental reactions to the child's visual impairment and of the manner in which these reactions can affect the social–emotional environment of the preschool child. Variations in the child's social development and personality characteristics are highly correlated with variations in the social–emotional environment (e.g., Dote-Kwan, 1991; Imamura, 1965; Lairy & Harrison-Covello, 1973, Norris et al., 1957; Sommers, 1944). Variation in the reactions of siblings is also evident (Jan et al., 1977). Moving beyond the family setting, it is also apparent that the child's opportunities to engage in peer relationships affect his or her development of peer-appropriate modes of social interaction (Kekelis, 1988).

The school experience

Some variation in social adaptation is associated with school placement (e.g., McGuinness, 1970). However, as we noted in previous discussions, school setting is a complex issue that has less to do with the type of school than it does with the social environments individual schools provide. Lukoff and Whiteman (1970) provided an excellent summary of factors that influence the choice of school setting, such as the parents' expectations of the child's independence, social role, and achievement.

One abiding fact about the school environment as an influence on social development falls under the heading of the self-fulfilling prophecy: simply put, when less is expected, less is delivered. Not surprisingly, the school environment also has an influence on the child's friendship patterns; attendance at a residential school increases the likelihood that the child's friends are also blind, for example. Placement in a public school setting does not guarantee that the child with a visual impairment will acquire sighted friends, however; much depends on the social characteristics that the visually impaired child brings to the interaction with sighted peers. It is also clear that adults, particularly teachers, can influence the child's integration into the larger social structure.

Comment

Some remarkable, though perhaps not surprising, patterns emerge from this review of environmental factors in the development of children with visual impairments. In particular, the social and physical environments interact in important ways. Many studies show that variations in the child's physical environment have a potential effect on the child's development of aspects of perceptual, motor, and cognitive adaptation. Potential effect is not necessarily actual effect, however, and the literature is much less clear on the factors that influence the child to engage the physical environment. It is here that the social environment comes into play. Parents and others have a great deal of influence on the degree to which the child is encouraged to explore, challenge, and learn. Unfortunately, the existing research is very weak on this issue.

In general, the literature is much stronger in assessing the relationships of adaptive skills to status variables such as visual characteristics than it is in evaluating the impact of the physical and social environments and the nature of their influence on development. This is a rich area for future research, and it is especially important given that it is just these aspects of the environmental context that are, unlike the visual impairment itself, under the potential control of parents and others who shape the child's experience.

Training

The studies of environmental factors that we have reviewed up to this point have evaluated the variation that occurs among parents, families, schools, and other social settings. Training studies are designed to provide a specific and intentional set of altered experiences. They represent variations, however temporary, in the environment of the child, and thus are a legitimate inclusion in this section on environmental factors. In the preceding chapters we reviewed research designed to evaluate the effects of specific and general training of various capabilities; a brief summary will suffice here.

Infancy. Various attempts have been made to elicit the expression of perceptual and motor behaviors in blind infants, generally without much success. For example, Fraiberg's (1977) program was designed in part as a research project but also as a program of education to facilitate the blind infants' development. While the project was not designed to evaluate the success of the educational program, it is evident that at least for perceptually based motor behaviors, such as reaching and locomotion, the impact was not great. Schwartz (1984) reported success in stimulating a blind infant with CP, who was generally delayed in motor development, to reach for sounding objects. The work of Nielsen (1991) is provocative in suggesting that reducing the stimulation from the external environment may facilitate the infant's attention to his or her hands and to events in near space. Aside from these instances, there is not much in the way of positive report of training intervention.

Studies using devices such as the Sonicguide to elicit reaching have been reported, and while success is cited in occasional instances (e.g., Ferrell, 1980; Sampaio, 1989), the general outcome is unsuccessful. It is likely that use of such devices to assist reaching is successful only when the infant is ready to reach without the device. Similarly, there is no evidence that use of the Sonicguide stimulates the development of locomotor abilities earlier than they might have been expected to emerge spontaneously.

Postinfancy. There is a small amount of literature on training of specific components of locomotor skills, such as balance and straight-line walking. Generally these studies (e.g., Cratty, 1969; Gipsman, 1979) have reported positive outcomes (although negative outcomes usually do not find their way into the literature). General programs of physical activity (e.g., Duehl, 1979) have also been found effective.

Several studies of training of concepts and cognitive abilities are also available, and these tend to show positive outcomes (note again the point about negative results). There has been some success in the training of spatial concepts both using nonassisted training (e.g., Hill, 1970, 1971) and using sensory aids such as the Sonicguide (e.g., Hornby et al., 1985).

The small amount of literature on the training of strategies of information processing (particularly the work of Berlá and Davidson and their colleagues) is impressive in its impact, showing not only that the quality of performance is affected by strategies, but also that effective strategies can be encouraged by training. It is also clear (e.g., Friedman & Pasnak, 1973b) that classification skills are amenable to training interventions.

Finally, several training studies of conservation and other areas of cognitive understanding have shown successful intervention (e.g., Lopata & Pasnak, 1976; Stephens & Grube, 1982).

Perhaps the most remarkable gap in the area of training studies has to do with social skills. It is evident that children with visual impairments sometimes lack the necessary skills of social interaction, and it is just as evident that these skills are a prerequisite to the child's effective social interaction, particularly with peers. Given the importance of this area, it is surprising that significant efforts have not been devoted to the specific training of social interactive skills.

Perspective. Several summary points about training are important. First, there is the issue of what the goal of training is, and how to evaluate its success. One possible goal is to have the child's capabilities at any given age match those of the sighted child. In general this is inappropriate; we should instead see training as a way of structuring the child's experience, with the goal of allowing each child to reach the positive limits of his or her own capabilities.

Thus, a training intervention is appropriate if a child is not showing behaviors or abilities of which he or she should be clearly capable, judged not against standards of sighted development but against the child's own potential. This kind of judgment is clearly more difficult and less concrete than judgment against sighted norms, but is a more legitimate quest.

Another implication, which seems self-evident but has sometimes been ignored, is that training programs should not attempt to induce behaviors before the child is developmentally ready for them. Again, developmental readiness should not be determined by reference to sighted children.

Services

Children with visual impairments and their families receive a variety of professional services including infant programs, preschool programs, programs of parent counseling, and special educational services. Many services have long been supported by private charitable sources, and with the advent of entitlement legislation additional public resources have been allocated to support the provision of services for children with visual impairments.

Different agencies are funded from distinct sources and serve discrete populations. Thus, there is variation in the services they provide. However, additional variation occurs because they are grounded in varying philosophies and have personnel with different professional orientations and backgrounds.

Presumably each agency thinks that its approach is appropriate, or it would change; yet they still differ. It is rarely asked which approaches are best. Evaluation research designed to compare programs is virtually nonexistent. For that matter, very little research evaluates the outcomes of any specific program.

It is not that evaluation is not done; administrators know how much time they spend in preparing reports! Nonetheless, the vast majority of the evaluation effort is directed to evaluating costs per client, successful "closures," and other administrative indices.

Nobody seriously doubts that children with visual impairments benefit from these services, or that their parents or the professionals who provide the services would judge their impact to be positive. In the end, however, it is not the opinions of service users or service providers that count; what counts is *impact*. What functional impact is produced by the services? In what ways are children better off with specific services than they would have been without them?

These questions are largely unanswered because there has not been a systematic evaluation of the relative impact of various kinds of services or service delivery programs for children with visual impairments. This is a serious gap in the research literature.

In the foregoing chapters, we have reviewed the literature to see what answers it can provide about the factors that influence the development of children with visual impairments. We have seen that there is variation in development that can be traced to *status factors* such as the age at visual loss and the presence of additional handicaps. We have seen that some variation can be attributed to *environmental factors* such as parental emotional reaction and the quality of the physical environment. I suggest that the nature and quality of services is one of the most important sources of individual differences among children with visual impairments; yet this is the area about which we know the least, *in terms of its impact on functional outcomes.*

Research on the impact of services to children with visual impairments must be added to the existing and future research on status factors and environmental factors in order to produce a body of knowledge that will allow us to intervene in an optimal way with these children. If we neglect to evaluate the impact of specific services and service models, we will in effect be ignoring one of the most potent influences that we have in our armory.

Conclusion

Using the comparative model, the development of children with visual impairments is evaluated against norms based on children with vision. The use of this research model has generated a considerable literature, which in turn has produced a particular view of children with visual impairments. In brief, this view is that the eventual level of their abilities may be adequate, but that their developmental progress is delayed. At any given age, they tend to show lags, so that their level of development is delayed by some time in relation to sighted children.

This view leads to a certain set of expectations of children with visual impairments. If a parent of a blind infant were to ask a social worker or other blindness professional what the prospects are for that infant (and later child), the professional would look to the comparative literature and would reassure the parent that the child will acquire a set of adaptive abilities, but that he or she will do so at a slower developmental pace than would be expected of a sighted child. The key sentence, intended to be both realistic and reassuring, might be, "You cannot expect a normal rate of development, and you should not be disappointed by a pace that is delayed in comparison to your sighted children."

The well-meaning professional is accurate in reading the existing literature this way. In normative terms, children with visual impairments are indeed delayed in many aspects of development. However, there is a most serious problem with this conclusion, no matter how well it is based in the comparative literature.

The problem lies in the implicit equation of norms and expectations. This professional opinion is based on norms. Based on these norms, the parents will expect no more of their own child than normative development *for blind children*.

The analysis presented in this book, oriented as it is to individual differences and to the factors that cause them, does not dispute the evidence generated by the comparative approach. But it does reveal that the conclusions drawn from it fall far short of "the whole truth." Differential analysis shows that in virtually every area of development, there are visually impaired children whose developmental progress is at least at the norm for, and often at the high end of the distribution for, sighted children.

What should we make of these examples? Unfortunately, most reports note only the exceptions without attempting to account for them. However, some of the reports do give us more, by examining variations among children as a function of differences in status variables – such as age at visual loss – and in environmental variations.

Aside from medical advances that will no doubt occur, we can do very little about status variables. We can encourage the child to make full use of residual visual capability, but we cannot remove an additional handicap or slow the loss of sight. We should certainly know about such factors, but they are essentially beyond our control.

Environmental variables are a different matter altogether. The relevant research, sparse though it is, tells us that variations in children's abilities and characteristics are related to variations in their environmental circumstances. Infants and young children who experience a rich physical environment, and who are encouraged to engage it rather than being protected from it, show more developmentally advanced perceptual–motor behaviors. Children whose parents have difficulty adjusting to the child's visual loss, and who neglect or otherwise reject the child, show aspects of emotional disturbance. Children who encounter a rich learning environment show a more advanced level of conceptual development for a given age than whose whose environment is restricted.

Since it is generally unethical to manipulate environmental variables experimentally, there is scarcely any rigorous experimental evidence on these issues. Using what is essentially a correlational approach, we can never be absolutely sure of the causal relationship between two variables, or whether there is a third factor that causes the covariation of the two. In short, we will never have a truly airtight scientific case that specific variations in the environments of children with visual impairments *cause* specific variations in their development.

However, if in the future enough parents are convinced of their children's potential and of the importance of the social and physical environments they provide for achieving it, then we may see a population of children with visual impairments who will show increasingly more adaptive patterns of development than the current norms indicate.

Parents of the future will never be convinced by the reference to the current normative literature, in which children with visual impairments are *on the average* less well developed than sighted children of comparable age. Reference to such research will only lower parents' expectations. It is clear from the psychological literature that low expectations generate low outcomes. On the other hand, reference to a literature that emphasizes the variation, and especially the high-end (as well as the low-end) extremes of development and the relationships of these to the quality of the child's environment, is likely to influence parents and professionals to be active in their quest for the best possible environments for their children with visual impairments.

To offer the children any less is to do less than our best for them.

References

Abang, T. B. (1985). Blindism: Likely causes and preventive measures. *Journal of Visual Impairment & Blindness, 79*, 400–401.

Achenbach, T. M. (1979). The Child Behavior Profile: An empirically based system for assessing behavioral problems and competence. *International Journal of Mental Health, 7*, 24–42.

Adelson, E., & Fraiberg, S. (1974). Gross motor development in infants blind from birth. *Child Development, 45*, 114–126.

Adi, H., & Pulos, S. (1977–1978). Conservation of number and the developmental lag among the blind. *Education of the Visually Handicapped, 9*, 102–106.

Adkins, S. D. W. (1965). Effects of visual deficit on acquisition of classification concepts. *Dissertation Abstracts, 26*, 1769A, 9, no. 4 (University Microfilms No. 65-08567).

Agrawal, R., & Kaur, J. (1985). Anxiety and adjustment levels among the visually and hearing impaired and their relationship to locus of control, cognitive, social, and biographical variables. *Journal of Psychology, 119*, 265–269.

Ainsworth, M. D. S., & Wittig, B. A. (1969). Attachment and exploratory behavior of one-year-olds in a strange situation. In B. M. Foss (Ed.), *Determinants of infant behavior* (Vol. 4, pp. 111–136). London: Methuen.

Aitken, S., & Bower, T. G. R. (1982). Intersensory substitution in the blind. *Journal of Experimental Child Psychology, 33*, 309–323.

Als, H., Tronick, E., & Brazelton, T. B. (1980a). Stages of early behavioral organization: The study of a sighted infant and a blind infant in interaction with their mothers. In T. M. Field (Ed.), *High-risk infants and children, adult and peer interactions* (pp. 181–204). New York: Academic Press.

(1980b). Affective reciprocity and the development of autonomy: The study of a blind infant. *Journal of the American Academy of Child Psychiatry, 19*, 22–40.

Andersen, E. S., Dunlea, A., & Kekelis, L. S. (1984). Blind children's language: Resolving some differences. *Journal of Child Language, 11*, 645–664.

Andersen, E. S., & Kekelis, L. S. (1986). The role of sibling input in the language socialization of younger blind children. *Southern California Occasional Papers in Linguistics, Vol. 11: Social and Cognitive Perspectives on Language* (pp. 141–156). Los Angeles: University of Southern California.

Anderson, D. W. (1979). *A descriptive analysis of language and cognition in congenitally blind children ages 3 through 9.* Unpublished doctoral dissertation, University of North Dakota.

(1984). Mental imagery in congenitally blind children. *Journal of Visual Impairment & Blindness,* 78, 206–210.

Anderson, D. W., & Olson, M. (1981). Word meaning among congenitally blind children. *Journal of Visual Impairment & Blindness,* 75, 165–168.

Asher, S. R., Renshaw, P. D., & Hymel, S. (1982). Peer relations and the development of social skills. In S. G. Moore & C. R. Cooper (Eds.), *The young child: Reviews of research* (Vol. 3, pp. 137–158). Washington, DC: National Association for the Education of Young Children.

Ashmead, D. H., Hill, E. W., & Talor, C. R. (1989). Obstacle perception by congenitally blind children. *Perception & Psychophysics,* 46, 425–433.

Avery, C. (1968). Play therapy with the blind. *International Journal for the Education of the Blind,* 18, 41–46.

Axelrod, S. (1959). *Effects of early blindness.* New York: American Foundation for the Blind (Research Series, No. 7).

(1968). *Basic and complex functions in the blind and the sighted.* Unpublished doctoral dissertation, New York University.

Ball, W., & Tronick, E. (1971). Infant responses to impending collision: Optical and real. *Science,* 172, 1161–1163.

Barraga, N. C. (1976). *Visual handicaps and learning: A developmental approach.* Belmont, CA: Wadsworth.

Battacchi, M. W., Franza, A., & Pani, R. (1981). Memory processing of spatial order as transmitted by auditory information in the absence of visual cues. *Memory & Cognition,* 9, 301–307.

Bauman, M. K. (1964). Group differences disclosed by inventory items. *International Journal for the Education of the Blind,* 13, 101–106.

Bauman, M. K., & Yoder, N. M. (1966). *Adjustment to blindness – reviewed.* Springfield, IL: Thomas.

Berg, J., & Worchel, P. (1956). Sensory contributions to human maze learning: A comparison of matched blind, deaf, and normals. *Journal of General Psychology,* 54, 81–93.

Berkson, G. (1973). *Animal studies of treatment of impaired young by parents and the social group.* Paper presented at Conference on The Blind Child in Social Interaction: Developing Relationships with Peers and Adults, New York.

Berlá, E. P. (1974). Tactual orientation performance of blind children in different grade levels. *American Foundation for the Blind Research Bulletin,* 27, 1–10.

(1981). Tactile scanning and memory for a spatial display by blind students. *Journal of Special Education,* 15, 341–350.

Berlá, E. P., & Butterfield, L. H., Jr. (1977). Tactual distinctive features analysis: Training blind students in shape recognition and in locating shapes on a map. *Journal of Special Education,* 11, 335–346.

Berlá, E. P., & Murr, M. J. (1974). Searching tactual space. *Education of the Visually Handicapped,* 6, 49–58.

(1975). Psychophysical functions for active tactual discrimination of line width by blind children. *Perception & Psychophysics,* 17, 607–612.

Bernstein, D. K. (1978). *Semantic development in congenitally blind children.* Unpublished doctoral dissertation, City University of New York.

Bigelow, A. E. (1986). The development of reaching in blind children. *British Journal of Developmental Psychology,* 4, 355–366.

(1987). Early words of blind children. *Journal of Child Language,* 14, 47–56.

(1988). Blind children's concepts of how people see. *Journal of Visual Impairment & Blindness,* 82, 65–68.

(1990). Relationship between the development of language and thought in young blind children. *Journal of Visual Impairment & Blindness,* 84, 414–419.

(1991). Spatial mapping of familiar locations in blind children. *Journal of Visual Impairment & Blindness,* 85, 113–117.

(1992). Blind children's ability to predict what another sees. *Journal of Visual Impairment & Blindness,* 86, 181–184.

Birns, S. L. (1986). Age at onset of blindness and development of space concepts: From topological to projective space. *Journal of Visual Impairment & Blindness,* 80, 577–582.

Blackhurst, A. E., Marks, C. H., & Tisdall, W. J. (1969). Relationship beween mobility and divergent thinking in blind children. *Education of the Visually Handicapped,* 1, 33–36.

Blank, H. R. (1959). Psychiatric problems associated with congenital blindness due to retrolental fibroplasia. *New Outlook for the Blind,* 53, 237–244.

Blasch, B. B. (1975). *A study of the treatment of blindisms using punishment and positive reinforcement in laboratory and natural settings.* Dissertation Abstracts International, 36, 3558A (University Microfilms No. DCJ 75–27236).

Block, C. (1972). *Developmental study of tactile–kinesthetic discrimination in blind, deaf, and normal children.* Dissertation Abstracts International, 33, 1781B (University Microfilms No. 72-25, 247).

Bower, T. G. R. (1974). *Development in infancy.* San Francisco: Freeman.

(1977). Blind babies see with their ears. *New Scientist, 73,* 255–257.

Bradway, K. P. (1937). Social competence of exceptional children: III. The deaf, the blind, and the crippled. *Exceptional Children, 4,* 64–69.

Brambring, M. (1988). *Assessment of developmental and educational problems in blind infants and preschoolers – limitations and potentials.* Presented at 1988 meetings of International Council for the Education of the Visually Handicapped, Edinburgh. University of Bielefeld, SBF Preprint No. 14.

Brambring, M., Dobslaw, G., Hauptmeier, M., Hecker, W., Latta-Weber, E., & Troester, H. (1989). *Assessment of blind infants and preschoolers – preliminary results with the Bielefeld Developmental Test.* University of Bielefeld, SFB Preprint No. 17.

Brambring, M., & Troester, H. (1992). On the stability of stereotyped behaviors in blind infants and preschoolers. *Journal of Visual Impairment & Blindness, 86,* 105–110.

Brekke, B., Williams, J. D., & Tait, P. (1974). The acquisition of conservation of weight by visually impaired children. *Journal of Genetic Psychology, 125,* 89–97.

Brennan, W. M., Ames, E. W., & Moore, R. W. (1966). Age differences in infants' attention to patterns of different complexities. *Science, 151,* 354–356.

Brieland, D. M. (1950). A comparative study of speech of blind and sighted children. *Speech Monographs, 17,* 99–103.

Brown, P. A. (1938). Responses of blind and seeing adolescents to an introversion–extroversion questionnaire. *Journal of Psychology, 6,* 137–147.

(1939). Responses of blind and seeing adolescents to a neurotic inventory. *Journal of Psychology, 7,* 211–221.

Bruner, J. (1966). On cognitive growth. In J. Bruner, R. Olver & P. Greenfield (Eds.), *Studies in cognitive growth* (pp. 7–32). New York: Wiley.

Buell, C. E. (1950). Motor performance of visually handicapped children. *Exceptional Children, 17,* 69–72.

Buell, C. E. (1982). *Physical education and recreation for the visually handicapped.* Reston, VA: The American Alliance for Health, Physical Education, Recreation and Dance.

Burlingham, D. (1961). Some notes on the development of the blind. *Psychoanalytic Study of the Child, 16,* 121–145.

(1964). Hearing and its role in the development of the blind. *Psychoanalytic Study of the Child, 19,* 95–112.

(1965). Some problems of ego development in blind children. *Psychoanalytic Study of the Child, 19,* 95–112.

(1967). Developmental considerations in the occupations of the blind. *Psychoanalytic Study of the Child, 22,* 187–198.

Bush-LaFrance, B. (1988). Unseen expectations of blind youth: Educational and occupational ideas. *Journal of Visual Impairment & Blindness*, 82, 132–136.

Caetano, A. P., & Kauffman, J. M. (1975). Reduction of mannerisms in two blind children. *Education of the Visually Handicapped*, 7, 101–105.

Caldwell, B. M., & Bradley, R. H. (1984). *Home observation for measurement of the environment*. Little Rock: University of Arkansas Center for Child Development and Education.

Canning, M. (1957). *Exploring the number concept in blind children*. Unpublished manuscript, University of Birmingham.

Carpenter, P. A., & Eisenberg, P. (1978). Mental rotation and the frame of reference in blind and sighted individuals. *Perception & Psychophysics*, 23, 117–124.

Casey, S. M. (1978). Cognitive mapping by the blind. *Journal of Visual Impairment & Blindness*, 72, 297–301.

Chase, J. B. (1972). *Retrolental fibroplasia and autistic symptomatology*. New York: American Foundation for the Blind (Research Series No. 24).

Chin, D. L. (1988). Dance movement instruction: Effects on spatial awareness in visually impaired elementary students. *Journal of Visual Impairment & Blindness*, 82, 188–192.

Clark, K. L. (1992). *A comparison of the effects of mobility training with a long cane and a precane device on the travel performance of preschool children with severe visual disabilities*. Unpublished doctoral dissertation, Ohio State University.

Cohen, J. (1966). The effects of blindness on children's development. *New Outlook for the Blind*, 60, 150–154.

Cohen, J., Alfano, J. E., Boshes, L. D., & Palmgren, C. (1964). Clinical evaluation of school-age children with retrolental fibroplasia. *American Journal of Ophthalmology*, 47, 41–57.

Cohen, J., Boshes, L. D., & Snider, R. S. (1961). Electroencephalographic changes following retrolental fibroplasia. *Electroencephalogical Clinical Neurophysiology*, 13, 914–922.

Coker, C. (1979). A comparison of self-concepts and academic achievement of visually handicapped children enrolled in a regular school and in a residential school. *Education of the Visually Handicapped*, 11, 67–74.

Colonna, A.B. (1968). A blind child goes to the hospital. *Psychoanalytic Study of the Child*, 23, 391–422.

Cook-Clampert, D. (1981). The development of self-concept in blind children. *Journal of Visual Impairment & Blindness*, 75, 233–238.

Cowen, E. L., Underberg, R. P., Verillo, R. T., & Benham, F. G. (1961). *Adjustment to visual disability in adolescence*. New York: American Foundation for the Blind.

Craig, E. M. (1973). Role of mental imagery in free recall of deaf, blind, and normal subjects. *Journal of Experimental Psychology*, 97, 249–253.

Crandall, V., Katkovsky, W., & Crandall, V. (1965). Children's beliefs in their own control of reinforcements in intellectual–academic situations. *Child Development*, 36, 91–109.

Crandell, J. M., Hammill, D. D., Witkowski, C., & Barkovich, F. (1968). Measuring form-discrimination in blind individuals. *International Journal for the Education of the Blind*, 18, 65–68.

Cratty, B. J. (1967). The perception of gradient and the veering tendency while walking without vision. *American Foundation for the Blind Research Bulletin*, 14, 31–51.

(1969). *Perceptual–motor behavior and educational processes*. Springfield, IL: Thomas.

Cratty, B. J., Peterson, C., Harris, J., & Schoner, R. (1968). The development of perceptual–motor abilities in blind children and adolescents. *New Outlook for the Blind*, 62, 111–117.

Cratty, B. J., & Sams, T. A. (1968). *The body-image of blind children*. New York: American Foundation for the Blind.

Cromer, R. F. (1973). Conservation by the congenitally blind. *British Journal of Psychology*, 64, 241–250.

Curson, A. (1979). The blind nursery school child. *Psychoanalytic Study of the Child*, 34, 51–83.

Cutsforth, T. D. (1932). The unreality of words to the blind. *Teachers Forum*, 4, 86–89.

(1951). *The blind in school and society*. New York: American Foundation for the Blind.

Czerwinski, M. H., & Tait, P. E. (1981). Blind children's perceptions of normal, withdrawn and antisocial behavior. *Journal of Visual Impairment & Blindness*, 75, 252–257.

Davidson, P. W. (1972). Haptic judgments of curvature by blind and sighted humans. *Journal of Experimental Psychology*, 93, 43–55.

(1976). Some functions of active handling: Studies with blind humans. *New Outlook for the Blind*, 70, 198–202.

Davidson, P. W., Barnes, J. K., & Mullen, G. (1974). Differential effects of task memory demand on haptic matching of shape by blind and sighted humans. *Neuropsychologia*, 12, 395–397.

Davidson, P. W., Dunn, G., Wiles-Kettenmann, M., & Appelle, S. (1981). Haptic conservation of amount in blind and sighted children: Exploratory movement effects. *Journal of Pediatric Psychology*, 6, 191–200.

Davidson, P. W., & Whitson, T. T. (1974). Haptic equivalence matching of curvature by blind and sighted humans. *Journal of Experimental Psychology*, 102, 687–690.

Davidson, P. W., Wiles-Kettenmann, M., Haber, R. N., & Appelle, S. (1980). Relationship between hand movements, reading competence and passage difficulty in braille reading. *Neuropsychologia*, 18, 629–635.

Davis, C. J. (1980). *Perkins–Binet Tests of Intelligence for the Blind.* Watertown, MA: Perkins School for the Blind.

Dekaban, A. S. (1972). Mental retardation and neurologic involvement in patients with congenital retinal blindness. *Developmental Medicine and Child Neurology*, 14, 436–444.

Dekker, R., Drenth, P. J. D., & Zaal, J. N. (1991). Results of the Intelligence Test for Visually Impaired Children (ITVIC). *Journal of Visual Impairment & Blindness*, 85, 261–267.

Dekker, R., Drenth, P. J. D., Zaal, J. N., & Koole, F. D. (1990). An intelligence test series for blind and low vision children. *Journal of Visual Impairment & Blindness*, 84, 71–76.

Dekker, R., & Koole, F. D. (1992). Visually impaired children's visual characteristics and intelligence. *Developmental Medicine and Child Neurology*, 34, 123–133.

Delia, J. G., & Clark, R. A. (1977). Cognitive complexity, social perception, and the development of listener-adapted communication in six-, eight-, ten-, and twelve-year-old boys. *Communication Monographs*, 44, 326–345.

DeMott, R. M. (1972). Verbalism and affective meaning for blind, severely visually impaired, and normally sighted children. *New Outlook for the Blind*, 66, 1–8.

Dershowitz, N. K. (1975). On connotative meaning of emotional terms to the blind: A contribution to the study of the phenomenology of emotion. *Perceptual and Motor Skills*, 41, 87–94.

Deutsch, F. (1940). The sense of reality in persons born blind. *Journal of Psychology*, 10, 121–140.

Dimcovic, N. (1992). Verbal competence and some other factors in the development of Piagetian concepts in blind children. *British Journal of Visual Impairment*, 10, 55–57.

Dodds, A. G., & Carter, D. D. C. (1983). Memory for movement in blind children: The role of previous visual experience. *Journal of Motor Behavior*, 15, 343–352.

Dodds, A. G., Howarth, C. I., & Carter, D. C. (1982). The mental maps of the blind: The role of previous experience. *Journal of Visual Impairment & Blindness*, 76, 5–12.

Dokecki, P. C. (1966). Verbalism and the blind: A critical review of the concept and the literature. *Exceptional Children*, 32, 525–530.

Dote-Kwan, J. (1991). *The relationship between early experiences and the development of young children with visual impairments.* Unpublished doctoral dissertation, California State University, Los Angeles/University of California, Los Angeles.

Drever, J. (1955). Early learning and the perception of space. *American Journal of Psychology*, 68, 605–614.

Duehl, A. N. (1979). The effect of creative dance movement on large muscle control and balance in congenitally blind children. *Journal of Visual Impairment & Blindness*, 73, 127–133.

Duncan, B. K. (1934). A comparative study of finger-maze learning by blind and sighted subjects. *Journal of Genetic Psychology*, 44, 69–95.

Dunlea, A. (1982). *The role of visual information in the emergence of meaning: A comparison of blind and sighted children*. Unpublished doctoral dissertation, University of Southern California.

   (1984). The relationship between concept formation and semantic roles: Some evidence from the blind. In L. Feagens, C. Garvey & R. Golinkoff (Eds.), *The origins and growth of communication* (pp. 224–243). Norwood, NJ: Ablex.

Duran, P., & Tufenkjian, S. (1970). The measurement of length by congenitally blind children and a quasiformal approach for spatial concepts. *American Foundation for the Blind Research Bulletin*, 22, 47–70.

Easton, R. D. (1985). Sonar sensory aid and blind children's spatial cognition. In D. H. Warren & E. R. Strelow (Eds.), *Electronic spatial sensing for the blind* (pp. 201–216). Dordrecht: Martinus Nijhoff.

Egland, G. O. (1955). Teaching speech to blind children with cerebral palsy. *New Outlook for the Blind*, 49, 282–289.

Eichel, V. J. (1979). A taxonomy for mannerisms of blind children. *Journal of Visual Impairment & Blindness*, 73, 167–178.

Eisenstadt, A. A. (1955). The speech status and the speech ability of visually handicapped children. *Speech Monographs*, 22, 199–200.

Elioseff, J. (1971). Training or education: Learning patterns of younger deaf–blind children. In *Fourth International Conference on Deaf–Blind Children* (pp. 85–106). Watertown, MA: Perkins School for the Blind.

Elonen, A. S., & Zwarensteyn, S. B. (1964). Appraisal of developmental lag in certain blind children. *Journal of Pediatrics*, 65, 599–610.

Fantz, R. L. (1964). Visual experience in infants: Decreased attention to familiar patterns relative to novel ones. *Science*, 146, 668–670.

Fernald, M. R. (1913). The mental imagery of two blind subjects. *Psychological Bulletin*, 10, 62–63.

Ferrell, K. A. (1980). Can infants use the Sonicguide? Two years' experience of Project VIEW. *Journal of Visual Impairment & Blindness*, 74, 209–220.

   (1984). A second look at sensory aids in early childhood. *Education of the Visually Handicapped*, 16, 83–101.

Ferrell, K. A., Trief, E., Dietz, S. J., Bonner, M. A., Cruz, D., Ford, E., &

Stratton, J. M. (1990). Visually Impaired Infants Research Consortium (VIIRC): First-year results. *Journal of Visual Impairment & Blindness*, 84, 404–410.

Flavell, J. H. (1963). *The Developmental Psychology of Jean Piaget*. Princeton, NJ: Van Nostrand.

(1985). *Cognitive Development* (2d edition). Englewood Cliffs, NJ: Prentice-Hall.

(1989). The development of children's knowledge about the mind: From cognitive connections to mental representations. In J. W. Asington, P. H. Harris & O. R. Olson (Eds.), *Developing theories of mind* (pp. 244–267). Cambridge University Press.

Fletcher, J. F. (1980). Spatial representation in blind children. 1: Development compared to sighted children. *Journal of Visual Impairment & Blindness*, 74, 381–385.

(1981a). Spatial representation in blind children. 2: Effects of task variations. *Journal of Visual Impairment & Blindness*, 75, 1–3.

(1981b). Spatial representation in blind children. 3: Effects of individual differences. *Journal of Visual Impairment & Blindness*, 75, 46–49.

Foulke, E., & Uhde, T. (1974). Do blind children need sex education? *New Outlook for the Blind*, 68, 193–200, 209.

Fraiberg, S. (1968). Parallel and divergent patterns in blind and sighted infants. *Psychoanalytic Study of the Child*, 23, 264–300.

(1970). Smiling and stranger reaction in blind infants. In J. Hellmuth (Ed.), *Exceptional infant* (pp. 110–127). New York: Brunner/Mazel.

(1972). Separation crisis in two blind children. *Psychoanalytic Study of the Child*, 26, 355–371.

(1974). Blind infants and their mothers: An examination of the sign system. In M. Lewis & L. A. Rosenblum (Eds.), *The effect of the infant on its caregiver* (pp. 215–232). New York: Wiley.

(1977). *Insights from the blind*. New York: Basic.

Fraiberg, S., & Adelson, E. (1976). Self-representation in young blind children. In Z. S. Jastrzembska (Ed.), *The effects of blindness and other impairments on early development* (pp. 136–159). New York: American Foundation for the Blind.

Fraiberg S., & Freedman, D. A. (1964). Studies in the ego development of the congenitally blind child. *Psychoanalytic Study of the Child*, 19, 113–169.

Fraiberg, S., Siegel, B., & Gibson, R. (1966). The role of sound in the search behavior of a blind infant. *Psychoanalytic Study of the Child*, 21, 327–357.

Fraiberg, S., Smith, M., & Adelson, E. (1969). An educational program for blind infants. *Journal of Special Education*, 3, 121–142.

Freedman, D. A. (1971). Congenital and perinatal sensory deprivation: Some studies in early development. *American Journal of Psychiatry,* 127, no. 11, 1539–1545.

(1972). On hearing, oral language, and psychic structure. In R. R. Holt & E. Peterfreund (Eds.), *Psychoanalysis and contemporary science* (pp. 57–69). New York: Macmillan.

Freedman, D. A., & Cannady, C. (1971). Delayed emergence of prone locomotion. *Journal of Nervous and Mental Disease,* 153, 108–117.

Freedman, D. A., Fox-Kolenda, B. J., Margileth, D. A., & Miller, D. H. (1969). The development of the use of sound as a guide to affective and cognitive behavior: A two-phase process. *Child Development,* 40, 1099–1105.

Freedman, D. G. (1964). Smiling in blind infants and the issue of innate vs. acquired. *Journal of Child Psychology and Psychiatry,* 5, 171–184.

Freeman, R. D., Goetz, E., Richards, D. P., & Groenveld, M. (1991). Defiers of negative prediction: A 14-year follow-up study of legally blind children. *Journal of Visual Impairment & Blindness,* 85, 365–370.

Freeman, R. D., Goetz, E., Richards, D. P., Groenveld, M., Blockberger, S., Jan, J. E., & Sykanda, A. M. (1989). Blind children's early emotional development: Do we know enough to help? *Child: Care, Health and Development,* 15, 3–28.

Friedman, J., & Pasnak, R. (1973a). Attainment of classification and seriation concepts by blind and sighted children. *Education of the Visually Handicapped,* 5, 55–62.

(1973b). Accelerated acquisition of classification skills by blind children. *Developmental Psychology,* 9, 333–337.

Gelber, A. H. (1980). *The development of social cognition in blind children.* Unpublished doctoral dissertation, City University of New York.

Gendel, E. S. (1973). Sex education of the blind child. Paper presented at Conference on the Blind Child in Social Interaction: Developing Relationships with Peers and Adults, New York.

Genn, M. M., & Silverman, W. A. (1964). The mental development of ex-premature children with retrolental fibroplasia. *Journal of Nervous and Mental Disease,* 138, 79–86.

Gerhardt, J. B. (1982). The development of object play and classificatory skills in a blind child. *Journal of Visual Impairment & Blindness,* 76, 219–223.

Gibbs, S. H., & Rice, J. A. (1974). The psycholinguistic characteristics of visually impaired children: An ITPA pattern analysis. *Education of the Visually Handicapped,* 6, 80–87.

Gibson, E. J. (1969). *Principles of perceptual learning and development.* New York: Appleton-Century-Crofts.

Gillman, A. E., & Goddard, D. R. (1974). The 20-year outcome of blind children two years old and younger: A preliminary survey. *New Outlook for the Blind,* 68, 1–7.

Gipsman, S. C. (1979). *Factors affecting performance and learning of blind and sighted children on a balance task.* Unpublished doctoral dissertation, University of California, Berkeley.

Gleitman, L. R. (1981). Maturational determinants of language growth. *Cognition,* 10, 103–114.

Gliner, C. R. (1966). *A psychophysical study of tactual perception.* Unpublished doctoral dissertation, University of Minnesota.

Goldman, H. (1970). Psychological testing of blind children. *American Foundation for the Blind Research Bulletin,* 21, 77–90.

Gore, G. V. (1966). Retrolental fibroplasia and I.Q. *New Outlook for the Blind,* 60, 305–306.

Gottesman, M. (1973). Conservation development in blind children. *Child Development,* 44, 824–827.

(1976). Stage development of blind children: A Piagetian view. *New Outlook for the Blind,* 70, 94–100.

Green, M. R., & Schecter, D. E. (1957). Autistic and symbiotic disorders in three blind children. *Psychiatric Quarterly,* 31, 629–646.

Greenberg, H. M., Allison, L., Fewell, M., & Rich, C. (1957). The personality of junior high school students attending a residential school for the blind. *Journal of Educational Psychology,* 48, 406–410.

Greenberg, H. M., & Jordan, S. (1957). Differential effects of total blindness and partial sight. *Exceptional Children,* 24, 123–124.

Groenveld, M., & Jan, J. E. (1992). Intelligence profiles of low vision and blind children. *Journal of Visual Impairment & Blindness,* 86, 68–71.

Guess, D. (1966). The influence of visual and ambulation restrictions on stereotyped behavior. *American Journal of Mental Deficiency,* 70, 542–547.

Hall, A. (1981a). Mental images and the cognitive development of the congenitally blind. *Journal of Visual Impairment & Blindness,* 75, 281–285.

(1981b). A developmental study of cognitive equivalence in the congenitally blind. *Journal of Mental Imagery,* 5, 61–74.

(1983). Methods of equivalence grouping by congenitally blind children: Implications for education. *Journal of Visual Impairment & Blindness,* 77, 172–174.

Hallenbeck, J. (1954a). Two essential factors in the development of young blind children. *New Outlook for the Blind,* 48, 308–315.

(1954b). Pseudo-retardation in retrolental fibroplasia. *New Outlook for the Blind,* 48, 301–307.

Halpin, G. (1972). The effects of visual deprivation on creative thinking abilities of children. Dissertation Abstracts International, 33, 3381A. (University Microfilms No. 72–34, 082).

Halpin, G., Halpin, G., & Tillman, M. H. (1973). Relationships between creative thinking, intelligence, and teacher-rated characteristics of blind children. *Education of the Visually Handicapped, 5*, 33–48.

Hammill, D. D., & Crandell, J. M., Jr. (1969). Implications of tactile-kinesthetic ability in visually handicapped children. *Education of the Visually Handicapped, 1*, 65–69.

Hammill, D. D., & Powell, L. S. (1967). An abstraction test for visually handicapped children. *Exceptional Children, 33*, 646–647.

Hanninen, K. A. (1970). The effect of texture on tactual perception of length. *Exceptional Children, 36*, 655–659.

  (1976). The influence of preference of texture on the accuracy of tactile discrimination. *Education of the Visually Handicapped, 8*, 44–52.

Hardy, R. E. (1968). A study of manifest anxiety among blind residential school students. *New Outlook for the Blind, 62*, 173–180.

Hare, B. A., Hammill, D. D., & Crandell, J. M. (1970). Auditory discrimination ability of visually limited children. *New Outlook for the Blind, 64*, 287–292.

Harley, R. K., Jr. (1963). *Verbalism among blind children.* New York: American Foundation for the Blind (Research Series, No. 10).

Harris, L., Humphrey, G. K., Muir, D. M., & Dodwell, P. C. (1985). The use of the Canterbury Child's Aid in infancy and early childhood: A case study. *Journal of Visual Impairment & Blindness, 79*, 4–11.

Hart, V. (1983). Characteristics of young blind children. Paper presented at the Second International Symposium on Visually Handicapped Infants and Young Children: Birth to 7. Aruba.

Hartlage, L. C. (1969). Verbal tests of spatial conceptualization. *Journal of Experimental Psychology, 80*, 180–182.

Haspiel, G. S. (1965). Communication breakdown in the blind emotionally disturbed child. *New Outlook for the Blind, 59*, 98–99.

Hatwell, Y. (1966). *Privation sensorielle et intelligence.* Paris: Presses Universitaires de France.

  (1985). *Piagetian reasoning and the blind.* New York: American Foundation for the Blind.

Hayes, C. S., & Weinhouse, E. (1978). Application of behavior modification to blind children. *Journal of Visual Impairment & Blindness, 72*, 139–146.

Hayes, S. P. (1929). The new revision of the Binet Intelligence Tests for the blind. *Teachers Forum, 2*, 2–4.

  (1930). *Terman's Condensed Guide for the Stanford Revision of the Binet–Simon Tests, adapted for use with the blind.* Watertown, MA: Perkins School for the Blind (Publication No. 4).

  (1933). New experimental data on the old problem of sensory compensation. *Teachers Forum, 5*, 22–26.

  (1935). Where did that sound come from? *Teachers Forum, 7*, 47–51.

(1942). Alternative scales for the mental measurement of the blind. *Outlook for the Blind,* 36, 225–230.

(1950). Measuring the intelligence of the blind. In P. A. Zahl (Ed.), *Blindness* (pp. 141–173). Princeton, NJ: Princeton University Press.

Head, D. (1979). A comparison of self-concept scores for visually impaired adolescents in several class settings. *Education of the Visually Handicapped,* 11, 51–55.

Heinze, A., Matson, J. L., Helsel, W. J., & Kapperman, G. (1987). Assessing general psychopathology in children and youth with visual handicaps. *Australia and New Zealand Journal of Developmental Disabilities,* 13, 219–226.

Herman, J. F., Chatman, S. P., & Roth, S. F. (1983). Cognitive mapping in blind people: Acquisition of spatial relationships in a large-scale environment. *Journal of Visual Impairment & Blindness,* 77, 161–166.

Hermelin, B. M., & O'Connor, N. (1971a). Right and left handed reading of braille. *Nature,* 231, 470.

(1971b). Spatial coding in normal, autistic and blind children. *Perceptual and Motor Skills,* 33, 127–132.

(1975). Location and distance estimates by blind and sighted children. *Quarterly Journal of Experimental Psychology,* 27, 295–301.

Higgins, L. C. (1973). *Classification in congenitally blind children.* New York: American Foundation for the Blind (Research Series, No. 25).

Hill, A., Spencer, C., & Baybutt, K. (1985). Predicting efficiency of travel in young, visually impaired children from their other spatial skills. *Journal of Visual Impairment & Blindness,* 79, 297–300.

Hill, E. W. (1970). The formation of concepts involved in body position in space. *Education of the Visually Handicapped,* 2, 112–115.

(1971). The formation of concepts involved in body position in space, Part 2. *Education of the Visually Handicapped,* 3, 21–25.

(1981). *The Hill performance test of selected positional concepts.* Chicago: Stoelting.

Hill, E. W., Guth, D. A., & Hill, M.-M. (1985). Spatial concept instruction for children with low vision. *Education of the Visually Handicapped,* 16, 152–161.

Hill, E. W., & Hill, M.-M. (1980). Revision and validation of a test for assessing the spatial conceptual abilities of visually impaired children. *Journal of Visual Impairment & Blindness,* 74, 373–380.

Hodapp, R. M., & Zigler, E. (in press). Past, present, and future issues in the developmental approach to mental retardation and developmental disabilities. In D. Cicchetti & D. Cohen (Eds.), *Manual of developmental psychopathology.* New York: Wiley.

Hopkins, K. D., & McGuire, L. (1967). IQ constancy and the blind child. *International Journal for the Education of the Blind,* 16, 113–114.

Hornby, G. Kay, L., Satherley, M., & Kay, N. (1985). Spatial awareness training of blind children using the Trisensor. In D. H. Warren & E. R. Strelow (Eds.), *Electronic spatial sensing for the blind*, pp. 257–272. Dordrecht: Martinus Nijhoff.

Hoshmand, L. T. (1975). "Blindisms": Some observations and propositions. *Education of the Visually Handicapped*, 7, 56–60.

Huckabee, M. W., & Ferrell, J. G., Jr. (1971). The Tactual Embedded Figures Test as a measure of field dependence–independence in blind adolescents. *Education of the Visually Handicapped*, 3, 37–40.

Humphrey, G. K., Dodwell, P. C., Muir, D. M., & Humphrey, D. W. (1988). Can blind infants and children use sonar sensory aids? *Canadian Journal of Psychology*, 42, 94–119.

Imamura, S. (1965). *Mother and blind child*. New York: American Foundation for the Blind (Research Series, No. 14).

Ittyerah, M., & Samarapungavan, A. (1989). The performance of congenitally blind children in cognitive developmental tasks. *British Journal of Developmental Psychology*, 7, 129–139.

Jan, J. E., Freeman, R. D., & Scott, E. P. (1977). *Visual impairment in children and adolescents*. New York: Grune & Stratton.

Jankowski, L. W., & Evans, J. K. (1981). The exercise capacity of blind children. *Journal of Visual Impairment & Blindness*, 75, 248–251.

Janson, U., & Merényi, A.-C. (1992). Social play between blind and sighted preschool children. Paper presented at the ICEVH Early Childhood Conference, Bangkok, Thailand.

Jervis, F. M. (1959). A comparison of self-concepts of blind and sighted children. In C. J. Davis (Ed.), *Guidance programs for blind children* (pp. 19–31). Watertown, MA: Perkins.

Jervis, F. M., & Haslerud, G. M. (1950). Quantitative and qualitative differences in frustration between blind and sighted adolescents. *Journal of Psychology*, 29, 67–76.

Jones, B. (1972). Development of cutaneous and kinesthetic localization by blind and sighted children. *Developmental Psychology*, 6, 349–352.

(1975). Spatial perception in the blind. *British Journal of Psychology*, 66, 461–472.

Jones, R. L., Lavine, K., & Shell, J. (1972). Blind children integrated in classrooms with sighted children: A sociometric study. *New Outlook for the Blind*, 66, 75–80.

Jones, R. L., & McGhee, P. W. (1972). Locus of control, reference group, and achievement in blind children. *Rehabilitation Psychology*, 19, 18–26.

Jordan, J. E., & Felty, J. (1968). Factors associated with intellectual variation among visually impaired children. *American Foundation for the Blind Research Bulletin*, 15, 61–70.

Kagan, J. (1970). Attention and psychological change in the young child. *Science*, 170, 826–832.

Kaplan, D. M., & Mason, E. A. (1960). Maternal reactions to premature birth viewed as an acute emotional disorder. *American Journal of Orthopsychiatry*, 30, 539–552.

Kay, L. (1974). A sonar aid to enhance spatial perception of the blind: Engineering design and evaluation. *The Radio and Electronic Engineer*, 44, 40–62.

   (1984). Learning to use the ultrasonic spatial sensor by the blind infant: Comments on Aitken and Bower. *Journal of Experimental Child Psychology*, 37, 207–211.

Kay, L., & Kay, N. (1983). An ultrasonic spatial sensor's role as a developmental aid for blind children. *Transactions of the Ophthalmological Society of New Zealand*, 35, 38–42.

Kay, L., & Strelow, E. R. (1977). Blind babies need specially-designed aids. *New Scientist*, 74, 709–712.

Keeler, W. R. (1958). Autistic patterns and defective communication in blind children with retrolental fibroplasia. In P. H. Hoch & J. Zubin (Eds.), *Psychopathology of communication* (pp. 64–84). New York: Grune & Stratton.

Kekelis, L. S. (1988). Peer interactions in childhood: The impact of visual impairment. In S. Z. Sacks, L. S. Kekelis, & R. J. Gaylord-Ross (Eds.), *The development of social skills by visually impaired children* (pp. 1–28). San Francisco: San Francisco State University.

Kekelis, L. S., & Andersen, E. W. (1984). Family communication styles and language development. *Journal of Visual Impairment & Blindness*, 78, 54–65.

Kekelis, L. S., & Sacks, S. Z. (1988). Mainstreaming visually impaired children into regular education programs: The effects of visual impairment on children's interactions with peers. In S. Z. Sacks, L. S. Kekelis, & R. J. Gaylord-Ross (Eds.), *The development of social skills by visually impaired children* (pp. 1–42). San Francisco: San Francisco State University.

Kenmore, J. R. (1965). *Associative learning by blind versus sighted children with words and objects differing in meaningfulness and identifiability without vision.* Unpublished doctoral dissertation, University of Minnesota.

Kennedy, J. M. (1980). Blind people recognizing and making haptic pictures. In M. Hagen (Ed.), *The perception of pictures* (pp. 263–303). New York: Academic Press.

   (1982). Haptic pictures. In W. Schiff & E. Foulke (Eds.), *Tactual perception: A sourcebook* (pp. 305–333). Cambridge University Press.

   (1983). What can we learn about pictures from the blind? *American Scientist*, 71, 19–26.

Kennedy, J. M., & Domander, R. (1981). Blind people depicting states & events in metaphoric line drawings. Paper presented at meeting of the Psychonomic Society, Philadelphia.

Kephart, J. G., Kephart, C. P., & Schwarz, G. C. (1974). A journey into the world of the blind child. *Exceptional Children*, 40, 421–427.

Kinsbourne, M., & Lempert, H. (1980). Human figure representation by blind children. *Journal of General Psychology*, 102, 33–37.

Klatzky, R. L., Lederman, S. J., & Reed, C. (1987). There's more to touch than meets the eye: The salience of object attributes for haptics with and without vision. *Journal of Experimental Psychology: General*, 116, 356–369.

Klaus, M. H., & Kennell, J. H. (1976). *Maternal–infant bonding: The impact of early separation or loss on family development*. St. Louis, MO: Mosby.

Knight, J. J. (1972). Mannerisms in the congenitally blind child. *New Outlook for the Blind*, 66, 297–302.

Knobloch, H., Rider, R., Harper, P., & Pasamanick, B. (1956). Neuropsychiatric sequelae of prematurity. *Journal of the American Medical Association*, 161, 581–585.

Knotts, J. R., & Miles, W. R. (1929). The maze-learning ability of blind compared with sighted children. *Journal of Genetic Psychology*, 36, 21–50.

Kohlberg, L. (1981). *The philosophy of moral development*. New York: Harper & Row.

Komisar, D., & MacDonnell, M. (1955). Gains in IQ for students attending a school for the blind. *Exceptional Children*, 21, 127–129.

Kool, V. K., & Rana, M. (1980). Tactual short term memory of blind and sighted children. *Psychologia: An International Journal of Psychology in the Orient*, 23, 173–178.

Lairy, G. C., & Harrison-Covello, A. (1973). The blind child and his parents: Congenital visual defect and the repercussion of family attitudes on the early development of the blind. *American Foundation for the Blind Research Bulletin*, 25, 1–24.

Land, S. L., & Vineberg, S. E. (1965). Locus of control in blind children. *Exceptional Children*, 31, 257–260.

Landau, B. (1983). Blind children's language is not "meaningless." In A. E. Mills (Ed.), *Language acquisition in the blind child: Normal and deficient*, pp. 62–76. London: Croom Helm.

(1986). Early map use as an unlearned ability. *Cognition*, 22, 201–223.

Landau, B., & Gleitman, L. R. (1985). *Language and experience: Evidence from the blind child*. Cambridge, MA: Harvard University Press.

Landau, B., Gleitman, H., & Spelke, E. (1981). Spatial knowledge and geometric representation in the child blind from birth. *Science*, 213, 1275–1277.

Landau, B., Spelke, E., & Gleitman, H. (1984). Spatial knowledge in a young blind child. *Cognition*, 16, 225–260.

Laurendeau, M., & Pinard, A. (1970). *The development of the concept of space in the child*. New York: International Universities Press.

Lebron-Rodriguez, D. E., & Pasnak, R. (1977). Introduction of intellectual gains in blind children. *Journal of Experimental Child Psychology*, 24, 505–515.

Lefcourt, H. (1976). *Locus of control: Current trends in theory and research*. Hillsdale, NJ: Erlbaum.

Leonard, J. A. (1969). Static and mobile balancing performance of blind adolescent grammar school children. *New Outlook for the Blind*, 63, 65–72.

Levitt, E. A., Rosenbaum, A. L., Willerman, L., & Levitt, M. (1972). Intelligence of retinoblastoma patients and their siblings. *Child Development*, 43, 939–948.

Ling, D., & Ling, A. (1976). Communication development in the first three years of life. In Z. Jastrzembska (Ed.), *The effects of blindness on early development* (pp. 160–172). New York: American Foundation for the Blind.

Linvill, J. G., & Bliss, J. C. (1971). A direct translation reading aid for the blind. *Proceedings of the IEEE*, 54, 40–51.

Lipsitt, L. P. (1958). A self-concept scale for children and its relationship to the children's form of the Manifest Anxiety Scale. *Child Development*, 29, 463–472.

Lister, C., Leach, C., & Walsh, M. (1989). The development of conservation concepts in children with visual impairment. *British Journal of Educational Psychology*, 59, 211–219.

Lockman, J. J., Rieser, J. J., & Pick, H. L., Jr. (1981). Assessing blind travelers' knowledge of spatial layout. *Journal of Visual Impairment & Blindness*, 75, 321–326.

Lopata, D. J., & Pasnak, R. (1976). Accelerated conservation acquisition and IQ gains by blind children. *Genetic Psychology Monographs*, 93, 3–25.

Lucas, S. A. (1984). Auditory discrimination and speech production in the blind child. *International Journal of Rehabilitation Research*, 7, 74–76.

Lukoff, I. F., & Whiteman, M. (1970). Socialization and segregated education. *American Foundation for the Blind Research Bulletin*, 20, 91–107.

Maas, E., Marecek, J., & Travers, J. R. (1978). Children's conceptions of disordered behavior. *Child Development*, 49, 146–154.

Markoulis, D. (1988). Moral and cognitive reasoning features in congenitally blind children: Comparisons with the sighted. *British Journal of Developmental Psychology*, 6, 59–69.

Martin, C. J., Boersma, F.J., & Cox, D. L. (1965). A classification of associative strategies in paired-associate learning. *Psychonomic Science*, 3, 455–456.

Martin, C. J., & Herndon, M. A. (1971). Facilitation of associative learning among blind children. *Proceedings of the American Psychological Association*, 629–630.

Matsuda, M. M. (1984). A comparative analysis of blind and sighted children's communication skills. *Journal of Visual Impairment & Blindness*, 78, 1–4.

Maxfield, K. E., & Buchholz, S. (1957). *A social maturity scale for blind preschool children: A guide to its use*. New York: American Foundation for the Blind.

Maxfield, K. E., & Fjeld, H. A. (1942). The social maturity of the visually handicapped preschoolchild. *Child Development*, 13, 1–27.

Mayadas, N. S. (1972). Role expectations and performance of blind children: Practice and implications. *Education of the Visually Handicapped*, 4, 45–52.

Mayadas, N. S., & Duehn, W. D. (1976). The impact of significant adults' expectations on the life style of visually impaired children. *New Outlook for the Blind*, 70, 286–290.

McAndrew, H. (1948a). Rigidity and isolation: A study of the deaf and the blind. *Journal of Abnormal and Social Psychology*, 43, 476–494.

(1948b). Rigidity in the deaf and blind. *Journal of Social Issues*, 4, 72–77.

McGlynn, N., & Phillips, G. (1987). Integrated pre-schooling: An overview of the literature. *Educational Psychology in Practice*, 7, 38–41.

McGraw, M. B. (1945). *The neuro-muscular maturation of the human infant* (reprint ed., 1963). New York: Hafner.

McGuinness, R. M. (1970). A descriptive study of blind children educated in the itinerant teacher, resource room, and special school setting. *American Foundation for the Blind Research Bulletin*, 20, 1–56.

McGuire, L. L., & Meyers, C. E. (1971). Early personality in the congenitally blind child. *New Outlook for the Blind*, 65, 137–143.

McGurk, H. (1983). Effectance motivation and the development of communication competence in blind and sighted children. In A. E. Mills (Ed.), *Language acquisition in the blind child: Normal and deficient* (pp. 108–113). London: Croom Helm.

McKay, B. E. (1936). Social maturity of the preschool blind child. *Training School Bulletin*, 33, 146–155.

McLinden, D. J. (1988). Spatial task performance: A meta-analysis. *Journal of Visual Impairment & Blindness*, 82, 231–236.

McReynolds, J., & Worchel, P. (1954). Geographic orientation in the blind. *Journal of General Psychology*, 51, 221–236.

Meighan, T. (1971). *An investigation of the self concept of blind and visually handicapped adolescents*. New York: American Foundation for the Blind.

Miletic, G., Hughes, B., & Bach-y-Rita, P. (1988). Vibrotactile stimulation: An educational program for spatial concept development. *Journal of Visual Impairment & Blindness*, 82, 366–370.

Millar, S. (1974). Tactile short-term memory by blind and sighted children. *British Journal of Psychology*, 65, 253–263.

(1975a). Effects of phonological and tactual similarity on serial object recall by blind and sighted children. *Cortex*, 11, 170–180.

(1975b). Effects of tactual and phonological similarity on the recall of braille letters by blind children. *British Journal of Psychology*, 66, 193–201.

(1975c). Spatial memory by blind and sighted children. *British Journal of Psychology*, 66, 449–459.

(1975d). Visual experience or translation rules? Drawing the human figure by blind and sighted children. *Perception*, 4, 363–371.

(1976). Spatial representation by blind and sighted children. *Journal of Experimental Child Psychology*, 21, 460–479.

(1978). Short-term serial tactual recall: Effects of grouping on tactually probed recall of braille letters and nonsense shapes by blind children. *British Journal of Psychology*, 69, 17–24.

(1979). The utilization of external and movement cues in simple spatial tasks by blind and sighted children. *Perception*, 8, 11–20.

(1981a). Crossmodal and intersensory perception and the blind. In R. D. Walk & H. L. Pick, Jr. (Eds.), *Intersensory perception and sensory integration* (pp. 281–314). London: Plenum Press.

(1981b). Self-referent and movement cues in coding spatial location by blind and sighted children. *Perception*, 10, 255–264.

(1982). The problem of imagery and spatial development in the blind. In B. de Gelder (Ed.), *Knowledge and representation* (pp. 111–120). London: Routledge & Kegan Paul.

(1983). Language and active touch: Some aspects of reading and writing by blind children. In A. E. Mills (Ed.), *Language acquisition in the blind child: Normal and deficient* (pp. 167–186). London: Croom Helm.

(1984). Strategy choices by young Braille readers. *Perception*, 13, 567–579.

(1985). Movement cues and body orientation in recall of locations by blind and sighted children. *Quarterly Journal of Experimental Psychology*, 37A, 257–279.

Miller, B. S., & Miller, W. H. (1976). Extinguishing "blindisms": A paradigm for intervention. *Education of the Visually Handicapped*, 8, 6–15.

Miller, C. K. (1969). Conservation in blind children. *Education of the Visually Handicapped*, 1, 101–105.

Miller, L. (1992). Diderot reconsidered: Visual impairment and auditory compensation. *Journal of Visual Impairment & Blindness*, 86, 206–210.

Miller, W. H. (1970). Manifest anxiety in visually impaired adolescents. *Education of the Visually Handicapped*, 2, 91–95.

Mills, A. E. (1983). The acquisition of speech sounds in the visually-handicapped child. In A. E. Mills (Ed.), *Language acquisition in the blind child: Normal and deficient* (pp. 46–56). London: Croom Helm.

Mills, R. J. (1970). Orientation and mobility for teachers. *Education of the Visually Handicapped*, 2, 80–82.

Miner, L. E. (1963). A study of the incidence of speech deviations among visually handicapped children. *New Outlook for the Blind*, 57, 10–14.

Mommers, M. J. C. (1980). Braille reading: Effects of different hand and finger usage. *Journal of Visual Impairment & Blindness*, 74, 338–343.

Morris, J. E., & Nolan, C. Y. (1963). Minimum sizes for areal type tactual symbols. *International Journal for the Education of the Blind*, 13, 48–51.

Morrissey, W. P. (1950). The fantasy life of the blind. *Outlook for the Blind*, 44, 195–198.

Muir, D. (1982). The development of human auditory localization in infancy. In R. W. Gatehouse (Ed.), *Localization of sound: Theory and applications* (pp. 22–46). Groton, CT: Amphora.

Muir, D., Abraham, W., Forbes, B., & Harris, L. (1979). The ontogenesis of an auditory localization response from birth to four months of age. *Canadian Journal of Psychology*, 33, 320–333.

Mulford, R. C. (1980). *Talking without seeing: Some problems of semantic development in blind children.* Unpublished doctoral dissertation, Stanford University.

Mulford, R. C. (1983). Referential development in blind children. In A. E. Mills (Ed.), *Language acquisition in the blind child: Normal and deficient.* London: Croom Helm, pp. 89–107.

(1988). First words of the blind child. In M. D. Smith & J. L. Locke (Eds.), *The emergent lexicon: The child's development of a linguistic vocabulary* (pp. 293–338). New York: Academic Press.

Nagera, H., & Colonna, A. B. (1965). Aspects of the contribution of sight to ego and drive development. *Psychoanalytic Study of the Child*, 20, 267–287.

Nelson, K. (1973). Structure and strategy in learning to talk. *Monographs of the Society for Research in Child Development*, 38, no. 149.

Nelson, K. (1981). Individual differences in language development: Implications for development and language. *Developmental Psychology*, 17, 170–187.

Newland, T. E. (1964). Prediction and evaluation of academic learning by blind children. *International Journal for the Education of the Blind*, 14, 1–7.

Newland, T. E. (1979). The Blind Learning Aptitude Test. *Journal of Visual Impairment & Blindness*, 73, 134–139.

Nielsen, L. (1991). Spatial relations in congenitally blind infants: A study. *Journal of Visual Impairment & Blindness*, 85, 11–16.

Nixon, H. L., II. (1988). Getting over the worry hurdle: Parental encouragement and the sports involvement of visually impaired children and youths. *Adapted Physical Activity Quarterly*, 5, 29–43.

Nolan, C. Y. (1960a). Roughness discrimination among blind children in the primary grades. *International Journal for the Education of the Blind,* 9, 97–100.

(1960b). On the unreality of words to the blind. *New Outlook for the Blind,* 54, 100–102.

Nolan, C. Y., & Morris, J. E. (1960). Further results in the development of a test of roughness discrimination. *International Journal for the Education of the Blind,* 10, 48–50.

Norris, M., Spaulding, P. J., & Brodie, F. H. (1957). *Blindness in children.* Chicago: University of Chicago Press.

Novikova, L. A. (1973). *Blindness and the electrical activity of the brain.* New York: American Foundation for the Blind (Research Series, No. 23).

O'Connor, N., & Hermelin, B. M. (1972a). Seeing and hearing in space and time. *Perception & Psychophysics,* 11, 46–48.

(1972b). Seeing and hearing in space time: Problems by blind and sighted children. *British Journal of Psychology,* 63, 381–386.

Ohwaki, Y., Tanno, Y., Ohwaki, M., Hariu, T., Hayasaka, K., & Miyake, K. (1960). Construction of an intelligence test for the blind. *Tohoku Psychologia Folia,* 18, 45–63.

Olson, M. R. (1983). A study of the exploratory behavior of legally blind and sighted preschoolers. *Exceptional Children.* 50, 130–138.

Osgood, C. E., Suci, G. J., & Tannenbaum, P. H. (1957). *The measurement of meaning.* Urbana: University of Illinois Press.

Paivio, A., & Okovita, H. W. (1971). Word imagery modalities and associative learning in blind and sighted subjects. *Journal of Verbal Learning and Verbal Behavior,* 10, 506–510.

Parmalee, A. H., Cutsforth, M. G., & Jackson, C. L. (1958). Mental development of children with blindness due to retrolental fibroplasia. *American Medical Association Journal of Diseases of Children,* 96, 641–654.

Parmalee, A. H., Fiske, C. E., & Wright, R. H. (1959). The development of ten children with blindness as a result of retrolental fibroplasia. *American Medical Association Journal of Diseases of Children,* 98, 198–220.

Parsons, S. (1986a). Function of play in low vision children (Part 1): A review of the research and literature. *Journal of Visual Impairment & Blindness,* 80, 627–630.

(1986b). Function of play in low vision children (Part 2): Emerging patterns of behavior. *Journal of Visual Impairment & Blindness,* 80, 777–784.

(1987). Locus of control and adaptive behavior in visually impaired children. *Journal of Visual Impairment & Blindness,* 81, 429–432.

Pereira, L. M. (1990). Spatial concepts and balance performance: Motor learning in blind and visually impaired children. *Journal of Visual Impairment & Blindness,* 84, 109–111.

Petrucci, D. (1953). The blind child and his adjustment. *New Outlook for the Blind*, 47, 240–246.

Piaget, J. (1946). *Le développement de la notion de temps chez l'enfant*. Paris: Presses Universitaires de France.

(1948). *The moral development of the child*. New York: Free Press.

(1952). *The origins of intelligence in children* (2nd ed.). New York: International Universities Press.

(1954). *The construction of reality in the child*. New York: Basic.

Pick, A. D., Thomas, M. L., & Pick, H. L., Jr. (1966). The role of grapheme–phoneme correspondences in the perception of braille. *Journal of Verbal Learning and Verbal Behavior*, 5, 298–300.

Pintner, R., & Forlano, G. (1943). Personality tests of partially sighted children. *Journal of Applied Psychology*, 27, 283–287.

Pitman, D. J. (1965). The musical ability of blind children. *American Foundation for the Blind Research Bulletin*, 11, 63–80.

Pring, L. (1982). Phonological and tactual coding of braille by blind children. *British Journal of Psychology*, 73, 351–359.

(1984). A comparison of the word recognition processes of blind and sighted children. *Child Development*, 55, 1865–1877.

(1987). Picture processing by the blind. *British Journal of Experimental Psychology*, 57, 38–44.

Pring, L., & Rusted, J. (1985). Pictures for the blind: An investigation of the influence of pictures on recall of text by blind children. *British Journal of Developmental Psychology*, 3, 41–45.

Prizant, B. M. (1984). Toward an understanding of language symptomatology of visually-impaired children. In A. M. Sykanda, B. K. Buchanan, J. E. Jan, M. Groenveld, & S. J. Blockberger (Eds.), *Insight in sight: Proceedings of the fifth Canadian interdisciplinary conference on the visually impaired child* (pp. 70–87). Vancouver: CNIB.

Read, L. F. (1989). An examination of the social skills of blind kindergarten children. *Education of the Visually Handicapped*, 20, 142–155.

Renshaw, S., Wherry, R. J., & Newlin, J. C. (1930). Cutaneous localization in congenitally blind versus seeing children and adults. *Journal of Genetic Psychology*, 38, 239–248.

Revesz, G. (1950). *Psychology and the art of the blind*. New York: Longmans, Green.

Reynell, J. (1978). Developmental patterns of visually handicapped children. *Child: Care, Health & Development*, 4, 291–303.

Robbins, N. (1971). The teaching of a manual-sign as a diagnostic tool with deaf–blind children. *Fourth International Conference on Deaf–Blind Children* (pp. 124–127). Watertown, MA: Perkins School for the Blind.

Robin, M., & Pecheux, M.-G. (1976). Problèmes posés par la réproduction de modèles spatiaux chez des enfants aveugles: Une étude expérimentale. *Perception*, 5, 39–49.

Rogers, S. J., & Puchalski, C. B. (1984a). Social characteristics of visually impaired infants' play. *Topics in Early Childhood Special Education*, 3, 52–56.

(1984b). Development of symbolic play in visually impaired young children. *Topics in Early Childhood Special Education*, 3, 57–63.

(1986). Social smiles of visually impaired infants. *Journal of Visual Impairment & Blindness*, 80, 863–865.

(1988). Development of object permanence in visually impaired infants. *Journal of Visual Impairment & Blindness*, 82, 137–142.

Rogow, S. M. (1972). Language acquisition and the blind retarded child. *Education of the Visually Handicapped*. 4, 36–40.

(1980). Language development in blind multihandicapped children: A model of co-active intervention. *Child: Care, Health & Development*, 6, 301–308.

(1981). The appreciation of riddles by blind and visually handicapped children. *Education of the Visually Handicapped*, 13, 4–10.

(1982). Rhythms and rhymes: Developing communication in very young blind and multihandicapped children. *Child: Care, Health and Development*, 8, 249–260.

Rothschild, J. (1960). Play therapy with blind children. *New Outlook for the Blind*, 54, 329–333.

Rowland, C. (1983). Patterns of interaction between three blind infants and their mothers. In A. E. Mills (Ed.), *Language acquisition in the blind child: Normal and deficient* (pp. 114–132). London: Croom Helm.

(1984). Preverbal communication of blind infants and their mothers. *Journal of Visual Impairment & Blindness*, 78, 297–302.

Salmon, P. J., & Rusalem, H. (1966). The deaf–blind person: A review of the literature. *Blindness 1966: American Association of Workers for the Blind Annual*, 15–63.

Sameroff, A. J. (1989). Commentary: General systems and the regulation of development. In M. R. Gunnar & E. Thelen (Eds.), *Systems and development: The Minnesota symposium on child psychology* (pp. 219–235). Hillsdale, NJ: Erlbaum.

Sampaio, E. (1989). Is there a critical age for using the Sonicguide with blind infants? *Journal of Visual Impairment & Blindness*, 83, 105–108.

Sandler, A.-M. (1963). Aspects of passivity and ego development in the blind infant. *Psychoanalytic Study of the Child*, 18, 343–360.

Sandler, A.-M., & Wills, D. M. (1965). Preliminary notes on play and mastery in the blind child. *Journal of Child Psychotherapy*, 1, 7–19.

Schaffer, H. R., & Callender, W. M. (1959). Psychologic effects of hospitalization in infancy. *Pediatrics*, 24, 528–539.

Schein, J. D., Kates, L., Wolf, E. G., & Theil, L. (1983). Assessing and developing the communications abilities of deaf–blind children. *Journal of Visual Impairment & Blindness*, 77, 152–157.

Schindele, R. (1974). The social adjustment of visually handicapped children in different educational settings. *American Foundation for the Blind Research Bulletin*, 28, 125–144.

Schlaegel, T. F. (1953). The dominant method of imagery in blind as compared to sighted adolescents. *Journal of Genetic Psychology*, 83, 265–277.

Schneekloth, L. H. (1989). Play environments for visually impaired children. *Journal of Visual Impairment & Blindness*, 83, 196–210.

Schnittjer, C. J., & Hirshoren, A. (1981). Factors of problem behavior in visually impaired children. *Journal of Abnormal Child Psychology*, 9, 517–522.

Scholl, G. T. (1974). The psychosocial effects of blindness: Implications for program planning in sex education. *New Outlook for the Blind*, 68, 201–209.

Schwartz, A. W. (1972). A comparison of congenitally blind and sighted elementary school children on intelligence, tactile discrimination, abstract reasoning, perceived physical health, perceived personality adjustment and parent–teacher perceptions of intellectual performance. *Dissertation Abstracts International*, 33, 5588A. (University Microfilms No. 73-9717.)

Schwartz, M. (1984). The role of sound for space and object perception in the congenitally blind infant. In L. Lipsitt & C. Rovee-Collier (Eds.), *Advances in infancy research* (pp. 23–56). Norwood, N.J.: Ablex.

Scott, R. A. (1968). *The making of blind men.* New York: Sage.

(1969). The socialization of blind children. In D. A. Goslin (Ed.), *Handbook of socialization theory and research* (pp. 1025–1046). Chicago: Rand McNally.

Seashore, M. J., Leifer, A. D., Barnett, C. R., & Leiderman, P. H. (1973). The effects of denial of early mother–infant interaction on maternal self-confidence. *Journal of Personality and Social Psychology*, 26, 369–378.

Seeyle, W. (1983). Physical fitness of blind and visually impaired Detroit public school children. *Journal of Visual Impairment & Blindness*, 77, 117–118.

Selman, R. L., & Byrne, D. F. (1974). A structural–developmental analysis of levels of role taking in middle childhood. *Child Development*, 45, 803–806.

Shagan, J., & Goodnow, J. (1973). Recall of haptic information by blind and sighted individuals. *Journal of Experimental Psychology*, 101, 221–226.

Shepard, R. N., & Metzler, J. (1971). Mental rotation of three-dimensional objects. *Science*, 171, 701–703.

Short, F. X., & Winnick, J. P. (1986). The influence of visual impairment on physical fitness test performance. *Journal of Visual Impairment & Blindness*, 80, 729–731.

(1988). Adolescent physical fitness: A comparative study. *Journal of Visual Impairment & Blindness*, 82, 237–239.

Sicilian, S. P. (1988). Development of counting strategies in congenitally blind children. *Journal of Visual Impairment & Blindness*, 82, 331–335.

Siegel, I. M., & Murphy, T. J. (1970). *Postural determinants in the blind.* Final Project Report, Grant RD-3512-SB-700C2.

Simpkins, K. E. (1979). Tactual discrimination of shapes. *Journal of Visual Impairment & Blindness*, 73, 93–101.

Simpkins, K. E., & Siegel, A. J. (1979). The blind child's construction of the projective straight line. *Journal of Visual Impairment & Blindness*, 73, 233–238.

Singer, J. L., & Streiner, B. F. (1966). Imaginative content in the dreams and fantasy play of blind and sighted children. *Perceptual and Motor Skills*, 22, 475–482.

Smith, M. A., Chethik, M., & Adelson, E. (1969). Differential assessments of "blindisms." *American Journal of Orthopsychiatry*, 39, 807–817.

Smits, B. W. G. M., & Mommers, M. J. C. (1976). Differences between blind and sighted children on WISC verbal subtests. *New Outlook for the Blind*, 70, 240–246.

Solntseva, L. I. (1966). Features peculiar to perception of the blind preschool children. In *Mental Development and Sensory Defects*, 18th International Congress of Psychology, 226–230.

Sommers, V. S. (1944). *The influence of parental attitudes and social environment on the personality development of the adolescent blind.* New York: American Foundation for the Blind.

Sparrow, S., Balla, D., & Cicchetti, V. (1984). *Vineland Adaptive Behavior Scales, Interview Edition.* Circle Pines, MN: American Guidance Service.

Spelke, E. (1976). Infants' intermodal perception of events. *Cognitive Psychology*, 8, 553–560.

Spiegelman, M. N. (1976). A comparative study of the effects of early blindness on the development of auditory–spatial learning. In Z. S. Jastrzembska (Ed.), *The effects of blindness and other impairments on early development* (pp. 29–63). New York: American Foundation for the Blind.

Spitz, R. A. (1945). Hospitalism. *Psychoanalytic Study of the Child*, 1, 53–74. (1946). Anaclitic depression. *Psychoanalytic Study of the Child*, 2, 313–342.

Stack, D. M., Muir, D., & Sherriff, F. (1986). "Reaching in the dark," poster presented at the International Conference on Infant Studies, Los Angeles, CA.

Stankov, L., & Spilsbury, G. (1978). The measurement of auditory abilities of blind, partially sighted, and sighted children. *Applied Psychological Measurement*, 2, 491–503.

Steinzor, L. V. (1966). School peers of visually handicapped children. *New Outlook for the Blind*, 60, 312–314.

Stephens, B., & Grube, C. (1982). Development of Piagetian reasoning in congenitally blind children. *Journal of Visual Impairment & Blindness*, 76, 133–143.

Stephens, B., & Simpkins, K. (1974). *The reasoning, moral judgment, and moral conduct of the congenitally blind* (Report No. H23–3197). Office of Education, Bureau of Education for the Handicapped.

Stephens, B., Simpkins, K., & Wexler, M. (1976). A comparison of the performance of blind and sighted subjects age 6–10 years on the Rotation of Squares Test. *Education of the Visually Handicapped*, 8, 66–70.

Stinchfield-Hawk, S. (1944). Moto-kinaesthetic speech training applied to visually handicapped children. *New Outlook for the Blind*, 38, 4–8.

Stone, A. A. (1964). Consciousness: Altered levels in blind retarded children. *Psychosomatic Medicine*, 26, 14–19.

Stone, N. W., & Chesney, B. H. (1978). Attachment behaviors in handicapped infants. *Mental Retardation*, 16, 8–12.

Strelow, E. R., & Warren, D. H. (1985). Sensory substitution in blind children and neonates. In D. H. Warren & E. R. Strelow (Eds.), *Electronic spatial sensing for the blind*, pp. 273–298. Dordrecht: Martinus Nijhoff.

Supa, M., Cotzin, M., & Dallenbach, K. M. (1944). "Facial vision": The perception of obstacles by the blind. *American Journal of Psychology*, 57, 133–183.

Swanson, L., Minifie, D., & Minifie, E. (1979). Conservation development in the partially sighted child. *Psychology in the School*, 16, 309–313.

Tait, P. E. (1972a). Behavior of young blind children in a controlled play situation. *Perceptual and Motor Skills*, 34, 963–969.

(1972b). A descriptive analysis of the play of young blind children. *Education of the Visually Handicapped*, 4, 12–15.

(1972c). The implication of play as it relates to the emotional development of the blind child. *Education of the Visually Handicapped*, 4, 52–54.

(1972d). Play and the intellectual development of blind children. *New Outlook for the Blind*, 66, 361–369.

(1972e). The effect of circumstantial rejection on infant behavior. *New Outlook for the Blind*, 66, 139–151.

(1990). The attainment of conservation by Chinese and Indian children. *Journal of Visual Impairment & Blindness*, 84, 380–382.

Tait, P. E., & Ward, M. (1982). The comprehension of verbal humor by visually impaired children. *Journal of Visual Impairment & Blindness*, 76, 144–147.

Taktikos, A. (1964). Association of retinoblastoma with mental defect and other pathological manifestations. *British Journal of Ophthalmology*, 48, 495–498.

Tanaka, N., Sato, H., & Matsui, H. (1987). An analysis of visually handicapped children's behavior: Walking in natural settings. *Japanese Journal of Special Education*, 25, 25–33.

Teare, J. F. (1984). Behavioral adjustment of children attending a residential school for the blind. *Developmental and Behavioral Pediatrics*, 5, 237–240.

Thelen, E. (1989). Self-organization in developmental processes: Can systems approaches work? In Gunnar & Thelen (Eds.), *Systems and development*, pp. 77–117.

Thomas, A., & Chess, S. (1981). The role of temperament in the contributions of individuals to their development. In R. M. Lerner & N. A. Busch-Rossnagel (Eds.), *Individuals as producers of their development* (pp. 231–256). New York: Academic Press.

Thurrell, R. J., & Josephson, T. S. (1966). Retinoblastoma and intelligence. *Psychosomatics*, 7, 368–370.

Thurrell, R. J., & Rice, D. G. (1970). Eye rubbing in blind children: Application of a sensory deprivation model. *Exceptional Children*, 36, 325–330.

Thurstone, L. L. (1938). Primary mental abilities. *Psychometric Monographs*, 1.

Tillman, M. H. (1967). The performance of blind and sighted children on the Wechsler Intelligence Scale for Children: Study II. *International Journal for the Education of the Blind*, 16, 106–112.

Tillman, M. H., & Osborne, R. T. (1969). The performance of blind and sighted children on the Wechsler Intelligence Scale for Children: Interaction effects. *Education of the Visually Handicapped*, 1, 1–4.

Tobin, M. J. (1972). Conservation of substance in the blind and partially sighted. *British Journal of Educational Psychology*, 42, 192–197.

Tomlinson-Keasey, C. (1985). *Child development: Psychological, sociocultural, and biological factors*. Homewood, IL: Dorsey.

Troester, H., Brambring, M., & Beelmann, A. (1991). Prevalence and situational causes of stereotyped behaviors in blind infants and preschoolers. *Journal of Abnormal Child Psychology*, 19, 569–590.

Tufenkjian, S. (1971). *A study of the meaningfulness of optical conceptions to congenitally blind persons*. Unpublished doctoral dissertation, California School of Professional Psychology.

Umezu, H. (1972). Formation of verbal behavior of deaf–blind children. *Proceedings of the 20th International Congress of Psychology*, Tokyo, 58–74.

Urwin, C. (1973). The development of a blind baby. Unpublished manuscript read at Edinburgh University. Cited by T. G. R. Bower (1974), *Development in infancy* (p. 169). San Francisco: Freeman.

(1978). The development of communication between blind infants and their parents. In A. Lock (Ed.), *Action, gesture and symbol: The emergence of language* (pp. 79–108). London: Academic Press.

(1983). Dialogue and cognitive functioning in the early language development of three blind children. In A. E. Mills (Ed.), *Language acquisition in the blind child: Normal and deficient* (pp. 142–161). London: Croom Helm.

Vander Kolk, C. J. (1977). Intelligence testing for visually impaired persons. *Journal of Visual Impairment & Blindness*, 71, 158–163.

Van Hasselt, V. B. (1983). Social adaptation in the blind. *Clinical Psychology Review*, 3, 87–102.

Walker, D. L. (1970). The effects of training on the body image of blind children of elementary school age: A pilot study. Unpublished manuscript, University of Virginia.

——— (1971). *The effects of training on the body image of blind children of kindergarten age*. Unpublished doctoral dissertation, George Peabody College for Teachers, Nashville, TN.

——— (1973). Body image and blindness: A review of related theory and research. *American Foundation for the Blind Research Bulletin*, 25, 211–232.

Wan-Lin, M.-W., & Tait, P. E. (1987). The attainment of conservation by visually impaired children in Taiwan. *Journal of Visual Impairment & Blindness*, 81, 423–428.

Warren, D. H. (1974). Early vs. late vision: The role of early vision in spatial reference systems. *New Outlook for the Blind*, 68, 157–162.

——— (1977). *Blindness and early childhood development*. New York: American Foundation for the Blind.

——— (1984). *Blindness and early childhood development* (2d ed., revised). New York: American Foundation for the Blind.

Warren, D. H., Anooshian, L. J., & Bollinger, J. G. (1973). Early vs. late blindness: The role of early vision in spatial behavior. *American Foundation for the Blind Research Bulletin*, 26, 151–170.

Watemberg, J., Cermak, S. A., & Henderson, A. (1986). Right–left discrimination in blind and sighted children. *Physical & Occupational Therapy in Pediatrics*, 6, 7–19.

Wattron, J. B. (1956). A suggested performance test of intelligence. *New Outlook for the Blind*, 50, 115–121.

Webster, R. (1983, February). What – no blindisms in African blind children? *Imfama*, 7, 16, 18.

Weinberg, B. (1964). Stuttering among blind and partially sighted children. *Journal of Speech and Hearing Disorders*, 29, 322–326.

Weiner, L. H. (1963). The performance of good and poor braille readers on certain tests involving tactual perception. *International Journal for the Education of the Blind*, 12, 72–77.

Wertheimer, M. (1961). Psychomotor co-ordination of auditory and visual space at birth. *Science*, 134, 1692.

White, B. L. (1971). *Human infants: Experience and psychological development*. Englewood Cliffs, NJ: Prentice-Hall.

Wilhelm, J. G. (1989). Fear and anxiety in low vision and totally blind children. *Education of the Visually Handicapped*, 20, 163–172.

Williams, C. E. (1978). Strategies of intervention with the profoundly retarded visually-handicapped child: A brief report of a study of stereotypy. *Occasional Papers of the British Psychological Society*, 2, 68–72.

Williams, M. (1968). Superior intelligence of children blinded from retinoblastoma. *Archives of Diseases of Childhood*, 43, 204–210.

Wills, D. M. (1968). Problems of play and mastery in the blind child. *British Journal of Medical Psychology*, 41, 213–222.

(1970). Vulnerable periods in the early development of blind children. *Psychoanalytic Study of the Child*, 25, 461–480.

(1979). Early speech development in blind children. *Psychoanalytic Study of the Child*, 84, 85–117.

Wilson, J., & Halverson, H. M. (1947). Development of a young blind child. *Journal of Genetic Psychology*, 71, 155–175.

Winton, C. A. (1970). On the realization of blindness. *New Outlook for the Blind*, 64, 16–24.

Wishart, J. G., Bower, T. G. R., & Dunkeld, J. (1978). Reaching in the dark. *Perception*, 7, 507–512.

Witkin, H. A., Birnbaum, J., Lomonaco, S., Lehr, S., & Herman, J. L. (1968). Cognitive patterning in congenitally blind children. *Child Development*, 39, 767–786.

Witkin, H. A., Oltman, P. K., Chase, J. B., & Friedman, F. (1971). Cognitive patterning in the blind. In J. Hellmuth (Ed.), *Cognitive studies* (Vol. 2, pp. 16–46). New York: Brunner/Mazel.

Worchel, P. (1951). Space perception and orientation in the blind. *Psychological Monographs*, 65, 1–28.

Worchel, P., Mauney, J., & Andrew, J. G. (1950). The perception of obstacles by the blind. *Journal of Experimental Psychology*, 40, 746–751.

Workman, S. H. (1986). Teachers' verbalizations and the social interaction of blind preschoolers. *Journal of Visual Impairment & Blindness*, 80, 532–534.

Zahran, H. A. S. (1965). A study of personality differences between blind and sighted children. *British Journal of Educational Psychology*, 35, 329–338.

Zigler, E., & Balla, D. (1982). Rigidity – a resilient concept. In E. Zigler & D. Balla (Eds.), *Mental retardation: The developmental-difference controversy* (pp. 61–82). Hillsdale, NJ: Erlbaum.

Zimler, J., & Keenan, J. M. (1983). Imagery in the congenitally blind: How visual are visual images? *Journal of Experimental Psychology: Learning, Memory, and Cognition*, 9, 269–282.

Zunich, M., & Ledwith, B. E. (1965). Self-concepts of visually handicapped and sighted children. *Perceptual and Motor Skills*, 21, 771–774.

Zweibelson, I., & Barg, C. F. (1967). Concept development of blind children. *New Outlook for the Blind*, 61, 218–222.

Author index

Subject index